BEYOND THE FIRM

General Editor
Professor Akira Kudo, Institute of Social Science, University of Tokyo.

Series Adviser
Professor Mark Mason, Yale University.

FUJI CONFERENCE SERIES II

BEYOND THE FIRM

Business Groups in International and Historical Perspective

Edited by

TAKAO SHIBA

and

MASAHIRO SHIMOTANI

OXFORD UNIVERSITY PRESS

1997

Oxford University Press, Great Clarendon Street, Oxford OX2 6DP

Oxford New York
Athens Auckland Bangkok Bogota Bombay
Buenos Aires Calcutta Cape Town Dar es Salaam
Delhi Florence Hong Kong Istanbul Karachi
Kuala Lumpur Madras Madrid Melbourne
Mexico City Nairobi Paris Singapore
Taipei Tokyo Toronto
and associated companies in
Berlin Ibadan

Oxford is a trade mark of Oxford University Press

Published in the United States
by Oxford University Press Inc., New York

British Library Cataloguing in Publication Data
Data available

Library of Congress Cataloging in Publication Data
Data available
ISBN 0–19–829060–8

1 3 5 7 9 10 8 6 4 2

Typeset by Hope Services (Abingdon) Ltd.
Printed in Great Britain
Biddles Ltd., Guildford and King's Lynn

ACKNOWLEDGEMENTS

THE eleven chapters of the present volume were originally papers presented at the 22nd International Conference on Business History. The Business History Society of Japan inaugurated these annual international conferences in 1974 with the generous financial backing of the Taniguchi Foundation, seeking to bring together scholars from around the world to address a variety of topics in the field of business history. The nickname 'Fuji Conference', by which these gatherings have come to be known in the business history community, is inspired by their location at the foot of Japan's most famous mountain.

The 22nd Conference was organized around the theme of interfirm relations, and was held on 5–8 January 1995 in sight of Mt. Fuji. Continued support from the Taniguchi Foundation made the 22nd Conference possible, and the editors and organizing committee wish to express their sincere appreciation.

A number of people gave unstintingly of their time during the process of compiling and publishing the present volume. Mark Mason, the series adviser, was in attendance at the Conference, and the editors extend their thanks for his insightful advice; the idea for the title of this volume, *Beyond the Firm*, was his. In addition to the eleven authors (David Hochfelder, co-author with Susan Helper, did not attend), sixteen other scholars were present at the Conference to provide valuable contributions to its overall framework and important suggestions that have been incorporated into the final versions of the papers. They were: Etsuo Abe, Jun Aso, Ken Hirano, Sachio Imakubo, Makoto Kasuya, Ken Kojima, Akira Kudo, Hideaki Miyajima, Hidemasa Morikawa, Keiichiro Nakagawa, Kiyoshi Nakamura, Izumi Nonaka, Jun Sakudo, Minoru Sawai, and Hiromi Shioji, all of Japan, and Jin Sung Chung, who journeyed from Korea in order to take part. All are the recipients of heartfelt gratitude.

In addition, Gakuya Hirai, Ha Hoimin, and Akira Tanaka served as behind-the-scenes staff to ensure that the Conference proceeded smoothly; the Conference would not have been nearly as effective without their tireless efforts. The editors would also like to offer their deepest appreciation to the two interpreters, Brendon Hanna and Mito Makkin. They ably facilitated the exchange of opinions across international barriers, and the stimulating discussion among the participants was due in large measure to their linguistic exertions. Edmund R. Skrzypczak also served as a copy-editor for the present volume, together with Brendon

Hanna. The readability of the book owes much to their criticism and corrections, and the editors offer well-deserved thanks.

There are a large number of scholars in the fields of business history, economic history, management theory, etc. who helped to bring about the Conference and to define the theme of the present volume, and, although they are too numerous to name individually, they are nevertheless the recipients of our gratitude.

Finally, the editors would like to express their profound sense of loss over the death of the Taniguchi Foundation's Mr Yuichiro Taniguchi, on 2 September 1995. The Foundation, established by his father, has supported the Fuji Conferences ever since the first gathering in 1974. Mr Yuichiro Taniguchi, succeeding his father as head of the Foundation, was particularly enthusiastic about the theme of the 22nd Conference, and the editors regret deeply that he was unable to see the publication of the resulting book.

T.S.
M.S.

CONTENTS

List of Contributors	ix
List of Figures	xi
List of Tables	xiii
Introduction	1
MASAHIRO SHIMOTANI AND TAKAO SHIBA	
1. The History and Structure of Business Groups in Japan	5
MASAHIRO SHIMOTANI	

PART I. THE CORPORATE COMPLEX

2. Diversification Process and the Ownership Structure of Samsung Chaebol	31
CHUL-KYU KANG	
3. From Zaibatsu to Corporate Complexes	59
KUNIO SUZUKI	
4. Structure and Strategy of Belgian Business Groups (1920–1990)	88
GINETTE KURGAN-VAN HENTENRYK	

PART II. THE CORPORATE GROUP

5. Growth via Politics: Business Groups Italian-Style	109
FRANCO AMATORI	
6. Business Groups in the German Electrical Industry	135
WILFRIED FELDENKIRCHEN	
7. A Path to the Corporate Group in Japan: Mitsubishi Heavy Industries and its Group Formation	167
TAKAO SHIBA	

PART III. ASSEMBLER–SUPPLIER RELATIONS

8. 'Japanese-Style' Supplier Relationships in the American
   Auto Industry, 1895–1920   187
   SUSAN HELPER AND DAVID HOCHFELDER

9. The Subcontracting System and Business Groups: The Case
   of the Japanese Automotive Industry   215
   HIROFUMI UEDA

PART IV. JAPANESE BUSINESS GROUPS

10. The Organizational Logic of Business Groups: Evidence from
    the Zaibatsu   245
    MICHAEL L. GERLACH

11. Learning to Work Together: Adaptation and the Japanese
    Firm   274
    W. MARK FRUIN

Afterword   291
MASAHIRO SHIMOTANI AND TAKAO SHIBA

Index   297

LIST OF CONTRIBUTORS

FRANCO AMATORI is Associate Professor of Economic History at Bocconi University, Milan.

WILFRIED FELDENKIRCHEN is a Professor and serves as the Chair for Economic and Business History at the University of Erlangen-Nuremberg.

W. MARK FRUIN is Hong Kong Bank of Canada Professor at the University of British Columbia.

MICHAEL L. GERLACH is an Associate Professor at Haas Business School, University of California at Berkeley.

SUSAN HELPER is Associate Professor of Economics and Research Associate at the Center for Regional Economic Issues, Case Western Reserve University.

DAVID HOCHFELDER is a Research Assistant at the Center for Regional Economic Issues and a Ph.D. candidate in the History of Technology at Case Western Reserve University.

CHUL-KYU KANG is a Professor in the Faculty of Economics at Seoul City University.

GINETTE KURGAN-VAN HENTENRYK is a Professor at Université Libre de Bruxelles.

TAKAO SHIBA is a Professor in the Faculty of Business Administration at Kyoto Sangyo University.

MASAHIRO SHIMOTANI is a Professor of Economics at Kyoto University.

KUNIO SUZUKI is Associate Professor of Social Science and Foreign Languages at the University of Electro-Communications (Tokyo).

HIROFUMI UEDA is an Associate Professor at the Institute for Economic Research, Osaka City University.

All four of the Japanese papers were translated by Brendon Hanna, who is a Ph.D candidate in the Faculty of Economics at Kyoto University.

LIST OF FIGURES

1.1.	The corporate complex, corporate groups, and subcontractors	6
1.2.	Structure of the Matsushita electrical group	10
1.3.	Tiered structure of Japanese corporate aggregates	20
1.4.	A two-by-two matrix analysis of corporate aggregates	21
2.1	Ownership and diversification of Korean chaebol	33
2.2.	Ownership structure of Samsung	48
3.1.	Structure of the Big Three zaibatsu	60
3.2.	Trademarks and logos of the Big Three zaibatsu banned by SCAP	81
4.1.	Tractebel's control of electrical power companies	103
5.1.	The system of state shareholdings: theory and reality	123
5.2.	Finsider: basic activity sectors	125
5.3.	ENI: basic activity sectors	127
6.1.	Sales of Siemens and AEG	138
6.2.	The concentration process in the German electrical industry	142
6.3.	Sales of the German electrical industry and its two major business groups	145
6.4.	Market shares in the German electrical industry	146
6.5.	Concentration in the telecommunications industry around 1930	148
6.6.	The structure of the Siemens concern in 1928	151
6.7.	Major joint ventures of Siemens and AEG, 1929	152
8.1.	Percentage of unit volume versus price class for cars 1903, 1907, and 1911	190
8.2.	Advertisement for Lindsay running gears, motors, and axles for electrical automobiles	192
8.3.	Advertisement for Lindsay running gears and completed cars	193
8.4.	Advertisement warning automobile assemblers of the dangers of placing late parts orders	194

9.1. Confederation of Japan Automobile Workers' Unions and
Federation of All Toyota Workers' Unions   225

10.1. The dominant techno-organizational chains in the Sumitomo and
Furukawa zaibatsu during the pre-war period   252

10.2. The organization of the Sumitomo konzern (*c.*1930)   254

10.3. Company history of Sumitomo Bank   256–7

10.4. Company history of Dai-Ichi Kangyo (Hypothec) Bank (DKB)   258–9

10.5. Company history of Nippon Electric Company (NEC)   260–1

10.6. Company history of Fujitsu   262

10.7. Sumitomo Chemical and associated business enterprises   268–9

A.1 Boundaries of a firm   294

LIST OF TABLES

1.1. The number of subsidiaries   8

1.2. The six largest corporate complexes   12

1.3. Nitchitsu Konzern in 1937   15

2.1. Number of keiretsu of the five largest chaebol   32

2.2. Interest rate in the official financial market, 1954–1994   36

2.3. Trend of establishment, acquisition, and extinction of Samsung firms   37

2.4. Change in Samsung subsidiaries   38–40

2.5. Trend of Samsung keiretsu firms' increase by industry   42

2.6. The ownership structure of the five largest chaebol as of April 1994   47

3.1. Positions of Mitsui complex directly controlled companies in terms of amounts of deposits and loans at/from Mitsui Bank (excluding colonial and overseas branches)   67

3.2. Ownership of directly controlled companies by Mitsui financial institutions   69

3.3. Ownership of directly controlled companies by Mitsubishi financial institutions   70

3.4. Ownership of directly controlled companies by Sumitomo financial institutions   71

3.5. Asset tax taxpayers (zaibatsu families)   75

3.6. Lateral cross-holdings within the Mitsui, Mitsubishi, and Sumitomo complexes   79

4.1. Electric power industry, Belgium, 1914–1992   101

5.1. IRI and ENI groups: employment and as % of the manufacturing sector employment, 1956–1991   129

5.2. Finsider group employment as % of IRI group total employment, 1939–1988   129

5.3. IRI and ENI groups: sales and as % of the manufacturing sector sales, 1956–1991   129

5.4. Finsider group sales as % of IRI group total sales, 1939–1988   130

5.5. Finsider group steel production as % of Italy's total steel output, 1939–1988 — 133

5.6. Finsider, IRI, and ENI groups' net profit/sales ratio, 1956–1991 — 134

5.7. ENI and IRI liabilities, 1950–1990 — 133

6.1. Germany's top thirty industrial companies according to their turnover rankings — 158

6.2. Interlocking relationships among the big nine in electricals — 159

7.1. Mitsubishi Heavy Industries group during the Second World War — 174

7.2. Subsidiaries of Mitsubishi Shipbuilding, Shin Mitsubishi Heavy Industries, and Mitsubishi Nippon Heavy Industries — 178

9.1. Types of group companies in the 1980s — 216

9.2. Changes in the number of Toyota suppliers — 221

9.3. Starting dates for transactions with Toyota Kyohokai association members — 225

9.4. Co-operative associations of the assemblers — 232

9.5. Introduction of the kanban system at Toyota group companies — 236

10.1 Modes of organizational growth and diversification — 255

10.2. Business relationships with affiliated and unaffiliated companies: unit sales of large-scale industrial products by Fuji Electric, 1924–1956 — 267

A.1. Boundaries of a firm — 296

Introduction

MASAHIRO SHIMOTANI AND TAKAO SHIBA

In the 1980s, when Japanese firms were still boasting impressive growth compared with their competitors in many other nations, their special brand of interfirm relations was cited as an important asset by observers from around the world in business, academia, and government. The word that was most commonly used to designate these 'special' Japanese interfirm relations was the term 'keiretsu', and they were seen as a major source of strength for Japanese firms. The 'keiretsu' organizations were also the targets of not a few complaints: e.g. 'Large Japanese firms engage in exclusive transactions within their "keiretsu" organizations, preventing firms from other countries from entering Japanese markets', or 'Costs that should be borne by Japanese firms are actually forced onto their "keiretsu" subsidiaries.' Prime examples of this type of representation were seen during the USA–Japan bilateral Structural Impediments Initiatives.

However, the word 'keiretsu' is extremely ambiguous; its exact content depends inordinately heavily on the person using it and on the context involved. Some commentators have used it to describe Japan's complexes of huge firms that are connected to each other via extensive mutual shareholdings. Others have used it to refer to the structure in which a major firm operates together with a group of subsidiaries more or less as a single entity. Still others have identified the word 'keiretsu' with the practice of a large firm establishing semi-permanent transactional relationships with small and medium-sized subcontractors. It should appear dubious that a single word can be used to describe such a diverse range of relationships. Which is the real 'keiretsu'? Is the Japanese language as vague as all that?

The source of the confusion is that there are at least three types or levels of interfirm relationships that coexist in the Japanese corporate environment. One is the corporate complex that consists of loosely bound groups of huge companies from different industries (including major banks); the second is the pyramid-structured corporate group with a major firm at the head of a large body of subsidiaries and affiliates; and the third is subcontractor-type assembler–supplier relations. Unfortunately, observers have attempted to apply the word 'keiretsu' to each of these three types of levels of interfirm relations, leading to unwarranted confusion.

This confusion needs to be sorted out, and an excellent first step is already being taken by a small number of Japanese scholars who are endeavouring to depict Japanese interfirm relations more accurately. Moreover, during this process, they have begun to doubt that the interfirm relationships found among Japanese firms are actually unique to Japan.

In the modern economic world, firms do not generally exist solely as independent entities. This is not because firms come into contact with each other as buyers and sellers in markets, or because competitors may attempt to come together to form cartels, but rather because legally independent enterprises often move beyond the framework of the 'firm' to form co-operative groups that function as if they were single organizations. For example, it is common in all countries for large firms to operate through various subsidiaries which respond to instructions from above, although there are necessarily differences of degree. Depending on the country, there can also be found holding companies under the auspices of which firms in various industries co-operate to support one another. That is, it is somewhat ridiculous to suppose that only in Japan does enterprise extend beyond the framework of the individual firm to create and maintain interfirm relations. However this may be, important questions still remain as to why Japanese interfirm relations can be pointed to as being somehow 'special', and how interfirm relations in other countries are to be best understood. These concerns naturally stem from expanded attempts to organize Japanese interfirm relations in a theoretical context, and they provided the inspiration for the theme of the 22nd Fuji Conference.

Accordingly, the Conference provided a forum for both approaches. The conference organizers, also serving as editors of the present volume, invited presentations by Japanese scholars of cases demonstrating Japanese interfirm relationships, and sought to balance these with the views of non-Japanese scholars researching the same subject from an outside perspective. This led to the enlightening presentations of Mark Fruin and Michael Gerlach. Meanwhile, business historians from a number of other countries were invited to present papers addressing representative interfirm relations and business groups in their nations, resulting in highly informative papers dealing with situations in Germany, Italy, Belgium, the USA, and Korea. All of these, as well as the four Japanese papers, elicited heated discussion over the four days of the Conference.

Preceded by a chapter by Masahiro Shimotani that seeks to provide a better framework for consideration of interfirm relations in the Japanese context, the present volume is divided into four main parts.

The first three correspond to the three types or levels of Japanese interfirm relationships as identified by Masahiro Shimotani; i.e. corporate complex, corporate group, and subcontracting system. Part I consists of chapters dealing with the subject of the corporate complex, or loose horizontal associations of large firms in differing industries. This section includes the chapter by Chul-Kyu Kang, utilizing the case of Samsung to examine the formation and ownership of the Korean chaebol groups, which continue to play important roles in Korea's economic development. In particular, Kang provides important points for use in comparing the chaebol organizations with the corporate complexes, often thought to be unique to Japan in the post-war period. Next, Kunio Suzuki looks at the transformation of the Japanese pre-war zaibatsu into the post-war corporate complexes, focusing attention on changes in the structure of ownership. The section concludes with the chapter by G. Kurgan-van Hentenryk, considering the managerial strategies adopted by bank-centred financial groups and entrepreneurial families in Belgium in order to organize and expand their industrial groups in the first country in the European continent to embark on industrialization.

Part II consists of three chapters concerned with the pyramid-type structure headed by a single industrial firm that we refer to as the corporate group. The chapter by Franco Amatori details the various group transitions that occurred in Italy after the First World War, using the state holding companies IRI and ENI to emphasize the importance of state actions on these types of groups in the Italian context.

The next chapter is by Wilfried Feldenkirchen, who explains the differences in the expansion strategies and underlying corporate structures of Siemens and AEG, two well-known participants in the German electrical industry. Takao Shiba then uses the case of a heavy equipment maker to demonstrate that industry-specific characteristics significantly influence corporate group formation even in Japan.

Part III contains two chapters that address assembler–supplier relations, with special attention given to the Japanese subcontracting system. Susan Helper and David Hochfelder offer a stimulating investigation into the role of Japanese-style supplier relations in the formative years of the American auto industry, while Hirofumi Ueda sheds light on the formation of supplier groupings and the subcontracting production system by assemblers in the Japanese auto industry.

Following up on the discussion of the three types or levels of interfirm relations presented in these three parts, Part IV consists of two chapters by Mark Fruin and Michael Gerlach that clarify the specifically Japanese characteristics of interfirm relations and corporate activity. Gerlach stresses that an important feature of the growth of Japanese firms is that the boundaries of the firm are loose, and that they continually shift in concert with growth; the case of the Sumitomo zaibatsu is a major focal point. Fruin, providing a new channel for future discussion of interfirm relations, describes how firms utilize the process of adaptation to the business environment in order to form networks, work together in the context of interfirm relations, and accomplish necessary learning.

Some readers may feel that the book has been too heavily sectionalized, but the editors are convinced that a clear structure is needed in response to the tendency to ignore type or level in discussion of interfirm relations. The present volume is intended to spark more meaningful debate over the wider issues involved.

1

The History and Structure of Business Groups in Japan

Masahiro Shimotani

The Debate Surrounding Business Groups and Keiretsu

The USA–Japan bilateral Structural Impediments Initiatives (SII), which began in 1989, marked the start of serious debate concerning business groups and keiretsu, as interest mounted in the nature of the special inter-firm networks formed by Japanese companies, and in their role in pro-moting Japan's resilient international competitiveness. Seemingly unique Japanese business practices, along with the closed or exclusive nature of Japanese corporate complexes, were also addressed. Specifically, the mutual stockholding arrangements forming the basis for the six major complexes became a focus of attention, and the exclusivity of intracom-plex transactions was made a target for criticism. However, the six major complexes are not the only significant constellations of firms in the Japanese economy. There are, for example, pyramid-like 'corporate groups' featuring a large enterprise at the apex, supported by a large num-ber of subsidiaries. These are generally known by the parent's name, as in the Toyota group, the Matsushita group, or the Sony group.

There are also groups of firms bound together by long-term 'Japanese' subcontracting relationships involving the production and processing of parts. Subcontractor groups are not necessarily bound together by capital ties and often represent the quasi-internalization of smaller firms by large enterprises.

These 'corporate complexes', 'corporate groups', and 'assembler–supplier relationships' each feature different aspects of Japanese business groups and interfirm relations and have differing structures. Accordingly, it is necessary both to clarify the make-up of each of these constellations of firms and to show clearly the mutual connections among them.

Here, in order better to facilitate discussion concerning the various types of business groups, let us order their relations to one another as in Fig. 1.1. This is necessary in order to establish a common semantic and

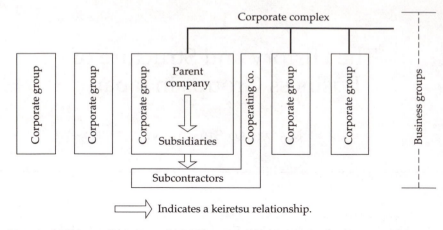

Note: ⇒ indicates a keiretsu relationship.

Fig. 1.1. *The corporate complex, corporate groups, and subcontractors.*

conceptual framework with which to undertake international and historical comparison.

   Currently there are in Japan approximately 2.3 million incorporated
enterprises (National Tax 1994). In terms of capitalization, however, the
vast majority (98.7 per cent) are small enterprises capitalized at 100 million
yen or under; very small firms capitalized at 5 million yen or less account
for 52.1 per cent of the total. At the other end of the scale, large companies
with capital of 1 billion yen or more constitute only 0.2 per cent of the total.
Further, joint-stock companies account for 48.7 per cent of the total
(1,115,000 firms), and virtually all of the companies capitalized at 1 billion
yen and over take this form of organization.

   The corporate picture, however, is not one in which these many companies are all floating independently in the immense sea of the economic
market. Instead, there are a number of corporate aggregates, made up of
various interfirm relationships, typically in the form of business groups or
keiretsu that are themselves bound together by capital ties and/or regular
transactional contact. Of course, businesses can be observed to come
together in various types of groups in virtually all countries, since operational systems can only be constructed in the context of a social division of
labour, or interfirm relationships. This in turn requires the establishment
of stable transactional ties. Enterprises typically seek to construct business
groups of one kind or another, and it very often happens that these bonds
are reinforced by the ownership of shares and the dispatching of top management personnel. Alternatively, these ties can be formed through such
means as long-term continuous transactions, the supply of technology, or
the provision of funding. (Note that we are not considering here groups

such as cartels made up of participants in the same industry that come together with monopolistic intent.)

It should also be recognized that business groups are not necessarily formed through the establishment of ties among already existing firms. That is, enterprises do not merely seek to make connections with outside firms that are already present in economic markets; many companies actively spin or hive off subsidiaries from within themselves, forming business groups in the process. This is because the birth of potentially independent units within companies generally accompanies the process of business development, both in the context of diversification and in that of vertical expansion. In addition, because organizational obesity brings about managerial inefficiencies, operational decentralization (decentralized management) becomes unavoidable.

While there are a number of methods of decentralization (e.g. operating divisions or intrafirm 'companies'), the spinning off of internal operations into separate subsidiaries is popular in Japan, and this results in the formation of 'groups' of enterprises. It is somewhat obvious in these cases that the subsidiaries remain organically connected with the parent company. In fact, the Japanese terminology is indicative of this type of organic, familial relationship, referring to 'parent', 'child', 'grandchild', and even 'great-grandchild' companies.

In observing Japanese corporate trends over recent years, we find that the majority of subsidiaries are of this type, having been formed through the spin-off of previously internal operations. This is representative of: (1) efforts by a company to create a slimmed-down central strategic or group headquarters through the spinning off of line functions such as manufacturing, sales, and service into a series of subsidiaries; and (2) efforts at forming a flexible organization of enterprises surrounding the parent that can, as a whole, effectively cope with changes in the external business environment (Shimotani 1991; 1993).

Corporate Aggregates: Two Types and Two Levels

Currently there are in Japan two types of corporate aggregates: the pyramid-type 'corporate groups' consisting of a parent company at the head of a large number of supporting subsidiaries, and the 'corporate complexes' that are made up of a number of corporate groups. These can be described as 'vertical' and 'horizontal' types, but it is important to remember that they produce two hierarchical levels or tiers (Sakamoto and Shimotani 1987; Sakamoto 1990–1).

Corporate Groups

The great majority of large Japanese enterprises are parent companies surrounded by large numbers of subsidiaries. Actually, a more precise term would be 'related companies'. The term subsidiary is used here to indicate cases in which the parent company holds a significant stake (20–100 per cent of the stock). Related companies can be subdivided by the stockholding ratio of the parent into true 'subsidiaries' (over 50 per cent) and affiliates (20–50 per cent), but, for the sake of convenience, these will be referred to together hereafter as 'subsidiaries' or 'group companies'.

Of course, large enterprises in all countries hold sway over a number of subsidiaries, but the numbers of these subsidiaries or group companies tend to be characteristically large in the case of Japan. The number of subsidiaries varies from parent company to parent company, but it is not unusual for there to be several hundred, and there are even a few huge enterprises with over 1,000 subsidiaries. Table 1.1 outlines post-war trends in the numbers of subsidiaries of several large Japanese enterprises, and indicates the impressive expansion that has taken place in this form. This trend can be seen to have accelerated from 1978, when the current consolidated accounting system was introduced.

The majority of these subsidiaries can be said to exist under the control, via capital, of the parent, or holding company. The parent, then, is a type of holding company, but one that conducts its own independent business operations, thus becoming what may be referred to as an 'operating hold-

Table 1.1.   *The number of subsidiaries*

	1955	1960	1965	1970	1975	1981	1985	1991
Sumitomo Metal	9	15	36	42	53	91	108	191
NKK	3	10	36	42	53	91	107	164
Sumitomo Chemical	8	13	28	39	45	98	102	132
Mitsubishi Kasei	7	28	27	48	66	109	124	170
Asahi Chemical	8	13	33	58	89	144	149	184
Teijin	4	8	12	13	34	114	84	100
Matsushita	70	187	332	562	656	476	435	671
NEC	8	19	28	49	93	121	143	235
Hitachi	13	55	90	111	129	190	210	764
Mitsubishi Heavy Ind.	11	19	19	35	42	120	137	272
Toyota Auto.	26	16	20	28	46	68	164	200
Nissan Auto.	20	24	27	86	80	209	217	590
Mitsui & Co.	28	37	59	88	150	488	501	723
Itochu	17	33	70	113	159	312	364	728

Sources: The annual reports of each company.

ing company'. The Anti-Monopoly Law of 1947 prohibits the establishment of pure holding companies, with the result that parent companies are forced to undertake some kind of operations on their own behalf. For example, Toyota is an operating holding company that manufactures automobiles while holding shares in its subsidiaries. Matsushita and Sony both manufacture electronics and simultaneously maintain holdings in their many subsidiaries.

It is also significant that the group of subsidiaries typically has intimate and organic relations to the parent company's main business, resulting in an intragroup division of labour, or specialized production system. They can be broadly classified as either: (1) entities engaged in areas representing diversification from the parent's main business, or (2) entities that perform a vertically supplementary role (e.g. parts supply, processing, sales, or service). In both of these cases, the operations of the subsidiary are organically connected to the main business of the parent. The term 'corporate group' will be used to identify the organic whole consisting of a parent company at the apex of a supporting cast of group companies, each linked to the parent by capital and operational ties. Virtually all major Japanese companies are organized in this corporate group form (Shimotani 1988).

Fig. 1.2 illustrates the structure of the Matsushita group, centring on Matsushita Electric Industrial, as a practical example. The Matsushita group is made up of nearly 700 subsidiaries, with the various intragroup functions divided among the group companies. Differences among these companies in terms of responsibilities and ratio of ownership by the parent can be ascribed to the relative importance of each company to the group as a whole, as well as to the degree of autonomy of each company and its relative scale. In particular, the six divisional companies, along with Matsushita Electric Industrial (MEI) itself, form the nucleus of the group. These six are all former operating divisions of the parent that were split off to form subsidiaries; they maintain an extremely high level of integration with MEI (the parent) (Shimotani 1993). The other group companies also take on various other roles within the framework of intimate relations with MEI.

As regards the circumstances of the establishment of these group companies, we find that they closely follow the development and expansion of the operations (both diversification and vertical integration) of the parent. From the standpoint of their relation to the parent, they can be roughly divided into two categories: (1) existing external enterprises that were absorbed and reorganized as group companies, and (2) parent operations that were spun off into separate subsidiaries. In Japan the latter (spin-offs) overwhelmingly outweigh the former (acquisitions). It is also important to note that the spin-offs are not restricted only to operating divisions and other units that are capable of standing alone; there is a distinct trend

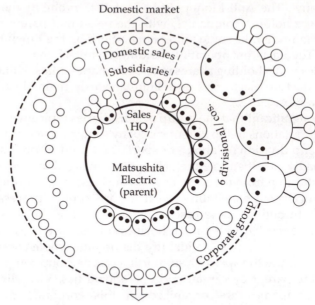

Domestic market

Overseas market

Note: All circles, excluding the parent, mean subsidiaries.

Fig. 1.2. *Structure of the Matsushita electrical group.*

toward the spinning off of small dependent units too, such as individual factories, sales offices, research facilities, and relatively small staff sections. On the one hand, this externalization of internal units allows the parent to transform itself into a slimmed-down 'strategic headquarters'; on the other, it increases the level of decentralization and turns the spun-off partial units into individual profit centres.

Large Japanese enterprises, then, generally exist in the form of corporate groups, and, while these are typically made up of large numbers of former operational units that have been made independent via the spin-off mechanism, the groups maintain their holistic identities. To repeat, there is a particularly strong trend in Japan for unitary capital entities to exist in the form of large numbers of nominally separate subsidiaries. Accordingly, analysis of the management of parent enterprises in isolation from their respective groups is essentially meaningless; the entire corporate group must be considered.

The Six Major Corporate Complexes

While many of the corporate groups operate independently (as independent corporate groups), a significant number of them (188 in total) are aligned at a higher level of organization as well, within the so-called 'six major corporate complexes' (in Japanese, *roku dai kigyo-shudan*).

Corporate complexes may be defined as collections of huge enterprises (i.e. corporate groups) from different industries that have been assembled into loose complexes. The six majors, as noted in Table 1.2, are the Mitsui, Mitsubishi, Sumitomo, Fuyo, Sanwa, and Dai-Ichi Kangin groups (complexes) (Fair Trade Commission 1994; Okumura 1983; Odagiri 1992b). The first three trace their origins directly to the prewar 'zaibatsu' business families, and had been more or less reformed by the end of the 1950s. The others were formed in the 1960s and 1970s in a series of catch-up efforts, and each is centred on one of the large commercial 'city' banks. The original three and the later three, then, differ significantly in terms of their origins and compositions, but they share the common denominator of each having a central city bank, 'sogo shosha' general trading company(ies), and insurance companies, as well as other giant firms representative of the Japanese industrial spectrum. Each of the six central city banks serves as the main bank to their respective member firms, and the sogo shosha general trading companies play pivotal roles in facilitating transactions for members.

The six majors are also characterized by their well-known mutual stockholding arrangements and central councils made up of the presidents of group companies. Mutual stockholding arrangements were originally constructed in order to provide stable ownership, particularly in the cases of the original three majors, which feature intracomplex holdings of an average near 30 per cent of all of the stock issued by member companies. The corresponding figures for the later three are comparatively low, ranging between 15 and 20 per cent, and intracomplex holdings tend to be centred on financial institutions; lateral mutual shareholding among industrial group members is generally lacking. The regular meetings of the presidents of complex companies, known as presidents' council meetings, occur as informal monthly luncheons, and are seen as forums for social interaction and the exchange of information. That is, they are not necessarily decision-making organizations standing at the helms of their respective corporate complexes; individual member companies maintain their own independent powers of decision. The pre-war 'control tower' organizations that guided the overall actions of the zaibatsu no longer exist, and have been supplanted by loose complexes.

Member firms do conduct intracomplex transactions among themselves, and, while these transactions are often preferential to members,

Table 1.2. *The six largest corporate complexes*

	Mitsui	Mitsubishi	Sumitomo	Fuyo	Sanwa	Dai-Ichi Kangin
Presidents' meeting	Nimokukai	Kin'yokai	Hakusuikai	Fuyokai	Sansuikai	Sankinkai
No. of member cos.	26	29	20	29	44	48
Year of est.	1961	1955	1951	1966	1967	1978
Mutual holding matrix density (%)	57.6	75.3	94.5	46.8	27.5	29.4
Intracomplex stock holding (%)	19.3	38.2	28.0	16.9	16.7	14.2
Intracomplex transactions (excluding financial inst.)						
Sale (%)	5.8	14.2	11.3	5.6	3.2	4.9
Purchase (%)	6.4	16.9	12.2	6.4	3.8	5.4

Source: Fair Trade Commission (1994)

member companies do not limit their transactions solely to other member-company counterparts. Were intracomplex transactions exclusive to the degree that has been asserted, and had the competitive mechanism been placed in abeyance, it is doubtful that the complexes could have played the leading roles that they did in Japan's rapid post-war economic development. Furthermore, complex members have almost always maintained their managerial independence, and instances of friction and competition among members of the same complex have not been unusual.

There are, therefore, two basic types of corporate aggregates in contemporary Japan: the vertical corporate group, made up of a parent company and its subsidiaries; and the loosely organized horizontal corporate complex bound together through mutual stockholding arrangements and the council of member-company presidents. However, these are not merely two types of aggregates; it is important to note that they represent two levels in a hierarchical structure. The following are the nineteen members of the Sumitomo complex, each of which is represented at the presidents' council meetings (Hakusuikai).

	Subsidiaries
Sumitomo Bank	49
Sumitomo Trust and Banking	15
Sumitomo Marine and Fire Insurance	27
Sumitomo Corporation	503
Sumitomo Coal Mining	50
Sumitomo Construction	31
Sumitomo Forestry	37
Sumitomo Chemical	172
Sumitomo Bakelite	40
Nippon Sheet Glass	152
Sumitomo Cement	88
Sumitomo Metal	287
Sumitomo Metal Mining	75
Sumitomo Light Metal	40
Sumitomo Electric	199
Sumitomo Heavy Industry	125
NEC	235
Sumitomo Realty and Development	54
Sumitomo Warehouse	36

These companies are connected to each other horizontally to form a corporate complex, but they also each stand at the apex of their own bodies of subsidiaries, forming independent corporate groups as well. Note for example that Sumitomo Chemical, a typical Hakusuikai member, is supported by its own group of 172 subsidiaries, making up the Sumitomo Chemical corporate group. The Sumitomo example is representative of the other complexes, and indicative of the Japanese group structure featuring two types of hierarchically arranged aggregates (Shimotani 1993). Next, let us examine the process of the birth of this dual-level hierarchical structure.

The Dual-Level Split of the 1930s

The decade of the 1930s is a significant and extremely interesting period in the history of the formation of Japanese corporate aggregates. While the 1930s began with economic crisis and proceeded toward wartime economic controls, it was also a period that saw new technologies, an active securities market, and a boom in military demand, all of which combined rapidly to advance private heavy and chemical industry and to offer a variety of business opportunities. There were also important changes in corporate organization as solutions came to be needed for new organizational problems and inefficiencies arising from diversification, vertical integration, and various *ad hoc* production arrangements. Organizational experimentation was also made in response to the need to procure funds, tax considerations, and the increasingly rigorous controls on the economy. The various problems that surfaced in the 1930s affected both zaibatsu and non-zaibatsu enterprises, and it was during this period that the dual-level hierarchical structure of Japanese corporate aggregates began to be formed.

The Appearance of the New Konzerns

One of the most noticeable phenomena on the business scene during the 1930s was the entry, one after another, of the New Konzerns. ('Konzern' is a German word, used as a direct loan-word in Japanese. A rough English equivalent would be 'combine'.) These were essentially corporate groups. They established large numbers of subsidiaries, each having some kind of connection to the parent company's main business, with the entire group operating as an organic whole (Shimotani 1986a).

The designation 'New Konzern' is normally applied to five specific groups: Nissan, Nitchitsu, Mori, Nisso, and Riken. Table 1.3 shows as an example the composition of the Nitchitsu Group. The parent company, Nippon Nitrogen Fertilizer (founded in 1908 and abbreviated 'Nitchitsu'), made a variety of electrochemical products, but mainly chemical fertilizers, and created a large number of subsidiaries as it rapidly diversified and expanded into Japan's colonial holdings in the 1930s. It soon became a major corporate group, growing from 10 companies in 1930, to 20 by 1935, and to 43 by 1940. The Nitchitsu Konzern, as it was known at the time, con-

Table 1.3. *Nitchitsu Konzern in 1937*

	Capital (10,000 yen)	Stockholding (%)
Nippon Chisso Fertilizer	20,000	—
Chosen Chisso Fertilizer	7,000	100
Choshinko Hydroelectric	7,000	100
Asahi Bemberg Silk	4,600	75
Chosen Coal Ind.	1,000	100
Nichitsu Securities	1,000	100
Nichitsu Mining	500	100
Nippon Magnesium Metal	420	70
Nippon Chisso Explosive	100	100
Chosen Chisso Explosive	100	100
Tanpo Railroad	500	100
Shinko Railroad	200	100
Chosen Building	200	100
Chosen 'Mite	10	100
Nippon Hydroelectric	2,000	20
Chosen Electric Supply	1,500	50
Chosen Petroleum	1,000	20
Shinetsu Chisso Fertilizer	500	40
Toyo Ind.	500	10
Toyo Mercury Mining	300	50
Kusatsu Sulfur Mining	150	50
Tomita & Co.	100	30
Chisso Fertilizer Sales	100	50
Yuki Electric	100	70
Nitto Explosive Parts	50	100
Nichitsu Explosive Sales	50	65
Nichitsu Jewels	50	65

Source: Oshio (1989).

structed huge electrochemical industrial bases in Minamata and Nobeoka in Kyushu, and in the colony of Korea, each of which was made up of the facilities of numerous subsidiaries. The operations of most of these subsidiaries were based on diversification from the parent's business, or contributed to vertical integration. That is, the entire combine functioned as an organic whole and was thus a prototypical corporate group. Significantly, the majority of the subsidiaries had been spun off from the parent and retained close ties in regard to both capital and personnel. These so-called subsidiaries, then, were actually little more than operating divisions or remote arms of the parent company (Shimotani 1982; Oshio 1989; Molony 1990).

In contrast with the older zaibatsu, the five New Konzerns were distinguished first by the fact that the spread of their businesses tended to be limited by their retention of close connections with the original business and industry of the parent company. The zaibatsu, on the other hand, particularly the largest three, were each involved in a very wide range of businesses and industries. It is also worth noting that possession of the capital behind the konzerns was comparatively more open (as will be shown later, ownership of zaibatsu capital was extremely exclusive). In addition, the konzerns aggressively pushed into new fields in the heavy and chemical industries that were avoided by the risk-averse zaibatsu. The konzerns were able to expand as rapidly as they did by exploiting the gaps left open by the zaibatsu, by pursuing new technologies, and by actively moving into the colonies.

The spectacular appearance of the New Konzerns was symbolic of the new economic stage that Japan entered in the 1930s. These five large groups, however, were not the only konzern-like structures to appear. It is important to stress that many other companies also began to establish impressive numbers of subsidiaries, moving towards the holistic corporate group paradigm. Far from being the only corporate groups on the scene, the five major New Konzerns were joined by many other large enterprises of the day forming such parent-centred groups. It would not be wrong to call these other groups New Konzerns as well, and this can be confirmed by the large number of special articles that appeared in contemporary economic publications about 'industrial konzerns' or corporate groups. Companies that were often featured include Toyobo, Kanebo, Matsushita, and Toyota, as well as many other familiar names in modern Japanese business. These were also referred to as 'industrial combines' or 'industrial groups', and, although wartime economic controls in the early 1940s served temporarily to reduce the numbers of their subsidiaries, they were in many cases the direct forebears of the post-war corporate groups (Shimotani 1994*a*).

The Organizational Structure of the Zaibatsu

Next, let us examine those pillars of the pre-war Japanese economy, the zaibatsu (Morikawa 1992). While the general zaibatsu (Mitsui, Mitsubishi, and Sumitomo) are the best known, there were also numerous small and medium-sized zaibatsu, along with a host of regional zaibatsu. It is important to note that the zaibatsu were not unchanging entities; they were not exempt from changes in appearance and composition resulting from Japan's economic development.

If we restrict our discussion to the general zaibatsu, however, we can observe that the process of capital formation among the zaibatsu families originally depended heavily on the policies and national industries of the government, stretching for almost fifty years from roughly the middle of the 1800s. Over this period, the zaibatsu gradually shed this direct dependence on government support, becoming able to undertake independent use of their own capital from about the turn of the century. While maintaining close connections with the government during this process of self-assertion, the zaibatsu also expanded aggressively into a variety of industrial areas, eventually gaining control of these industries to a great degree. Their growth paralleled Japan's rapid economic expansion, and they experienced consequent enlargement of their respective organizations. However, the traditional organization of the zaibatsu structure(s) was geared to maintaining business opportunities for family members; as their sway over the Japanese economy increased, they found it necessary to revamp this family approach to organizational structure. Major structural adjustments occurred in the 1910s, resulting in the transformation of their various businesses into individual joint-stock companies. This resulted in turn in pyramid-like structures, with a zaibatsu family occupying the top position, supported by a holding company (the zaibatsu headquarters), below which came the various joint-stock companies (Kikkawa 1987).

In the case of Mitsui, which was the largest zaibatsu in the pre-war period, the central headquarters was founded in 1909 as Mitsui Gomei (Mitsui Partnership). Mitsui Partnership developed from a clan organization that had served to promote the interests of the collective family business, and, as the various branches of its business were turned into individual joint-stock companies, it became a holding company. The eleven houses (families) of the Mitsui clan maintained 100 per cent control over Mitsui Partnership, which in turn held significant stakes in the subsidiary joint-stock companies and had major influence over their management. The pre-war zaibatsu were based on the closed nature of zaibatsu family ownership, and the respective zaibatsu headquarters were typically able to maintain extremely tight control over their subsidiaries. Still, this did not necessarily mean that clan members directly managed the subsidiary companies. While details differed in the cases of each zaibatsu, the zaibatsu headquarters generally worked to recruit and develop non-family talent, and actual affairs of business were often left to these non-family managers. Known literally as 'clerk managers', a term that gives us an idea of the clear delineation of family from non-family, these individuals typically had strong ties of loyalty to the zaibatsu clan and families.

The level of actual control that the zaibatsu exercised over Japanese industry took a dramatic leap in the 1920s. By the end of the year 1930, the swath of industries in which the three largest zaibatsu interests (Mitsui, Mitsubishi, and Sumitomo) alone accounted for more than 60 per cent of the total capital involved, embraced the mining, chemical fertilizer, paper, fishing, transport, trading, and warehousing industries. The key areas for investing zaibatsu funds were banking, trading, mining, and shipping. In the case of Mitsui, for example, Mitsui Bank, Mitsui Bussan (trading), and Mitsui Mining were the three principal member companies. In addition, the various industrial interests of the zaibatsu took leading roles in the formation of cartels, and the huge monopoly profits that resulted were sufficient to permit virtual self-financing, at least until the late 1920s (Shibagaki 1965).

By the end of the 1920s, the zaibatsu headquarters companies had essentially become pure holding companies at the apexes of respective pyramids of large numbers of substantial member subsidiaries. In the cases of the general zaibatsu, composed of ten or more large member companies, the members were involved in a tremendous range of industrial activity, meaning that they could also be described as huge multi-industry pyramid structures, i.e. corporate complexes.

Changes in the Zaibatsu

The zaibatsu underwent further dramatic change in the 1930s, and it was this structural transformation that gave rise to the dual-level hierarchical nature of Japan's corporate aggregates.

The economic crisis that swept the country in the early 1930s impoverished the general population (especially farmers), but left the huge capital holdings of the zaibatsu intact or even enlarged. As a result, the zaibatsu became targets of social resentment, and managers of the leading zaibatsu became subject to terrorist attack. This forced the zaibatsu to institute a number of countermeasures, known collectively as the 'zaibatsu conversion'. A limited amount of stock in zaibatsu member companies was made available to the public, contributions were made to social causes, family members retired from the front lines of business involvement, and other changes were made to give the impression that the zaibatsu organizations were no longer the possessions of a select number of families. These changes were essentially cosmetic, intended to ward off social attack; they were also sarcastically called the 'fake conversion'.

However, with the rapid development of heavy and chemical industries transforming the Japanese economy over the course of the 1930s, the zaibatsu began full-scale entry into these industries, and it was this process more than anything else that worked against the principle of zaibatsu cohesiveness (particularly towards the end of the decade) (Hashimoto 1984). That is, the process of heavy and chemical industrialization required such prodigious funding that even the zaibatsu were forced to sell significant blocks of shares in their member companies. This gradually broke the exclusive grip that they had maintained on these

holdings. Meanwhile, the technological requirements of the new industries, together with the accumulation of company-specific managerial
resources on the part of the member companies, led to larger measures of
de facto independence from the zaibatsu headquarters holding companies.
The concentrated, exclusive control of stockholdings and the centralized
organizational structures began to weaken. More diverse ownership and
a transition towards decentralized structure crept in, influenced by higher
levels of member-company autonomy. These trends were further reinforced by the strengthening of wartime economic controls at the end of the
decade, and the centripetal force exerted by the zaibatsu headquarters
began to wane, because controls were administered at the industry level
and served to weaken the multi-industry pyramid structure of the
zaibatsu organizations.

It is significant that the zaibatsu organizational transformation
described above occurred at the same time as the conversion of zaibatsu
member companies into 'corporate groups'. The forces that were bringing
about the creation of the previously mentioned New Konzerns (corporate
groups) were also pushing zaibatsu member companies in the same direction.

In practical terms, this meant that the various zaibatsu member companies formed subsidiaries of their own, thus becoming operating holding
companies. That is, each original member company became its own small
constellation of enterprises within the larger zaibatsu constellation of
member companies (Shimotani 1993). In the Mitsui case, Mitsui Bussan,
Mitsui Mining, Mitsui Lines, Mitsui Chemicals, and other member companies each actively formed its own diversified and vertically integrated
group of subsidiaries that took the form of an organic 'corporate
group'. Just as the New Konzerns had developed, so similar organizations
began to appear in large numbers within the larger constellations of the
zaibatsu.

The transformation of the zaibatsu member companies into 'holding
companies' can be confirmed from their self-compiled official corporate
histories. Additional confirmation is supplied by their inclusion in the
ranks of holding companies that were identified immediately following
the war (Holding Company 1951). In November 1945, as part of the
zaibatsu dissolution process, GHQ (General Headquarters of the Occupation Forces) issued its 'Memorandum Concerning the Dissolution of
Holding Companies', and a total of eighty-three major holding companies
were named in five initiatives undertaken from September 1946 to
September 1947. The first round focused on four major 'holding companies of the first order', including the Mitsui and Mitsubishi headquarters
companies. The second round identified 'holding companies that have
operating divisions and which invest in and control large numbers of
related subsidiaries'; that is, forty of the New Konzerns and corporate

groups described earlier. Significantly, the third round targeted zaibatsu-affiliated 'major subsidiaries with strong holding company-like characteristics', and twenty member companies of the major zaibatsu were named.

As we have seen, the mounting independence of the zaibatsu member companies, along with their development as holding companies through the establishment of subsidiaries of their own, both of which became pronounced from the late 1930s, worked to transform the zaibatsu into collections of corporate groups. Thus, the organizational structure of the zaibatsu became hierarchically separated into the larger constellations of the zaibatsu member companies and the smaller constellations of their subsidiary corporate groups.

Fig. 1.3 provides a comparison of Japanese corporate aggregates now and as they existed in the 1930s. Corporate groups (New Konzerns before the war) can be seen to be common to both periods, and it is important to consider this from the standpoint of what kinds of corporate complexes these corporate groups created on the higher level. It is difficult to grasp the process properly if one sees it simply as a one-track switch from zaibatsu to corporate complex (Hashimoto and Takeda 1992). A dual-level corporate group/complex two-track view, which takes into account both the pre-war (late 1930s) and post-war situations, is needed. The same approach would be necessary in international comparisons, too; differences among corporate groups in each country would have to be analysed, as well as the kind of corporate complexes they produced on a higher level.

Two-tiered structure		1930s ⟶	Present
Corporate complexes		General zaibatsu	6 largest complexes
		⇩	⇩
Corporate groups	(members of complex)	Member companies	Member companies
	(independent)	New Konzerns	Corporate groups

Fig. 1.3. *Tiered structure of Japanese corporate aggregates.*

However, there is a need to reconsider the traditional definition of the zaibatsu, generally taken to mean an entity that is both (1) a group of diversified businesses, and (2) owned exclusively by a family or clan (Morikawa 1992). This definition seems to be too narrow to facilitate sufficient understanding of Japanese corporate aggregates in both the pre-war and post-war periods, nor does it allow effective cross-national comparison. For example, use of the traditional definition complicates treatment of the various New Konzerns of the 1930s and of Korea's chaebol aggregates, as it has required the two conditions to be met simultaneously. As illustrated in Fig. 1.4, however, a two-by-two matrix that treats conditions of diversification and family ownership in a two-dimensional manner provides a more dynamic framework for consideration of historical shifts and for making international comparisons.

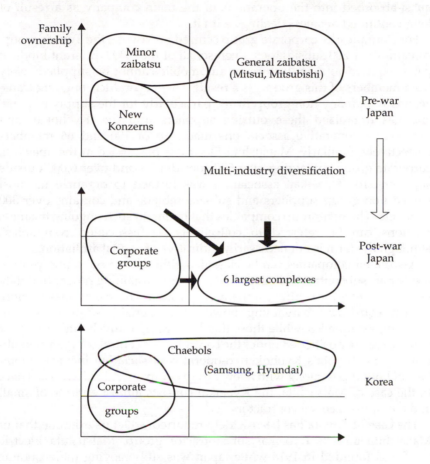

Fig. 1.4. *A two-by-two matrix analysis of corporate aggregates.*

The Subcontracting System and Subcontractors

As has been made clear, the formation of both corporate complexes and corporate groups was based on capital ownership. The zaibatsu of the prewar period were owned by families; the post-war six major complexes were built on mutual stockholding arrangements, while the scale of the

corporate groups was defined primarily by stock ownership on the part of
the central company. However, there is another kind of stable interfirm
relationship prevalent in Japan that does not rely solely on capital ties. It
shows up in the organization of subcontractors, or a cluster of businesses
that, while outside the strict domain of the corporate group, has been
quasi-absorbed into the operations of the main company as a result of
long-continued business dealings with it.

For example, the corporate group centred on Toyota, the Toyota group,
contains over 200 subsidiaries. Even so, all of the 8,000 different kinds of
parts required to manufacture an automobile cannot be supplied solely
from members of this group. As a result, Toyota conducts ongoing transactions with many non-group firms, particularly for the supply of parts,
and has organized these outside suppliers into the 'Kyōhokai' and
'Eihokai', co-operative associations made up of 190 and 66 members
respectively. Similarly, Matsushita Electric is positioned at the apex of a
corporate group containing over 600 subsidiaries and over 6,000 outside
suppliers. Its 'Kyoeikai' association was formed to organize its most
valued non-group suppliers and sub-assemblers, and contains over 300
members. The non-group companies that maintain such ongoing business
relations can be referred to collectively as 'associated companies',
although the term is not necessarily indicative of capital affiliation.

Associated companies can be classified either as 'co-operating companies' or as 'subcontractors', depending on the bargaining power that they
possess *vis-à-vis* the central company in question. Those that possess more
or less equivalent bargaining power (managerial resources) are co-
operating companies, while those that have comparatively little room for
manœuvre are positioned under the control of the central company as subcontractors. Toyota's Kyohokai co-operative association includes members of both types (along with a few group company subsidiaries as well).
In the case of Matsushita, the Kyoeikai consists almost entirely of small
and medium-sized subcontractors.

The case of Toyota has been widely reported, so let us examine that of
Matsushita and its Kyoeikai subcontractor group. Matsushita Electric
itself was founded in 1918 while Japan was still enjoying the economic
boom associated with the First World War. It started out as nothing more
than a small local factory, but by the early 1930s it was producing more
than 200 products, including wiring supplies, lamps, dry-cell batteries,
and radios, with over 1,000 employees working in 18 factories. In 1933
Matsushita became the first company in Japan to introduce the decentralized divisional system, and it adopted the joint-stock form of organization
in 1935. In the same year it began to spin off divisions and factories into
separate companies, forming what became the Matsushita Electric group.
Known at the time as the 'Matsushita Industrial Group', it contained over
thirty subsidiaries by the early 1940s (Shimotani 1986*b*).

Meanwhile, the implementation of wartime economic controls was changing the original transitory nature of subcontractors into something more fixed. The 1940 introduction of the Subcontracting Factory Assignment System, intended to increase wartime industrial output, forcibly aligned small and medium-sized enterprises with specific major companies. Several hundred subcontractors were assigned to the Matsushita Electric group (Shimotani and Nagashima 1992), and many of these wartime assignees remained associated with Matsushita even after the war.

Following the war, major Japanese companies again rushed to establish subsidiaries and set up corporate groups, but at the same time they also began to enhance the continuity of their transactions with selected outside small and medium-sized enterprises, incorporating them into a sort of external 'keiretsu' organization. In the area of sales, for example, home appliance and electronics makers had formed keiretsu chains of whole-salers and retailers throughout the country by the end of the 1950s. Matsushita boasted the largest network and was able to attract the most capable distributors, primarily because it had already begun this process in the 1930s. The sales keiretsu had been set up under a theme that can be loosely translated as 'mutual co-operation and mutual prosperity' for the three levels of manufacturer, wholesaler, and retailer, but wartime controls had prevented the keiretsu from functioning and it was abandoned (Son 1992; Shimotani 1995).

On the manufacturing side, the process of keiretsu formation for the purpose of parts supply took place through the sytematization of the subcontractors; the Matsushita group's official subcontractor organization, the 'Kyoeikai', was formed in 1971. The home appliance and electronics makers had begun addressing the issue of realignment of subcontractors from the late 1960s to deal with concerns over capital liberalization and international competitiveness. This realignment consisted of selecting the most capable subcontractor companies and reinforcing them by supplying technological and managerial expertise. Matsushita selected about 300 members for its newly founded Kyoeikai, and concentrated on their development through various seminars and competitions.

Today, the Kyoeikai has 307 member companies, only 12 of which are capitalized at 1 billion yen or more; over half (56 per cent) of the membership consists of small companies capitalized at 50 million yen or less, and 82 per cent of the member companies employ 300 people or less. Therefore most of the member companies are not particularly large in scale. And yet Matsushita conducts transactions with some 6,000 subcontractors in total, so this means that there is a huge body of even smaller companies positioned below the members. It should also be noted that there is no stockholding or dispatch of personnel from the Matsushita group to any of the Kyoeikai member firms.

Matsushita Electric conducts its operations within the corporate group
known as the Matsushita Electric group, yet simultaneously maintains
ongoing transactions with a large number of outside subcontractors. That
is, the Kyoeikai members have no capital and personnel connections with
the Matsushita group, but continue to receive technology infusions and
are provided with production equipment from the group, thus functioning nearly as internal units of the central company (Shimotani 1994*b*). In
other words, outside companies are quasi-internalized and treated as if
they were internal members of the corporate group.

Conclusion: Corporate Aggregates and Keiretsu

The foregoing analysis has divided Japanese corporate aggregates into
three types: corporate complexes, corporate groups, and subcontractors.
These various entities are indicative of different facets of interfirm relationships, and express different features of business groups. Of the three
types, the one that occupies the most central position is the corporate
group, composed of a large number of subsidiaries and forming a fundamental unit of business enterprise.

The majority of subsidiaries making up a given corporate group have
been spun off from their parent, and are thus quasi-externalized organic
structures that were formerly internal units of the parent. Virtually all
large enterprises in today's Japan are corporate groups of this type, meaning that there are approximately as many corporate groups in Japan as
there are large enterprises. It was in the 1930s that such corporate groups
began to form in significant numbers; originally known as the New
Konzerns, they attracted much attention. At the same time, the member
companies of the zaibatsu also began to establish large numbers of subsidiaries, thus themselves developing into corporate groups.

A number of these corporate groups can come together in a loose
arrangement to form a larger corporate complex, and Japan's current six
major corporate complexes are indeed of this nature. Corporate complexes
existed in zaibatsu form in the 1930s; although the pre-war zaibatsu and
the post-war six major complexes are dissimilar in terms of capital ownership and organizational structure, both types of corporate complex are
found to consist of a number of corporate groups.

On the other hand, the corporate group also functions as a unit of capital with lines of control flowing down from the central parent company.
Because these capital units are divided into a large number of decentralized managerial entities, Japan's corporate groups have proven to be quite
flexible, contributing to the avoidance of what might be called 'big company disease'. Still, at the operating level, corporate groups are not always

complete in and of themselves. This is because completeness requires transactions with other outside entities (co-operating companies and subcontractors). In addition, the securing of capable transaction partners and the construction of long-term, stable, ongoing transactional relationships have been necessitated by the business environment. This has led central parent companies to select some of their outside subcontractors for 'quasi-internal' organizational status, thereby forming a complete operational system. The influence of the central parent companies on these outside subcontractors is comparable to that which is observed in parent–subsidiary relations within a corporate group, so that this type of intimate assembler–supplier relationship has also come to be indicated in Japanese by the term 'keiretsu'. This quasi-incorporation of outside subcontractors into the internal structure of central parent companies or their corporate groups appears to be a distinguishing feature of Japanese business. Such subcontractors are neither internal organizations nor simply a part of the general market *per se*; they possess characteristics of both, and can be seen, accordingly, as 'intermediate organizations' (Imai *et al.* 1982).

Large Japanese enterprises have actively sought to quasi-externalize internal units into subsidiaries, while simultaneously quasi-internalizing numerous outside smaller companies and subcontractors. By taking advantage of these processes of quasi-externalization and quasi-internalization, Japan's large enterprises have been able to expand their boundaries beyond the limits of the firm and have created more flexible organizational structures.

While the term 'keiretsu' can indicate both parent–subsidiary and assembler–supplier subcontracting relationships, it is not used as a general term to describe all interfirm relations. Rather, it refers specifically to relationships that feature an imbalance of bargaining power, demonstrating a gap in relative managerial resources (see Fig. 1.1) (Shimada 1993). It should also be noted that the term 'keiretsu' refers to the interfirm transactional 'relationship' itself, and that the corporate 'aggregate' exists on a fundamentally different level. Strictly speaking, then, it is not correct to use the term 'keiretsu' to refer to the six major complexes.

Finally, let us take a brief look at the current activities of Japanese business groups. First, in the case of corporate groups, major Japanese companies are placing increasing emphasis on 'group strategy'. While the subsidiary establishment boom of the 1970s and 1980s seems to be waning, the old problem of balancing decentralization and vertical integration has resurfaced in the form of post-bubble recession restructuring strategy. While the focus of 'group strategy' is shifting from expansion to reorganization, the fundamental nature of Japanese corporate groups is likely to continue as it is for the foreseeable future.

On the other hand, major changes are being seen in the six major corporate complexes and in the subcontracting system. Japan's corporate complexes have been much criticized as symbols of exclusivity and closedness, and they have responded by consciously reducing mutual shareholding ratios and intracomplex transactions. Also, while the giant corporate complexes were appropriate in the rapid economic growth of the 1960s spurred on by the chemical and heavy industries, subsequent changes in Japan's industrial structure have gradually reduced the importance of their role. In the case of the subcontracting system, rapid economic growth saw dramatic transfers of technology and managerial resources from central parent companies to their main subcontractors. As a result, many subcontractor firms have already begun to pull away from domination by the central parent. This process, which might be described as 'de-keiretsufication', has been a phenomenon worth noting in recent years. Thus, large Japanese companies (corporate groups) are currently facing the need for new organizational strategies as the business environment continues to change.

REFERENCES

Aoki, Masahiko (ed.) (1984), *The Economic Analysis of the Japanese Firm*, Amsterdam: North-Holland.

Asanuma, Banri (1989), 'Manufacturer–Supplier Relationships in Japan and the Concept of Relation-Specific Skill', *Journal of the Japanese and International Economies*, 3.

Chandler, Alfred D., Jr. (1962), *Strategy and Structure*, Cambridge, Mass.: MIT Press.

Fair Trade Commission (Japan) (1994), *Nihon no roku dai-kigyo-shudan no jittai* [*The Status Quo of Japan's Six Largest Corporate Complexes*], Tokyo: Toyo Keizai Shimpo-sha.

Fruin, W. Mark (1992), *The Japanese Enterprise System: Competitive Strategies and Cooperative Structures*, Oxford: Clarendon Press.

Gerlach, Michael (1992), *Alliance Capitalism: The Social Organization of Japanese Business*, Berkeley and Los Angeles: University of California Press.

Hashimoto, Jiro (1984), *Dai-kyoko-ki no Nihon shihon-shugi* [*Japanese Capitalism During the Great Depression*], Tokyo: Tokyo Daigaku Shuppankai.

—— and Takeda, Haruhito (eds.) (1992), *Nihon keizai no hatten to kigyo shudan* [*The Development of the Japanese Economy and Corporate Complexes*], Tokyo: Tokyo Daigaku Shuppankai.

Holding Company Liquidation Commission (Japan) (1951), *Nihon zaibatsu to sono kaitai* [*Japanese Zaibatsu and Their Dissolution*], Tokyo.

Imai, Ken'ichi, *et. al.* (1982), *Naibu soshiki no keizai-gaku* {*Economics of Internal Organization*], Tokyo: Toyo Keizai Shimpo-sha.

Kikkawa, Takeo (1987), 'Daiichiji-taisen zengo ni okeru konzern keisei undo no rekishi-teki igi' ['The Historical Meaning of Konzern Formation during the First World War Period in Japan'], *Aoyama-keieironshu*, 22/1.

Molony, Barbara (1990), *Technology and Investment*, Cambridge, Mass.: Council on East Asian Studies, Harvard University.

Morikawa, Hidemasa (1992), *Zaibatsu: The Rise and Fall of the Family Enterprise Group in Japan*, Tokyo: University of Tokyo Press.

National Tax Administration Agency (Japan) (1994), *Zeimu tokei kara mita hojin kigyo no jittai* [*The Present Status of Corporations as Revealed by Taxation Statistics*], Tokyo.

Odagiri, Hiroyuki (1992a), *Growth through Competition, Competition through Growth: Strategic Management and the Economy in Japan*, Oxford: Oxford University Press.

—— (1992b), *Nihon no kigyo senryaku to soshiki* [*Corporate Strategy and Structure in Japan*], Tokyo: Toyo Keizai Shimpo-sha.

Okumura, Hiroshi (1983), *Shin Nihon no roku dai-kigyo-shudan* [*The Six Largest Corporate Complexes in Japan*] (new edn.), Tokyo: Daiyamondo-sha.

Oshio, Takeshi (1989), *Nitchitsu Konzern no kenkyu* [*A Study of the Nitchitsu Konzern*], Tokyo: Nihon Keizai Hyoron-sha.

Sakamoto, Kazuichi (1979), 'A Survey of Corporate Group Theories', *Gendai to Shiso*, 35.

—— (1990–1), 'Enterprise Groups in Modern Japan', *Japanese Economic Studies*, Winter.

—— and Shimotani, Masahiro (eds.) (1987), *Gendai Nihon no kigyo group* [*Corporate Groups in Modern Japan*], Tokyo: Toyo Keizai Shimpo-sha.

Sheard, Paul (ed.) (1992), *International Adjustment and the Japanese Firm*, Sydney: Allen & Unwin.

Shibagaki, Kazuo (1965), *Nihon kinyu shihon bunseki* [*An Analysis of Japanese Finance Capital*], Tokyo: Tokyo Daigaku Shuppankai.

Shimada, Katsumi (1993), *Keiretsu shihon-shugi* [*Keiretsu Capitalism*], Tokyo: Nihon Keizai Hyoron-sha.

Shimotani, Masahiro (1982), *Nihon kagaku-kogyo-shiron* [*Historical Theory Regarding the Japanese Chemical Industry*], Tokyo: Ochanomizu Shobo.

—— (1986a), 'Shinko konzern to kigyo group' ['New Konzerns and Corporate Groups'], *Keizai-ronso* (Kyoto University), 137/2.

—— (1986b), '1930 nendai Matsushita Sangyodan no keisei katei' ['Formation of the Matsushita Group in the 1930s'], *Keieishigaku*, 21/3.

—— (1988), 'Corporate Groups and Industrial Fusion', *Kyoto University Economic Review*, 124.

—— (1991), 'Corporate Groups and Keiretsu in Japan', *Japanese Yearbook on Business History*, 8.

—— (1993), *Nihon no keiretsu to kigyo group* [*Japanese Keiretsu and Corporate Groups*], Tokyo: Yuhikaku.

—— (1994a), '1990 nendai no shinko konzern keisei to zaibatsu no henshitsu' ['Zaibatsu, Konzerns, and New Corporate Groups in 1930s Japan'], *Chosa to kenkyu* (Kyoto University).

—— (1994b), 'Matsushita Denki Group no kyoei kaisha to Kyoeikai' ['On the Subcontractor System of the Matsushita Group'], *Chushokigyo-kiho*, 3.

—— (1995), 'The Formation of Distribution Keiretsu', *Business History* (London), 37/2.

—— and Nagashima, Osamu (1992), *Senji Nihon keizai no kenkyu* [*Studies on the Japanese Wartime Economy*], Kyoto: Koyo Shobo.

Son, Il-Sun (1992), 'Kodo-seicho-ki ni okeru kaden ryutsu kozo no henka' ['The Distribution System for Home Appliances in Japan in the 1960s'], *Keizaigaku-kenkyu* (Tokyo University), 35.

PART I

THE CORPORATE COMPLEX

2

Diversification Process and the Ownership Structure of Samsung Chaebol

CHUL-KYU KANG

Introduction

The Korean economy has grown rapidly during the last three decades. The annual GNP growth rate from 1963 to 1993 was 9.4 per cent on average, which was the fastest in the world compared with either the developing countries in the same period or the developed countries in the nineteenth century (their early developing period).[1]

The leading type of business group in this rapid economic growth was the chaebol, which can be defined as 'a business group which is owned and controlled by a person and that person's family'. This definition coincides for the most part with Morikawa's definition of a zaibatsu,[2] as 'exclusively owned and controlled by the family', and probably also fits the rest of the definition, 'diversified industrial firms', since it is a business group.

In Korea thirty chaebol are famous; their names are announced officially as 'the thirty largest business groups' every year on the first day of April. They account for 35.7 per cent of total shipments in the mineral and manufacturing sector, 31.6 per cent of value-added, and 15.9 per cent of employment in the same sector.[3] More than one-half of this share falls to the five largest chaebol. These chaebol are the leading factor in Korean economic development. If the Korean economy has developed successfully, then it is due to the chaebol's success. However, strong negative criticism of the chaebol is also widespread in Korea. People think that the chaebol's accumulation process is not justified even if they have succeeded in production. Meanwhile, university graduates usually get jobs in chaebol firms even if they previously criticized chaebol injustice as university students. This indicates that the chaebol are succeeding in the competition, but this is not necessary being done fairly.

This article concentrates on the case of Samsung, one of the five largest chaebol. A short history of Samsung's diversification will be studied, and both the ownership structure and the governance structure will be analysed. Samsung has expanded from a small trading company to one of the largest chaebol, including several corporate groups, within a generation. Through this study, that is, examining how the Samsung chaebol has expanded, we can understand how the Korean economy has grown so rapidly during the past several decades. This chapter may show the secret of its rapid success, its characteristics of both ownership and governance structure, and how they have formed. And finally we will show the present problems and prospects of the Samsung chaebol.

Characteristics of Samsung Chaebol

The Samsung chaebol is one of the most important business groups in Korea (see Table 2.1). The weight of the Samsung group is critical in the national economy. The total number of Samsung keiretsu firms is 55,[4] with annual sales of 37.9 trillion won (48.1 billion dollars); its production of added value occupied 2.5 per cent of the GNP in 1992. Samsung's share of the GNP was 1.5 per cent in 1986, rising to 2.5 per cent in 1992. Samsung's total employees numbered 180,000 as of 1992, comprising 0.9 per cent of the total national employment; its total assets are 38 trillion won, and its liabilities are 33 trillion won.

Table 2.1. *Number of keiretsu of the five largest chaebol*

Chaebol	1990.4	1991.4	1992.4	1993.4	1994.4	1995.4
Hyundai	39	42	43	45	48	48
Samsung	45	48	52	55	50	55
Daewoo	27	24	22	22	24	22
LG	58	62	58	54	53	50
Sunkyung	24	26	31	32	33	32
Total	193	202	206	208	208	207

Source: The Fair Trade Committee.

It has grown rapidly. The annual average growth rate of sales was 35.5 per cent during 1963–1992, while the nominal GNP growth rate was 23.7 per cent during the same period. So the share of the Samsung group in the national economy has increased.

Compared with internationally known big firms, Samsung Electronics Company reaches 11.6 per cent of IBM in sales, and Samsung Chemicals Company reaches 3.7 per cent of Dupont in sales. Samsung's trade volume is 8.1 per cent that of Itochu. These statistics tell us that Samsung firms are still small compared with bigger firms known world-wide.

R. & D. investment by Samsung is concentrated in three sectors: electronics, machinery, and chemicals. Its R. & D. investment is top-level in Korea, but is not so high compared to the world level. In the case of the electronics industry, R. & D. investment by Samsung is only 20 per cent as much as Matsushita, and 5 per cent as much as Mitsubishi Heavy Industries Company in the machinery sector. The technical manpower per project is 10.4 persons in Samsung compared with 16 persons in Toshiba. The contribution rate of new commodities to sales is 33.4 per cent for Samsung, but for Hewlett Packard it is 70 per cent (Jun and Han 1994: 266).

The Samsung group covers a wide area of industries, from food to electronics and now automobiles. Having started out as a trade company, it has entered almost all the manufacturing and service sectors, step by step. Samsung's corporate governance style is that of the owner Lee and his family management system, which has never changed. The owner is the dominant shareholder through both his own shareholdings and the keiretsu's shareholdings. The total shareholdings of the owner were 48.9 per cent as of 1 April 1994 (see Table 2.5). In order to control its many subsidiaries efficiently the group has used a secretarial office.

The Samsung chaebol belongs to the first quadrant of Shimotani's diagram (see Fig. 1.4), where the concentration of ownership is very high and the subsidiaries are multi-diversified (see Fig. 2.1). Most Korean chaebol are in both this and the second quadrant, like the Samsung chaebol. One or two chaebol, for example, Kia Motors, are in the third quadrant, where

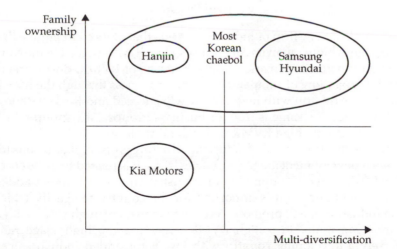

Fig. 2.1. *Ownership and diversification of Korean chaebol.*

ownership is dispersed and the subsidiaries are diversified within a single industry.

Diversification Process

Value-Added Margin Ratio Competition

To analyse the development process we have chosen the Value-added Margin Ratio (VMR) model as a criterion. Any firm or country will succeed if it wins the VMR competition with its rivals. That is, the higher the relative VMR, the more of the market share will be achieved.

The VMR is defined as value-added margin over added value as in equation (1). Value-added Margin Ratio is defined as

$$m = 1 - A/v, \tag{1}$$

where v represents added value per manhour, A is factor costs and taxation per manhour, and m is the value-added margin ratio. A includes wage rate (w), financial cost (f), rent expenses (l), and taxes (t), as shown in (2).

$$A = w + f + l + t \tag{2}$$

The commodity or the industry which has the relatively higher value-added margin ratio among the competitors has the comparative advantage. So we define the relative VMR (RVMR) as $R = m/m^*$, where m^* is the world average VMR of the commodity or the industry in question. Then the market share S will be a function of the RVMR.

$$S = F(R), f' > 0 \tag{3}$$

If the RVMR of one firm or industry exceeds that of its competitors, that is, if R becomes higher than its competitors, then it will succeed in the competition and increase its market share. In terms of RVMR, development means the expanding of comparative competitiveness through the RVMR competition. Any firm with high RVMR will succeed and those with low RVMR will fail. The same is true for business groups. Any group which has many firms with high RVMR will expand rapidly.

In general, the differential of industrial structure is one of the reasons for the uneven development among countries, since it is related to differences in added value. Every commodity or industry produces different added value per manhour. So it is important for the country to specify which band of industries it will promote. A country with many high value-added industries can maintain a high RVMR even under a high wage rate. Conversely a developing country with low value-added industries can achieve high RVMR if its industries' added value greatly exceeds the factor costs A. Thus, what the major industries are in terms of the added value in each period is important for each country. A desirable industry always produces added value high enough to succeed in the VMR competition. As seen in equations (1) and (2), the determinants are the wage rate (w), financial cost (f), rent (l), and taxes (t). While the added value of the firm or industry is positively related to the VMR, the factor costs are negatively related.

The wage rate is inversely related to the VMR. In a developed country where the wage rate per manhour is more than $10, the VMR tends to decrease, so that it is important to select appropriate industries bringing enough added value per manhour. If any country fails to exploit appropriate industries with high VMR, then it experiences rapid de-industrialization like the hollowing out of US industry in the middle of the 1980s. The emergence of the Newly Industrializing Economies (NIEs) since the late 1970s, and the rapid growth of China and the South-East Asian countries since the late 1980s, are thought to be due mainly to the low wage rate, which makes the RVMR high enough to be competitive in the low value-added industry.

The rental cost of capital influences the VMR, and it can be measured by the interest rate. The firm or industry with relatively low interest produces relatively high VMR, so that it can increase its market share. The same is true for the rent expenses.

The 'low' interest rate means that the differential between the official rate and the black market rate was large. As illustrated in Table 2.2, the gap between the official interest rate and the curb market was about 30 percentage points in the 1960s, ranged from 20 to 30 points in the 1970s, declined to 20 points in the 1980s and 10 points in the early 1990s. Any firm that can borrow from financial institutions gets rent from the interest differential; those firms with easy access to the official financial market became the current chaebol. This explains why the debt/equity ratio of Korean firms has been so high (around 3 for average firms and 5 for chaebol firms), and it is one of the reasons why the Korean official financial market has faced chronic excess demand.

Another factor determining the VMR is the efficiency of the institution or organization. It affects the RVMR indirectly by reducing A. A country or firm whose institutions and organizations are efficient enough to reduce the transaction cost can maintain a relatively high VMR. Government policy affects the VMR in this way.

Both the domestic and the foreign conditions were favourable to the enhancement of the RVMR of the Korean firms, especially of the chaebol, and thus increased the share of Korean products in the world export market. Since VMR is determined by such factors as wage rate, added value, interest rate, rent, taxes, etc., the above various factors affected the RVMR of chaebol firms, directly or indirectly. The chaebol's exclusive enjoyment of this environment, together with their information gathering power,

Table 2.2. *Interest rate in the official financial market 1954–1994* (%)

Year	Bank lending rate (A)[a]	Inflation (B)[b]	Real interest rate (A–B)	Curb market lending rate[c]	Debt/ equity ratio[d]
1954	18.3	31.8	−13.5	n.a.	n.a.
1955	18.3	62.1	−43.8	n.a.	n.a.
1956	18.3	34.0	−15.7	n.a.	n.a.
1957	18.3	22.0	−3.9	n.a.	n.a.
1958	18.3	−1.3	19.6	n.a.	n.a.
1959	17.9	1.3	16.6	n.a.	n.a.
1960	17.9	11.7	5.8	n.a.	n.a.
1961	17.5	14.0	3.5	n.a.	1.36
1962	16.6	18.4	−1.8	n.a.	1.54
1963	15.7	29.3	−13.6	52.6	0.92
1964	16.0	30.0	−14.0	61.8	1.01
1965	26.0	6.2	19.8	58.9	0.94
1966	26.0	14.5	11.5	58.7	1.18
1967	26.0	15.6	10.4	56.5	1.51
1968	25.2	16.2	9.1	56.0	2.01
1969	24.0	14.8	9.2	51.4	2.70
1970	24.0	15.6	8.4	50.2	3.28
1971	22.0	13.9	8.1	46.4	3.94
1972	15.5	16.1	−0.6	39.0	3.13
1973	15.5	13.4	2.1	33.2	2.73
1974	15.5	29.5	−14.0	40.6	3.16
1975	15.5	25.7	−10.2	47.9	3.40
1976	18.0	20.7	−2.7	40.5	3.65
1977	16.0	15.7	0.3	38.1	3.51
1978	19.0	21.9	−2.9	41.7	3.67
1979	19.0	21.2	−2.2	42.4	3.77
1980	20.0	25.6	−5.6	45.0	4.88
1981	17.0	15.9	1.1	35.3	4.52
1982	10.0	7.1	2.9	30.6	3.86
1983	10.0	5.0	5.0	25.8	3.60
1984	10.0	3.9	6.1	24.7	3.43
1985	10.0	4.2	5.8	n.a.	3.48
1986	10.0	2.8	7.2	n.a.	3.51
1987	10.0	3.5	6.5	22.95	3.40
1988	10.0	5.9	4.1	22.68	2.96
1989	10.0	5.2	4.8	23.10	2.54
1990	10.0	10.6	−0.6	19.86	2.86
1991	10.0	10.2	0.2	23.39	3.09
1992	10.0	6.1	3.9	17.16	3.20
1993	9.5	4.8	4.7	15.72	2.95
1994	9.5	6.2	3.3	15.84	3.02

[a] At year-end, one year's maturity. Bank of Korea, Economic Statistics Yearbook (Seoul, various years).
[b] Change of GNP deflator, Bank of Korea, Price Survey (Seoul, various years).
[c] Cole and Park (1983: 131); non-published data of the Bank of Korea.
[d] Bank of Korea, *The Statistics Yearbook*, various years.
Sources: The sources shown in the notes and Kim (1987).

rent-seeking activities, and government subsidies, made them the leaders of Korean economic growth during the last three decades.

Samsung, which is one of the five largest chaebol, is known for its reasonable management, high quality of employees, and high-tech. industrial development (for example semi-conductors). By analysing Samsung chaebol we will discover the backbone of the development process of the Korean economy. The diversification process of Samsung will be scrutinized in this section and its ownership structure in the next section.

Diversification Process

Samsung expanded rapidly through diversification. Diversification of modern enterprises is defined as 'the expanding of business activities over the current commodity, market, or industry' (Cosh 1986). It can usually be measured by counting the numbers of commodities or industries in which a firm participates. This chapter will deal only with the expansion of the number of firms or industries.

Samsung established or took over 97 firms in 56 years, and 52 firms remained in 1993. Its establishment of 62 firms, 64 per cent of the total, is almost twice the 35 firms it took over. Among the 45 vanishing firms, 25 were merged with Samsung firms, 5 were sold out, and 15 were bankrupted or given to a partner or the government (see Tables 2.3 and 2.4) (Kim 1993: 34).

Horizontal diversification (1938–1968)

The diversification of Samsung can be divided into several stages. The first stage lasted until 1968, just before entering the electronics industry. In this period Samsung diversified horizontally to various sectors. Interested at first in the import substitution industry, Samsung expanded to trade, textiles, and food. In the 1950s three major firms, Samsung Corporation, Cheil Foods and Chemicals Inc., and Cheil Wool and Textile Co., were founded.

Table 2.3. *Trend of establishment, acquisition, and extinction of Samsung firms* (no. of firms)

	1938–59	1960–8	1969–75	1976–80	1981–93	1938–93
Establishment	9	8	16	5	24	62
Acquisition	12	9	1	9	4	35
Extinction	8	14	8	7	8	45
Total	13	3	9	7	20	52

Sources: Samsung Economic Institute (1986); Kim (1993).

Table 2.4. *Change in Samsung subsidiaries*

Industry	1938–59	1960–68	1969–75	1976–80	1981–93
Until 1968 Trading	S. General Store (1938)* S. Tading Co. (1951) Keunyoung (1958)				
Food and beverage	Chosun Brewery (1939)* Chosun Yeast (1948)* Cheil Sugar Refinery (1953) Pungkuk Liquor (1953)* Taehan Sugar (1955)* Hyosung Trading (1957)* Tongyang Sugar (1957)*	Cheil Sugar Sale (1969)* Sunil Dextrose (1972)*	Donglip Industry (1978)*	Hankuk Coking (1982) Cheil Frozen Food (1987)	
Textiles	Cheil Wool (1954) Tongil Textile (1958)* Cheil Costume (1958)*	Hanil Nilon (1963)* Samyoung Inc. (1968)*	Cheil Synthetics (1972) Samri Textile (1973)*		Hicreation (1988)
Finance and insurance	Heungup Bank (1957)* Chunil Securities (1957)*	Dongbang Life Insurance (1963) Dongnam Securities (1963)*			S. Winners Card (1988) Dongsung Investment Consulting (1988)

	Commercial Bank (1958)* Anguk Fire Insurance (1963)* (1958) Choheung Bank (1959)*	Dongyang Fire & Marine Insurance (1963)*		
Distribution and advertisement	Shinsegae Dept. Store (1963)	Shinsegae Store (1974) Cheil Communications (1973)		Cheil Bozel (1989) Shinsegae Taejun Station Store (1990)
Other services	Joon-Ang Development Co. (1963) Dongyang Broadcast (1963)* Joong-Ang TV Broadcast (1963)* Joong-Ang Daily News (1965) Seoul FM Broadcast (1966)*	Hotel Shilla (1973)	Kyungju Hotel Shilla (1977) Yunpo Leisure Development (1979)	S. Lions (1982) Hankuk Safety System (1981) Chosun Hotel (1983) Dongbang Building Maintenance (1988) Daekyung Building (1989) S. Economic Research Institute (1986)
Other manufacturing	Samchuck Cement (1956)* Honam Fertilizer (1958)* Hankook Tier (1958)* Korea Hungjin (1966) Ulsan Fertilizer (1961)* Taehan Oil (1963)* Hankook Fertilizer (1964)* Junju Paper (1965)			
From 1969 to present				
Electric and electronics	S. Electronics (1969) S. Sanyo Electric (1969)		Joong-Ang SVP (1979)* S. GTE Communication (1977)*	SS Watch (1983) SS H.P. (1984)

Industry	1938–59	1960–68	1969–75	1976–80	1981–93
From 1969 to present					
			S. Display Devices (1970)	S. Semi-conductor (1977)*	SS Medical Systems (1984)
			S. Electric Parts (1973)	Hankuk-Electro Communication (1980)	SS Data Systems (1985)
			Hankuk Computer (1971)		Hankuk Shinyets Silicon (1986)
			Electro-Mechanics (1973)		SS Emerson Electrics (1988)
			S. Corning (1973)		Kwangju Electronics (1989)
					Samtech (1990)
Heavy industry			S. Heavy Industry (1974)	S. Precision (1977)	SS United Aerospace (1985)
				S. Shipbuilding (1977)	SS Clark (1987)
				S. Aerospace (1977)	SS Kloekner (1989)
				Taisung Heavy Industries (1977)*	
Petrochemicals			S. Petrochemicals (1974)		Taehan Precision Chemicals (1988)
					SS General Chemicals (1988)
					Cheil Sibagaigi (1988)
					BP-Chemicals (1989)
Construction			Joong-Ang Engineering (1975)	Korea Engineering (1978)	
				S. Engineering & Construction (1977)	

Notes: S. represents Samsung. Firms marked * are now defunct.
Sources: Samsung Economic Institution (1986); Kim (1993).

Based on these three parent companies, several related companies were taken over.

Samsung was also interested in the financial industry in this period, for smooth financing.[5] It took over three of the five commercial banks, one every year from 1957 to 1959: Hanil Bank in 1957, Commercial Bank of Korea in 1958, and Chohung Bank of Korea in 1959. At the end of the 1950s the total number of Samsung keiretsu was 13 (Kim 1993: 28).

However, three banks owned by Samsung were taken over by the military government in 1963, as Samsung's owner Lee was charged as an illicit money-maker. That same year, Samsung took over Tongbang Life Insurance Co. for its continuous financial purposes.[6]

With its new financial firm, Samsung attempted to diversify to the fertilizer industry by building Korea Fertilizer Co. in 1964, but this ended in failure when it was charged with saccharin smuggling. Samsung gave up on the fertilizer industry by offering the Korea Fertilizer Co. to the government in the middle of the 1960s, but took it over in 1994 through participation in the privatization of public enterprises.

Samsung also participated in the mass media industry of TV and radio broadcasting. As a result seventeen firms were newly built and twenty-one firms were acquired during this period (see Table 2.3).

Penrose (1959) has shown that diversification occurs as a response to special opportunities. The special opportunities related to new commodities come from current R. & D. or production activity, from market activity, or from existing extra factors, and sometimes from normal business activity. Firms also diversify for risk avoidance or in response to competitors' diversification, and sometimes diversification comes from the general strategy of growth.

The early diversification of Samsung came from the opportunity for profit or rent from market activity in new fields where nobody had yet entered rather than from R. & D. activity. This is shown by the early diversification mainly in the fields of light industry, trade, and banking rather than in high-tech. industry.

Diversification to heavy and chemical industries (1969–1980)

From 1969 when it entered the electronics industry, Samsung diversified to heavy and chemical industries throughout the 1970s. During this period the government's declaration of a policy to promote heavy and chemical industries stimulated investment in this field nation-wide. Samsung, like other top chaebol, participated in such industries as electrical and electronic goods, shipbuilding, heavy machinery industry, and petrochemicals.

New establishment was the main method of diversification until 1975. During 1969–75 there were 16 firms established, while only one firm was taken over. Among these, 9 belonged to the heavy and chemical industry. This period was the first step in heavy and chemical industry in Korea. Samsung itself was entering the field for the first time and there were not enough firms to be merged or acquired yet. But the situation changed in the later half of the 1970s. Samsung added 14 firms from 1976 to 1980, 9 of them being taken over and 5 newly built. This means that when ailing firms began to appear, Samsung, already having a parent company in the electronics industry, could positively take over the related firms. According to Penrose's explanation, Samsung found opportunities and diversified in the heavy and chemical industry and also had to diversify to compete with other chaebol in this field. The character of the diversification was not different from the former period in terms of horizontal diversification. However, the diversification field was changed as shown by Table 2.5. The main field of diversification was changed from light industry until the late 1960s, to heavy and chemical industry during the 1970s. Vertical diversification began to appear in the electronics and electrical industry in the late 1970s, as Kim's study shows. He concludes that the diversification of Samsung was horizontal until the 1960s, but vertical in the 1970s.[7]

In this period Samsung began to form corporate groups[8] in several industries. Before entering the heavy and chemical industries Samsung's diversification was directed mainly to horizontal expansion. After enter-

Table 2.5. *Trend of Samsung keiretsu firms' increase by industry* (no. of firms)

Industry	1938–59	1960–8	1969–75	1976–80	1981–93	1938–93
Trade	3	—	—	—	—	3
Food	7	—	2	1	2	12
Textiles	3	2	2	—	1	8
Paper	—	1	—	—	—	1
Fertilizers etc.	3	3	—	—	—	6
Petrochemicals	—	—	1	—	3	4
Electric and electronics	—	—	7	4	9	20
Heavy machinery	—	—	1	4	3	7
Construction	—	—	1	3	—	4
Financing	5	4	—	—	2	11
Sales and advertising	—	1	2	—	2	5
Other services	—	6	1	2	6	15
Total	21	17	17	14	28	97

Sources: Samsung Economic Institute (1986); Kim (1993).

ing the electronics and heavy machinery industries, however, it began to form corporate groups in these sectors.

Although the 1970s diversification was vertical in such fields as electronics, it was not yet a spin-off diversification, that is, producing subsidiaries from the parent company,[9] since it had just begun from the assembling and simple fabricating process, whose capital and technologies were not enough to build up new subsidiaries yet.

Spin-off diversification appeared in the 1980s. In any event, the electronics industry with Samsung Electronics Co. as the central figure became the main part of the Samsung group.

Both horizontal and spin-off diversification (1981–1990)

Diversification from 1980 on seems to consist of many spin-off subsidiaries from the core father company, especially in the electronics industry. Spin-off diversification was not significant until the 1970s. Samsung added 28 firms in this period. Among them 24 were newly built and only 4 were taken over. The electronics and electric industry accounted for 9 of them, heavy machinery industry for 3, and petrochemicals for 3, which means that spin-off diversification occurred mainly in heavy and chemical industry (see Table 2.5). Seen in terms of the production process the diversification field was changed from the parent company producing final goods to the related subsidiary producing parts, components, and materials. That is, it resulted in production keiretsu in several core firms. According to Penrose, this was a response to special opportunities coming from current R. & D. or production activity and opportunities from existing extra factors.

Together with its vertical diversification, Samsung has expanded horizontally into the service area for the high-income and advanced-age society. It has expanded into such areas as hotels, building maintenance, economic institutes, baseball teams, commodity circulation, and fashion, which are typical of capital keiretsu.

In summary, Samsung diversified to heavy and chemical industry in the 1970s by establishing core companies in the earlier part of the 1970s and then taking over the related firms or splitting the core companies into related subsidiaries from the later half of the 1970s. The above facts show that Samsung's diversification began in light industry, reached easily to capital and technology, then went into heavy and chemical industry following the government policy trend, and finally began trying to enhance its VMR by deepening the production process from the 1980s on.

Restructuring plan (1995–)

Samsung announced its restructuring plan on 27 October 1994. According to the plan Samsung was to sector its business structure into four core

groups: electronics, chemicals, machinery, and banking and insurance.
Subsidiaries were regrouped with 7 in electronics, 2 in chemicals, 2 in
machinery, 6 in banking and insurance, and 7 in others so that the total
number of subsidiaries would become 24, down from 50. Of course this is
only a plan which has not yet been executed.

This restructuring plan was announced both as a response to the government's specification policy and according to Samsung's own needs.
The core groups might coincide with the concept of Shimotani's 'corporate
group', since they make a group around the parent company. If Samsung
enters this core group era, then it will be characterized as a chaebol with
several typical corporate groups.

The Sources of Rapid Diversification

There are several reasons for Samsung, and for the other Korean chaebol,
to diversify rapidly. Most importantly, Samsung chose the right industries
at the right time. Korea was an agricultural society, with 63 per cent of the
population engaged in the agricultural sector in the early 1960s. In this
kind of society anyone who had some business acumen could find plenty
of opportunities in the manufacturing sector, because the VMR of the
manufacturing sector was usually very high compared with that of the
agricultural sector. Under the situation in which manufacturing firms
were few in most industries and were completely protected from foreign
competitors, one with a business mind who could afford to invest got the
opportunity to manage a modern manufacturing firm and won the VMR
competition. Samsung found the opportunity to raise the VMR in the manufacturing sector.

The decision to begin with light industry such as textiles and food was
due to the shortage of those products at the time, which was a sufficient
condition to raise the VMR with these products.

The second reason for the rapid diversification of Samsung was its positive response to the government's policy. The Korean government chose
a growth strategy based on foreign capital and technology so that it always
needed foreign exchange for amortization. This choice made Korea follow
the export-led growth policy from the early period of development. In the
1970s the heavy and chemical industry-drive policy was forwarded.
Various subsidies of both financing and taxation were supplied whenever
a firm exported and tried to invest in heavy and chemical industry in the
1970s. The policy gave an opportunity to firms to diversify horizontally.
Samsung was one of the firms with enough sense to follow government
policy.

In the 1980s government policy moved toward an emphasis on R. & D.
investment and the forming of industries producing both parts and com-

ponents, and new materials. For the firms this changeover was inevitable because the wage rate was hiked so rapidly. Otherwise the VMR of the existing firms would decline so that they would lose their competitiveness against the low-wage developing countries. As a result, vertical diversification was widely prevalent from the late 1980s on.

Thirdly, diversification was closely related to rent-seeking activity. Since the financial market was distorted, rent from the interest rate margin was possible. The more firms in a chaebol, the more rent they could produce. Thus octopus-like expansion prevailed widely in most chaebol, which could make false capital through mutual investment and get substantial loans at low interest from the official bank through mutual guarantees of payment. Once a firm is established in a chaebol, it is unlikely to leave the industry even if it accumulates a deficit, because it produces a good amount of rent. There are several kinds of rents for the chaebol, including large amounts of loans with interest rate differential, entry barriers, exit protection, land holdings with tax exemption, subsidies, etc. Normally, even an existing firm should be sold out if it is badly run, but this does not happen in a rent-producing society. That is, the rent restricts exit. The rents come from the distortion of the financial market and the excessive government intervention. In any event the rent can raise the VMR of the rent-seeking firms.

Appraisal

Samsung's diversification has progressed through three stages. In the first stage it expanded horizontally to the trade, textile, and banking industries during the period from 1938 to the 1960s. From the 1970s it entered the heavy and chemical industry and expanded mainly in this sector. This is the second stage. In the third stage, beginning in the 1980s, Samsung's diversification can be characterized as the formation of corporate groups in several sectors, in such fields as electronics, chemicals, and heavy machinery. In 1994 it announced that it would build four corporate groups in the near future.

Samsung's diversification was done by forming intra- and inter-industry relationships of affiliated companies, producing a keiretsu relationship. Shimotani's (1993) definition is true for this case: 'The keiretsu is an asymmetric relationship between the parent company and the subsidiaries, or the fixed channel itself between them in the long-run transaction.' And 'The keiretsu is not the group itself, but the vertical transaction relationship centering around big enterprises.'

Samsung is not a horizontally related corporate group, but a vertically related corporate group. This becomes clearer when we observe its ownership relations in the next section. Most firms in electronics and heavy machinery industries are production keiretsu with a vertical relationship. Most firms of the Samsung keiretsu are invested in by the core or the sub-core enterprises. So even Samsung firms which are not production keiretsu also belong to the capital or distribution keiretsu.

If diversification is usually accompanied by stockholding by the parent enterprises, that is, capital keiretsu, then most Samsung firms have a dual structure, with relationships of both production or distribution and capital.

Recently the Samsung chaebol has sectored its firms, which means a strategic organizational attempt to reduce the inefficiency and to create a synergy effect among related firms by using their mutual relationship (Jun and Han 1993: 277). Dividing into sectors can be called a restructuring of the diversification. Samsung divided fifty firms into five sectors: electronics, engineering, chemicals, financial and information, and consumer products.

Ownership Structure

Characteristics of a Chaebol's Ownership

A Korean chaebol is in general governed by an owner and his/her family. The ownership structure is not the same among different chaebol. There are several studies on the Korean chaebol ownership structure. Hattori (1982) classifies three types; Kang, Chang, and Choi (1991) also three types but a little different from Hattori's; and Kong (1994) five types. However it is common among all types that owner-and-family are the accountable top bosses. This is similar to the pre-war Japanese zaibatsu. The ownership of Korean chaebol is quite different from both the Anglo-Saxon type, owned by many small shareholders, and the German or Japanese type, owned by the bank or by cross-shareholders.

The shareholding by owners and their families of the five largest chaebol was 9.8 per cent as of 1 April 1994, and that of keiretsu owned by owners and their families, directly or indirectly, was 38.4 per cent, so that the total share of the dominant stockholders became 48.2 per cent. This makes the owner's decision-making power absolute. The dominant stockholder's average share in the thirty largest chaebol was 42.7 per cent, which was a little lower than that in the five largest chaebol. In the case of Samsung, the stockholding share of the owner and his family was 3.9 per cent and that of the keiretsu 45 per cent, so the total share of the dominant stockholders was 48.9 per cent (see Table 2.6).

Compared with the Japanese or German type of ownership structure, Korean chaebol show higher shareholding by the owners themselves.

Table 2.6. *The ownership structure of the five largest chaebol as of April 1994* (%)

Chaebol	The owner and his family (A)	Keiretsu (B)	Total (A+B)
Hyundai	16.8	44.5	61.3
Samsung	3.9	45.0	48.9
Daewoo	6.5	35.9	42.3
LG	5.4	32.3	37.7
Sunkyung	16.6	34.3	50.9
Average of 5 largest chaebol	9.8	38.4	48.2
Average of 30 largest chaebol	9.7	33.1	42.7

Source: The Fair Trade Committee.

Owners can exercise absolute power over decision-making. Another difference is found in the ownership of banks. Commercial banks rarely hold shares in chaebol firms. Mutual investment was prevalent until 1987, when the Fair Trade Law was reformed to prohibit direct mutual investment between the keiretsu in a chaebol. The custom of mutual investment was formally similar to the Japanese chaebol (zaibatsu), but they are quite different from each other. While Japanese keiretsu firms invest mutually and independently among themselves, Korean keiretsu firms invest in each other under the control of the owner. That is, Korean mutual investment between keiretsu may be characterized as the proxy investment of the owner. Direct mutual investment is not permitted by the law, but indirect mutual investment is still permitted, and instead the amount of total mutual investment is limited to the level of 25 per cent of the net assets of any chaebol firm.

Change in Ownership Structure

The ownership structure of Korean chaebol can be described as several types. However, this does not change the fact that they are owned by one family. The ownership of Korean chaebol is divided into two types: one type owned by the owner directly, and the other owned by the owner through core enterprises.[10]

In the case of a direct-control chaebol the owner is a dominant shareholder of most of its keiretsu firms. Although some chaebol have one or two big core enterprises that own other keiretsu firms, those big enterprises share ownership together with the owner. Hanjin, Lotte, Miwon, Tong-A Construction, Halla, and Haitai groups belong to this category. The other corporate groups belong to the second case, owned by the owner through core enterprises. The owner holds one or several core enterprises at the first stage, and then those core enterprises own the other keiretsu firms. A cultural foundation is usually established, besides the core enterprises. It holds shares of the keiretsu firms' stock (Kang, Chang, and Choi 1991: 44–5).

The present Samsung ownership structure belongs to the second case, owned by an owner through core enterprises (see Fig. 2.2). The owner and his family have invested directly in the eight core enterprises: Cheil Sugar Co., Cheil Wool Textiles, Cheil Synthetic Textiles, Samsung Electronics, Samsung Electronic Devices, Samsung Corporation and Marine Insurance, Samsung Life Insurance. The owner and his family hold the stock of these eight core enterprises, but do not hold the stock of the other keiretsu firms directly. The core enterprises are owned both by the owner himself and by each other, through cross-shareholding.

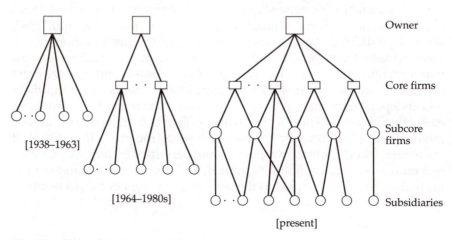

Fig. 2.2. *Ownership structure of Samsung.*

These core enterprises invest in ten subcore enterprises, separately or jointly. The meaning of 'subcore' does not indicate weight, but refers to cases in which the owner does not hold any share of stock. They are jointly invested in by the core enterprises and also have mutual shareholdings among them.

The subcore enterprises hold the shares of low-rank subsidiaries. The subsidiaries do not invest in other firms. The ownership of subsidiaries is of three types: investment by core enterprises directly, investment by sub-core enterprises, and investment by both core and subcore enterprises jointly.

It is clear that the Samsung owner and his family have invested in the 8 core enterprises, the 8 core enterprises own the 10 subcore enterprises, and then the 10 subcore enterprises own 34 subsidiaries. The ownership strategy of Samsung can be called one in which 'the owner owns the core enterprises directly, and controls the non-core firms through the core enterprises' (Kim 1993: 100).

The cross-shareholdings among the keiretsu firms become higher as we move from the core to the subsidiary. The owner's shareholding in the core enterprises is only 3.9 per cent, while the shareholdings between the core and subcore enterprises are much higher than that of the owner, but much less than those for the subsidiary. Kim's study says that mutual investment between the keiretsu firms has appeared since 1964, when horizontal diversification began to speed up. The weight of the cross-shareholdings between the keiretsu among the total inside shareholdings was 84 per cent as of 1 April 1991, and 92 per cent in 1994. Compared with this, such core enterprises as Samsung, Cheil Sugar, Cheil Wool Textiles, and Chonju Paper were recording relatively low cross-shareholdings of 6.2 per cent, 5.6 per cent, 22.3 per cent, and 17.1 per cent respectively among the keiretsu firms. However, the dominant stockholders' share, including that of the owner and the executives and staff, was much higher than this. On the other hand cross-shareholdings between the core enterprises have declined since the early 1980s. This tendency endorses the proposition that the owner owns the core enterprises directly, and controls the non-core firms through the core enterprises (Kim 1993: 100–1).

As for Samsung's ownership structure, Hattori (1982) classifies it as a cross-shareholding type on the ground of mutual investment between the core enterprises and the cultural foundation. Kong (1994) also classifies Samsung's ownership structure as a mutual owning type. But their proposition is hardly acceptable. Even if mutual investment takes place between the core enterprises, the basic ownership belongs not to any keiretsu firm but to the owner himself. The owner exercises ownership through the keiretsu firm. Direct mutual investment was widened from 1964 to the middle of the 1980s, when direct mutual investment was prohibited by the Fair Trade Law. Now we can rarely find direct mutual investment, but indirect mutual investment is still allowed. Thus the ownership structure of Samsung is classified as a type of governing by the owner through the core enterprises, which is a modified type of owner governance. The core or semi-core enterprises invest in each other and they invest in other keiretsu firms, but this is done only as proxies for the owner. In this sense, for Korean chaebol including Samsung, mutual investment does not coincide with that of the Japanese corporate complex.[11]

The role of the cultural foundation was strong through the 1970s: after the 1980s it was reduced continuously and became a minor object in the ownership structure.[12]

To sum up, the ownership structure of Samsung is basically considered to be a modified type of owner governance.[13]

Relation of Ownership Structure to Diversification

The formation of the above ownership structure is closely related to Samsung's diversification. Without losing the owner governance system, Samsung wanted to expand rapidly, which produced the modified ownership structure. A concentration of the economic power in the owner is convenient for rapid diversification. The owner can display his dynamism of expansion with such concentrated power. One problem was the shortage of the owner's financial assets for expansion, which was solved by making the double structure of direct and indirect ownership. That is, the core firms were dominated directly by the owner, and the subsidiaries were dominated not by the owner but by the core enterprises indirectly. Some of the keiretsu firms were opened to the public in the capital market and thus the small stockholders participated in ownership, but this was done within the limits of non-violation of the owner governing system. The owner's capital alone was not enough to expand or to diversify so rapidly. To make many keiretsu firms, like the octopus's tentacles, despite the owner's small amount of capital, it was necessary to create false capital through mutual investment. The owner used the core enterprises to establish new firms by making investment in non-core subsidiaries. It is natural and efficient for diversification that the share of the owner's stockholding reduces, while that of the keiretsu increases.

One reason for the rapid expansion came from rent-seeking. Rent increases as the number of keiretsu firms increases, since a chaebol's keiretsu firms are usually credited by the banks and so able to get bank loans at a lower interest rate than that of non-chaebol firms. Thus diversification was useful for rent-seeking, and Samsung's owner-governing system was a convenient system for rapid diversification (Kang and Shin 1993).

Such factors as the immaturity of the capital market, unlimited use of mutual investment and mutual payment guarantees, the government's chaebol-centred growth strategy, rent-seeking in the distorted financial market, and land speculation, etc., also contributed towards a favourable environment for the formation of this ownership structure of Samsung.

Managerial Structure

In the management of Korean chaebol, typically the ultimate authority is always the owner and his family, no matter who manages. The management of the Samsung group is such an owner-manager system, in which the owner's family holds the final responsibility. That is, all the employed managers have to account to the owner. Owner Lee and his family participate in the management directly. Routine affairs are entrusted to professional managers who have full powers except for personnel and financial management, where they are limited. In any case the final authority is President Lee.

The Owner-Manager System

The president of the Samsung group participates in management directly. This has not changed through two generations of Lees. The Lee family exercises its management power by both direct and indirect participation. As the dominant stockholder, Lee's family usually appoints and dismisses executives, which is typical indirect participation. Lee's family members also directly participate in routine management affairs as the presidents of groups, sectors, or core enterprises. In other words, Lee's family governs the Samsung group completely through its domination of the general meeting of stockholders and the executive committee (Kim 1993: 131).

A specific characteristic of the Korean chaebol's corporate governance lies not in management control through appointing and dismissing executives, but in direct participation in management, being the president or the executive. Lee Byung Chul, the founding owner of Samsung Group, exercised his final decision-making authority as the president of Samsung Group in addition to his indirect management control, for example the changing of executives. Most of the important new investments, such as the fertilizer industry in the 1960s, shipbuilding and precision industry in the 1970s, and the semi-conductor industry in the 1980s, followed the decision of President Lee. It is said that the professional managers are entrusted with matters other than strategic decision-making, such as the reshuffle of executives, financial management, and crucial new investment. This is true to some extent, but Lee has supervised and appraised the management results through the president's year-end council meeting, the results of which are reflected in the next year's reshuffle of the keiretsu presidents. By using the secretarial office furthermore, Lee gets information on the ordinary management affairs of the keiretsu and controls them as the real decision maker. Lee and his family are said to govern Samsung totally, in terms of both ownership and management. (Kim 1993: 133)

The corporate governance system of Samsung is different from that of Anglo-Saxon firms, which are accountable to many small stockholders at their general meeting, or that of Japanese or German firms, which are accountable to the banks or the cross-shareholders.[14]

The problem when the owner participates directly in management is how to control the many firms efficiently. The owner must organize a secretarial or planning office for assistance, and might also need a periodical meeting of keiretsu presidents.

Secretarial Office

Samsung's secretarial office, composed of élite staff from the core and keiretsu firms, has played an important role in assisting the president since it was organized in 1959. Its function is much more than that of staff.

The general staff of a big US company is only a staff office advising and assisting the executive committee for a better business environment and co-ordination between sectors, while the secretarial office of Samsung intervenes in business activities such as personnel affairs and management of both the chaebol group itself and the keiretsu firms.

The secretarial office of Samsung assists President Lee and his family with four functions: first, research and study; second, planning and co-ordinating; third, appraising results; and fourth, drafting plans and improving the institution (Jun and Han 1994).

The main function of the secretarial office has changed according to the times. Financing, personnel affairs and education, and management advising were the main functions from 1959 to the middle of the 1970s; the planning function was strengthened from the mid-1970s to the mid-1980s. Since then, routine managerial affairs have been transferred to the individual sector, while the functions of planning, public information, internationalization, and R. & D. at the group level have been exercised by the secretarial office. In the early founding period the secretarial office played the role of 'other self' to the top manager. In the 1970s when Samsung diversified to the heavy and chemical industry, it strengthened its function of control and co-ordination through concentration of management power. The functions of planning, research, auditing, and management advising were greatly enhanced, as in Chandler's central office.[15]

However, since the beginning of the term of the second President Lee, the functions of the secretarial office have been transferred to the individual sectors or firms. It is said that the function of the secretarial office is being reduced. The size of the office reveals this. In the 1970s there were 60–70 people in its seven teams, which increased to 150 in 1985, and peaked at 250 in 1990. After that the size of the office was reduced sharply, to 100 in 1993, as a result of the policy of autonomous management by sector, and affairs were run by a select few.

President's Council

The president's council is one of the tools by which the owner governs the corporate group. There are two kinds of president's council: group level and sector level. The president's council at the sector level specifies the co-ordination of related business processes and the exchange of information between the production keiretsu firms. In the president's council at the group level, the owner presides to receive reports, co-ordinate, and appraise the top managers. This meeting does not occur so often, but it may be compared to a council in the king's presence, where the participants are in a high state of tension. The president's council at the group level shows that the owner exercises simultaneously the power of appointing and dismissing executives, as the dominant stockholder, and the power of management control, as the president of the group (Kim 1993: 164).

Prospects for the Owner-Manager System

The owner-manager system has played a certain role in enhancing the RVMR during the expansion period. Concentration of managing power might be the most efficient way to diversify rapidly. However, this system is hardly the best in the long run. When the environment changes, the owner-manager system is likely to be changed. Especially in the period of deepening of diversification, when experts are needed, the owner-manager system is not appropriate for enhancing or maintaining the VMR.

Conclusion

The Samsung chaebol has fast become a leading part of the country's GNP growth. However, the chaebol have been criticized by the people with regard to both the legitimacy of their past wealth accumulation and the possibilities for their future development.

The first criticism comes from the assertion that a crucial part of the past accumulation of Korean chaebol did not originate from fair competition, but from government subsidies and favouritism, and from the chaebol's rent-seeking activity. The eager desire by the illegitimate government for rapid economic growth led it to grant subsidies of various types to chaebol which were big exporters, and in the 1970s to the chaebol which participated in the heavy and chemical industries drive. This resulted in the rapid formation of chaebol, but restricted the appearance and growth of non-chaebol firms. The vulnerability of Korea's small and medium industry is due in part to this historical process.

Secondly, it became customary for the chaebol to seek rent. The government created favourable conditions for the chaebol and protected them from new foreign and domestic competitors by erecting entry barriers. This encouraged the chaebol to lobby the government and to be inclined to government-led management.

Thirdly, the policy distorted the industrial structure, making it one in which large-scale assembling and fabricating industries have flourished, while small and medium-sized firms producing parts and components, new materials, and machinery have become vulnerable. Capital and intermediate goods have been imported from Japan and the USA. The added value of the assembling and fabricating industries is not nearly as high as that of the capital and intermediate goods industries. This situation has trained many blue-collar workers and welders in the assembly lines, but has rarely produced the planners and designers that are needed for the production of capital and intermediate goods.[16]

Fourthly, the chaebol itself is inefficient, responding slowly to environmental change because of its pre-modern ownership structure. Most of the important decision-making is done by the owner and his family, so that the professional managers have little space to demonstrate their ability. In spite of the managerial inefficiency, the chaebol have maintained their high RVMR level in the past, with the aid of the low wage rate and acquisition of rent. In the future, as rent-seeking is restricted and the wage rate goes up, it is doubtful whether the traditional owner management can survive and respond to the never-ending competitive situation. Moreover, the large-scale chaebol which led the growth of the economy could be an obstacle to change in the future. Samsung must now solve at least two problems: how to survive in a high factor cost environment, and how to expand in a non-rent society. The wage rate per manhour of Korean workers will rise from $5.37 to a two-digit number in dollar terms in the early twenty-first century; then Samsung must raise its added value two or three times. For this, first, Samsung must decide which industry should be chosen as central. Second, it must study how to improve the ownership structure. These two are critical parameters for Samsung's further development. One possible direction for improvement is to disperse ownership to small stockholders like the Anglo-Saxon type. The alternative is to go to a mutual ownership structure like the Japanese corporate complex.

The future of the Korean economy depends on how many firms have VMR competitiveness. If the chaebol do, it will be because they have changed their ownership structure. If not, they may lose their position as the leading groups in Korean development. It is the firm or group with relatively high VMR that will lead Korea's further development.

NOTES

1. The average annual GDP growth rate of low- and middle-income countries was recorded as 5.9% during 1965–80 and 3.3% during 1980–90. The average annual GDP growth rate of high-income economies was recorded as 3.7% during 1965–80 and 2.9% during 1980–91. However, the annual average GDP growth rate of Korea was 9.9% during 1965–80 and 9.6% during 1980–91 (World Bank 1992; 1993).
2. Morikawa (1980) repr. from Shimotani (1993: 210).
3. According to a report of KDI (Korea Development Institute 1994), the share of the ten largest chaebol is so crucial that shipments rank at 29.3%, added value is 25.4%, and employment 12.5%.
4. The number of Samsung's subsidiaries was 55 as of 1 Apr. 1995, compared to 52 as of the previous year, even as it announced the restructuring plan to build up four corporate groups while reducing the keiretsu firms to 24. See section on sectoring plan.
5. Samsung's bank ownership was aimed at acquiring reliable financing sources, and, as a result of it, bank loans to Samsung increased. The share of Heung Up Bank's loans to Samsung increased annually to 5.6% for 5 years after it was acquired in 1957 by Samsung, compared with 2.3% before the acquisition. The share of Chohung Bank's loans to Samsung increased from 0.6% for 6 years before the acquisition to 2.9% for the 3 years after the acquisition. The total amount of Samsung's bank loans as of May 1954 became 5.1 times that of the end of 1957, while the total loans of the 5 largest banks increased 2.1 times during the same period (Kim 1993).
6. As of the 1990 fiscal year the loan to the Samsung keiretsu firms by Tongbang Insurance Co. was 22.6% of Samsung keiretsu firms' total short-term loans (Kim 1993: 48).
7. Kim (1993) analysed the vertical diversification of the Samsung chaebol as having begun in the middle of the 1970s.
8. See Ch. 1 above.
9. Although the related diversification of the Samsung chaebol dated from the middle of the 1970s, the spin-off diversification seems to have begun in the 1980s since the number of acquisitions was much higher than that of establishment in the late 1970s.
10. Hattori classifies it into three types: the owner monopoly type, the core enterprises dominating type, and the mutual dominating type. Kang, Chang, and Choi classify it into three different types: the owner direct dominating type, the single core enterprise dominating type, and the multiple core enterprises dominating type. Recently Kong has divided it in more detail, as: the owner dominating type, the complex dominating type, the two-stage dominating type, the parent company dominating type, and the mutual owning type.
11. Hattori (1982) agreed on this point.
12. According to Kim (1993: 110) the share of the non-profit foundation increased sharply just before going public. For example, its share increased from 4.2% in 1970 to 33.5% in 1974 in the case of Cheil Wool and Textile, and from 0% to

43.8% in the case of Samsung. However, the share decreased heavily from the 1980s.

13. Since the 1980s the shareholdings of the executives and staff have increased rapidly, which is closely related to the opening of the Samsung keiretsu to the capital market and limited public ownership. After that opening, the system of stockholding by employees and the Saemaul Fund were established and have enhanced their shares. For example, the shareholdings of employees and the Saemaul Fund amount to 46% of total employee and staff share in the case of Cheil Wool and Textile Co., and 55% in the case of Cheil Sugar.

14. *The Economist*, 14 Jan. 1994.

15. The three functions of Chandler's central office: first, acquisition, distribution, and co-ordination for capital and manpower; second, gathering information, analysing, and planning; and third, controlling through auditing. Quoted in Jun and Han (1993: 114–16).

16. Korea is comparable to Switzerland or Singapore on this point.

REFERENCES

Bank of Korea (1993), *National Income Accounts and New SNA*, Seoul.

Choo, H. (1991), 'Hankuk jejoup ui energy hyoyulsung bunseok' ['Energy Efficiency Analysis of Korea's Manufacturing Industries'], Seoul: KIET.

Clark, C. (1940), *The Conditions of Economic Progress*, London: Macmillan.

Cole, D., and Park, Y. C. (1983), *Financial Development in Korea, 1945–1978*, Cambridge, Mass.: Harvard University Press.

Cosh, A. (1986), 'Diversification of Activities', in R. Harry and I. Palgrave, *A Dictionary of Economics*, London: Macmillan.

Economic Planning Board (EPB) (various years), *Korean Economic Indicators*, Seoul.

—— (1993), *Report on Mining and Manufacturing Survey*, Seoul.

Falvey, R. E. (1981), 'Commercial Policy and Intra-industry Trade', *Journal of International Economics*, 11.

Hattori, Tamio (1982), 'Concerning the Ownership of Korean Chaebol', *Social Science*, 30 (The Institute of Cultural Science, Doshisha University).

—— (1987), 'Comparison of Large Corporate Groups between Korea and Japan' (Korean), in Lee and Chong.

Hoffman, W. (1958), *The Growth of Industrial Economies*, trans. W. O. Henderson and W. H. Chaloner, Manchester: Manchester University Press.

ILO (1980–90), *Yearbook of Labor Statistics*.

IMF, *IFS*, various versions.

Jun, Yong-Wook, and Han, Jong-Wha (1994), *Choilyu ro ganun gil: Samsung ui seong-jang gwa jeonhwan* [*The Way to the Ultra-top-rank: The Growth and Transformation of Samsung*], Seoul: Kimyong Co.

Kang, C. K. (1988), *Industrial Policy in Korea: Review and Perspective*, Seoul: KIET.

—— (1992), *Hankuk ui 1990 yondae bigyouwi sanup* [*Comparatively Advantaged Industries of Korea in the 1990s*], Seoul: Daewoo Economic Institutes.

—— Chang, C. S., and Choi, J. P. (1991), *Chaebol: seongjang ui juyeok inga tamyok ui hwasin inga?* [*Chaebol: The Leading Actors of Growth or the Incarnation of Avarice?*], Seoul: Bibong Press Co.

—— and Shin, B. H. (1993), 'Kumli gyuje haui kumlicha jidae mohyung' ['Estimation of the Rent from the Interest Rate Differential under the Interest Regulation'], in Korean Economic Association, *Kyong Je Hak Yon Gu* [*Economic Studies*], 41/2.

Kim, J. C., and Yoo, B. H. (1987), 'Structural Changes in the Korean Manufacturing Industry', *Quarterly Economic Review*, June (Bank of Korea).

Kim, Seok Ki (1987), 'Business Concentration and Government Policy: A Study of the Phenomenon of Business Groups in Korea, 1945–1985', DBA dissertation, Harvard University.

Kim, Yeong-Ook (1993), 'Samsung chaebol ui dagakhwa wa jibae gujo ye daehan yongu' ['A Study on the Diversification and Control Structure of Samsung Chaebol'], Ph.D. dissertation, Seoul National University.

Kong, B. H. (1994), 'Hankuk chaebol ui soyu gujo ye daehan yongu' ['A Study of the Ownership of Korean Chaebol'], *Proceedings of the Korean Economic Association*.

Korea Development Institute (KDI) (1994), 'The Policy against the Corporate Group and Improvement for the Fair Trade System', mimeo.

Kuznets, S. (1966), *Modern Economic Growth: Rate, Structure, and Spread*, Clinton, Mass.: The Colonial Press, Inc.

—— (1971), *Economic Growth of Nation: Total Output and Production Structure*, Cambridge, Mass.: Bellknap Press of Harvard University Press.

Lee, H. J., and Chong, K. H. (1987), *Hankuk giup ui gujo wa chunlyak* [*Structure and Strategy of Korean Firms*], Bumoonsa.

Ministry of Science and Technology (1993), *Yearbook of Science and Technology*, Seoul.

Morikawa, E. (1980), *A Managerial Study of Zaibatsu* (Japanese), Tokyo: Toyo Keizai Shimpo-sha.

Morishima, M. (1984), *The Economics of Non-resource Countries* (Japanese), Iwanami Press.

OECD (1983), *The Positive Adjustment Policy: Managing Structural Change.*

Penrose, E. T. (1959), *The Theory of the Growth of the Firm*, Oxford: Basil Blackwell.

Petty, W. (1969), *Political Arithmetick* (1899), repr. in W. Petty, *The Economic Writings of Sir William Petty*, 2 vols., ed. C. H. Hull, Cambridge: Cambridge University Press.

Samsung Economic Institute (1986), *Samsung Group 50 yonsa* [*The 50-Year History of Samsung Group*], Seoul.

—— (ed.) (1988), *Hoam ui kyongyong cheolhak* [*Hoam's Philosophy of Management*], Seoul.

Shimotani, M. (1988), 'Corporate Groups and Industrial Fusion: Development of Corporate Restructuring in Japan', *Kyoto University Economic Review*, 58/1, Apr.

—— (1991), 'Corporate Groups and Keiretsu in Japan', *Japanese Yearbook on Business History*, 8 (Japan Business History Institute).

—— (1993), *Keiretsu of Japan and Corporate Groups: History and Theory* (Japanese), Tokyo: Yuhikaku.

UN (1993), *Industrial Statistics Yearbook*, i: *General Industrial Statistics*, New York: United Nations.

Vernon, R. (1966), 'International Investment and International Trade in the Product Cycle', *Quarterly Journal of Economics*, 80.

World Bank (1992, 1993), *World Development Report*, Oxford: Oxford University Press.

3

From Zaibatsu to Corporate Complexes

KUNIO SUZUKI

Introduction

Until the end of the Second World War, the zaibatsu wielded enormous economic power within the Japanese economy. The 'Big Three' zaibatsu in particular, Mitsui, Mitsubishi, and Sumitomo, had assembled powerful firms in wide-ranging areas such as finance (banking, insurance, and trust operations), mining, machinery manufacture, and chemicals, with the Mitsui and Mitsubishi zaibatsu each including a global trading company (Mitsui Bussan Kaisha and Mitsubishi Shoji Kaisha, respectively). These zaibatsu were broken up in the economic reforms that followed the war, only to re-emerge later as corporate complexes in the form of the Mitsui group, the Mitsubishi group, and the Sumitomo group. Further, these corporate complexes became major components of the Japanese economy, just as their zaibatsu predecessors had been.

This chapter will provide an analysis of the Big Three zaibatsu and the Big Three corporate complexes from, fittingly, three standpoints. The first will be the methods of control exercised by the zaibatsu holding companies (headquarters) over their subsidiaries, along with the role of the banks within the zaibatsu. The second will be that of the process of transformation from zaibatsu to corporate complex. Thirdly, the characteristics of intracomplex ties among firms (including the role of the banks) will be compared with the characteristics of similar ties in the zaibatsu. Because it was stock ownership that bound together the individual zaibatsu and that continues to hold together the corporate complexes, stock ownership will serve as a focus of analysis.

The Zaibatsu and the Banks

Zaibatsu Holding Companies' Control of Subsidiaries

The basic pyramid structure used by all of the Big Three zaibatsu is illustrated in Fig. 3.1. The position at the very top of the pyramid is occupied by the zaibatsu families (the Mitsui family, the Iwasaki family, and the Sumitomo family), under which follow, in descending order, the holding companies (controlled directly by the zaibatsu families), the subsidiary directly controlled and quasi-controlled subsidiary companies, their subsidiaries, and even subsidiaries of these subsidiaries. Each of the zaibatsu holding companies was charged with the functions of safeguarding zaibatsu family assets, controlling subsidiary operating companies, and co-ordinating contacts among operating companies. The precise nature of these functions, however, differed considerably among the several zaibatsu.

The Mitsui, Mitsubishi, and Sumitomo zaibatsu had 10, 11, and 15 subsidiaries, respectively, under their direct control, as well as being responsible, respectively, for 12, 16, and 6 quasi-controlled subsidiaries. When it came to financial institutions, directly controlled subsidiaries did not necessarily include the full four-institution complement of bank, trust

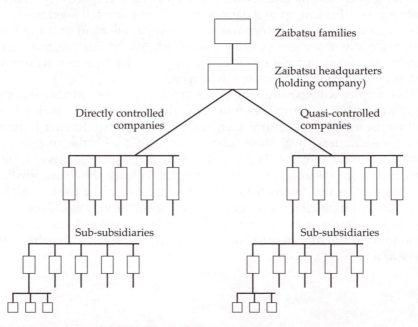

Fig. 3.1. *Structure of the Big Three zaibatsu.*

company, life insurance company, and casualty insurance company. Sumitomo maintained banking, trust operations, and life insurance under direct control, relegating its casualty insurance subsidiary (Osaka Sumitomo Marine & Fire Insurance) to quasi-controlled status. Mitsui had directly controlled trust and life insurance subsidiaries, and a quasi-controlled casualty insurance subsidiary (Taisho Marine & Fire Insurance), but Teikoku Bank (formed in 1943 from the combination of Mitsui Bank and Dai-Ichi Bank) was not designated as within either category. Mitsubishi operated directly controlled banking and trust subsidiaries, but ran quasi-controlled life insurance (Meiji Life Insurance) and casualty insurance (Tokio Marine & Fire Insurance) subsidiaries. Especially interesting is the fact that Teikoku Bank was neither directly controlled nor quasi-controlled (Holding Company 1951*a*: 90, 111, 124).

Each holding company established a number of regulations *vis-à-vis* the subsidiaries that it controlled directly. Of the Big Three zaibatsu, Sumitomo provided the strongest directives, going as far as hiring all necessary white-collar personnel and allocating them to the directly controlled subsidiaries until as late as 1943. Because directly controlled subsidiary personnel were hired in this manner, they were subject to rules laid down by the holding company, Sumitomo Honsha, which carried out a unified system of personnel and compensation policies. This made intercompany personnel transfers fairly straightforward. Additionally, holding company consideration and approval were required for all major board decisions at directly controlled subsidiaries, and the chairmen (or presidents in companies without chairman positions) were all officers of the holding company. In 1945, at the time of Japan's defeat, Shunnosuke Furuta, the representative officer of Sumitomo Honsha, served as chairman of nine subsidiaries, while three other officers were each chairman (or president) of one subsidiary. The three companies of which Furuta was not chairman were operations in Korea and Manchuria, and Sumitomo Trust. Thus, the limits of independent discretion were extremely tight, such that Sumitomo's directly controlled subsidiaries were virtually internal divisions of the holding company (Holding Company 1951*a*: 126–9).

Mitsubishi regulations were somewhat more relaxed than those of Sumitomo, with directly controlled subsidiaries allowed to make their own hiring decisions from 1932. However, compensation decisions had to be made in consultation with the holding company (and were required to conform to holding company norms), thereby easing interfirm transitions, and significant board decisions had to be ratified. Proposals that pertained to more than one directly controlled subsidiary, or to all of them, were reviewed by the Mitsubishi Council, established within the holding company. This group consisted of the head or the chief director and the executive director of the holding company, along with the chairmen (or presidents, in companies without chairmen) of the subsidiaries, and served to strengthen lateral connections (Holding Company 1951*a*: 106; Ohtsuki 1987: 18–19).

Mitsui's *de facto* directly controlled subsidiaries were only officially designated as such in September 1944, and regulations were even more relaxed than at Mitsubishi. During the 1930s, moreover, there were only five of these *de facto* directly controlled subsidiaries: Mitsui Bussan Kaisha, Mitsui Mining, Toshin Warehouse, Mitsui Bank, Mitsui Trust, and Mitsui Life Insurance. Of these, Mitsui Bussan, Mitsui Mining, and Toshin Warehouse were required to submit board decisions to the holding company, Mitsui Partnership Co. (Mitsui So-motokata after its merger with Mitsui Bussan), but the others were merely required to submit minutes of their board meetings. This was due to the public nature of the three financial subsidiaries. Each of the companies was free to make its own personnel decisions, and each had its own compensation system, making intercompany personnel transfers extremely difficult. Further, because there was no forum for discussion of proposals among the chairmen (or presidents), lateral co-operation was not particularly close. Following the examples of Sumitomo and Mitsubishi, Mitsui made the companies into officially directly controlled entities in 1944, intending to strengthen controls (eliminating special treatment for the trust and life insurance companies). It also attempted to standardize personnel and compensation policies, and to encourage more intercompany transfers and lateral co-operation. Japan's defeat less than a year later cut short these efforts, however, with few results to be seen (Mitsui Bunko forthcoming).

In short, the Sumitomo zaibatsu fostered the tightest organizational and personnel connections among its subsidiary companies, followed by Mitsubishi, with Mitsui having comparatively weak ties. The effects of this background were readily seen after the war and the dissolution of the zaibatsu, when the Sumitomo group started regular meetings of company presidents most rapidly, followed by Mitsubishi, with Mitsui taking the longest to reassemble.

The Case of the Mitsui Zaibatsu

A concrete look at the Mitsui zaibatsu provides an opportunity to see a form of control different from the straightforward control of subsidiaries by a zaibatsu holding company. This is because the Mitsui zaibatsu was characterized by noticeable contrasts in its internal control mechanisms, and because a number of huge enterprises can be seen to have split away. Availability of historical material also makes the Mitsui example more complete.

In the case of Mitsui Mining, presidents of its own subsidiaries were all dispatched officers of the parent, and all major board decisions of the subsidiaries were submitted for review. Appointment of subsidiary officers and division chiefs were approved or rejected by Mitsui Mining as well, and capital investment was heavily scrutinized, with requisite funding provided from above (Mitsui Bunko, forthcoming). In short, Mitsui Mining and its subsidiaries functioned rather like a miniature Sumitomo zaibatsu, operating almost as a single unit.

On the other hand, Mitsui Bussan, prior to its unorthodox absorption by the Mitsui Partnership holding company in August 1940, treated its subsidiaries in a manner almost opposite to that of Mitsui Mining. As an independent entity, Mitsui Bussan was itself a holding company central to the Mitsui zaibatsu, on top of its role as a trading company. In a sense, Mitsui Bussan was a zaibatsu within the larger Mitsui zaibatsu, holding shares in a large number of enterprises. Of the companies that were designated as directly controlled or quasi-controlled subsidiaries of Mitsui So-motokata (the organization resulting from the merger of Mitsui Partnership and Mitsui Bussan), many had been directly under the control of Mitsui Bussan. These included Toyo Precision Machine (later Mitsui Precision Machinery & Engineering), which received the directly controlled designation in 1944, as well as Toyo Rayon, Taisho Marine & Fire, Toyo Menka Kaisha, Sanki Engineering, and Kyodo Oil & Fats (later Mitsui Oil & Fats Chemical Ind.), which were made quasi-controlled subsidiaries at the same time. Additionally, a number of subsidiaries originated from internal divisions of Mitsui Bussan, including the directly controlled Mitsui Shipbuilding & Engineering (formerly Mitsui Bussan's shipbuilding division), Mitsui Steamship (formerly the shipping division), and the quasi-controlled Mitsui Timber Ind. (formerly the wood products division). Mitsui Bussan had a strong tradition of hands-off control of its subsidiaries (sub-subsidiaries of the main holding company), meaning that the influence wielded over them by Mitsui Bussan was even weaker than in the cases of the three financial subsidiaries. After they were made subsidiaries, it became standard practice for directors of (the former) Mitsui Bussan to be sent in to manage them (Mitsui Bunko forthcoming). This hands-off approach of Mitsui Bussan toward its subsidiaries was one factor in the delay of the Mitsui group's reorganization after the war, and in its comparatively loose structure.

As for companies that became independent, it should first be noted that Mitsui Partnership (and the less formal clan investment council that preceded it) invested in and dispatched personnel to a large number of enterprises besides those bearing the Mitsui name. Representative among these were Kanegafuchi Spinning, Oji Paper, Hokkaido Colliery & Steamship, and Tokyo Shibaura Electric (through one of its predecessor companies, Shibaura Engineering Works). All of these grew to very large proportions, and all assembled significant keiretsu organizations of their own. These firms underwent major mergers and/or capital increases during their respective growth processes, but Mitsui Partnership was not particularly aggressive in its purchases of stock, exercising control instead through the customary dispatch of chairmen and presidents. However, with the important exception of Tokyo Shibaura Electric, the dispatched officers generally built independent kingdoms under their own control and stopped submitting to the directives of Mitsui Partnership.

In the case of Kanegafuchi Spinning, Mitsui Bank set about restructuring the ailing company by sending in Sanji Muto as general manager of its Hyogo factory. Following his promotion to executive director in 1908, Muto assumed control of the company and became increasingly less responsive to the will of Mitsui Partnership. By 1916, when stockholdings in Kanegafuchi were transferred from Mitsui Bank to the holding company, Mitsui Partnership's interest was a mere 7.5 per cent, and a scant 8.4 per cent even when Mitsui Bussan's holdings were added in (Mitsui Bunko 1980).

The story of Oji Paper is somewhat similar; Mitsui Bussan's wood products division chief Ginjiro Fujiwara was sent in in 1911, also on a restructuring assignment. His leadership saw the company return to financial health by the time of the First World War, but Mitsui Partnership sold half of its 66 per cent stake in November 1916. Subsequently, Fujiwara chose to chart his own course for Oji, often independently of the holding company (Mitsui Bunko 1980, 190–7).

At Hokkaido Colliery & Steamship, Mitsui Partnership general director Takuma Dan served concurrently as chairman from 1913 until his assassination in 1932, at which point managing director Toyotaro Isomura (originally of Mitsui Bussan) was made president. In 1934, because Mitsui Partnership sold off shares in Hokkaido Colliery & Steamship, Isomura, who had been made chairman in 1934, began running the company as he saw fit, with little reference to Mitsui Partnership. By 1937, the total holdings of Mitsui companies (Mitsui Partnership, Mitsui Mining, Mitsui Trust, Mitsui Bussan, and Mitsui Life Insurance) had declined to 33.3 per cent. Upon Isomura's death in October 1939, however, Mitsui Partnership was successful in placing Katsunosuke Shimada (then a managing director of Mitsui Partnership) as chairman, thereby regaining control (Mitsui Bunko, forthcoming).

In the case of Tokyo Shibaura Electric, created through the combination of Shibaura Engineering Works and Tokyo Electric, the total holdings of Mitsui companies (Mitsui Partnership and Mitsui Bussan) were reduced from an original 34.3 per cent stake in Shibaura Engineering Works to a 14.5 per cent share in the company that emerged from the combination in 1939. Kisaburo Yamaguchi, in his capacity as president of both Shibaura Engineering Works and Tokyo Electric, had exercised leadership before the merger, but he consolidated this even more afterwards with his assumption of the chairmanship of the newly enlarged firm. Further, comparison of the Mitsui stake in June 1941 with that in June 1942 reveals that, owing to the absorption of several other companies, it declined from 16.3 per cent to 16.1 per cent, while the share of Yamaguchi and his associates rose from 11.5 per cent to 20.0 per cent over the same period, making them the primary stockholders. Intending to increase its share of ownership, Mitsui Bussan tried to acquire half of the stake held by International General Electric Co. (IGEC), which the latter was forced to sell off because of wartime legislation, but this plan ended in failure. Additionally, Yamaguchi oversaw changes to Tokyo Shibaura's articles of incorporation in June 1943 that further hindered Mitsui attempts at domination by stipulating that the chairman, vice-chairman, president, and vice-president of the company must have served at least five years with the company before being thus appointed, and by lengthening the terms of directors from one year to three years. These changes made it more difficult for Mitsui to put its own men into these positions (Mitsui Bunko forthcoming).

Aside from Yamaguchi, dispatchees from Mitsui companies occupied the other three top positions, but, because the Mitsui companies did not hold a majority of the shares, Mitsui Partnership controls concerning personnel, sales, and purchasing were ineffectual, and an independent line was taken. Had Mitsui Partnership seen to it that Mitsui companies held a majority of the shares before this situation arose, it would have been able to prevent the independent activities of the three officers that it had dispatched. Alternatively, had it increased its holdings in Tokyo Shibaura Electric, it would have been able to limit the scope of Yamaguchi's discretion. Instead, Mitsui Partnership took the opposite course, selling off 83,000 shares in Shibaura in 1936, and another 6,650 shares in 1938.

There were, in fact, a number of reasons making it difficult for the four Mitsui companies to achieve a majority stake. One of these was that there were limits on the financial resources available even to Mitsui Partnership (that is, to the Mitsui family). A second fundamental reason was the lack of availability of sufficient supplemental funding. Had the financial institutions, particularly Mitsui Bank, which had the greatest resources, invested more aggressively, they would have played an important supplementary role. Even before the First World War, however, Mitsui Bank, which had previously engaged in this type of investment, concentrated on commercial banking as opposed to institutional banking, and, as will be discussed below, tried to minimize the long-term commitment of its assets to investments in stock. The managers of Mitsui Bank believed that it should be first and foremost a commercial bank. Additionally, Mitsui Partnership continued to place emphasis on the public responsibility of the three financial institutions (including Mitsui Bank), and thus maintained more liberal controls than it did with Mitsui Bussan, Mitsui Mining, and the other non-financial firms. For these reasons, it proved difficult to change the bank's managerial direction in order to gain co-operation in the control of other companies.

The Roles of the Banks within the Big Three Zaibatsu

In a broad sense, the roles of the financial institutions within the Big Three zaibatsu in the interwar period to 1936 differed significantly from the roles that they played in the wartime economy from 1937 onward. With regard to the banks, which had the most impressive financial resources, post-1937 dependence on firms with zaibatsu ties for deposits lessened, just as dependence on these same firms for loans grew (Asajima 1968: 368–91; 1983: 572–82). Table 3.1 outlines the situation of Mitsui Bank, where the ratio of loans to deposits of the five Mitsui companies (Mitsui Partnership and the four *de facto* subsidiaries) ballooned from 49 per cent in 1938 to 163 per cent in 1941. During the same period, the ratio for the bank's general customers declined from 61 per cent to 56 per cent. It can also be surmised that, from the second half of 1940, the bank held down the expansion of general lending in order better to meet the needs of the five Mitsui companies. Comparing deposits from and loans to these companies in mid-1940, it can be seen that there is still a positive balance, but loans then grew to exceed deposits by the end of 1940. Thus, from the standpoint of the Mitsui zaibatsu, the role of Mitsui Bank shifted from that of providing zaibatsu funds for external use to that of raising funds for internal use. Similar changes can also be observed in the characteristics of Mitsubishi Bank and Sumitomo Bank.

On the other hand, the commercial banking approach of Mitsui Bank was quite different from that of Mitsubishi Bank and Sumitomo Bank. Comparison of the financial statements of the three banks as of December 1937 reveals that, while Mitsui Bank owned stockholdings worth only 350,000 yen, Mitsubishi Bank had investments in stock worth 27.06 million yen, and Sumitomo Bank had 25.44 million yen worth. Not only that, but Mitsui's holdings were composed merely of 10,000 shares in Mitsui Trust, originally founded in large measure by Mitsui Bank itself, and 20,000 shares in Showa Bank, an institution that had been jointly established by the major Japanese banks in order to help deal with the effects of the 1927 financial crisis. Accordingly, Mitsui's maintenance of its status as a commercial bank is readily apparent (*Kabushiki* 1938: 906–9; Mitsui Accounting Dept. 1938).

These differences are clearly visible immediately following Japan's defeat in the Second World War. Teikoku Bank, which had been created in March 1943 from the merger of Mitsui Bank and Dai-Ichi Bank, went on to absorb Daijyugo National Bank in August of 1944. Teikoku Bank, then, inherited the stockholdings of all three of its predecessor banks, but the

Table 3.1. *Positions of 5 Mitsui companies in terms of amounts of deposits and loans at/from Mitsui Bank (excluding colonial and overseas branches)* (ten million yen)

Date	Deposits			Loans			Balance		
	5 Mitsui Companies	General	Total	5 Mitsui Companies	General	Total	5 Mitsui Companies	General	Total
31 Dec. 1938	8 (7)	103 (93)	111 (100)	4 (6)	63 (94)	67 (100)	4 [49]	40 [61]	44 [60]
30 June 1939	5 (4)	115 (96)	120 (100)	3 (5)	69 (95)	72 (100)	2 [67]	46 [60]	48 [60]
31 Dec. 1939	8 (6)	125 (94)	133 (100)	4 (5)	78 (95)	82 (100)	4 [47]	47 [62]	51 [61]
30 June 1940	6 (4)	139 (96)	144 (100)	5 (5)	84 (95)	89 (100)	1 [81]	55 [61]	56 [61]
31 Dec. 1940	9 (6)	146 (94)	155 (100)	11 (11)	88 (89)	100 (100)	−2 [123]	58 [61]	55 [64]
30 June 1941	13 (8)	159 (92)	173 (100)	17 (17)	87 (84)	104 (100)	−4 [127]	73 [54]	69 [60]
31 Dec. 1941	11 (6)	163 (94)	174 (100)	17 (16)	91 (84)	109 (100)	−7 [163]	72 [56]	65 [63]
30 June 1942	11 (6)	193 (94)	204 (100)	18 (15)	98 (85)	116 (100)	−7 [158]	95 [51]	88 [57]

Notes: The five directly controlled companies were Mitsui Partnership (Mitsui So-motokata), Mitsui Bussan, Mitsui Mining, Mitsui Trust, and Mitsui Life Insurance. Parentheses indicate percentages of deposits or loans. Square brackets indicate ratios of loans to deposits.

Sources: Mitsui Bank Accounting Dept. (1939–42); Mitsui Bank Domestic Dept. (1939–40).

holdings of Mitsui origin consisted only of token shares in Mitsui Partnership and Mitsui Trust, with a more significant stake in Japan Steel Works (a subsidiary of Hokkaido Colliery & Steamship that had been acquired by Teikoku Bank in a somewhat accidental manner) (Mitsui Bunko forthcoming).

In the case of Mitsubishi Bank (which had absorbed Daihyaku Bank in 1943), however, holdings were maintained in the Mitsubishi zaibatsu holding company, as well as in Meiji Life Insurance, Mitsubishi Heavy Industries, and Mitsubishi Mining (all directly controlled subsidiaries), and Tokio Marine & Fire Insurance and Mitsubishi Trust (both quasi-controlled). It should be noted that the stakes in Tokio Marine & Fire, and Mitsubishi Heavy Industries were quite substantial.

Meanwhile, Sumitomo Bank (which absorbed Hannan Bank in July 1945) held shares in the zaibatsu holding company, 11 directly controlled subsidiaries, and 2 quasi-controlled subsidiaries, with particularly large stakes in Sumitomo Trust, Sumitomo Mining, and Sumitomo Metal Industries (all directly controlled). Sumitomo Bank had total paid-in holdings in related companies of 55.37 million yen, roughly double the corresponding 24.18 million yen figure for Teikoku Bank or the 25.27 million yen amount for Mitsubishi Bank. From a commercial banking standpoint, this was rather unhealthy. Sumitomo Bank began acquisitions of stock in Sumitomo Trust in 1925, Nippon Sheet Glass in 1926, Sumitomo Kyodo Electric Power and Sumitomo Chemical in 1934, Osaka Sumitomo Marine & Fire Insurance in 1935, and the Sumitomo zaibatsu holding company (Sumitomo Honsha) in 1945, with other holdings thought to have been initiated between 1936 and 1945 (Asajima 1983: 536–40). This would indicate that Sumitomo Bank played an important supplementary role in the control of the subsidiaries of Sumitomo Goshi Kaisha (subsequently Sumitomo Honsha) from fairly early on. It was because of the strict control measures over Sumitomo Bank instigated by the holding company, and because of the bank's consequent lack of independence, that it took on this type of supplementary role. Although not to the same extent as Sumitomo Bank, Mitsubishi Bank can also be seen to have played a similar supplementary role from well before the war. Mitsui Bank (later Teikoku Bank) was the only one of the three not to act in this manner.

Next, Tables 3.2–3.4 record the shares held by the zaibatsu financial institutions in their zaibatsu subsidiaries immediately following the war. Mitsui financial institutions can be seen to have shares in three directly controlled subsidiaries, but the total stakes in even these subsidiaries come to less than 2 per cent, meaning that the financial institutions did not have much of a supplementary role in terms of assisting the holding company to maintain control of the subsidiaries.

In contrast, Mitsubishi financial institutions maintained shares in ten

Table 3.2. *Ownership of directly controlled companies by Mitsui financial institutions (1,000 shares)*

Issue	Shareholders						No. of shares issued
	Teikoku Bank	Mitsui Trust	Mitsui Life Insurance	Taisho Marine & Fire Insurance	Subtotal	Mitsui Honsha	
Trading (MBK)	—	—	30	—	30 (2)	1,028 (51)	2,000
Mining	11	—	49	22	70 (1)	4,980 (62)	8,000
Trust	—	—	—	—	11 (2)	96 (16)	600
Life Insurance	—	—	—	—	—	30 (75)	40
Agriculture	—	—	—	—	—	189 (90)	209
Shipbuilding	—	—	—	—	—	994 (83)	1,200
Precision Machinery	—	—	—	—	—	1,993 (100)	2,000
Chemical	—	—	—	—	—	972 (40)	2,430
Real Estate	—	—	—	—	—	100 (100)	100
Steamship	—	—	—	—	—	1,020 (73)	1,400
Mitsui total	11	—	78	22	111 (1)	11,401 (63)	17,979

Notes: The figures of Mitsui Honsha include shares of Mitsui families. Figures in parentheses indicate percentages. MBK stands for Mitsui Bussan Kaisha.

Source: Holding Company (1951*b*).

Table 3.3. *Ownership of directly controlled companies by Mitsubishi financial institutions* (1,000 shares)

Issue	Shareholders						No. of shares issued
	Mitsubishi Bank	Mitsubishi Trust	Meiji Life Insurance	Tokio Marine & Fire Insurance	Subtotal	Mitsubishi Honsha	
Trading (MSK)	—	—	44	22	66 (3)	827 (41)	2,000
Mining	22	—	281	109	412 (1)	3,515 (43)	8,148
Trust	1	—	87	—	88 (15)	151 (25)	600
Heavy Industries	340	28	1,044	700	2,113 (11)	4,616 (23)	20,000
Electric Manufacturing	—	—	168	—	168 (7)	1,072 (45)	2,400
Bank	—	6	5	171	182 (7)	872 (32)	2,700
Chemical Industries	—	39	83	140	262 (12)	575 (26)	2,216
Oil	—	—	—	—	—	180 (45)	400
Steel Manufacturing	—	—	56	45	101 (5)	1,021 (51)	2,000
Estate	—	40	30	50	120 (32)	247 (67)	370
Warehouse	—	—	40	13	53 (13)	189 (47)	400
Mitsubishi total	363	113	1,837	1,251	3,564 (9)	13,264 (32)	41,234

Notes: The figures of Mitsubishi Honsha include shares of Iwasaki families. Figures in parentheses indicate percentages. MSK stands for Mitsubishi Shoji Kaisha.
Source: Holding Company (1951b).

Table 3.4. *Ownership of directly controlled companies by Sumitomo financial institutions (1,000 shares)*

Issue	Shareholders						No. of shares issued
	Sumitomo Bank	Sumitomo Trust	Sumitomo Life Insurance	Osaka Sumitomo M. & F. Insurance	Subtotal	Sumitomo Honsha	
Mining	112	48	64	48	272 (17)	1,279 (80)	1,600
Bank	—	40	13	2	55 (8)	261 (35)	737
Trust	161	—	—	2	163 (41)	17 (25)	400
Life Insurance	—	—	—	—	—	15 (100)	15
Metal Industries	578	187	114	32	911 (11)	2,117 (25)	8,375
Communication Industries	6	—	62	5	73 (2)	393 (13)	3,000
Electric Industries	24	35	30	11	100 (4)	696 (29)	2,400
Shikoku Machinery Works	48	49	57	—	154 (19)	226 (28)	800
Chemical	11	59	64	4	138 (6)	554 (25)	2,240
Aluminium Reduction	10	5	10	—	25 (6)	140 (35)	400
Real Estate & Building	65	—	—	—	65 (8)	509 (61)	830
Warehouse	100	—	20	—	120 (40)	180 (60)	300
Kyodo Electric Power	12	24	12	6	54 (14)	119 (30)	400
Sumitomo total	1,127	447	445	111	2,130 (10)	6,507 (30)	21,497

Notes: The figures of Sumitomo Honsha include shares of Sumitomo families. Figures in parentheses indicate percentages.
Source: Holding Company (1951b).

directly controlled subsidiaries, with total shares exceeding 10 per cent in Mitsubishi Heavy Industries, Mitsubishi Warehouse, Mitsubishi Trust, Mitsubishi Estate, and Mitsubishi Chemical Industries. Thus, the Mitsubishi financial institutions, particularly Meiji Life Insurance and Tokio Marine & Fire Insurance, played important supplementary control roles.

Sumitomo financial institutions held shares in twelve of Sumitomo Honsha's directly controlled subsidiaries, with total stakes exceeding 10 per cent in six of these. Sumitomo Trust, Sumitomo Life Insurance, and Sumitomo Bank all played equivalently significant roles in supplementing the control exercised by Sumitomo Honsha.

The foregoing analysis indicates that, while the Mitsui financial institutions provided virtually no supplementary support to the holding company, Mitsubishi and Sumitomo financial institutions were mobilized to a significant degree in reinforcing control over zaibatsu subsidiaries. Additionally, in contrast to the collective face value holdings in zaibatsu subsidiaries of 5.53 million yen by Mitsui financial institutions, the respective figures for Mitsubishi and Sumitomo had grown to 177.09 million yen and 109.27 million yen.

The large holdings of the Mitsubishi and Sumitomo institutions came to have important significance when the zaibatsu were dissolved and the financial institutions were ordered to conduct preferential sales of their holdings in zaibatsu subsidiaries to the officers and employees of the individual issuing companies. In comparison with the unilateral actions taken with regard to the stock held by the holding companies, the financial institutions were given some freedom in selecting the timing, methods, and buyers involved, which meant that they were (it has been surmised) able in many cases to sell their holdings back to the original issuing companies themselves.

Zaibatsu Dissolution and the Formation of Corporate Complexes

Zaibatsu Dissolution and the Assets of the Zaibatsu Families

Following Japan's defeat in the Second World War, the General Headquarters of the Allied Powers set about dismantling the zaibatsu by cutting the personnel and financial chains that linked them together. In addition, large monopolistic firms were broken up in order to eliminate or weaken their power.

The first strong movement in the direction of zaibatsu dissolution came in the form of a Japanese government memorandum addressed to the General Headquarters of the Supreme Commander for the Allied Powers (GHQ/SCAP) dated 4 November 1945, proposing 'voluntary dissolution' of the Big Four zaibatsu (including Yasuda). This voluntary dissolution was to consist of the elimination of zaibatsu control over subsidiaries, the disestablishment of the holding companies, and the disposal of the assets of the zaibatsu families. A memorandum in response, dated 6 November 1945, expressed approval of the plan. While the memorandum of 4 November had been written as if proposed by the Japanese government, its true author was the Economic Science Section of SCAP, suggesting that the dissolution of the Big Four zaibatsu was not voluntary but imposed. The stockholdings of the holding companies and of the zaibatsu families were subsequently sold off by the Holding Company Liquidation Commission (established on 22 August 1946) (Memorandum 1945*a*; 1945*b*; Holding Company 1951*a*: 163–5; Mitsui Bunko, forthcoming).

The Commission was also ordered by SCAP to dissolve, or sell off the holdings of, seventy-nine other holding companies, and to dispose of the assets of six other zaibatsu families (Aikawa/Nissan, Asano, Furukawa, Okura, Nakajima, and Nomura). The promulgation of the Corporate Securities Holdings Limitation Order (25 November 1946) and the Anti-Monopoly Law (14 April 1947) also brought about the disposal of stock-holdings held by a variety of other enterprises. The elimination of stockholding arrangements and the purge of the officers of large firms served to sever completely the capital and personnel ties that had formerly bound together the zaibatsu.

SCAP not only dissolved the pyramid-like organizations of the zaibatsu and broke up the keiretsu ranks of subsidiaries controlled by large mono-polistic firms, but from July 1947 set about liquidating or disintegrating these huge firms themselves. On 3 July, SCAP ordered the Japanese gov-ernment to dissolve Mitsui Bussan and Mitsubishi Shoji, and this directive was immediately executed. These two companies had not only been vying with each other for the top position in Japan, but were among the top-ranked trading companies in the world prior to the outbreak of the war. SCAP then ordered the Japanese government to address over-concentration of economic power, resulting in the promulgation on 18 December 1948 of the Elimination of Excessive Concentrations of Economic Power Law. On the basis of this legislation, 325 companies were designated as targets for dissolution, but, as fundamental American goals for the Occupation shifted from demilitarization and democratization towards establishing an anti-Communist base, these designations were retracted one after the other. Eventually, the only firms to which the dissolution orders were actually applied were eighteen firms positioned at the top of their respective indus-tries, including Nippon Steel, Tokyo Shibaura Electric, Mitsubishi Heavy Industries, Mitsui Mining, and Seika Mining (formerly Sumitomo Mining). These companies were ordered to be broken up into smaller entities and/or disbanded with their facilities to be sold off (Ministry of Finance 1977: 282–5, 504–67).

SCAP thus oversaw the thorough dissolution of the zaibatsu and of those large firms judged to be extremely monopolistic. The question remains, however, as to the changes in the assets held by the zaibatsu families. The memorandum of 4 November 1945 stipulated that the stocks, bonds, etc. held by the zaibatsu holding companies were to be converted into national bonds, the sale of which was to be prohibited for ten years, and this method was also to be applied to the assets of the zaibatsu families. While this measure was intended to prevent the re-formation and resurgence of the zaibatsu, it was never actually implemented. This was because the establishment of a new tax on assets guaranteed that the zaibatsu would not reappear.

The instigator of the asset tax was not SCAP but the Ministry of Finance (MOF) within the Japanese government. In order to secure a base of funds with which to pay off huge issues of government bonds made during the war, MOF planned extremely progressive taxes on both individuals and corporations, meaning that the origin of the tax actually had nothing to do with zaibatsu dissolution. After modifying the plan in response to SCAP directives that only individuals were to be made subject, the corresponding legislation was passed by the Diet (parliament) on 12 November 1946. The resulting asset tax was, as noted, extremely progressive, with minimum taxation of 25 per cent on the portion of personal assets exceeding 100,000 yen, rising to a maximum of 90 per cent (on assets in excess of 15 million yen). This made it legally possible for the state to siphon off a considerable portion of the wealth of the zaibatsu and other wealthy families in the form of taxes (Ministry of Finance 1982: 69–174).

Table 3.5 indicates the amounts of assets that were taken from the ten largest zaibatsu families in accordance with the new legislation. The dubious distinction of first place went to Kichizaemon Sumitomo; on total assessed taxable assets of 117.38 million yen, he was forced to pay 104.26 million yen in taxes. The honour of second place went to Takakimi Mitsui, of the Mitsui zaibatsu, with Hisaya Iwasaki of the Mitsubishi zaibatsu coming in fourth. The eleventh spot went to Jujun Furukawa and family, of the Furukawa zaibatsu, with position number thirty-nine going to Kishichiro Okura and family, of the Okura zaibatsu. Because the net assets of the main families in the Yasuda and four other zaibatsu were below 5 million yen, it is not clear how much they had to pay. Yoshio Tatsu'uma, who ranked a distant third behind Takakimi Mitsui, had stockholdings in a large number of enterprises, but the scale of the companies that they actually controlled (primarily in the sake brewing and shipping industries) was much smaller than those of the ten largest zaibatsu.

Next, because the greater portion of each zaibatsu branch family's assets was combined with those of the other branch families in running the various zaibatsu, it is useful to add up total branch family assets in determin-

Table 3.5. *Asset tax taxpayers (zaibatsu families)* (1,000 yen)

Name of taxpayer of zaibatsu families	Final amount		Remainder	(b)/(a) (%)
	Taxable amt. (a)	Tax (b)	(a)–(b)	
Rank				
1 Kichizaemon Sumitomo	117,383	104,261	13,122	
2 Takakimi Mitsui	96,275	85,264	11,011	
4 Hisaya Iwasaki	53,483	46,750	6,733	
5 Takanaru Mitsui	47,726	41,569	6,157	
6 Takanaga Mitsui	46,797	40,733	6,064	
7 Takaharu Mitsui	44,218	38,412	5,806	
9 Hikoyata Iwasaki	41,895	36,322	5,573	
10 Takaosa Mitsui	41,089	35,596	5,493	
11 Jujun Furukawa	38,201	32,997	5,204	
19 Takahiro Mitsui	29,344	25,025	4,319	
24 Takako Iwasaki	24,275	20,464	3,811	
39 Kishichiro Okura	16,885	13,812	3,073	
46 Takaakira Mitsui	14,793	11,940	2,853	
70 Takaatsu Mitsui	12,592	10,069	2,523	
85 Takaya Iwasaki	11,619	9,242	2,377	
88 Tsuneya Iwasaki	11,349	9,012	2,337	
110 Takaosa Mitsui	9,960	7,832	2,128	
278 Takateru Mitsui	5,901	4,381	1,520	
297 Tadao Iwasaki	5,763	4,264	1,499	
309 Kan'ichi Sumitomo	5,663	4,178	1,485	
No. of families				
Mitsui: 10 families	348,695	300,821	47,874	86
Iwasaki: 6 families	148,384	126,054	22,330	85
Sumitomo: 2 families	123,046	108,439	14,607	88
Furukawa: 1 family	38,201	32,997	5,204	86
Okura: 1 family	16,885	13,812	3,073	82

Note: In this source, 393 taxpayers were listed whose taxable assets were more than 5 million yen. Those of the other five largest zaibatsu families were under 5 million yen.

Source: Tax Administration Agency (1954).

ing overall scale. When assets are thus added together, the Mitsui family as a whole had far and away the greatest total assets, followed by those of the Iwasaki and Sumitomo families, which were also quite substantial. The ten Mitsui branch families turned out to have total taxable assets of 348.69 million yen, of which 300.82 million yen was confiscated in asset taxes, for an effective tax rate of about 86 per cent, leaving only 47.87 million yen to the family as a whole. The six Iwasaki branch families were taxed at an effective rate of 85 per cent, leaving 22.33 million yen, and the two branches of the Sumitomo family at a rate of 88 per cent, leaving only 14.60 million yen. Also, because the assets of greatest liquidity were encashed in order to pay the taxes, the assets that were left were of comparatively low liquidity. The Mitsui families, for example, were left with family residences and land, burial plots, and works of art, but with hardly any cash. The situations of the Iwasaki and Sumitomo families were much the same, crushing any subsequent hope of reassembling their holdings for zaibatsu resurgence.

The Mitsuis, Iwasakis, Sumitomos, and other zaibatsu families originally identified by the Holding Company Liquidation Commission, as has been shown, saw the great majority of their fortunes disappear in the form of asset taxes. In fact, all holders of assets in excess of 100,000 yen were subject to taxation, such that all financially influential individuals and families (such as the Tatsu'uma family) saw their assets significantly diminished. This was compounded by the fact that most such individuals and families found themselves forced to divest themselves of stocks in order to pay the taxes. Asset taxation, then, along with the dissolution of the zaibatsu, eliminated major individual shareholders in Japan's largest firms.

Treasury Stock and Mutual Shareholdings

The Holding Company Liquidation Commission expected a total of 42 per cent of all the stock that had been issued in Japan to be removed from the hands of its former individual and corporate owners through the processes of zaibatsu dissolution and asset taxation. It was the decision of SCAP to order the Japanese government to transfer these holdings on preferential terms to the managers and employees of the issuing firms, in order to encourage democratization of securities ownership, that is, ownership of stock by the general public. The issuing companies responded by moving to place stock in the hands of managers and employees, and securities dealers acted to see that large numbers of individuals became stock owners (Holding Company 1951a: 433–5).

However, the sudden increase in individual stock owners did not necessarily translate into a larger body of stable, long-term stockholders. Even in the case of employee-stockholders, it was feared that spot sales would occur when lower stock prices were anticipated, because of the fact that many had taken out loans in order to make their original stock purchases. This meant that there was a general danger of eventual corporate takeover, which led the issuing companies to request financial institutions (banks, trust banks, and life insurance companies) to purchase their stock. While the 1947 anti-monopoly legislation had outlawed corporate ownership of stock, financial institutions were treated as exceptions and were allowed to hold up to 5 per cent of the stock of issuing companies. But because the Corporate Securities Ownership Limitation Order (25 November 1945) and other rules prevented cross-ownership among companies that had belonged to the same zaibatsu, former zaibatsu companies made their requests to other financial institutions. This meant that the new owners of stock in former zaibatsu companies were in fact financial institutions with comparatively weak historical ties to the issuing companies (Ministry of Finance 1977: 339–53).

The Anti-Monopoly Law was modified on 18 June 1949, removing the prohibition against ownership of stock by corporations, and the beginnings of cross-shareholding relationships were established as various companies purchased shares in formerly non-related financial institutions. Then, in the wake of the signing of the Peace Treaty on 28 April 1952, the Corporate Securities Ownership Limitation Order and many other Occupation-imposed rules were abrogated, clearing the way for the former zaibatsu financial institutions and same-zaibatsu firms to purchase shares in their old zaibatsu member companies. This resulted in a strengthening of ties along former zaibatsu group lines through the rapid establishment of mutual share ownership. Thus, the emergence of mutual shareholding came about in two stages. The fact that today's large corporate complexes, such as the Mitsui, Mitsubishi, and Sumitomo groups, feature cross-ownership between member firms and non-member financial institutions stems from this historical process.

To the question of whether the pre-1952 ownership of company shares by former non-member financial institutions ensured peace of mind for management, the answer would have to be 'no'. The surest way of guarding managerial independence was the accumulation of treasury stock. This was obviously illegal because of the prohibition of treasury stock by Article 210 of the Commercial Code, but managers none the less saw treasury stock as the most stable vehicle for stock ownership. Thus, many large enterprises, in knowing violation of the law, secretly purchased treasury shares.

Mitsui Real Estate provides a good example of this type of behaviour. The stock of the company, which was wholly owned by the Mitsui family, was transferred to the Holding Company Liquidation Commission following zaibatsu dissolution. Immediately after Mitsui Real Estate increased its capital from 5 million yen (100,000 shares) to 50 million yen (1 million shares) in March 1949, the Commission allotted 60,000 of the newly issued 900,000 shares to company managers, employees, and their relatives at par (50 yen per share). The remaining 840,000 shares were sold to the public at a price of 400 yen per share. In order to prevent takeover of the company, the management of the company secretly purchased 280,000 of the publicly issued shares (28 per cent of the company) through Nomura Securities, using a large number of names 'borrowed' from individuals for this purpose. The names were then changed over, making Nomura the apparent owner of the shares. It was technically permitted to do this, since securities companies were allowed to surpass the 5 per cent ownership rule (still in place) in the case of shares for resale.

Mitsui Real Estate needed about 120 million yen in order to accomplish this large-scale purchase of illegal treasury stock. Because Dai-Ichi Bank had been split off and made independent of Teikoku Bank (soon to be given back its former name, Mitsui Bank), the company was able to procure only 20 million yen from this source. Mitsui Real Estate officers managed to round up additional sums of 30 million yen from Chiyoda Bank (soon to revert to its old name, Mitsubishi Bank), 30 million yen from Joyo Bank, and 40 million yen from a variety of other financial institutions (trust banks and life insurance companies). In doing so, they used the names of Japan Steel Works and several other companies, and offered the subsequently purchased shares to the financial institutions as collateral (Edo 1994: 149–56; Suzuki 1992).

As this shows, Mitsui Real Estate, with capital of only 50 million yen, was able to manœuvre over twice this amount in order to gain control over its own stock. Other companies employed similar methods to effect protection against takeovers, and it is for this reason that the major securities houses are found listed as major stockholders in these companies around 1950.

It was through the co-operation of the banks, trust banks, insurance companies, and securities houses that large-scale, secret, and illegal purchases of treasury stock were made. Former members of the Mitsubishi zaibatsu relied on Chiyoda Bank for such funding, and Sumitomo members relied on Osaka Bank (formerly, and soon to be again, Sumitomo Bank). Mitsui members can be assumed to have relied on Teikoku (Mitsui) Bank as well as on other banks. Additionally, there is a strong likelihood that the financial institutions of the old Mitsubishi zaibatsu and of the old Sumitomo zaibatsu were easily able to convert their large-scale shareholdings (that had served to supplement the control exercised by their respective holding companies) into treasury stock for the companies concerned. This is because the financial institutions were given considerable latitude in selecting buyers for these holdings and were not required to dispose of them publicly.

As to the question of how these illicit caches of treasury stock were later handled, firms were again permitted to hold shares in their former zaibatsu cousins after the conclusion of the Peace Treaty in April 1952. This provided a legal means of takeover prevention through cross-shareholdings along former zaibatsu lines. Table 3.6 compares intragroup mutual ownership among former zaibatsu members of the Mitsui, Mitsubishi, and Sumitomo groups in October 1953 and March 1957. Only eighteen months after the Peace Treaty, overall cross-shareholdings

Table 3.6. *Lateral cross-holdings within the Mitsui, Mitsubishi, and Sumitomo complexes* (%)

Issuing Companies	Ratio of same complex shareholding	
	Oct. 1953	Mar. 1957
Mitsui (21 companies)	9.6	11.4
Mitsubishi (24 companies)	10.4	14.6
Sumitomo (17 companies)	11.4	18.7

Note: Ratio of same complex shareholding is as follows: (No. of shares owned by same complex companies including one mutual life insurance company) ÷ (Total of shares issued by same complex companies) × 100.

Source: Fair Trade Commission (n.d.).

totalled 9.6 per cent of all shares for the Mitsui group, 10.4 per cent for the Mitsubishi group, and 11.4 per cent for the Sumitomo group. The likely reason for this impressively fast realignment following former patterns is the existence of treasury stock that could be easily assigned to new (or, perhaps more accurately, old) owners. By March 1957 the intragroup mutual ownership ratio had jumped to 18.7 per cent for the Sumitomo group, followed by Mitsubishi at 14.6 per cent, and distantly by Mitsui at 11.4 per cent. The order of these figures is strongly affected by the relative strength (or weakness) of lateral ties among the firms that had been the directly controlled subsidiaries of the former zaibatsu.

The Formation of the Corporate Complexes and the Role of the Banks

The horizontal ties among firms that resulted in the formation of corporate complexes must be considered in two contexts. One of these is the banding together of firms in opposition to the prohibition of the use of zaibatsu names and trademarks, and the other is the assembly of firms radiating like spokes from a hub of common financial institutions, primarily banks. The former served as an active element in forming corporate complexes in the beginning, while the latter served as the objective foundation for continued promotion of the formation process.

SCAP ordered the Japanese government on 18 September 1949 to prohibit the use of the names, trademarks, and corporate logos of the Mitsui, Mitsubishi, and Sumitomo companies. The deadline for cessation of use was 30 June 1951. SCAP had already stipulated that restructured entities created by means of the Financial Institution Restructuring Law and of the Elimination of Excessive Concentrations of Economic Power Law were not to use zaibatsu names. Thus, Mitsubishi Bank became Chiyoda Bank,

Sumitomo Bank became Osaka Bank, Mitsui Trust became Tokyo Trust & Banking, Mitsubishi Trust became Asahi Trust & Banking, Sumitomo Trust became Fuji Trust & Banking, Mitsui Life Insurance became Chuo Life Insurance Co., and Sumitomo Life Insurance became Kokumin Life Insurance Co. Of all the financial institutions the only one to continue use of its former name was Osaka Sumitomo Marine & Fire Insurance.

SCAP, which had intended to eliminate the names of the Big Three zaibatsu completely, instead unwittingly encouraged the realignment of former zaibatsu enterprises into corporate complexes. While almost all of the financial institutions had already changed their names, Osaka Sumitomo Marine & Fire Insurance and the non-financial firms that had been using former zaibatsu names came together in opposition to the order. The presidents and managing directors of eight former Mitsui companies convened a meeting immediately following the SCAP order in order to contemplate countermeasures, and a series of meetings was subsequently held to consider how the order might be reversed, with the management of Mitsui Mining and Mitsui Real Estate in the lead. The final decision, handed down in March 1950, was crafted in large measure by Walter R. Hutchinson, who had worked to influence SCAP and the US government. Hutchinson, who had been dispatched from the US government to serve on the Deconcentration Review Board, and who had remained in Japan as a lawyer following the expiration of his term in March 1950, was retained by the Mitsui companies. His fee, if successful, was to be 40 million yen, in addition to travel and other expenses.

A group of three Sumitomo companies retained the Japanese lawyer Gunji Hosono to act on their behalf in approaching SCAP, and a group of eight Mitsubishi companies retained another Japanese lawyer, Kenzo Takayanagi, for the same purpose. The Mitsubishi companies also appealed to the US government through Westinghouse Electric Corp., with which Mitsubishi Electric Mfg. had a technical tie-up. The leaders of the Mitsubishi group were the executors of the Mitsubishi holding company and the management of Mitsubishi Electric. Following Mitsui's decision to retain Hutchinson, the three Sumitomo companies and the eight Mitsubishi companies also moved to support the Hutchinson approach and decided to contribute to the associated expenses, and, subsequently, the three groups acted in concert with each other. Meanwhile, the three groups endeavoured to have Prime Minister Yoshida approach Supreme Commander MacArthur concerning the matter. The result of these actions was to have the order postponed twice for periods of one year each, following which the April 1952 signing of the Peace Treaty brought about the order's annulment. The trademarks and logos of the Big Three zaibatsu are shown in Fig. 3.2.

The zaibatsu names, trademarks, and logos were seen as expressions of long years of trust and commitment. That is, they symbolized social trust

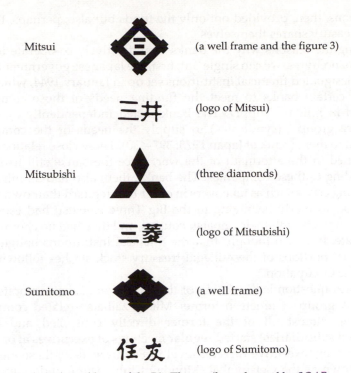

Mitsui (a well frame and the figure 3)

(logo of Mitsui)

Mitsubishi (three diamonds)

(logo of Mitsubishi)

Sumitomo (a well frame)

(logo of Sumitomo)

Fig. 3.2. *Trademarks and logos of the Big Three zaibatsu banned by SCAP.*

in products and businesses of the companies concerned, and the companies fought bitterly against the order to abandon these important business tools. Many of those firms that did not join in the struggle to oppose the order later came to recognize the value of the zaibatsu names, trademarks, and logos, choosing one after another to re-adopt them from May 1952 onward. Thus it was that the original prohibition triggered the formation of the corporate complexes (Mitsui Real Estate 1980).

With regard to the second context of formation, the orientation of group firms around central financial institutions, we can begin by recalling that the policy of democratization of securities ownership increased owner fears of corporate takeovers. To prevent this eventuality, many large enterprises besides the former zaibatsu companies sought to secure quantities of treasury stock. To facilitate such purchases, former zaibatsu-related financial institutions provided the necessary funds. The Mitsubishi and Sumitomo financial institutions, which had played important roles in helping their respective zaibatsu holding companies to control subsidiaries, were particularly well positioned to place these shares in friendly hands during the zaibatsu dissolution process. These financial institutions, then, provided not only the funds but also, perhaps, the targeted treasury shares themselves.

Among the reasons why the banks would actively co-operate in such illegal manœuvres, we can single out, first, the Japanese government's system of designated financial institutions set up in January 1944, which designated certain banks to meet the funding needs of those companies engaged in military supply. The banks acted independently or in 'co-operative groups' (syndicates) to supply the needs of the companies assigned to them (Bank of Japan 1973: 397–430). These close relations were maintained in the aftermath of the war, since the banks still had loans outstanding to these companies. The banks, then, also had an interest in preventing crises such as takeovers in order to safeguard their own assets. The banks formerly belonging to the Big Three zaibatsu had especially lengthy contacts with their zaibatsu cousins, and they had no choice but to co-operate. It is also thought that the financial institutions bought back substantial portions of these illegal treasury stock stashes following the end of the Occupation.

The next question is the timing of the formation of the corporate complexes. A group of nineteen former Mitsui zaibatsu-related companies (including almost all of the former directly controlled and quasi-controlled subsidiaries) started regular meetings of executives at or above the managing/executive director level in February 1950; these meetings were known as the Getsuyokai (Monday Club). The founders were the executives of Teikoku/Mitsui Bank and the management of Mitsui Mining and Mitsui Real Estate, who were organizing resistance to the order to drop the use of the Mitsui name. A group of eleven former Sumitomo members started regular meetings of company presidents, known as the Hakusuikai (White Water Club—'water' also referring to Wednesday), in October 1951; this group also consisted mainly of former directly controlled and quasi-controlled companies. The Mitsubishi companies began their Shacho Kondankai (Presidents' Round Table) around April 1952, and it was renamed the Mitsubishi Kin'yokai (Friday Club) in 1954; it had a membership similar to that of the Mitsui and Sumitomo groups. Again, the executors of the Mitsubishi holding company and the management of Mitsubishi Electric, motivated by the assault on the Mitsubishi name, initiated the original contacts. These high-level discussion groups, founded during the period 1950–2, held regular, members-only meetings; while the Mitsui meetings were held for both social and co-operative purposes below the presidential level, the top-level Mitsubishi and Sumitomo meetings were held not only for social and co-operative purposes but also to decide on their companies' contributions to various group causes. The regular meeting of Mitsui presidents, known as the Nimokukai (Second Thursday Club), was delayed by difficulties in the unification of Dai-Ichi Bussan and Mitsui Bussan, but was eventually established for the same purpose as its Mitsubishi and Sumitomo counterparts.

With the resolution of the turmoil over use of zaibatsu names and trademarks, Sumitomo drew up an 'All Sumitomo Name Basic Agreement' that was ratified by the various companies, with the Hakusuikai given the authority to approve or deny use. Mitsubishi also formed a 'Name and Trademark Management Committee', the deliberations of which resulted in the decision to give powers of approval or rejection to the Kin'yokai. Because the establishment of the Mitsui presidents' council was delayed, an interim 'Name and Trademark Preservation Committee' was formed in 1956; when the council was finally formed in October of 1961, it assumed the role of granting permission for use (Edo 1986: 91–4; Ohtsuki 1987: 71–4; Tsuda 1988: 91–9; Mitsui Real Estate 1980).

The three presidents' councils continue to this day to exist solely for the promotion of friendship and co-operation, for the allotment of contributions to common causes, and for decisions over the use of names and trademarks. Some see these councils as powerful assemblies of top decision-makers, or of top stockholders, but these views read too much into the formation and continuation of council meetings (Okumura 1988: 100–5). Council-fostered introductions of personnel have taken place in cases where a managerial crisis has threatened the integrity of the entire group, or where internal conditions in a subsidiary formed jointly by council member companies have warranted such action. The former is highly unusual, and the latter is an issue concerning regulation of a subsidiary, rather than deals between or among council members. All the members of the presidents' councils are equals among equals, and, except in unusual circumstances, there is no interference in the management of the affairs of members by other members. Thus, while the councils represent the apexes of their respective corporate complexes, and it may appear as if each complex is run on the basis of unified decisions, in reality there is no single, unified will.

The primary reason why the presidents of companies that are members of a corporate complex take part in these meetings is the maintenance of the goodwill associated with the name of the complex. When the name is used by a company outside the group, the council takes joint action to halt the unauthorized use. The council also upholds the complex's good name by sponsoring joint contributions to social causes, and therefore needs to confirm each member company's level of support. A second reason is friendship and co-operation. The mutual contact fostered by the council often proves useful in promoting joint projects later on and in facilitating the required negotiations. Generally speaking, such arrangements for co-operative projects are rarely made during the actual council meetings, but in settings in which only the member companies concerned with the project under discussion are in attendance.

Next, consideration of the roles of the banks in the Big Three corporate complexes is warranted. First, as mentioned previously, the banks secretly assisted in the procurement of treasury stock during the (re-)formation process, then subsequently assisted in establishing mutual shareholding patterns. In the 1920s and 1930s Mitsui Bank did not maintain large, long-term holdings but operated primarily as a commercial bank, with strict limits on the tying up of assets in long-term investment vehicles. Thus, it did not supplement the Mitsui zaibatsu holding company in its control of subsidiary enterprises. In contrast, Mitsubishi Bank and Sumitomo Bank played important supplemental roles, and Sumitomo Bank in particular held large numbers of shares in the holding company's directly controlled subsidiaries. As a result, the managerial direction of Mitsui Bank changed more dramatically than that of the other two following the Second World War. Kiichiro Sato, a former president of the bank, recalled;

Because companies' funding needs increased dramatically following the Second World War, the old commercial banking approach crumbled; the extending of loans, the purchasing of corporate bonds, and the maintenance of stockholdings all came to have the same significance as far as providing financial assistance from the bank to an enterprise was concerned. (Sato 1975: 302–3)

As for the common changes that took place at all three banks, the zaibatsu holding companies and directly controlled subsidiaries had maintained only small lateral mutual shareholdings prior to Japan's defeat, and this was true of the banks as well. In 1949, however, the way was opened for mutual holdings in companies that had different former zaibatsu affiliations, and in 1952 for mutual ownership of former zaibatsu-related companies, and the banks strengthened these ties accordingly. The banks became influential stockholders, they encouraged intragroup cross-ownership, and they played important roles in funding these purchases.

Secondly, the banks functioned as 'main banks', structuring the syndicates necessary to meet member companies' capital investment funding needs. Previously, when government designation had linked main banks with firms engaged in military supply, the designated banks had formed such loan syndicates in about one-third of the cases. The largest of these was the twenty-two-bank syndicate put together for Nippon Steel, but most of them were of ten banks or fewer. The membership of such syndicates in the post-war period, however, was rather larger. For example, a syndicate organized by Teikoku Bank on behalf of Tokyo Shibaura Electric consisted of about thirty banks. Another syndicate put together for Mitsubishi Electric by Mitsubishi Bank also totalled about thirty members. This meant, in the case of the Teikoku syndicate for Tokyo Shibaura, that the main bank (Teikoku) had only to supply 20 per cent of the requisite funds (Sato 1975: 306). Thus, the banks of the Big Three corporate complexes, acting as main banks on a scale even bigger than in the wartime years, continued their role of collecting funds from outside the complex (zaibatsu) for use within.

Thirdly, to prevent over-investment in particular sectors by firms in the same complexes, the banks worked to establish jointly owned enterprises. Representative of these were firms in the petrochemical and nuclear reactor manufacturing sectors. This role faded in the 1960s, however, and by the early years of the 1970s had almost disappeared. For example, the intervention of Kakuei Tanaka, the then Minister of International Trade and Industry, was required to sort out a dispute between two Sumitomo companies squabbling over investment in the aluminium business (Tsuda 1988: 161–4).

Finally, the banks became rescuers of companies in trouble, sending in top personnel in cases involving presidents' council members. These dispatches of personnel were not aimed at control so much as at monitoring in order to safeguard assets in the form of funds already extended. For example, in 1955 Mitsui Bank sent in its vice-president to serve as chairman of Mitsui Real Estate, and his monitoring role did not involve him deeply in the company's managerial policies. Actual connection with management occurred in cases of crises at council member firms. In the 1950s Sumitomo Machinery was overshadowed by crisis, and a Hakusuikai subcommittee was formed to provide restructuring assistance. In 1960 a full complement of directors drawn from a number of the companies in the Sumitomo complex was sent in, with the one from Sumitomo Bank assuming the presidency of the troubled company in 1965. In the case of companies that were not council members, there are numerous cases of banks leading the reconstruction efforts independently (Tsuda 1988: 100–1; Okumura 1988: 213–16).

Conclusion

The Mitsui, Mitsubishi, and Sumitomo corporate complexes all stem from zaibatsu heritages. Other major complexes in Japan are the Fuyo, Sanwa, and Dai-Ichi Kangin complexes, but these differ in terms of their lineage and formation from the zaibatsu complexes. First, the later three complexes have no distinct ties to the pre-war zaibatsu. While the companies belonging to the six mid-ranked zaibatsu (including Yasuda, Aikawa/Nissan, Nomura, and Furukawa) planned to initiate their own post-war corporate complexes, they were unable to form complexes on the scale of the Big Three. Second, it was not the issue of name, or trust, that initially brought together the later three complexes, but rather a desire to compete with the former three, which were already well established. The presidents' council of the Fuyo complex was formed in 1966, that of the

Sanwa complex in 1967, and that of the Dai-Ichi Kangin complex as late as 1977. Third, the leadership role in the formation of the later three can be seen to have rested very clearly with the banks, namely Fuji Bank (formerly Yasuda Bank of the Yasuda zaibatsu), Sanwa Bank, and Dai-Ichi Kangyo Bank (formed in 1971 through the merger of the Dai-Ichi Bank and the Nippon Kangyo Bank). The fact that the banks initiated formation of the complexes, however, does not mean that they obtained the power to run the complexes as they pleased. Additionally, the mutual shareholdings of the later three are rather weaker than in the cases of the former zaibatsu complexes, as are the co-operative ties in the presidents' councils (Okumura 1988: 217–53).

The Mitsui, Mitsubishi, and Sumitomo complexes have maintained their top positions even since the appearance of the latter three, but it should be noted in closing that even the ties binding Mitsui, Mitsubishi, and Sumitomo are weaker today than they were in the 1950s and 1960s.

REFERENCES

Asajima, S. (1968), *Mitsubishi zaibatsu keiei-shi* [*A Business History of the Mitsubishi Zaibatsu*], Tokyo: Ochanomizu Shobo.

—— (1983), *Senkan-ki Sumitomo zaibatsu keiei-shi* [*A Business History of the Sumitomo Zaibatsu in the Interwar Period*], Tokyo: Tokyo Daigaku Shuppankai.

Bank of Japan Research Agency (ed.) (1973), *Nihon kinyu-shi shiryo* [*Japanese Financial History Materials*], Showa edn., 34, Tokyo.

Edo, H. (1986), *Watashi no Mitsui Showa-shi* [*A Personal History of Mitsui in the Showa Era*], Tokyo: Toyo Keizai Shimpo-sha.

—— (1994), *Mitsui to ayunda 70 nen* [*70 Years with Mitsui*], Tokyo: Asahi Shimbun-sha.

Fair Trade Commission Economic Department (n.d.), *Shuyo-kaisha no kabushiki toshi to kyu-shuyo-zaibatsu no genkyo ni kan suru shiryo* [*Documents Concerning the Stock Investments of Major Companies and the Current State of Major Former Zaibatsu*], Tokyo.

Holding Company Liquidation Commission (ed.) (1951*a*), *Nihon zaibatsu to sono kaitai* [*Japanese Zaibatsu and their Dissolution*], Tokyo.

—— (ed.) (1951*b*), *Nihon zaibatsu to sono kaitai shiryo* [*Japanese Zaibatsu and their Dissolution: Documents*], Tokyo.

Kabushiki nenkan [*Stocks Annual*] (1938), Tokyo.

Memorandum (1945a), From the Japanese Minister of Finance to SCAP, 4 Nov.

—— (1945b) From SCAP to the Japanese government, 6 Nov.

Ministry of Finance, Public Finance History Office (ed.) (1977), *Showa zaisei-shi; shusen kara kowa made* [*A History of Public Finance in the Showa Era; From the End of the War to Normalization*], ii, Tokyo: Toyo Keizai Shimpo-sha.

—— (ed.) (1982), *Showa zaisei-shi; shusen kara kowa made* [*A History of Public Finance in the Showa Era; From the End of the War to Normalization*], vii, Tokyo: Toyo Keizai Shimpo-sha.

Mitsui Bank Accounting Department (1938), *1938 nen shimo-ki hokoku* [*1938 Second Half Report*], Dec.
—— (1939–42), *Gyomu hokoku* [*Operating Reports*], Tokyo.
Mitsui Bank Domestic Department (1939–40), *Mitsui kakusha kankei kaisha yotaikin zandaka-hyo* [*Balances of Deposits and Loans for Companies Affiliated with Mitsui Companies*], Tokyo.
Mitsui Bunko [Mitsui Research Institute for Social and Economic History] (ed.) (1980), *Mitsui jigyo-shi* [*A History of Mitsui Enterprises*], 3/1, Tokyo.
—— (ed.) (forthcoming), *Mitsui jigyo-shi* [*A History of Mitsui Enterprises*], 3/3, Tokyo.
Mitsui Real Estate Public Relations Office, (ed.) (1980), *Zaibatsu shogo shohyo goji ni kan suru kondankai kiroku* [*A Record of Roundtable Discussions Concerning the Preservation of Zaibatsu Names and Logos*], Tokyo.
Ohtsuki, B. (1987), *Watashi no Mitsubishi Showa-shi* [*A Personal History of Mitsubishi in the Showa Era*], Tokyo: Toyo Keizai Shimpo-sha.
Okumura, H. (1988), *Shin-Nihon no roku dai kigyo shudan* [*The 6 Big Japanese Corporate Complexes of the New Japan*], Tokyo: Daiyamondo-sha.
Sato, K. (1975), *Zoku: ori ni furete* [*Memoirs*, vol. ii], Tokyo: Kinyu Keizai Kenkyusho [Finance and Economics Research Institute].
Suzuki, Kunio (1992), 'Companies' Acquisition of their Own Shares after the Liquidation of the Zaibatsu', *Tochi seido shi-gaku* [*Journal of Agrarian History*], 135.
Tax Administration Agency (ed.) (1954), *Zaisan zei dai nozei-sha meibo* [*List of Top Payers of the Asset Tax*], Tokyo.
Tsuda, H. (1988), *Watashi no Sumitomo Showa-shi* [*A Personal History of Sumitomo in the Showa Era*], Tokyo: Toyo Keizai Shimpo-sha.

4

Structure and Strategy of Belgian Business Groups (1920–1990)

G. KURGAN-VAN HENTENRYK

As the first country of continental Europe where the process of industrialization was initiated, Belgium experienced early in the nineteenth century the concentration of some industrial branches under banking control. The early development of universal banks, with the prominent Société Générale, profoundly shaped the structure of the Belgian economy. During the last third of the nineteenth century, a number of industrial groups emerged, becoming powerful after the First World War.

Financial Groups versus Industrial Groups

Origins

The origin of financial groups goes back to the 1830s, the first decade of Belgian independence. Two factors were decisive: the high amount of debts owed to Société Générale by the coal producers in the south of the country, and the new state's decision to build a railway network for economic, political, and strategic reasons. Since there was no industrial capital market, banks became the main suppliers of funds for three capital-intensive industries: mining, iron and steel, and railroads. A grasp of the involvement of banks in heavy industry is essential to the understanding of the evolution of financial groups in the twentieth century. It should also be kept in mind that the small size of the domestic market resulted in the Belgian economy's export orientation from the 1850s through to the present.

From 1880 onward the country's chief banks were no longer exclusively investment banks or holding companies and began to combine these activities with those of deposits banks (Kurgan-van Hentenryk 1992: 316–27). Finance capitalism took off by the end of the century, thanks to an ever closer link between banks and industry and a growing dissociation of capital and its management. The increased participation in industrial enterprises was connected both with the growing number of universal banks, which numbered about thirty in 1914, and the rapid rise of the finance companies, a kind of proto-holding company.

In spite of this expansion, the Belgian banking system was dominated by the Société Générale's group and its subsidiaries. Because of its historical role in Belgian economic development and its prestige on the national market, the Société Générale's shareholding was widely dispersed. Thus the main shareholders, who were only known by the lists of stocks registered at the extraordinary general meetings, owned 1 to 4 per cent of the capital. Some of them were insurance companies of which the Société Générale itself was a shareholder. Given this mutual shareholding and the wide dispersion of the stock, up to 1985 the ownership of 10 per cent of the stock ensured the main shareholders control of the company. (This is why the Société Générale was so vulnerable to Carlo de Benedetti's raid in 1988.)

The development of the Société Générale was characterized by its activities as a deposit bank, the diversification of its financial and industrial interests both in Belgium and abroad, and a tendency to leave the exploration of new sectors to others, although it was quite ready to move in on them once they had shown themselves to be profitable. But on the eve of the First World War the Société Générale no longer stood as the sole and undisputed leader in industrial finance, despite its prominence in financial markets. At the beginning of the 1880s it had indeed been the only banking institution to supply large amounts of new money to joint-stock companies. Thirty years later it was sharing this task with several universal banks, the most energetic being the Banque de Bruxelles, the Banque d'Outremer and the Banque de Paris et des Pays-Bas, whose Brussels branch had become an integral part of the Belgian financial market.

On the other hand, one cannot fail to notice that even in those sectors in which the Société Générale had, or was acquiring, a dominating interest, it rarely functioned as a trailblazer. Thus although several tramway holdings were set up from the 1880s onward, it was not until 1911 that it gained a foothold in one of the most dynamic concerns of that period, the Compagnie Mutuelle des Tramways. Similarly, it was not until 1905 that it entered the electricity sector, ten years behind the Banque de Bruxelles.

The Société Générale's entrance on the colonial scene is quite typical of its caution and its ability to profit from the experience of the pioneers who had gone before. It actually took King Leopold II twenty years to persuade it to commit itself in the Congo by creating the so-called '1906 companies' for the development of the Katanga (Shaba today) and the exploitation of the Congo's mineral resources. By that time some Antwerp financiers, along with the group of Banque d'Outremer, were already firmly established in Africa at the King's instigation.

The First World War wrought profound disruption on the Belgian economy. Not only was the industrial base pillaged or destroyed in large measure, but the state's need for money caused a transfer of banking activity from the industrial and commercial sectors to the financing of state enterprises. Inflation, penury, and lack of investment swelled bank deposits while the country became poorer in real terms. The interwar period was thus marked by a reintegration of banking activities into the national economy, a concentration of banking and industrial undertakings into powerful finance groups, and the replacement of exports of capital abroad by an interest in colonial enterprise.

Contrary to financial groups whose development started from joint-stock banks, industrial groups originated in family business, and some of them were created before the First World War. Ernest Solvay built the first family group in Belgium, the chemical group Solvay, on the exploitation of a new manufacturing process of soda from the 1860s onward. By 1913 the group already employed 20,000 people and was established all over the world (Bolle 1963).

Another case was the Coppée family, producers of coke ovens with a world-wide reputation, who developed a subsidiary activity of producing coke and coal aimed at supplying their coking plant. Their success relied on continuous technological innovation and the development of engineering activities. On the eve of the First World War they entered a partnership with the Banque de Bruxelles, which was willing to expand its interests in the coal industry (Dubois 1988: 182). Meanwhile, the Empain group built its wealth on the development of transport and electricity (Jeanjot 1967: 265–7; CRISP 1966: 279–302).

With reference to the typology proposed by Professor Shimotani, the financial groups developed as corporate complexes, while the industrial groups, especially those controlled by families like Solvay and Coppée, look more like zaibatsu. Both have a pyramid-like structure, with a family at the top, supported by a holding company and by various joint-stock companies. The Empain case is somewhat different. It may be viewed as a zaibatsu up to the 1950s, but owing to the nationalization of its companies in France and Egypt, it had to restructure its interests and convert into a financial group. By taking a large interest in the French Schneider group and the Banque de l'Indochine, and by converting its operating companies into holdings, it built a corporate complex with mutual stockholding arrangements and interlocking directorates, not only with corporate groups from various industries but also with other financial groups.

In analysis of the financing, organization, and control of Belgian business groups, it must be noted that the typology proposed with reference to the Japanese case does not fit perfectly. Moreover, the study of the energy sector stresses the importance of alliances between companies belonging to different business groups in industrial organization. The monopolization of the electric power industry at the end of the twentieth century by a powerful corporate group, Tractebel, also reveals strained relations with the Société Générale, the top company of the corporate complex to which it belongs.

Financing

Prior to the banking reform of 1934–1935

Reconstructing the economy presented the banks with numerous lending and investment opportunities at a time when the accumulation of savings during the war and the redistribution of fortunes had increased the banks' supply of current and deposit accounts. In the decade from 1920 to 1930 banks increased their aid to industry both through the raising of their current-account credits and by direct participation in industrial companies. In order to increase their resources, the universal banks favoured the collection of long-term deposits as opposed to bond issues. Apart from the Société Générale, which had set up a network of branches via its sponsored banks, the collection of deposits had been exceedingly haphazard. After the war all universal banks competed for the collection of deposits more systematically, not only by extending their own networks but also by acquiring and incorporating other institutions. Among the main players, namely the Société Générale, the Banque de Bruxelles, and the Banque d'Outremer, the Société Générale was to emerge as victor.

Another way to raise funds was to issue stocks in companies in which the banks subscribed a large share. However, by the end of the 1920s the banks found it increasingly hard to find fresh capital on the Belgian market because successive public offerings had dried up the supply.

Meanwhile, the industrial groups created their own banks, not only to preserve their independence, but also to provide banking services to their subsidiaries. Thus, the Solvay family founded the Société Belge de Banque, while the Banque Industrielle Belge concentrated the financial interests of the Empain group.

In 1932 Belgium experienced the tremors of the world economic crisis. For several months the banks had been able to cash their investments only with heavy losses. They had also been trying to recover their debts from industrialists. Whereas the older banks had enough reserves to ride out the crisis, the smaller ones born in the boom years had not. Having a smaller number of depositors, they quietly disappeared. Then, from 22 August 1934, the mixed banks were compelled by royal decree to exercise their functions of deposit banks separately from those of investment banks (Vantemsche 1980: 389–435).

Consequences of the banking reform

The mixed banks split up into deposit banks and holding companies. The new deposit banks were forbidden to have business interests, and the holding companies took charge of the industrial banking activities of the mixed banks and gained a controlling interest in the deposit banks issued from the division. They monitored powerful financial groups whose main investments were in the basic industries of mining, iron and steel, transport equipment, electrical energy, and colonial enterprises in Zaïre.

Since the interwar period holding companies have been extremely stable institutions for co-ordinating and controlling capital management. The holding company has maintained a key position in the Belgian capital market by issuing shares to buy stakes in industrial and financial companies. By this substitution of securities, they have been able to control the flow of capital to industry and to broaden corporate control. They have relied strongly on the public to finance their activities (Daems 1977: 33).

Although industrial groups also created holding companies, they preferred to rely primarily on self-financing in order to keep a tight rein on their subsidiaries. It took more than a century, until 1967, for the Solvay firm to transform itself into a joint-stock company with access to the capital market. None the less only 12 per cent of its capital was issued to the public (Vincent 1990: 312–13).

Organization and Control

With respect to organization and control, major differences exist between financial and industrial groups. In the case of financial groups, the banks had been creating holding companies to manage their interests in transport firms even before the war. After the war, this practice became much more widespread, especially between 1925 and 1930. It had the advantage of relieving the bank of the management of part of its industrial activities by entrusting it to specialist managers, and it reduced the lock-up of capital while extending the bank's control by means of indirect intervention. In this way the practice of creating holding companies stimulated the development of given sectors of industry by forcing them to modernize their techniques and concentrate their enterprises. A clear case of this is the glass industry; the traditional manufacturing in the Charleroi region was swept away in a few years by the bank-led introduction of the mechanized production of glass panes, and by the 1930s restructuring of the industry was being conducted under the auspices of the Société Générale (Delaet 1986).

Comparing Belgian control techniques with those of Japanese corporate complexes, both use common ownership, personnel, and credit. In

Belgium, as in Japan, the corporate complexes have a central bank and insurance companies, but they have no general trading company which centralizes buying and organizes selling for the member firms. This means that they lack an important instrument for co-ordinating and improving their position on the market, and it further weakens managerial corporate control because, contrary to the Japanese case, the structure and strength of member firms are heterogeneous (Daems 1977: 35).

The financial holdings have a controlling interest, albeit with a minority ownership through cross-holding or shares in a hierarchy of specialized holdings and subsidiaries. The process of concentration is stimulated by interlocking directorates inside each sector and between all sectors and the financial holding company. But this process does not result in fully integrated management and centralized decision-making. The violent crisis that hit the Société Générale during the spring of 1988 revealed the absence before the 1980s of any integrated management system in Belgium's number one financial conglomerate (Cottenier *et al.* 1989: 179).

While financial groups had long maintained loose organizations, industrial groups founded by entrepreneurs and their families have generally owned their subsidiaries outright and controlled the majority of shares in the holdings that they set up in order to preserve family prerogatives. Thus in 1983 the members of the Solvay family consolidated their control of the Solvay Company by founding the holding Solvac, wherein they regrouped 25 per cent of its capital. The family shareholding currently numbers about 4,000 people who hold directly or through Solvac 55 per cent of the company's shares. The distribution of the shares between the descendants of Ernest Solvay and their allies is very uneven (Vincent 1990: 313).

Similarly, in the 1970s, one of their allies, the Boël family, whose fortune was built in the iron and steel industry, organized its interests in various branches of industry, finance, and services around four holding companies controlled and managed by members of the family (*La Libre Entreprise* 1993).

Family or Managerial Control

The emergence of salaried managers occurred at the end of the nineteenth century in some financial groups. Very often the directors of the holding company are seen to have built their careers in a subsidiary where they have obtained a strong technical skill. Sometimes they have experienced mobility, but only inside a specific sector, with the consequence that upon reaching the board of the holding company, they have tended to work for the benefit of their particular sector instead of conceiving a global strategy for the group. The balance of power between the various sectors is therefore very important.

After the Second World War the diversification of the banking and industrial interests of the Société Générale resulted in the creation of so-called 'baronies' within the group. From 1950, each member of the board was put in charge of a particular sector of the company's activity. This meant that conflicting interests within the group regularly caused clashes between the 'coal men' and the 'electricians', the steel-makers and the cement manufacturers, etc. As a result, strong tensions arose in times of crisis and compromises could only be reached according to the balance of power within the management.

The story of Tractebel illustrates the strain between strong corporate groups belonging to a highly diversified corporate complex. Following the Second World War Tractebel, which heads electricity and engineering activities, decided to expand in the non-ferrous metal industry and in the nuclear sector. This launched a clash with the powerful Union Minière, which exploited the Congolese copper and uranium ore deposits and developed mining operations in other areas of the world. Both corporate groups belonged to the Société Générale which arbitrated the conflict in 1956. Consequently, Tractebel gained control of the entire energy sector, oil included, in addition to aluminium smelting, which is also a major consumer of electric power. The Société Générale then tried from the 1960s to tighten its control on Tractebel's management by enlarging the executive board with its own representatives. Consequently, Tractebel's managers have been inclined to feel that membership in a corporate complex has been more detrimental than advantageous (CRISP 1959; Joye 1960; *La Société Générale* 1972: 197; Tractebel 1995).

When a group is founded by a family, whatever its structure and organization may be, the family exerts a tight control. The case of the Empain group is, however, outstanding. To penetrate French markets without arousing opposition from the authorities, Empain established a rather loose judicial and financial structure of his numerous companies while maintaining strong concentration of the production and management-related decision-making processes. In its global strategy it relied on a federation of holding companies, the main holding companies were supranational in character and were under direct family control. The Empain group behaved essentially as a zaibatsu up until the 1950s, after which it was transformed into a corporate complex (Lanthier 1988: 432).

The very authoritarian and paternalistic management of the Coppée family group was quite different and supported truly dynastic power over four generations. During the first decade of the twentieth century when the group took shape, baron Évence II Coppée, the main shareholder and managing director of the group, created the 'Cabinet d'Administration', a true staff with legal and judicial competence closely associated with the process of decision-making, while the 'Département Industriel' developed the engineering activities. The 'Cabinet d'Administration' controlled the large companies of the group whose boards were made up of members of the Coppée family only. The salaried managers of these companies enjoyed significant autonomy but the ultimate decisions were made by the leader and his staff. This organization was changed after the Second World War, following conflicts within the Coppée family. A managerial board of five family members was substituted for the formerly all-powerful chief of the family, and all the seats on the subsidiaries' boards were occupied by the family without any power devolved to salaried managers (Dubois 1988: 191).

The Role of Business Groups in the Energy Sector

Distinct from the case of Japan, alliances have often played important roles in Belgian business history. In fact, one striking feature of the development of Belgian business groups is the growth of mutual shareholding and interlocking directorates *between* financial and industrial groups, i.e. between or among corporate complexes, zaibatsu-type family holdings, and corporate groups.

The study of the energy sector is a revealing one. Through just two case studies, one on coal mining and the other on electric power, the main features of the Belgian business groups and their influence on the national economy can be seen. Let us take a cross-sectional approach to their structure and strategy.

Coal Mining

Diversity of ownership

The Belgian coal industry was based in five coalfields. Four of them, the Walloon coalfields (Borinage, Centre, the Low Sambre, and Charleroi, Liège) were located in the south of the country; their modern development dates back to the early nineteenth century. The exploitation of the fifth one, the Campine coalfield, started only after the First World War.

An analysis of the structures of ownership in the Walloon coalfields in the early twentieth century shows great diversity linked to the history of their exploitation (Kurgan-van Hentenryk and Puissant 1990: 214–20). In 1900 there were 119 mines occupying an area of 95,000 hectares, which produced a total of about 23 million tons. Even though the majority of concessionnaires organized their enterprises as joint-stock companies at this time, this legal form concealed important differences with respect to both the ownership and management of capital. Despite the presence of a score of enterprises, the coal industry in the Borinage was dominated in reality by the Société Générale. It owned five of the main coal companies and thereby controlled half of the production of this coalfield. Within the Société Générale, the Division of Industry centralized the auctions of state railway contracts. These auctions served as a basis for fixing the prices of the various types of coal on the Belgian market, and the Société Générale thus exercised considerable influence over prices.

The management of each company in the Société Générale's group was put in the hands of a managing director who kept in touch with his colleagues in the coalfield in order to take concerted action with respect to transport, distribution, and labour conflicts. He reported to the board of directors which was chaired by a member of the Société Générale's board. At a lower level, the chief engineers of the coal-workings of the Société Générale met once a month to co-ordinate production and to come to an agreement on workers' wages, in order to avoid competition. In this way, the Société Générale set the tone for industrial relations in the whole coalfield.

Of all the Walloon coalfields, the Centre was the one where the concessions were the most extensive and coal production was linked to the development of local industry. Several family enterprises were involved; two of them, respectively run by the Warocqué and Coppée families, were the main Belgian producers.

The Charleroi and Liège coalfield areas, both of which were highly industrialized but which were also producers of domestic coal, were characterized by being broken down into many small concessions and by the small size of the coal-workings. The Société Générale was also involved in the Charleroi coalfield, but its position was less dominant because the production there was spread between forty or so companies, a fair number of which belonged to local industrialists and had customers in the immediate vicinity.

Concentration

A new stage in the concentration of the Walloon coal industry was reached in 1914 when the two largest concerns in the country, those of Raoul Warocqué and Évence Coppée, entered into an association with the Banque de Bruxelles. Although the Société Générale's involvement in industry had begun in the coal sector, the new group of coal interests resulted from a different strategy; the Coppée family had developed coal mining as a subsidiary activity of its coke ovens production, and it sought special links with bankers in order to finance its investments in Belgium and abroad. The Société Générale was barred from such links by its conflicting interests in the coal business.

For its part, the Banque de Bruxelles, which had become the second most important universal bank in the country, sought stable industrial customers and wanted to extend its interests in the coal industry, which was considered to be essential at that time. The association took off after the First World War; with the assistance of Coppée, the Banque de Bruxelles acquired a share in the control of various coal companies, assuring it a dominant position in the Centre coalfield. Management of the companies owned by the Banque de Bruxelles was put in the hands of the Coppée group, which charged a fee related to output.

At the time of the banking reform of 1934–5, the industrial interests of the Banque de Bruxelles were transferred to a new holding company, Brufina. In 1937, the arrival as chairman of Brufina of baron Paul de Launoit, the architect of the transfer of the largest steel company in Belgium to the Cofinindus holding company, provoked a loosening of the association, and in 1946 the management contract with the Coppée group came to an end. Brufina then returned the management of the coal companies that it owned to its own coal division.

As early as the interwar period, the degree of concentration resulting from the initiative of the financial groups, as well as the crisis of the 1930s, brought a reduction in the number of coal companies in all the Walloon coalfields except the Centre. The number fell from 98 in 1913, to 55 in 1939, and to 46 in 1958 at the time of the coal crisis. This crisis brought about the merger of companies belonging to the Société Générale and to de Launoit in the Borinage, similarly to the merging of the Coppée and Brufina interests in the Centre. With 76 per cent of Belgian mines considered to be dependent on financial groups, i.e. corporate complexes, there were none the less 16 independent companies, mainly situated in the Liège and Charleroi coalfields.

From the 1920s onwards, the exploitation of the Campine coalfield was organized on a quite different model from that of the Walloon coalfields. The geological conditions only allowed extraction from a limited number of centres and required large investments. Consequently, from the outset, the principle of concentration of resources was established and the state granted concessions of several thousands of hectares to groups of companies which had sound financial backing. The number of companies active in Campine was limited to seven, for an output which reached at least 10 million tons at the beginning of the 1960s. These seven companies were made up of the principal coal companies of the Walloon coalfields, in addition to Belgian and French steel companies looking for a better energy supply. At the end of the 1930s, as a result of the rapid turnover of participants, the Société Générale controlled three companies, Brufina two, while Coppée and the Cockerill steel company were the dominant influences in each of the other two. This division of influence was accompanied by an interlinking of the principal investors in the Campine coalfields companies. It was not unusual for a director of the Société Générale to sit on the board of a Brufina coal company next to representatives of the major industrial customers of the Campine coal companies. The interpenetration of the interests of the financial groups and the steel-makers increased after the Second World War and was further accelerated following the creation of the European Coal and Steel Community (ECSC).

However, it would be quite wrong to believe that the control of coal companies by the financial groups was exercised according to a single model and in a neatly integrated and systematic fashion. We have already noted the conflicting interests of the various fiefdoms or baronies within the Société Générale, whereas the Coppée family exhibited extremely dynamic centralized management up to the end of the Second World War. Its coal companies were part of an integrated industrial strategy which left a lasting mark on the company until its merger with Lafarge in 1980. And yet, in the course of time, rivalry with the Société Générale stimulated an expansion of Coppée's coal interests, wherein preoccupation with integration was eclipsed by the desire to control the largest possible tonnage and thereby to improve the balance of power in the coal industry.

Alliances and cartelization

The sensitivity of the coal market to fluctuations in the economy also pushed the business groups involved in coal mining toward the building of a network of alliances during the interwar period. This tendency was strengthened by the enacting of collective agreements in the coal industry, which profoundly altered the relationship between sales price and cost price, in so far as the employers were no longer completely free to fix wages. The price of labour was the principal element in the cost price, accounting for 65 per cent, so it is no surprise that the main argument put forward by the industry to explain its difficulties was that the charges levied to finance the post-war social reforms had weakened it *vis-à-vis* its key competitors (Coppé 1940: 229).

From the 1920s, coal companies, particularly those of the Société Générale and the Coppée family groups, attempted to make up for the uncertainties of the market. For example, the Coppée group set up a central sales bureau for all its coal output, strengthening the links between the coal industry and the steel industry, its principal industrial customer. However, it was through the production of synthetic coal and coke, through the carbon-based chemical industry, and through the by-products of the coking plants that the owners attempted to improve their market position. In 1930, 28 per cent of Belgian coal was consumed in the coal processing industries (Coppé 1940: 185). At the end of the 1920s, on the initiative of Coppée and the Société Générale, the cartelization of industrial coal producers was undertaken; two limited companies were set up on 5

January 1929, the Belgian Industrial Coal Agency and the Belgian Coke and Coking Coal Union.

The Belgian Industrial Coal Agency brought together all the coal companies of the two promoting groups plus four independent owners from the Charleroi coalfield, centralizing the sale and purchase of coal by its shareholders. The John Cockerill steel company, which had an important coal division, joined later, as did several other independent coal mines. The Belgian Coke and Coking Coal Union brought together producers and consumers of coke and coking coal belonging to the two promoting groups. In addition to commercial operations connected with coke and coking coal, it had the authority to have a stake in all enterprises aimed at creating outlets or developing any of its areas of activity.

The worsening of the economic crisis after 1932 and the extent of the depression in the coal sector encouraged the government to promote the setting up of a compulsory cartel; the National Coal Office was accordingly created in 1935. The weight of the Société Générale and of the Coppée–Banque de Bruxelles group in the coal sector, and the fact that their coal interests were deployed both in the coalfields of the south and in those of the north, had greatly facilitated this concentration. The result was that from 1935 to 1944 Belgian coal policy was conducted by Alexandre Galopin, the governor of the Société Générale, along with Évence Coppée. Cartelization brought about by the state left an enduring mark. The architect of the agreements and sales agencies, which succeeded one another in different forms until the beginning of the 1950s, was Herman Capiau, a former director of one of the Société Générale's coal companies and then director general of the Coal Federation, the employers' association (Kurgan-van Hentenryk and Puissant 1990: 240–1).

After the Second World War, there was a strong belief in the need to maintain coal as a vital sector in order to provide for the energy needs of the country. At that time, the Campine coal mines were considered to be the future of Belgium. Even though they resigned themselves to the setting up of the ECSC, the employers had fought energetically against the Schuman plan from its announcement on 9 May 1950 (Devos 1989). Nevertheless, the adherence of Belgium to the ECSC exercised an undoubtedly stimulating effect on the efforts agreed to by the coal industry to increase its productivity and thereby reduce its costs.

Unfortunately the crisis of 1958 hit the European coal industry with devastating force. Not only had the consumption of oil products grown significantly compared to coal and its derivatives, but the massive reduction of transport costs for American coal threw the European coal market, which until then had enjoyed protection afforded by its geography, into complete disarray. In these circumstances, the Belgian industry, despite all its efforts, found itself a position even worse than that of its partners in the ECSC because its costs remained higher. From then on, the employers, led by the financial groups Société Générale and Brufina together with the Coppée group, the unions, and the state conducted a concerted policy to close the Walloon coalfields. A similar process began in the Campine coalfield a few years later (Kurgan-van Hentenryk and Puissant 1990: 266–9).

Electric Power Industry

Contrary to coal mining, which was a state privilege conceded to private companies, the electric power industry originated both from industrialists' initiative and municipal monopoly (Kurgan-van Hentenryk 1987: 119–33). In fact, in the 1880s when electric power generation became a technical and economic possibility, some industrialists involved themselves in electricity production in order to supply their own plants; they were known as 'autoproducers'. Meanwhile, the municipal monopoly on lighting was extended to electricity distribution, so by the end of the nineteenth century some municipalities produced and supplied electric power under municipal control while others conceded it to private companies. It was only from 1895 onward that the universal banks became interested in this sector. Thus, on the eve of the First World War, 77 per cent of the capacity and 88 per cent of the output lay with the autoproducers.

After the war public authorities and private companies became aware of the strong limitations the legal system imposed on electrification. Two laws were subsequently passed to change the conditions of electricity generation and distribution. The first of these, issued in 1922, authorized the municipalities to enter into partnership with each other and/or with private companies. The second limited in 1925 the distribution monopoly of the municipalities, thereby allowing the standardization, the interconnection, and the extension of the grid (see Table 4.1).

Under these circumstances the interwar tendency toward concentration was most strongly felt, and it gave rise to extremely heated competition. Without lingering over the details of the organization of the electricity industry during this period—the scene of rivalry between the public authorities, autoproducers, and private firms—we should note that the private firms themselves experienced a technical and financial concentration. In the case of finance, an enormous restructuring took place between 1928 and 1935 resulting in the creation of large specialized holdings, including Sofina (reorganized in 1928), Electrobel and Tractionel (set up in 1929), and Electrorail (1930).

While Electrobel was a corporate group resulting from an amalgamation of firms originally launched by the Banque de Bruxelles and of a redistribution of interests of the five groups involved in the electricity industry (the Banque de Bruxelles, the Banque de Paris et des Pays-Bas, the Société Générale, the Mutuelle Solvay, and Sofina), Tractionel was a subsidiary of

Table 4.1. *Electric power industry (1914–1992)*

(a)

Year	Capacity			
	Capacity (1,000 kw)	Private cos. (%)	Public cos. (%)	Autoproducers (%)
1914	562	21	2	77
1925	1,027	41	5	54
1955	3,063	55	6	39
1992	14,860	87	7	6

(b)

	Output			
	Output (million kw)	Private cos. (%)	Public cos. (%)	Autoproducers (%)
1914	1,392	10	2	88
1925	2,191	36	5	59
1955	10,949	51	3	46
1992	68,379	93	3	4

(c)

	Distribution		
	Private cos. (%)	Mixed intermunicipal partnership (%)	Public cos. (%)
1939	82	5	13
1955	57	24	19
1992	38	51	11

the Société Générale, which was regrouping all its interests in tramways and electricity. It worked very independently from the start and soon became the most powerful corporate group in the electricity industry. Electrorail, however, was the outcome of the Empain group's desire to unify the management of its companies' financial services.

By the end of the 1930s, these four holding companies were in virtually complete control of the private producers and suppliers of electric power, with 95 per cent of the available power capacity and 85 per cent of the assets of the suppliers. It should be kept in mind that, as early as 1939, private companies provided 82 per cent of electric power. By reason of their complex and multiple connections with gas, tramway, electrical equipment manufacturing, and foreign electricity companies, these four holdings exercised a *de facto* monopoly hinging on Tractionel.

Undoubtedly the electricity industry's growth benefited from the 1920s inflation and from savers' increasing faith in its future. Nevertheless, during the 1930s crisis a fierce political debate arose over the control of such public utilities, with the Socialists claiming that electric power production and supply had to be provided by public companies. At the same time the private companies entered into partnership with municipalities to supply electricity. In these mixed intermunicipal partnerships, the private firm took charge of the exploitation and management under the control of a board of directors including representatives of the municipalities and the private company; the municipalities were paid fees and a portion of the profits. This type of partnership became increasingly successful, especially after the Second World War.

Unlike the cases of France and Britain, the Belgian electric power industry was able to avoid nationalization despite political attack from the Socialist and Communist left. To prevent any further possibility of nationalization, the private sector proposed a compromise, which is reminiscent of the plan drawn up after the war by the leader of the reorganization of Japan's electric power industry, Yasuzaemon Matsunaga (Kikkawa 1993: 155–61).

From alliances of business groups to corporate group

Following the negotiations between the employers and unions known as the 'Table Ronde de l'Électricité', an agreement was reached in July 1955. This agreement aimed at a reduction in the price of electric power implemented via a rationalization of the industry through a co-ordinated and unified management. Thus, the private companies created a 'Management Committee' to which they delegated significant powers on investments, production co-ordination, pricing unification, and the system of accounting. In these respects the companies were managed as a single firm and had to obey the Management Committee's decisions. To avoid a monopolistic position, the private companies signed an agreement with the unions and the Federation of Belgian Industry, which defended the customers. This agreement created a Controlling Committee including representatives of the different partners and of the state. It was allowed to collect all the information it needed about the industry and to recommend any measure aiming at reducing the prices.

Following this reform, concentration and rationalization accelerated dramatically under pressure from the large electrical holding companies.

In 1949 there were still 236 private firms; in 1956 there remained 36; and only 8 in 1965. By the end of the 1960s intense competition was faced by the private companies and the autoproducers, who were also selling their surplus electric power to industrial consumers. However, most of the autoproducers were linked to the financial groups involved in the electrical sector. These circumstances led in 1976 to further mergers into three electric power companies, which were controlled by two holding companies, Tractionel and Electrobel, and their shareholdings were restructured and stabilized. Ten years later the merger of these two holding companies into Tractebel, controlled by the Société Générale, was the next step to the creation of a corporate group. The process was completed after the Société Générale fell under the French Suez Group control. In 1990 the three remaining electric power companies were merged into a single new one, Electrabel, controlled by Tractebel, which now owns directly and indirectly 42 per cent of the shares.

While producing 93 per cent of Belgium's electricity output, Electrabel supplies directly and through its partnership with municipalities 88 per cent of their electric power, 92 per cent of their gas, and serves 51 per cent of all cable television customers. Its links with Tractebel are strengthened by their partnership in Powerfin, which exports their know-how in engineering and electrical exploitation abroad (Vincent 1990: 96). In September 1994, the privatization of the public company Société Nationale d'Investissement provided Tractebel with the opportunity to control the supply of natural gas (see Fig. 4.1).

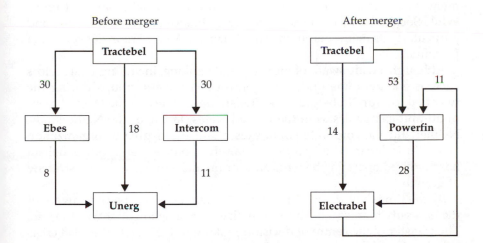

Fig. 4.1. *Tractebel's control of electrical power companies (%).*

Conclusion

The development of business groups in Belgium during the twentieth century seems to confirm the tendency of financial groups to consolidate via merger and acquisition, and the preference of family industrial groups to spin off subsidiaries. As financial groups may be defined as corporate complexes with looser trading organizations than in other countries, especially Japan, the family groups appear more like zaibatsu.

Another striking feature of the Belgian case is the importance of alliances between financial groups mostly in strategic industries like energy. Some corporate groups, like the former Electrobel or Petrofina, do not belong to particular corporate complexes, but are controlled by several of them. Consequently, the operations of the corporate group may sometimes be hindered by their main shareholders' rivalries. For example, Tractionel, which belonged to the Société Générale corporate complex, became stronger in the long term than Electrobel, whose management was often disturbed by differences among the three or four business groups represented on the executive board. In the case of Petrofina, the foremost corporate group in Belgium and the twentieth oil group in the world, it was controlled from the start by several groups. Although it achieved a certain amount of autonomy owing to its technological development, its size, and a policy of allocating stocks to the employees, the control of the group was still being negotiated in 1989 between two corporate complexes, Société Générale and Groupe Bruxelles Lambert (GBL). Following the takeover of the Société Générale by the French group Suez, Société Générale and GBL signed an agreement on the distribution of their influence in Tractebel and Petrofina. While Société Générale consolidated its influence on Tractebel, GBL, and particularly its main shareholder the financier Albert Frère, got control of Petrofina.

Although a wide swath of industry and banking, including vital sectors such as energy, came under the control of business groups during the twentieth century in Belgium, capitalism never reached the level of giant multi-unit companies as in the United States, Japan, or the Netherlands. Neither did the corporate complexes attain the degree of organization observed in Japan. The tradition of family capitalism and individualism has favoured operating benefits and/or financial interests over a strategy of growth.

By the time the former board of the Société Générale became aware of the necessity to integrate and rationalize its management, it was too late. The transfer of the centre of decision-making to Paris after the 1988 crisis is indicative of the increasing influence of foreign companies in strategic sectors of the Belgian economy. It raises the question of whether Belgian firms will be able to safeguard decision-making centres in a small open economy as we proceed in an era of global business.

REFERENCES

Bolle, P. (1963), *Solvay: L'Invention, l'homme, l'entreprise industrielle*, Brussels.

Chlepner, B. S. (1930), *Le Marché financier belge depuis cent ans*, Brussels.

Coppé, A. (1930), *Problèmes d'économie charbonnière*, Bruges.

Cottenier, J., De Booser, P., and Gounet, T. (1989), *La Société Générale 1822–1992*, Brussels.

CRISP (Centre de Recherche et d'Information Socio-politique), (1959), 'L'Organisation du patronat charbonnier belge et son influence politique', *Courrier hebdomadaire*, 7, 20 Feb.

—— (1966) *Morphologie des groupes financiers*, lst edn. Brussels, 1962.

Daems, H. (1977), *The Holding Company and Corporate Control*, Boston.

—— and Van de Weyer, P. (1993), *L'Économie belge sous influence*, Brussels.

Delaet, J.L. (1986), 'La Mécanisation de la verrerie à vitres à Charleroi dans la première moitié du XXe siècle', in G. Kurgan-van Hentenryk and J. Stengers, (eds.), *L'Innovation technologique facteur de changement (XIXe–XXe siècles)*, Brussels.

Devos, E. (1989), *Le Patronat belge face au Plan Schuman (9 mai 1950–5 fevrier 1952*, Brussels.

Devroey, M. (1973), *Propriété et pouvoir dans les grandes entreprises*, Brussels.

Dubois, L. (1988), *Lafarge Coppée: 150 ans d'industrie*, Paris.

Durviaux, R. (1947), *La Banque mixte: Origine et soutien du développement économique de la Belgique*, Brussels.

Jeanjot, P. (1967), 'Empain Édouard', *Biographie nationale*, xxxiv / 1, Brussels.

Joye, P. (1960), *Les Trusts en Belgique: La Concentration capitaliste*, 2nd edn. Brussels.

Kikkawa, T. (1993), 'La Réorganisation de l'industrie électrique au Japon en 1951', *Bulletin d'histoire de l'électricité*, 22, Dec.

Kurgan-van Hentenryk, G. (1987),'Le Régime économique de l'industrie électrique belge depuis la fin du XIXe siècle', in F. Cardot (ed.), *1880–1980: Un siècle d'électricité dans le monde*, Paris.

—— (1992), 'Finance and Financiers in Belgium, 1880–1940', in Y. Cassis (ed.), *Finance and Financiers in Europe 1880–1960*, Cambridge.

—— and Puissant, J. (1990), 'Industrial Relations in the Belgian Coal Industry since the End of the Nineteenth Century', in G. D. Feldman and K. Tenfelde (eds.), *Workers, Owners, and Politics in Coal Mining: An International Comparison of Industrial Relations*, New York.

Lanthier, P. (1988), 'Les Constructions électriques en France: Financement et stratégie de six groupes industriels internationaux, 1880–1940', thesis in history, Université Paris X.

La Libre Entreprise (1993), 27 Nov.

Répertoire permanent des groupes d'entreprises (1979–1989).

Répertoire permanent des groupes financiers et industriels (1967–1978).
La Société Générale 1822–1972 (1972), Brussels.
Tractebel 1895–1995. Les Métamorphoses d'un groupe industriel (1995), Antwerp.
Vantemsche, G. (1980), 'L'Élaboration de l'arrêté royal sur le contrôle bancaire (1935)', *Revue belge d'histoire contemporaine*, 11.
Vincent, A. (1990), *Les Groupes d'entreprises en Belgique: Le Domaine des principaux groupes privés*, Brussels.

PART II

THE CORPORATE GROUP

5

Growth via Politics: Business Groups Italian-Style

FRANCO AMATORI

Introduction

A business group is defined as an ensemble of enterprises which, while operatively or juridically independent, are subjected to some manner of unified control or, at the very least, co-ordination. It is a form of industrial organization constantly present in the past century's economic scenario, not only in what are classified as the 'advanced' countries but also in those which try to catch up with them.[1] There are various elements which outline a typology of a business group, such as the quantity of companies that refer to it, their belonging to related sectors, or their extension into unrelated fields of economic activity, the mechanisms through which control or co-ordination is obtained, etc. Considered from this viewpoint—i.e. as tools for control or co-ordination—we may distinguish between *associational groups*, alliances often cemented by cross-shareholdings that should be characterized by co-ordination and co-operation, and *hierarchical groups*[2] structured as a pyramid on top of which there is a mother company which, thanks to property rights, has the power to allocate resources, even transferring them from one company to another.

While there is no doubt that this distinction is important as it allows one to get a first orientation among these companies' 'archipelagos' or constellations, it is also important to keep in mind that it can lead to some fallacies. For example, *associational groups* such as the British federations of the beginning of this century, and the post-1950 Japanese keiretsu, are corporate aggregates whose economic results are deeply different. At the same time, *hierarchical groups* are multidivisional corporations, like the DuPont of Pierre duPont or the General Motors of Alfred Sloan, cornerstones of American supremacy in the twentieth century and the conglomerates that have seriously weakened American industrial apparatus in the past thirty years. It is necessary then to go beyond exterior forms and research the heart of the matter—i.e. the relationship between business groups and the wealth of a nation—in an analysis of the interface between the group headquarters and the organizational capabilities that operate in the companies. A headquarters can present itself in various forms—from a skyscraper in Manhattan with an extended managerial hierarchy to an exclusive hotel in Tokyo where the 'Thursday meetings' of a keiretsu take place—in any case it is the locus inhabited by those who can exercise the property rights and so determine the group's strategies. The company's organizational capabilities are formed by workers and technicians, possibly competent and motivated, and, above all, by managers who, given their many years of experience in a company or a sector, can correctly evaluate its specifications and its time horizons. The job of a headquarters is to put the organizational capabilities in the condition to operate at their best, to count on financial resources to invest in appropriate technologies, to be able to intensify the penetration in promising markets and to retreat from those saturated, to be committed to the R. & D. required for the company's particular needs, even if economic returns will become visible only after a long time span.

A group, like a single company, must face two implacable indicators: costs per unit and market shares of its products. If organizational capabilities do not get their way, or if a headquarters wants to expand the group towards sectors for which it cannot count on organizational capabilities, those indicators make their opinions heard and the headquarters turns out to be a serious cost for the group.

This is the situation captured by economist Piero Sraffa, commenting on the crisis of the two major Italian groups—Ilva (steel) and Ansaldo (heavy mechanics)—in the post-First World War period. Sraffa points out the contrast between the interests of the groups' leaders and those of the companies that they control. 'Both in the Ilva and in the Ansaldo groups there was a so-called "drainage corporation" whose shares were all in the hands of the leaders of each group, and whose only function was that of drying up the profits of its "daughter companies", hiding these unmistakable thefts with the most varied financial operations.'[3]

The goal of this chapter is to focus on the relationships between headquarters and organizational capabilities in Italian industrial groups between First World War and the 1980s. The groups considered are those for which the relationship with the state was a decisive one, either because the state's action served as a constant reference point for their strategies or because they became part of the state-owned enterprise system through the gigantic rescue of the 1930s and the following period of expansion of public intervention in the Italian industry. The chapter is divided into three parts. In the first part will be recounted the stories of the major groups between the First World War and the Great Crisis, many of whom in the 1930s would become part of the state holding IRI (Institute for Industrial Reconstruction). This does not include companies such as Fiat and Montecatini (even if, for the latter, IRI will be the major shareholder for a long time). The second part will analyse the phase—from the 1930s to the beginning of the 1960s—in which IRI acted as a weak headquarters, leaving room for the action of organizational capabilities in the sectorial subholdings and in the companies (IRI's structure will be explained in the second section), while a new state holding (ENI—National Hydrocarbon Corporation) was created to operate as a compact corporate group in a limited number of fields including natural gas, oil, and petrochemicals. This latter was independent but at the same level as IRI. The third part begins with the mid-1960s when IRI became a strong headquarters, pushed by goals inspired by the political powers, the same inputs that moved ENI to enlarge the scope of its activities in sectors unrelated to those of its origins. The relevance of the cases of IRI and ENI is due not only to their quantitative weight within Italian industry (as will be illustrated from data in the following pages as well as tables) but also to the fact that some of the sectors in which they operate (steel, oil, and petrochemicals) are central to the economic history of an advanced nation.

Italian Business Groups from the First World War to the Great Crisis

Even though at the beginning of the century the phenomenon of industrial concentration was already visible in Italy, it is with the First World War that we can observe a proliferation of corporate groups. A powerful incentive was represented by legislation which taxed reinvested profits at a much lower rate and pushed companies to acquire new production capacities not only to realize processes of vertical integration but also to expand into 'distant' sectors. A noticeable diversification could not be avoided as companies were cash laden thanks to military orders, while the possibilities of exploiting economies of scale in core sectors were limited given the extension of the markets.[4]

Even medium or small-sized companies turned themselves into corporate groups. Alfa Romeo, for example, on the eve of the war was an automobile company producing just a few hundred cars each year. Within a few months of the beginning of the conflict, it expanded its plants enormously to produce munitions, compressors, aeroplane engines, and agricultural machinery. Later it entered into the field of railway materials, incorporating Costruzioni Meccaniche di Saronno, a subsidiary of the German Maschinenfabrik Esslingen, and controlling two independent companies located in Rome and Naples, far from the Milan headquarters. Profits were exceptional during the war years but the difficulties of the post-war industrial reconversion for excess expansion were so insurmountable that the company was bankrupt by 1926 and could continue to survive only because the prime minister, Benito Mussolini, was fond of its speedy cars and ordered the Bank of Italy to guarantee promissory notes which would rescue the company.[5]

Problems of post-war industrial reconversion seriously damaged the major part of Italian enterprises. Fiat, the Turin based company which was already the number one automobile manufacturer before the war, was one of the few exceptions. Its expansion during the war years had been spectacular. While 22,500 units were produced between 1901 and 1914, 68,000 units were manufactured between 1915 and 1918. Employees increased from 4,000 in 1914 to 40,000 four years later. In addition, for Fiat product diversification during the war had a noticeable importance, especially as it expanded into the manufacture of aeroplanes and their engines, arms, and munitions. But, most especially, profits were reinvested to complete the vertical integration of the productive cycle; for this goal, in 1917 three major metal machinery companies in the Turin area were taken over. In addition, in the post-war years most of Fiat's holdings in activities external to its core sector—automobile production—were sold off so that by the mid-1920s their weight on total sales accounted for no more than 10%. War profits were mostly absorbed by the construction of a new plant—Lingotto—active since 1923 and, with its vertically designed layout, considered one of the most advanced in Europe.

Fiat could base its well-balanced development on a solid organizational structure. Already in the fifteen years preceding the war the company had made the necessary three-pronged investment in production, distribution, and management. Both during the war and in the post-war period, the corporation was solidly organized by functional departments which referred to a headquarters dominated by the strong personality of the company's leader, Giovanni Agnelli.[6] At the end of the war Fiat had moved from the position of thirtieth to that of third in the ranking by capital of Italian corporations. The first two, Ilva and Ansaldo, were not as successful in their post-war restructuring programmes.

Ilva[7] was the creation of a Roman banker and industrialist, Max Bondi, who in 1909 succeeded in setting up his steel plant in the Tuscan town of Piombino, a complete cycle steel mill. By 1918, thanks to the large profits accumulated during the war, and thanks to a series of shrewd agreements, Bondi took over the control of his major rivals. The outcome of these tactics should have been the legal premiss of a true rationalization of the Italian steel industry, whose productive apparatus in the first ten years of the century had grown in a chaotic manner, absolutely disproportionate when compared with the demand. There were managers and technicians in the companies which were taken over who pushed for rationalization but, *de facto*, the various plants remained independent entities. After having created Ilva, Bondi started a series of acquisitions in enterprises such as shipyards, railway and electric material producers, and automobile companies, with the declared intention of obtaining a forward integration in order to bring together the steel producer with his consumers. In reality, Bondi was overwhelmed by his very nature as a financial tycoon, a tendency which brought about the failure in 1921 of an attempt which could have attained rationalization and modernization of the Italian steel sector thirty years before it actually occurred.

Ansaldo[8] emerged from the war as the first corporation of the country with more than 110,000 employees. It had been founded in Genoa in 1853 by the most prestigious entrepreneurs of the town to produce locomotives but, since its beginnings, had effectively been supported by the state in an attempt to create a national railway system. The company knew a phase of considerable dynamism at the beginning of the century under the leadership of the Perrone family, launching itself in almost any field of the heavy machinery sector as well as shipyard production. The Perrones were different from Bondi; they were not financial raiders but, rather, technocrats. In 1915, supported by French capital, they created their own bank, the Banca Italiana di Sconto, and, envisioning a grand design, aimed to create a giant vertically integrated enterprise which could serve the country in times of war as well as peace and which would be able 'to produce and sell the finished products of a powerful industrial nation: electric systems from telephones to street cars and electrified railways; vehicles from automobiles to trucks and airplanes; ships of every dimension and category for the high seas'.[9]

The experiences of the Perrones' Ansaldo are similar to those of the British armament producer Vickers during the same years: an uncontrolled expansion in unrelated sectors for which the company did not have the organizational capabilities.[10] The Perrones were finally overthrown in 1922 by their excessive expansion and by the bankruptcy of the Banca Nazionale di Sconto. They perceived this defeat as deeply unjust. Since the state had been its principal customer, and Ansaldo embodied a lasting national interest, the Perrones and their managers considered it acceptable to make long-range plans that the state would then be obligated to protect from eventual market fluctuations.

The idea that in Italy a company considered strategic for the industrial national apparatus could enjoy a financial protective network was not new. It appeared in the 1880s when the state fostered a real infraction of the mechanisms of market economy so as to channel the country towards the industrialization process. Up to that point the Italian economy had been based on agriculture and its exports, both dramatically challenged during the 1880s by the flood of agricultural products from overseas made possible by the revolution in transportation means. The substantial drop in the prices of agricultural products rendered obsolete a model of economic development which had been valid in Italy since the beginning of the eighteenth century. It was now possible to respond to the emerging challenge with consistent political choices intended to direct the country towards industrialization. But in this period the word 'industrialization' was synonymous with the word 'steel', meaning that decisions had to be (1) protective tariffs in favour of cast iron and steel products; (2) convincing efforts so that national railways and shipyards would buy Italian made steel; and (3) privileges for Italian steel companies in the use of local iron ore. The state did this and something more. In 1884 it promoted the birth of an enterprise Terni (taking its name from the town near Rome where it was located) to become Italy's largest steel producer. The state largely financed the purchase of the machinery and, as was mentioned previously, set up tariffs intended to discourage steel imports, and guaranteed orders from shipyards and railroads. The entrepreneur to whom the state entrusted the project, Vincenzo Stefano Breda (not, by chance, a businessman involved in major public works projects financed by the state), envisioned an audacious plan to build up an integral-cycle steel production process, the only mass producer of steel in Italy. But Breda underestimated the technical, financial, and organizational complexity of his project. In addition, the entire affair was not lacking in speculative aspects. Thus the firm, unable to fulfil contracts signed with the Navy for the supply of battleship armour, found itself on the brink of bankruptcy in 1887, only three years after its founding. The government, however, was committed to a policy aimed at self-sufficiency in steel production and, therefore, intervened and rescued the company. The Navy paid in advance for 2,500 tons of battleship armour and the Banca Nazionale, through the distribution of new paper money, granted additional loans.[11] This episode was not an isolated event. If in 1887 the state had arranged the rescue of a large corporation, by 1911, under the aegis of the Bank of Italy (central bank), the entire steel sector (whose crisis risked ruining the major banks of the nation) was the recipient of the same cure. At the beginning of the century the leaders of the steel trust (which included Terni) and Max Bondi knew perfectly well that their intention of enlarging production capacity was economically irrational but they also realized that greater growth would guarantee preferential treatment from the state for their own companies. It happened just as expected: the cartel imposed by the central bank accepted all the plants of the various participants and shared profits according to the respective production capacities.[12]

It is not by chance that a company with the history and so with the corporate culture of Terni gave birth in the years between the two wars to a multi-sector group that held its advantage by positioning in sectors which were either protected or strongly regulated by the state. In the years between the wars the company's new leader, Arturo Bocciardo—appointed to his position by Banca Commerciale Italiana, the major shareholder—was a manager who had acquired his most important experiences as a civil servant during the war in the agency committed to supplying raw materials to companies engaged in the war production effort. Through that experience he understood the importance of an energy supply for a large corporation and so positioned Terni in the production of electric energy, utilizing the unsold stock for electrochemical manufacture. At the same time he kept alive the activities in the steel industry for war purposes—the original core sector—and the military shipyards that Terni had acquired at the beginning of the century. With Bocciardo, the Terni group became something more than the sum of its parts. A headquarters committed to a substantial policy of rationalization and centralized administration emerged. *De facto*, Bocciardo knew perfectly well that his plan of expansion in all three sectors would have been unsustainable if simply based on the features of the market. In reality, Terni's headquarters, more than fostering the full development of organizational capabilities, needed to be dedicated to bargaining work with the government. Terni kept the wartime steel production alive in times of peace with strong liabilities, but the state in return provided a good regulation of electricity prices to be distributed to all public utilities, good conditions for loans by the financial institutions that the state had created to support the electric industry, and a favourable position to Terni in the chemical cartels imposed by law at the beginning of the 1930s. Bocciardo's strategic goal was to draw large profits from the electric sector once the enormous initial investments had been amortized and, in any case, to occupy a strong position of power in Italy's 'limited suffrage' capitalism, given the centrality of the sectors in which Terni operated for the country's economy.

Like Terni, Montecatini (the giant of the Italian chemical industry) also grew in the years between the two wars, thanks to a form of do ut des with the political powers. Montecatini,[13] a mining company producing pyrites, accumulated notable profits during the First World War by supplying the manufacturers of explosives. Immediately after the war a process of forward integration (pyrites is the base component of sulphuric acid production which is, in turn, essential to making fertilizers) was begun so that in 1920 the company acquired the country's two largest producers of super phosphates. Montecatini, under the leadership of Guido Donegani, a real empire builder, activated a strong rationalization of the sector, shutting down old plants, opening new ones, framing the new productive reality inside an organization based on functional departments. But super phosphates production was a labour-intensive sector. Montecatini entered the age of the Second Industrial Revolution in the mid-1920s with the production of synthetic nitrogen, obtained thanks to an original patent, by an electrolitic method. All this required conspicuous investment in the construction of hydroelectric plants, realized with the help of the major Italian banks and with American loans, investment that could be justified only by complete control of the domestic market for synthetic fertilizers. Farmers'

associations were opposed to this since they wanted to be able to import
the product freely from abroad. Donegani was able to convince Mussolini
that synthetic nitrogen production was of supreme interest to the nation;
by 1931 strong protective tariffs eliminating any chance for foreign
competition had been issued. But 'there are no free lunches'. The government from that point on ordered Montecatini to follow a series of expan-
sive moves for which either it was not technically and organizationally
prepared (as in the case of dyestuffs) or did not make sense from an economic perspective (as in the rescuing of numerous mining companies).
Unlike the most important chemical corporations of the advanced countries, Montecatini would not adopt a multidivisional structure until the
early 1960s. In the 1930s the company did not own a surplus of organizational capabilities to export in related sectors, nor was this kind of growth
(i.e. in related sectors) possible in Italy for the spontaneous growth of markets. For the new initiatives commanded by the regime, juridically independent subsidiaries were created, but these were strictly controlled by
Donegani's headquarters as the resources to decentralize control did not
exist.

On the eve of the Second World War Montecatini was a major power in
the Italian economy, with 60,000 employees, consuming 10 per cent of the
country's electric power, and with its shares considered as equal to state
bonds. But the excessive expansion of the 1930s brought about by a political command laid a burden on the company that was to prove fatal in the
dynamic environment of the immediate post-war period.

To summarize: the First World War was the occasion for the expansion
of the major Italian companies out of their core sectors. But the element
that made this expansion permanent was the goal of attaining an importance in the national economic scenario which the government could not
ignore if it wanted to save the country's well-being. The growth had such
an extension that in the case of companies such as Terni and Montecatini
it is more appropriate to talk of corporate complexes than of corporate
groups. The growth occurred due to internal expansion, with the creation
of new plants and activities, via the acquisition and the incorporation of
other companies, or through the control of juridically independent subsidiaries. At any rate, the expansion overwhelmed the capacity of headquarters effectively to supervise and co-ordinate the process.

From what has been written up to this point the major difference
between Italian big business and that of the most advanced countries
becomes evident. In the latter, the enterprise grows for economic reasons
(i.e. to cut costs per unit) while in Italy it often grows for strategic purposes
(i.e. to be in a stronger bargaining position *vis-à-vis* the political powers).
If American capitalism can be defined as managerial, British as personal,
and German as co-operative,[14] then the Italian model can be termed
political.

Business Groups within the 'State as Entrepreneur' between the 1930s and the 1950s

The birthdate of the State as Entrepreneur in Italy can be proclaimed as 24 June 1937 when IRI (Istituto di Ricostruzione Industriale) was declared a permanent institution.[15]

IRI was a public holding company formed four years earlier with the purpose of freeing the Italian banking system from the close ties with major industry that threatened to sweep it away and to create economic chaos in the country. In 1933 IRI had two tasks: to grant long-term loans to the companies affected by the Depression and to take over the industrial securities held by the three major Italian banks, selling them to private buyers. It soon became apparent that it would be impossible to achieve the latter goal since no economic forces, except the state, were capable of not only purchasing the banks' shareholdings in sectors such as steel, shipyards, and public utilities but also financing the continual investments these activities required. Therefore, IRI could not be only a temporary owner. On the eve of the Second World War, IRI controlled 80 per cent of the production in shipbuilding, 45 per cent in steel, 39 per cent in the electro-mechanical industry, 23 per cent in the mechanical, and 16 per cent of the country's electric power generation.

As we have seen, IRI was deeply rooted in Italian history. It brought to an end a process begun in 1887 with the rescue of a large corporation, Terni, continued in 1911 with an entire sector (steel), and in 1922 with the industrial activities controlled by the major financial institution Banca Italiana di Sconto. IRI came to control all the groups we have mentioned so far, except Fiat, so that by the time its birth became official in 1933, it controlled an industrial shareholding equal to 42 per cent of the national total. But, according to the original goal, IRI's companies would not be insulated from the challenges of the marketplace, as had happened with companies under public administration.

The latter idea was deeply rooted in the entire career of Alberto Beneduce,[16] IRI's creator and first president as well as a civil servant since the turn of the century and chief economic adviser of Mussolini. Beneduce conceived a form of state intervention under which companies had to be managed according to entrepreneurial criteria. To achieve this goal, Beneduce first chose his collaborators at IRI on the basis of their managerial competence, providing them with complete liberty in hiring, rewarding, and firing personnel rather than subjecting them to the constraints typical of public administration. In addition, together with his staff, he designed a structure wherein IRI should serve as a 'bridge' between the state (which set the broad economic goals) and the industrial sectors under control. IRI became a central holding company with various sectorial holding companies whose task was to support financially and co-ordinate the management of firms remaining under the legal form of private corporations. Crucial to its structure, IRI considered the industrial sector as the only framework within which to pursue a strategy of order and rationality. From this perspective, it is highly significant to examine the clash between IRI and Terni which, as has been said, fell under IRI's control in 1933. IRI wanted to divide Terni's operations according to sectorial lines. This contrasted deeply with Bocciardo's bargaining logic and quickly encountered harsh opposition from Terni's management. Bocciardo was too powerful to lose but IRI's vision proved to be more appropriate in the long run.

One of Beneduce's major concerns was to limit the borders of his empire and, hence, to sell back to the private sector as many activities as possible in the period between 1933 and 1937. This attitude was motivated by two factors. First, Beneduce did not want to alter the delicate balance between public and private—in 1936 Italy was, after the Soviet Union, the second nation in the world in terms of state ownership of industrial properties. Second, IRI's founder was perfectly aware of the scarcity of managerial resources to control such a vast conglomerate. In its first twenty-five years, IRI was a loose corporate complex with a very weak headquarters and with much room for the initiative of sectorial holdings and companies. Certainly Beneduce's original imprint made possible this series of developments. On the other hand, the great turbulence of the war and the postwar period made uncertain the political power which provided room for professional management. There is no doubt that these were the best years for IRI, a real component of the so-called 'economic miracle' of the 1950s.

The story of the steel sector is a perfect illustration of this last concept. In the first half of the twentieth century the problem of steel was probably Italian industry's most severe challenge. After Terni's failure to build up its integral cycle plant (intended to become Italy's only mass producer), there was a proliferation of steel works absolutely disproportionate to the limited domestic market. The crisis of the sector, especially for Ilva, its most important player, was particularly apparent in the 1930s. At the beginning of this period in Sofindit (the holding company which oversaw the industrial shareholdings of the Banca Commerciale Italiana, the bank which controlled Ilva) there was a group of managers firmly intent on creating a modern steel industry in Italy. Their leader, Oscar Sinigaglia,[17] started to envision a plan based on three points: first, the creation of a new, large, complete-cycle plant in Genoa able to supply the most industrialized area of the country; second, rigorous productive specializations of all the other factories and modernization of techniques and organization; and, third, a shut-down of the old and inefficient plants and dismissal of unnecessary personnel. Sinigaglia anticipated that the workers laid off would be absorbed by the growing mechanical industry which at that point enjoyed the supply of cheaper steel. His central idea was that a large steel sector in Italy could justify its existence only by being competitive at the international level. Sinigaglia tried to rationalize the sector in 1933 when he was named president of Ilva. But he was soon forced to resign due to a conflict with the old company's management, which strongly believed in protectionism, cartels, and orders from the state. Sinigaglia's struggle was taken over by his pupil Agostino Rocca, who in 1937 was elected chief executive officer of Finsider, IRI's steel holding company. In fact, after serious battles with the old management and with some of the private steel companies such as Falck and Fiat, Rocca was able to build a complete cycle plant at Cornigliano near Genoa. Nevertheless, the project had some technical flaws and perished in 1943 when the German army completely dismantled the works. Sinigaglia returned at the end of the war as the president of Finsider, intent on realizing his own plan (notwithstanding strong opposition by the leftist parties and unions due to the lay-off of workers) which would utilize ERP funds. In 1953, the year of Sinigaglia's death, the Cornigliano plant was fully operative. Italy, which had never exceeded an output of 3 million tons of steel, reached by 1960 an annual output of 8.2 million tons, moving from ninth to sixth position in the world. Especially important was that under Sinigaglia a cohesive, competent, aggressive managerial team (which was also familiar with American industrial practices) emerged. Cornigliano's inner organization was designed by the American consultancy Booz-Allen and Hamilton and hundreds of workers and engineers received their training at ARMCO's plant in Middletown, Ohio.

Sinigaglia's Finsider was a multidivisional corporation. The headquarters issued a unitary policy for the corporate group and strongly opposed external pressure that attempted to modify it. IRI, for example, was favourable to strengthening existing plants, rather than building new ones, but was unable to get its way. The chief executives of the companies of Finsider were members of a president's committee which was part of the headquarters. In turn, this committee was equipped with ample functional staff and was clearly independent and superior to the companies which, on the other end, could rely on all the functional departments and, hence, could cope autonomously with their specific problems. Also worth noting is the fact that Sinigaglia wanted to put the new plant of Cornigliano under the roof of a newly created company, Cornigliano Corporation, given his fear that the old management of Ilva might choose to boycott an essential component of his plan. Following the war, Ilva controlled the other two integral-cycle plants of Piombino (Tuscany) and Bagnoli (Naples). In 1961 Ilva and Cornigliano merged to form Italsider, a company clearly dominated by the second, an indication that the philosophy of Sinigaglia's plan had been fully successful.

At the beginning of the 1950s, ENI (the National Hydrocarbon Corporation), another state holding completely independent of IRI but at the same level in the state shareholding system, was established. ENI, as has been stated earlier in this chapter, was created to act specifically in the fields of energy sources, oil, and petrochemicals. From its birth in 1953 through its first ten years of existence, we see the most complete expression of an entrepreneurial vision for a public enterprise. It is possible to state that ENI was a private initiative by a public entrepreneur, Enrico Mattei.[18] To put this new state business group in its proper historical framework, it is important to understand Mattei's charismatic personality.

The oil problem is a more recent issue for Italy, if compared with the steel industry. In 1926 the state founded AGIP (Azienda Generale Italiana Petroli), a company intended to research, process, and sell oil. AGIP had the merit of forming a group of highly specialized technicians but, business-wise, it was not a great success. By the end of the Second World War the government decided to liquidate the company as a residue of the Fascist regime. But the decision was completely overthrown by Mattei, the executive in charge of closing down the company. From experiences acquired prior to entering public life, he held the strong conviction that there was need for an active role of the state in the economy. Mattei had experienced the life of the emigrant when the 1929 Depression compelled him to move from a small town in central Italy (where he had become the general manager of its largest factory, a tannery, by his early twenties) to Milan. In the Lombard metropolis he soon developed a successful chemical firm which was nevertheless affected by the difficulties (typical of other Italian companies in the field) of supply of raw materials, controlled by multinationals. Thus, he was attracted by the theories of economic nationalism but, at the same time, opposed to the Fascist use of nationalistic concepts aimed more towards achieving a superficial *grandeur* than at creating consistent national prosperity. Familiarity with the progressive Lombard Catholicism formed his cultural and political ideas based on social justice, ideals that were strengthened by his struggle during the Resistance as a leader of the Christian Democrat partisans.

From these influences and experiences Mattei conceived of the state's role as undertaking broad economic action to overcome Italy's historical backwardness, i.e. its inferiority in comparison with the big industrialized countries and the poor living conditions of a large segment of the population. Such an action had to be free from any bureaucratic burdens. It would utilize the most advanced techniques, the finest managerial skills, and, above all, the most talented entrepreneurs available. For this it was necessary to assure the required flexibility: the economic risks and even the aggressive lobby towards political power inevitably connected with entrepreneurial activity were justified in Mattei's mind by the interest of the majority of the people and the consent of a wide range of political forces.

It is not feasible in the limits of this short essay to follow the complicated story of Enrico Mattei from his appointment as 'commissary' at AGIP in 1945 to his death in a plane crash in 1962 at the peak of his career. I will, however, deal with some of the crucial aspects of Mattei's strategy. After having greatly increased AGIP's capacity in mining research and distribution of natural gas in the Po Valley, following a tough political battle, Mattei obtained the monopoly on these activities from the government. Consistent with his concept of public interest, Mattei did not take advantage of this situation by raising prices but was still able to guarantee financial independence to the company. Starting from this basis, when AGIP became part of the larger holding ENI, he attempted to build up a vertically integrated oil corporate group. ENI already owned an oil distribution network which drew its supply from American and British multinationals. Mattei looked for new suppliers and started new ventures with the producing nations for oil mining in order to overcome the initially inferior position and reach a backward integration. The limits of the Italian oil market and the political issue of increasing employment in southern Italy pushed ENI into the chemical sector. Here, starting from the basis of natural gas, Mattei attained a major success by building up a petrochemical plant in Ravenna (a town in central Italy on the east coast) to an adequate scale dimension which, *de facto*, was able to put an end to the quasi-monopoly previously enjoyed by Montecatini in the field of nitrogen fertilizers. Mattei, however, was not interested in pursuing diversification beyond a certain point, recognizing that it could become a serious source of weakness for his creation. By the beginning of the 1960s the image of ENI was that of a pivotal element of the 'Italian big spurt', a company run in the best interests of the nation.

In the final analysis, the structure of Mattei's ENI was rather similar to that of Sinigaglia's Finsider. It was a compact corporate group where a headquarters, ENI, provided a powerful unified pulse to four vertically integrated sectorial subholdings. They were AGIP Mineraria (mining), with the task of mining for raw materials, oil, and natural gas; SNAM (National Natural Gas Pipeline Company) charged with transporting natural gas; ANIC (Oil Hydrogenation National Company) for refining and chemically processing gas; and AGIP for the marketing of the finished product. One of the most important jobs of headquarters was the interface with the political powers so that the subholdings were free to cope with the challenges created by technologies and the markets.[19]

The Involution of the State Entrepreneur after the 1960s

In 1956 the constitution of the Ministry of State Shareholdings seemed to offer the final step in the design of Beneduce and Mattei. In this way, there was a well-defined 'chain of command' (see Fig. 5.1). The Ministry fully controlled public holdings such as IRI and ENI, and in the following years added others including EFIM (primarily heavy mechanics) and EGAM (mining). In turn, the public holdings controlled partially (but always more than 50 per cent) their sector holdings, which in turn controlled the operating companies, all of whom were answerable to the holding's management and the Ministry in the final analysis. All this could have compensated for the lack of co-ordination that up to that point had characterized the system of state-owned enterprises. But, in this respect, the new Ministry did not act as a superior headquarters. For example, at the end of an intense decade Mattei's goal was to integrate within one corporation the nation's public energy policy, including electric and nuclear energy. Such an ambitious project was defeated on the one side by the opposition of the leftist parties (who feared excessive concentration of power) and, on the other side, by the lobby of the electric industry which fought to avoid expropriation. It is interesting to consider the fact that the latter group also included IRI's electric holding company.

Discussing the Italian state's policy of intervention, Franco Bonelli, one of the best authorities on the country's contemporary economic history, rightfully talks of 'State capitalisms'.[20] To express the same concept, Giuliano Amato (Italy's former Prime Minister but also an excellent scholar interested in relations between business and government) used the expression 'liberal protectionism', meaning that state intervention in Italy's economy guaranteed all manner of favours to the enterprises but was hardly co-ordinated and harmonized in a plan of economic development for the country.[21]

But more damaging than the scarce co-ordination of the system was the fact that the state was not an absent shareholder. In Italy the state does not signify a body of civil servants acting according to universalistic rules. Rather, given the cultural and economic fragmentation of the country, the relationship between universalistic rules and social action had to be mediated by politics. After the instability of the years following the Second World War, the pyramid-like system established with the birth of the Ministry of State Shareholdings reconfirmed the role of command of the politicians; something especially dangerous in a political system such as Italy's, in which an American-style change in the 'spoil system' was impossible since the leading opposition force (the Communist Party) was permanently excluded from the government. Political demand was for a continuous growth of productive capacities above all in the depressed areas in order to get higher levels of employment and to maximize consensus (as an example: a famous legislative bill in 1957 obliged state-owned companies to set up 40 per cent of their new investments in the southern part of the country). In a climate such as this, a managerial strategy like the one enacted with Sinigaglia's plan, implying the dismissal of

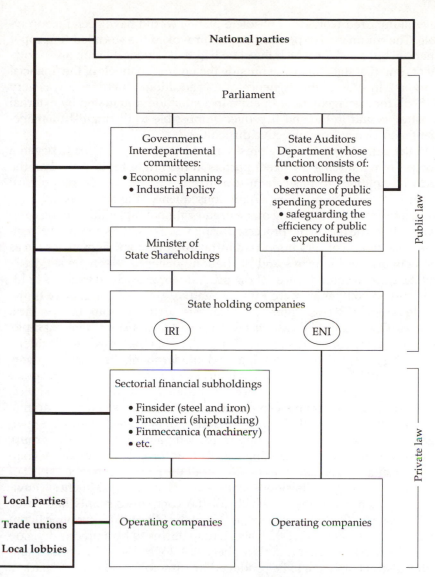

Fig. 5.1. *The system of state shareholdings: theory and reality.*

several hundred workers at obsolete plants, would have been inconceivable. The commands of political power provoked the so-called 'improper financial burdens' for which the state had to compensate with an endowment fund (i.e. state financing outside the normal channels of the financial markets). In spite of the existence of this additional funding, it was very difficult for management to operate in a situation dominated by external constraints and in the end it proved impossible to distinguish management inefficiency from objective difficulties.[22]

In the early 1960s, the new president of IRI, Giuseppe Petrilli, began a process of reinforcing the headquarters. It held tight to its control on the sectorial holdings to push them toward the growth which the political powers insisted on attaining. As a consequence, the sectorial holdings started to limit the autonomy of the organizational capabilities in the companies. It is true that in the process, during the 1960s, IRI's companies realized the building of very important infrastructures for the country such as the networks of highways and of the long-distance telephone service.[23] But the general consequences of the pressure for growth on sectorial holdings and on companies were rather negative, given the incapacity of the headquarters (IRI) to 'filter' the requests arriving from the political powers. Once again the case of the steel sector is a significant example. After the excellent results of the 'Sinigaglia plan' obtained by Finsider's leadership, instead of reinforcing and modernizing its existing plants (which would have been the most logical choice from an economic point of view) top management was forced in the late 1950s, by 'political' choice, to build up a new complete-cycle plant in the southern city of Taranto. This facility subsequently became the largest Italian steel plant. The management of Italsider, the most important company of the Finsider group, which was in charge of realizing the Taranto project, accepted the challenge, trying to overcome the constraints of the localization in the spirit of Sinigaglia's heritage. Italsider's chief executive, Mario Marchesi, envisioned a plan according to which all the company's plants had to be strengthened—the Italian market at the peak of the 1950s economic boom was all but saturated—but they also had to be linked by a precise division of production tasks. In this design, sheet steel for ships, welded pipes, and slabbed steel bars were to be produced in Taranto for sale on the market. Marchesi's plan was fiercely opposed by the 'new' IRI and by the 'new' sectorial holding it had shaped, Finsider. There was little tolerance for a company which would be perceived as too strong, as would have been the case with Marchesi's Italsider if his plan had succeeded. 'When I was hired by Finsider (in the late 1940s)', writes GianLupo Osti, Marchesi's assistant, in a beautiful first-person account, 'companies were much more autonomous and Finsider had to deal with them with great respect. At the end of my career in the 1970s, the scenario was so significantly different that Finsider "bossed" the companies. IRI did the same with its sectorial

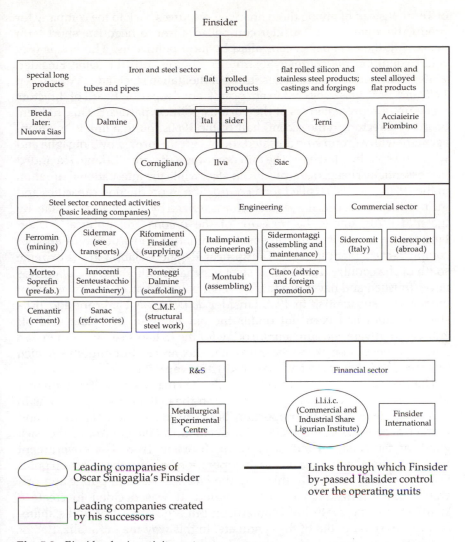

Fig. 5.2. *Finsider: basic activity sectors.*

holdings. Many organizational studies by consultants pointed out that the pyramid made by ministry, holding, sectorial holdings, and companies represented an excessive weight and a duplication of functions. Every independent observer could not but have reached this same conclusion.'[24] Finsider had a powerful means to bend the companies at will: the financial tool. Take the case of Terni, which was controlled by Finsider. The latter was cash laden after the nationalization of the electric energy industry since it could get the indemnities paid by the state to the electric division

of Terni. Instead of giving these financial resources back to the company for
productive investment, Finsider compelled Terni to negotiate short term
debts with the local banks controlled by local politicians, who in this way
could condition the company's strategic choices. But the same Finsider,
writes Margherita Balconi in her study of the Italian steel industry between
1945 and 1990, was subjected to an 'occult' and 'superior' board of directors
made up of representatives of the various political parties.[25] This 'hidden'
board of directors in the second half of the 1960s found a link to the management with a group who defeated the old group formed by Sinigaglia and
which was led by Marchesi. The outcome was a disaster. Taranto expanded
into essentially cheap, mass-produced steel while the international situation
in the 1970s and 1980s called for a contraction in production capacities and
the production of specialized steels characterized by a high added value. By
the mid-1970s, under the pressure of the unions and political parties,
Finsider even accepted the prospect of initiating construction of another
complete-cycle plant in Gioia Tauro, near Reggio Calabria in the extreme
south of the country. Reality was stronger than politics and the plant was
never finished and never produced even a pound of steel, but the waste of
money was substantial. In 1988 Finsider *de facto* was bankrupt and IRI's
steel activities had been put under the old name of Ilva, later sold off
entirely to private entrepreneurs. Today for the Italian steel sector there is a
new key decision-maker—the European Economic Community—which
imposes precise limits to national production capacities.

The story of the past thirty years of ENI has many similarities with that
of Finsider. As ENI was more involved in the chemical sector, and as in
this field there was a disproportion between production capacities and
market necessities in the 1960s, ENI decided to take control of the 'sick
giant' of the chemical industry, Montedison, in 1968. The government
soon intervened and put a halt to the operation because the common political judgement was that in this way the balance between public and private capitalism would have been altered. It was decided to create a
syndicate for the control of Montedison but a good part of ENI's shareholdings were kept out of the syndicate. In this way the rationalization of
the sector was impossible. At the end of the 1970s another political command imposed that ENI take over all the 'smoking ruins' of the Italian
chemical industry, the result of the failure of companies such as SIR,
Liquigas, and parts of Montedison itself: in their strategies of expanding
plants, the behaviour of these companies is quite similar to that of the steel
tycoons at the beginning of the century.[26] But the government did not
impose on ENI only the chemical 'ruins'. In 1962 ENI was forced to take
over an old textile company, Lanerossi, for 'social' reasons. Lanerossi was,
in its turn, the leader of another group of inefficient companies. Fifteen
years later the Italian Parliament issued a bill to compel ENI to take over
all the activities of EGAM (an acronym for the Authority which managed

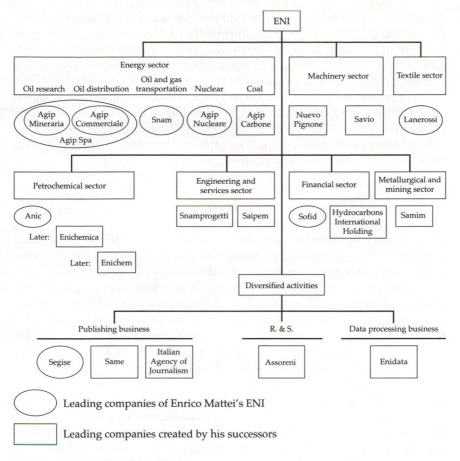

Fig. 5.3. *ENI: basic activity sectors.*

mining companies), another state holding of the same level as IRI and ENI which had been created in 1958. In the years following its creation, EGAM had become a conglomerate, expanding—again for 'social' reasons—in a variety of fields including metallurgy, mechanics, and textiles. As these industries were completely unrelated to ENI's traditional interests, Mattei's creation had become more a 'public holding for economic development'[27] than a true corporation.

Nowadays, the state of crisis of the 'formula' of state intervention begun in the early 1930s is a commonplace. The Ministry of State Shareholdings has been dismantled, public holdings such as EGAM and EFIM (the authority for the financing of the mechanics industry, founded in 1962) have been liquidated, a process of privatizing IRI's companies has been initiated (an important case is Alfa Romeo, bought out by Fiat), and the same IRI and ENI will be transformed into common corporations open to private shareholders. Pertinent is the fact that a decision taken by the government in 1992 abolished the executive committees of the boards of directors of ENI and IRI which had been filled with representatives of the various political parties. Decisions such as these have been welcomed by commentators and public opinion in general. But no one can deny that it will be difficult to find private shareholders interested in debt-ridden corporations such as IRI and ENI. Equally difficult after years of the less than correct relationship between politics and management will be to render the latter competitive in an unprotected market.

Conclusions

In the history of industrial Italy business groups can be found not only around the 'State Entrepreneur' but also in private hands. Especially in the last twenty years, the saturation or the difficulties of competition in some core sectors has moved family holdings or individual tycoons towards the creation of corporate complexes. Thus IFI, the financial holding company of the Agnelli family, added to its control of Fiat companies such as La Rinascente (retailing), SNIA (chemicals), Toro (insurance), etc. Carlo De Benedetti, an entrepreneur who for a short period in 1976 served as CEO of Fiat, took control of Olivetti (office machinery and equipment) in 1978 and then started to acquire companies in the mechanics, food, and publishing sectors. In 1986 the Ferruzzi family, one of the world's major grain traders, took over Montedison, which, in addition to its activities in the chemical sector, was involved in mass retailing, insurance, and publishing. But even within these private groups, which are comparable in dimensions to those controlled by the state, the conflict between ownership and management is apparent. Ownership is restricted in a few hands and it tends to obstruct management every time the strategies of the latter attempt to challenge its control. Even in these cases the state's role emerges. In order to finance its increasing intervention in the national economy, the state needs to offer high rates of interest to the buyers of its bonds and this drains private savings, thus preventing the rise of large corporations with diffused ownership/shareholders.[28]

Italy has made outstanding progress since its political unification in the middle of the nineteenth century. It was then an underdeveloped nation, exporting raw materials and importing finished goods manufactured by others. Now it is a full-fledged member of the 'G-7', the club of the most industrialized western nations whose policies affect the world's economy. The difficulties of big business that have been outlined in this essay constitute a serious obstacle not only to further development but also to Italy's maintaining membership in this exclusive club.[29]

Table 5.1. *IRI and ENI groups: employment and as % of the manufacturing sector employment, 1956–1991*

Year	Manufacturing sector total employment (thousands)	IRI group total employment (thousands)	ENI group total employment (thousands)	IRI and ENI groups: employment as % of the manufacturing sector
1956	5,376	227.4	17.6	4.56
1961	6,249	271.5	29.7	4.82
1971	6,553	406.7	65.7	7.21
1981	6,470	520.5	106.4	9.69
1991	6,120	408.0	110.3	8.47

Source: STAT; IRI and ENI balance sheets.

Table 5.2. *Finsider group employment as % of IRI group total employment, 1939–1988*

Year	IRI group employment (thousands)	Finsider group employment (thousands)	Finsider as % of IRI
1939	230.0	63.45	27.59
1956	227.4	59.30	26.08
1961	271.5	68.70	25.30
1971	406.7	94.50	23.24
1981	520.5	81.80	15.72
1988	408.0	60.30	14.70

Source: IRI and Finsider balance sheets.

Table 5.3. *IRI and ENI groups: sales and as % of the manufacturing sector sales, 1956–1991* (current prices)

Year	Manufacturing sector total total sales (billion lire)	IRI Group total sales (billion lire)	ENI Group total sales (billion lire)	IRI and ENI groups: sales as % of the manufacturing sector sales
1956	14,710	835.6	205.0	7.07
1961	22,883	1,401.7	406.0	7.90
1971	36,595	4,024.6	1,865.2	16.09
1981	274,505	29,106.1	37,021.0	24.11
1991	331,339	79,454.0	50,883.0	39.34

Source: ISTAT; IRI and ENI balance sheets.

Table 5.4. *Finsider group sales as % of IRI group total sales, 1939–1988* (current prices)

Year	IRI group sales (billion lire)	Finsider group sales (billion lire)	Finsider as % of IRI
1956	835.6	286.4	34.27
1961	1,401.7	471.9	33.67
1971	4,024.6	1,085.9	26.98
1981	29,106.1	9,674.0	33.24

Source: IRI and Finsider balance sheets.

Table 5.5. *Finsider group steel production as % of Italy's total steel output, 1939–1988*

Year national steel output	Finsider as % of
1939	45.0
1956	49.6
1961	54.8
1971	55.2
1981	51.5
1988	51.5

Source: Finsider balance sheets.

Table 5.7. *ENI and IRI liabilities, 1950–1990* (current prices)

Year	ENI debts and bonds	IRI debts and bonds
1950	n.a.	134.56
1955	8.33	242.51
1960	133.50	604.31
1965	475.19	832.42
1970	668.92	794.18
1975	1,156.24	809.79
1980	2,171.95	3,199.00
1985	5,548.83	10,405.30
1990	25,916.20	20,169.20

Source: ENI and IRI balance sheets.

Table 5.6. *Finsider, IRI, and ENI groups' net profit/sales ratio, 1956–1991 (current prices)*

Year	Finsider group Net profits (billion lire)	Profits/sales ratio (%)	IRI group Net profits (billion lire)	Profits/sales ratio (%)	ENI group Net profits (billion lire)	Profits/sales ratio (%)
1956	4.75	1.66	0.07	0.01	4.58	2.24
1961	9.94	2.11	0.33	0.02	6.21	1.53
1971	0.67	0.06	1.56	0.04	0.19	0.01
1981	−592.83	−6.13	−273.66	−0.94	−264.70	−0.71
1991	−3,608.51	−0.66	−343.25	−0.43	1,081.00	2.12

[a] For Finsider 1987.
Source: Finsider balance sheets.

NOTES

1. My theoretical reference in dealing with the subject of business groups is the work of Alfred D. Chandler, Jr. In addition to his best-known works, *Strategy and Structure* (Cambridge, Mass.: MIT Press, 1962), *The Visible Hand* (Cambridge, Mass.: Harvard University Press, 1977), and *Scale and Scope* (Cambridge, Mass.: Harvard University Press, 1990), I find two of his articles on this topic to be extremely useful. They are 'The M-Form Industrial Groups American Style', *European Economic Review*, 19 (1982) and 'The Functions of the HQ Unit in the Multibusiness Firm', *Strategic Management Journal*, 12 (1991).

    A good review of the literature on business groups in industrialized nations can be found in F. Brioschi, *et al.*, *Gruppi di imprese e mercato finanziario* (Rome: La Nuova Italia Scientifica, 1990).

    A good survey on Italian economic history from the middle of the past century to today can be found in V. Zamagni, *Dalla periferia al centro* (Bologna: Il Mulino, 1990).

2. I have borrowed the expressions 'associational' and 'hierarchical' groups from Brioschi *et al.*, *Gruppi di imprese*, 13.

3. P. Sraffa, 'La crisi bancaria in Italia', in id., *Saggi* (Bologna: Il Mulino, 1986), 237–8.

4. On Italian industry during the First World War, see A. Caracciolo, 'La crescita e la trasformazione della grande industria durante la prima guerra mondiale' in id. (ed.), *La formazione dell'Italia industriale* (Bari: Laterza, 1969).

5. On Alfa Romeo, see D. Bigazzi, *Portello* (Milan: Angeli, 1988).

6. On Fiat's story, see V. Castronovo, *Giovanni Agnelli* (Turin: UTET, 1971) and B. Bottiglieri, 'La Fiat tra il 1915 e il 1930: Alcune linee evolutive', in Progetto Archivio Storico Fiat, *Fiat 1915–1930: Verbali dei consigli d'amministrazione* (Milan: Fabbri, 1991).

7. On Ilva, see A. Carparelli, 'La siderurgia italiana nella prima guerra mondiale: Il caso dell'Ilva', in AA.VV., *La siderurgia italiana dall'Unità ad oggi* (Florence: CLUSF, 1978).

8. On Ansaldo, see M. Doria, *Ansaldo: L'impresa e lo Stato* (Milan: Angeli, 1989).

9. R. A. Webster, 'La tecnocrazia italiana e i sistemi industriali verticali: Il caso dell'Ansaldo (1914–1921)', *Storia contemporanea*, 2 (1978), 227.

10. Chandler, *Scale and Scope*, 342–3.

11. On Terni, see F. Bonelli, *Lo sviluppo di una grande impresa in Italia: La Terni dal 1884 al 1962* (Turin: Einaudi, 1975).

12. On the steel cartel of 1911, see D. Bigazzi, 'Grandi imprese e concentrazioni finanziarie', in AA.VV., *Storia della società italiana: L'Italia di Giolitti*, vol. xx (Milan: Teti, 1981).

13. On Montecatini, see F. Amatori and B. Bezza (eds.), *Montecatini 1888–1966: Capitoli di storia di una grande impresa* (Bologna: Il Mulino, 1990).

14. Chandler, *Scale and Scope*.

15. On IRI's origins, see E. Cianci, *Nascita dello Stato Imprenditore in Italia* (Milan: Mursia, 1977).

16. On Beneduce and his 'philosophy', see F. Bonelli, 'Alberto Beneduce', in A. Mortara (ed.), *Protagonisti dell'intervento pubblico in Italia* (Milan: Angeli, 1984).
17. On Sinigaglia's plan and the story of Finsider, see G. L. Osti and R. Ranieri, *L'industria di Stato dall'ascesa al degrado* (Bologna: Il Mulino, 1993).
18. On Enrico Mattei and the first decade of ENI, see M. Colitti, *Energia e sviluppo in Italia: La vicenda di Enrico Mattei* (Bari: De Donato, 1979).
19. On ENI's structure, see F. Carnevali, 'Il gruppo ENI dalle origini al 1985', in G. Sapelli and F. Carnevali, *Uno sviluppo tra politica e strategia (1953–1985)* (Milan: Angeli, 1992).
20. F. Bonelli, 'Il capitalismo italiano: Linee generali di interpretazione', in AA.VV., *Storia d'Italia. Annali I: Dal feudalismo al capitalismo* (Turin: Einaudi, 1978), 251.
21. G. Amato (ed.), *Il governo dell'industria in Italia* (Bologna: Il Mulino, 1972), 15–17.
22. P. Saraceno, *Il sistema delle imprese a partecipazione statale nell'esperienza italiana* (Milan: Giuffrè, 1975).
23. See B. Amoroso and A. J. Olsen, *Lo Stato imprenditore* (Bari: Laterza, 1978).
24. Osti and Ranieri, *L'industria di Stato*, 213.
25. M. Balconi, *La siderurgia italiana: 1945–1990* (Bologna: Il Mulino, 1991).
26. See G. F. Lepore Dubois and C. Sonzogno, *L'impero della chimica* (Rome: Newton Compton, 1990). Montedison is the new name of the entity which emerged from the merger in 1966 of Montecatini and Edison, the major Italian electric company which had directed to the chemical industry the indemnities received from the state in 1962 with the rationalization of the electric industry.
27. Carnevali, *Il gruppo ENI*, 100.
28. On Italian private groups, see R. Pavan, *Strutture e strategie delle imprese italiane* (Bologna: Il Mulino, 1976), and the more recent Brioschi *et al.*, *Gruppi di imprese*.
29. On Italy's position in the international competitive scenario, see M. E. Porter, *The Competitive Advantage of Nations* (New York: The Free Press, 1990), 421–53.

REFERENCES

Amato, G. (ed.), *Il governo dell'industria in Italia* (Bologna: Il Mulino, 1972).
Amatori, F., and Bezza, B. (eds.), *Montecatini 1888–1966: Capitoli di storia di una grande impresa* (Bologna: Il Mulino, 1990).
Amoroso, B., and Olsen, A. J., *Lo Stato imprenditore* (Bari: Laterza, 1978).
Balconi, M., *La siderurgia italiana: 1945–1990* (Bologna: Il Mulino, 1991).
Bigazzi, D., 'Grandi imprese e concentrazioni finanziarie', in AA.VV., *Storia della società italiana: L'Italia di Giolitti*, vol. xx (Milan: Teti, 1981).
—— *Portello* (Milan: Franco Angeli Editore, 1989).
Bonelli, F., *Lo sviluppo di una grande impresa in Italia: La Terni dal 1884 al 1962* (Turin: Einaudi, 1975).
—— 'Il capitalismo italiano: Linee generali di interpretazione' in AA.VV., *Storia d'Italia. Annali I: Dal feudalesimo al capitalismo* (Turin: Einaudi, 1978).
—— 'Alberto Beneduce' in A. Mortara (ed.), *Protagonisti dell'intervento pubblico in Italia* (Milan: Franco Angeli Editore, 1984).

Bottiglieri, B., 'La Fiat tra il 1915 e il 1930: Alcune linee evolutive', in Progetto Archivio Storico Fiat, *Fiat 1915–1930: Verbali dei consigli d'amministrazione* (Milan: Fabbri, 1991).

Brioschi, F., Buzzacchini, L., and Colombo, M. G., *Gruppi di imprese e mercato finanziario* (Rome: La Nuova Italia Scientifica, 1990).

Caracciolo, A., 'La crescita e la trasformazione della grande industria durante la prima guerra mondiale', in id. (ed.), *La formazione dell'Italia industriale* (Laterza: Bari, 1969).

Carnevali, F., 'Il gruppo ENI dalle origini al 1985', in G. Sapelli and F. Carnevali, *Uno sviluppo tra politica e strategia (1953–1985)* (Milan: Franco Angeli Editore, 1992).

Carparelli, A., 'La siderurgia italiana nella prima guerra mondiale: Il caso dell'Ilva', in AA.VV., *La siderurgia italiana dall'Unità ad oggi* (Florence: CLUSF, 1978).

Castronovo, V., *Giovanni Agnelli* (Turin: UTET, 1971).

Chandler, A. D., Jr., *Strategy and Structure* (Cambridge, Mass.: MIT Press, 1962).

—— *The Visible Hand* (Cambridge, Mass.: Harvard University Press, 1977).

—— 'The M-Form Industrial Groups American Style', *European Economic Review*, 19 (1982).

—— *Scale and Scope* (Cambridge, Mass.: Harvard University Press, 1990).

—— 'The Functions of the HQ Unit in the Multibusiness Firm', *Strategic Management Journal*, 12 (1991).

Cianci, E., *Nascita dello Stato Imprenditore in Italia* (Milan: Mursia, 1977).

Colitti, M., *Energia e sviluppo in Italia: La vicenda di Enrico Mattei* (Bari: De Donato, 1979).

Doria, M., *Ansaldo: L'impresa e lo Stato* (Milan: Franco Angeli Editore, 1989).

Lepore, G. F., and Sonzogno, C., *L'impero della chimica* (Rome: Newton Compton, 1990).

Osti, G. L., and Ranieri, R., *L'industria di Stato dall'ascesa al degrado* (Bologna: Il Mulino, 1993).

Pavan, R., *Strutture e strategie delle imprese italiane* (Bologna: Il Mulino, 1976).

Porter, M. E., *The Competitive Advantage of Nations* (New York: The Free Press, 1990).

Saraceno, P., *Il sistema delle imprese a partecipazione statale* (Milan: Giuffrè, 1975).

Sraffa, P., 'La crisi bancaria in Italia', in id., *Saggi* (Bologna: Il Mulino, 1986).

Webster, R. A., 'La tecnocrazia italiana e i sistemi industriali verticali: Il caso dell'Ansaldo (1914–1921)', *Storia contemporanea*, 2 (1978).

Zamagni, V., *Dalla periferia al centro* (Bologna: Il Mulino, 1990).

6

Business Groups in the German Electrical Industry

WILFRIED FELDENKIRCHEN

Big Business and Business Groups in the Context of Recent Research into the History of Corporations

The international debate on the phenomenon of big business has been linked directly for several decades to research into American business history and to the name of Alfred D. Chandler, who produced the first comprehensive hypotheses on the development of large corporations. The empirical content of these hypotheses constituted a challenge to produce an international and intertemporal comparison, as they claimed, *expressis verbis*, not only to be applicable to the USA but also to the highly industrialized states of west and central Europe and Japan.[1]

Studies have been carried out into the development of corporations in Germany along the same lines as Chandler's, who was able to verify his theoretical constructs through examples taken from major US enterprises.[2] In an international context the question of which forms big business took still tends to be viewed against the background of the three 'big' industrial nations at the end of the nineteenth century. On balance, Britain, Germany, and the USA appear not to have undergone the same process of development, but one which is similar in orientation and derives its own particular character from unique and specific aspects.[3] With an eye on Japan, an interesting problem arises with regard to the period in question: even though distinct horizontal and vertical concentration was manifest in Germany in the period examined, there was neither extensive lateral diversification, nor were conglomerates formed in the manner typical of the Japanese zaibatsu.[4]

The object of this account is therefore to describe the form taken by business groups in Germany—specifically, in the German electrical industry— their expansion strategies, and the underlying corporate structures. Two limitations must be made in order to achieve this object. The compound

causes of an economic, political, legal, or cultural nature behind the inti-
mated developmental differences can only be loosely outlined in the context of this account, rather than discussed in detail. Even a mere
comparison of competition legislation and economic realities in Germany,
Britain, and the USA demonstrates the difficulty involved in clearly iso-
lating causal factors in company development.[5] The inclusion of Japan
additionally directs the focus onto the role of the state in the industrialization process, structural and sectoral differences in growth, the much-cited
mentality differences, and the effects of late industrialization.[6]

Taking the German term 'Unternehmenskonzentration', or business
concentration, in the sense of a 'concentration of economic forces',[7] it can
be understood to refer not only to concerns[8] but also to cartels. In the following, the term 'business groups' does not extend to these cartels,
because of the fact that cartels can demonstrate different degrees of intensity and different binding effects.[9] Nevertheless an assessment of the business groups should bear in mind that their structure and their formation
are also dependent on the scope and the reach of cartels and the alternative they present. What is certain is that, parallel to the disabling of market functions internally by big companies, the participation in cartels
offered a second established means of escaping the mechanisms of the
market, at least in Germany.

The Development of Siemens and AEG and the German Electrical Industry before the First World War

Assisted by the favourable consequences of Germany's late entry into the
take-off period, the growth of the German economy proceeded without
major interruptions from the middle of the nineteenth century until the
First World War with an average annual growth rate of GNP of 2.6 per
cent, growth rates in industry being much higher. This development
turned Germany from a dominantly agrarian, poor, and, compared to its
Western neighbours, backward country into one of the leading industrial
nations, ranking second only to the United States in 1913. While railways,
mechanical engineering, and heavy industry were the leading sectors until
the 1870s, the so-called second industrialization, which was particularly
fast in Germany by international comparisons, was led by the electrical
and chemical industries. Even though their production and their work-
force remained smaller than those of the 'old' industries before 1914, their
growth potential could already be seen.[10] The 'new' industries were based
on science and technology.[11]

The electrical industry has been characterized by its concentration in a
few highly industrialized countries. Germany has always been prominent

in the development and manufacture of electrical equipment. As a nation, she has played an outstanding role in early developments of electrical engineering. In 1913 Germany's share in the world's electrical production was about one-third, her share in the world trade in electricals even bigger at nearly 47 per cent. By 1939 the relative importance of the German electrical industry was second only to that in the United States, with Great Britain ranking third.

From its founding in 1847 through to the 1880s Siemens & Halske, the parent company of today's Siemens AG, was undeniably the leading firm in the German electrical industry as Siemens could make use of the first mover advantage.[12] The company diversified early and developed a mix of electrical products and systems, the latter often long term and tailored to fit specific customers' needs. The German post office was a major customer. That diversity of output has given the company the flexibility to shift emphasis to other product and system lines when one began to experience problems.

Competition started to build up in the 1880s, particularly in power generating, and the company's main rivals were Schuckert and, even more so, AEG, which was formed out of Deutsche Edison Gesellschaft. AEG, which in the early years after its foundation had an agreement with Siemens & Halske[13] that ensured that there was no, or only limited, competition between S. & H. and AEG until 1894, soon enlarged the scope of its activities to include the manufacture of heavy-current equipment (see Fig. 6.1).

While Siemens & Halske at first focused exclusively on products utilizing low-voltage electricity, and expanded the range of products only after the invention of the dynamo, AEG primarily marketed products utilizing Thomas Edison's light-bulb patents in the beginning.

The new company, pursuing an aggressive business policy under the leadership of Emil Rathenau, soon threatened the supremacy of the established firm. Although primarily a manufacturing company, AEG had numerous interests in public utilities, banks, and various companies not only connected with the manufacture of electric equipment. Turning to the capital markets to finance internal as well as external growth, AEG grew at such a pace that Siemens & Halske was forced to react.

In an altogether characteristic way, Siemens and AEG embody precisely those two types of corporation defined by Chandler as diametrical opposites. Siemens, the conservative, technology-oriented family enterprise, stands opposite AEG, a company without start-up advantages, but also without traditions, which in an aggressive and finance-oriented attack seized temporary leadership of the electricals market. At the same time, internal historical but unavoidable weaknesses in the area of organization and management at Siemens & Halske contributed to allowing AEG to become a serious competitor. Emil Rathenau may not have known how to develop the possibilities of power engineering technically and industrially,

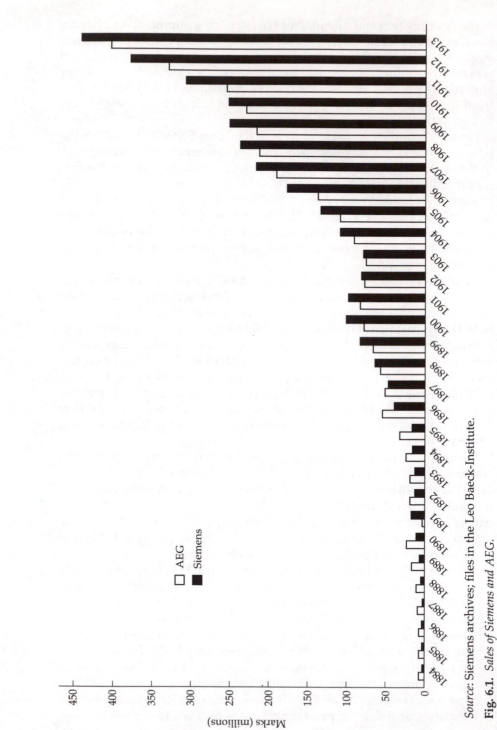

Source: Siemens archives; files in the Leo Baeck-Institute.

Fig. 6.1. *Sales of Siemens and AEG.*

but he did know how to establish it industrially and commercially, whereas Werner von Siemens gave high priority to technical innovations themselves than to their actual application, and this lost Siemens ground to its main competitor. The company's family-centric nature, its personal style of management, and its orientation according to early industrial practices that in the past had contributed to the company's success now proved a hindrance in view of the altered conditions, while manager-run enterprises along the lines of AEG were considerably less impeded and trod a path of uncompromising expansion.[14] Initially a general partnership, Siemens & Halske became a limited partnership in 1890 and then went public—with considerable help from Deutsche Bank—in 1897 with a capital of 35 million marks, the family holding all the shares.[15]

The electrical industry of that era was characterized by two structure-giving characteristics. High capital requirements meant that the sole and original owners were joined by new shareholders in the form of banks, which brought an additional influence to bear. While the might of the banks in the process of industrialization was regarded for a long time as an incontrovertible truth,[16] particularly in connection with Germany, it is now more important to differentiate, not just from a global point of view, but specifically with regard to the electrical industry.[17] As a family-run enterprise, Siemens did not allow Deutsche Bank to have the same kind of influence that AEG allowed the Berliner Handelsgesellschaft. Nor, in principle, is the Hilferding theory of the supremacy of the banks over industry, particularly the electrical industry, tenable. However, the fact that banks in Germany were able, at least for a time, to achieve a relatively strong position in relation to industrial enterprises was due not least to the fact that many German companies covered their capital requirements on the money market. This made it possible for the main banks to bring an influence to bear on the business policy of companies through underwriting and the provision of loans.[18] So-called *Unternehmergeschäft* in the form of BOT- or BOO-business[19] formed the second line of development at that time. The electrical companies went over to not just planning and constructing electricity generation and distribution centres but also financing and, in some cases, operating them, which at the same time led to vertical integration.[20] What played a key role in the rise of that BOT-/BOO-type of business were the high capital requirements associated with infrastructural measures, which as a rule overstretched customers (mainly public offices), combined with the hope of electrical companies involved in that kind of business of being able to obtain follow-up orders and linked deals. The first enterprise of this kind was Berlin's Städtische Elektrizitätswerke, founded by Deutsche Edison Gesellschaft in 1884. With the primary aim of providing finance for AEG's foreign enterprises, the company founded the Bank für elektrische Unternehmungen in Zurich in conjunction with Deutsche Bank, Berliner Handelsgesellschaft, Schweizerische

Kreditanstalt, and other German and Swiss banks in 1895. Schweizerische Gesellschaft für elektrische Industrie, Basel (founded jointly by S. & H. and German, Swiss, and Austrian banks) and Siemens Elektrische Betriebe AG in Berlin were founded in 1896 with Siemens's involvement, and were followed in 1897 by Elektrische Licht- und Kraftanlagen-Aktiengesellschaft, Berlin, which Siemens & Halske AG co-founded with the Deutsche Bank group.[21]

As a result of the enormous demand for electrical products and installations in the 1890s, Schuckert & Co., founded in 1873 and involved exclusively in the power engineering sector, was jointed by a rash of newly founded companies that were quick to expand. What all these companies had in common was that they were able to establish themselves next to the all-rounders Siemens and AEG as major companies before the turn of the century and attain a strong position in specific market segments—Schuckert in plant engineering, Union in the construction of electric street-car installations, Helios in alternating-current engineering, and Lahmeyer in three-phase-current engineering. Something else these companies had in common was their dependence on plant engineering.[22]

As the financial basis of most of the newly founded companies was too weak for the risky, capital-intensive business, most of them did not survive the general economic crisis in Germany around the turn of the century, and Siemens and AEG emerged from the concentration process as the dominant concerns of the German electrical industry. Enterprises in financial straits were either taken over by AEG or Siemens, or were jointly liquidated by these two key players in order to eliminate competition and increase their dominance of a market in which they finally had a joint market share of about 70 per cent.

When Union-Electrizitätsgesellschaft and Elektrizitätsgesellschaft AG vorm. S. Schuckert & Co. (Schuckert) met with difficulties in 1902, Siemens & Halske, in an effort to counterbalance AEG's merger with Union, transferred its own activities in the field of electric power to the newly founded Siemens-Schuckertwerke GmbH, after Schuckert first had entered into negotiations with AEG.[23] Siemens rather unwillingly performed this step in the development of the enterprise, and the aim in the long run was only to prevent a further growth of AEG. Siemens-Schuckertwerke (SSW) GmbH, a limited partnership under German law, founded in 1903 and turned into a stock company in 1927, was an integration of all activities in the field of electric power of Siemens & Halske AG and Elektrizitäts-AG form. S. Schuckert & Co., which dominated a substantial part of the market, above all in Bavaria.[24] By pooling all its own divisions in the field of electric power with Schuckert, the Siemens concern, which through Siemens & Halske had had a leading position in the market in the communication engineering field ever since its foundation, also advanced into a strong position in the field of the principal activities of AEG, almost drawing level with Emil Rathenau's enterprise, even though substantial funds had to be invested during the first years. Within the Siemens concerns, Siemens & Halske AG and Siemens-Schuckertwerke GmbH formed the core. Siemens & Halske and Siemens-Schuckertwerke GmbH were actually directed by a common management, even though they remained two legally independent companies,[25] and the chairman of the board of both companies was always the same family member.[26] The capital of Siemens-Schuckertwerke GmbH amounted to 90 million marks and was split almost equally between S. & H. and Schuckert, with S. & H.'s stake exceeding Schuckert's by 100,000 marks to give it the final say and avoid deadlock on matters of uniform management of the enterprise. With the foundation of Siemens-Schuckertwerke and the ensuing transfer of the electric power business, Siemens & Halske AG became a mixture of a manufacturing company and a holding company, but preferred to see itself as a 'technical holding company'.[27]

The concern was then rebuilt in the tradition of the restructuring measures that had been implemented since Wilhelm Siemens had taken over the running of the company in 1890 and had modernized the organizational and managerial structures. A function-oriented structure gave way to the principle of divisional organization, which was based on product lines or regions.[28]

After 1903 the only serious competitor was the rapidly expanding Bergmann-Elektricitätswerke AG. But at Bergmann, too, the financial assets hardly matched the company's growth rates, one of the main reasons being that earnings were not ploughed back into the company in favour of paying high dividends. When Bergmann ran into difficulties in 1911, Siemens, in co-operation with the Deutsche Bank, bought a major part of the newly issued shares and *de facto* dominated its former competitor, whose board was now run by a Siemens delegate.[29] AEG had taken control of the Cologne-based Felten & Guilleaume company in 1910 (see Fig. 6.2).

As Siemens and AEG increasingly co-ordinated their sales and pricing policies after 1900, either by direct mutual understandings, or through a so-called 'confidential convention' (Vertrauliche Convention', VC), or by establishing joint ventures like Telefunken, Deutsche Betriebsgesellschaft für Drahtlose Telegraphie mbH, or Deutsche Überseeische Elektricitäts-Gesellschaft, they were able to establish what contemporaries termed an 'incomplete monopoly', i.e. an effective monopoly in major markets that coexisted with the continued operations of several small- and medium-sized speciality firms.

Relations between Siemens and AEG had an ambiguous character. While co-ordinating sales and prices in some areas, and even entering into a joint venture in the form of Telefunken,[30] they competed fiercely in other areas of business. The striving for a monopoly position, the key to which

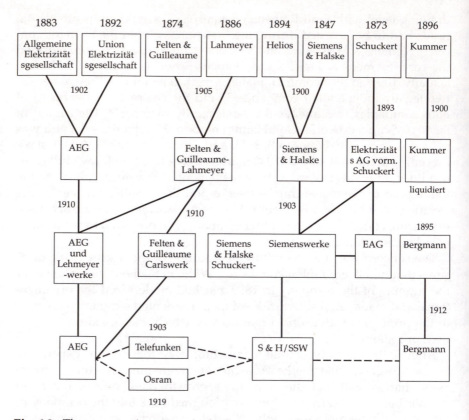

Fig. 6.2. *The concentration process in the German Electrical industry.*

lay in patents, led to bitter patent infringement lawsuits. The outcome of these lawsuits was often out-of-court settlements in which the rivals agreed either to exchange their patents or to pool their manufacturing facilities in a certain field and invest in a jointly owned new corporation, Telefunken being just one but perhaps the most important pre-1914.

The German Economy 1918–1945

The years 1918–45 can be seen as a development from a severe to the ultimate crisis in the German economy. There were hardly any 'normal' years in which the economy could progress without being decisively influenced by the overall conditions in Germany. Hyperinflation in the early 1920s, a short and shaky reconstruction period in the years 1924–9, the Depression, an artificial, debt-financed upswing based on rearmament after 1933 to 1939, and finally the Second World War can be taken as the milestones which left their impact on the German economy, the major companies, and their strategies to cope with the effects of such a framework.

The interwar period in the German economy can be characterized as a period of concentration, rationalization, and of international cartelization as a suitable means of offsetting the effects of the First World War. The German government, which held large entities to be useful to further exports in order to pay the country's reparation debts, promoted the foundation of huge concerns, for instance by lowering the associated taxes or levies. The formation of huge combines, as well as cartels, was also furthered by the fact that German inflation in the early 1920s provided a tremendous stimulus for takeovers, mergers, and *Interessengemeinschaften* (communities of interest), and the formation of huge combines. The German tax system also favoured the big combines to the disadvantage of the medium- and small-sized businesses. Special tax privileges were granted to so-called *Organgesellschaften* (i.e. wholly owned subsidiaries), and those companies which were owned to 25 per cent or more by another company fell under the so-called 'Schachtelprivileg'. Sales taxes, which did not have to be paid for transactions between wholly owned companies of a combine, and the privilege of offsetting losses of wholly owned subsidiaries against profits realized by the combine as a whole resulted in savings of many more million reichsmarks annually for combines. The possibility of thus offloading part of the tax burden onto the general public gave combines an advantage over their competitors.[31]

The German Electrical Industry in the Interwar Period

During the First World War the German electrical industry expanded vertically and horizontally[32] as it adapted to the war economy and attempted to secure adequate supplies of raw materials. Uncertain political and economic conditions in the country immediately following the war then made long-term corporate policy planning difficult. Production had to be changed, sales increased, and earnings optimized, all in the face of increasing industry-wide overproduction and an unfavourable development in prices.

A number of factors made it extremely difficult for the German electrical industry to regain its pre-war position in the world market: the establishment of new electrical industries[33] in former customer countries during and immediately following the war, an extensive loss of foreign possessions and patents,[34] the closing off of foreign markets to German products,[35] the increasing problem of raw material supplies, and the country's clearly deteriorating financial situation. In real terms, production surpassed the pre-war figures in the mid-1920s. In 1928 75 per cent of the world's electrical production once again came from the USA, Great Britain, and Germany. Market shares, however, had shifted in favour of the United States, while Germany's share had gone down from 34.9 per cent in 1913 to 23.3 per cent in 1925, even though production had increased.[36] Prior to the Second World War, Germany was the largest exporter and the second-largest producer of electrical equipment in the world (see Fig. 6.3).

As one of the world's leaders in both low- and high-voltage products, Siemens was the only major producer in the world to market a full line of production; the notable exception here was the production of batteries, an area in which it had a joint venture with AEG (AFA). Its share of the German market fluctuated from around 80 per cent between 1860 and 1890 to 30–40 per cent after the turn of century. When a new technology was introduced, its market share frequently ran up to 100 per cent.[37] As the new technology became standardized, its market share would typically decline, but in the field of telecommunications 60 per cent of all Deutsche Reichspost orders always went directly to Siemens & Halske in the interwar years.[38] The overall market share of the Siemens combine by the late 1930s was about 38 per cent, AEG ranked second in terms of market share with about 16 per cent, while others were only important in some sectors (see Fig. 6.4).[39]

Domestic cartels were of lesser relevance in electricals in the interwar period, although they were relatively high in number.[40] The effectiveness of most agreements should not be overestimated. Quite important were the international agreements that aimed at dividing the world market.[41]

The Development at Siemens and AEG

Even though the two electrical concerns Siemens and AEG dominated the German electrical market in principle, the heterogeneity of the individual lines of production merits detailed examination. In terms of the number of persons employed and their share in production within the overall electrical industry, the group referred to in official statistics as engaged in 'production of electrical machinery and transformers' topped the list. At the same time this is a line of production which, because capital intensiveness, was dominated by the all-rounders AEG and Siemens, which together accounted for more than 50 per cent of production. If BBC, Mannheim and Sachsenwerk, Licht und Kraft AG, which was controlled by AEG, are taken into consideration, these four companies accounted for roughly 80 per cent of production. In telegraphy and telephony, a mere handful of companies dominated the market, the main players being Siemens & Halske, C.

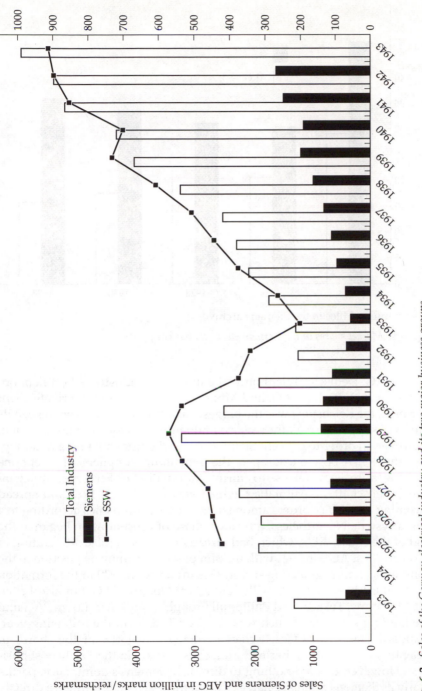

Fig. 6.3. *Sales of the German electrical industry and its two major business groups.*

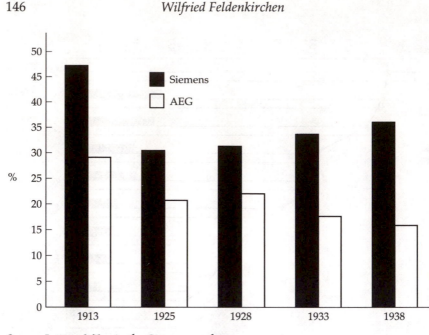

Source: Internal files in the Siemens archives.

Fig. 6.4. *Market shares in the German electrical industry.*

Lorenz AG, Deutsche Telephonwerke und Kabelindustrie AG, Telephonfabrik vorm. J. Berliner AG, and Mix & Genest AG. Next to private client
business, the Reichspost was the biggest customer and was keen to keep its
group of suppliers small for reasons of quality and ease of administration.
However, in order to prevent Siemens & Halske from obtaining a monopoly, the Reichspost encouraged the remaining suppliers of telephone
exchanges to join forces to form Automatische Fernsprechanlagen-
Bau-Gesellschaft, or Autofabag, which was founded in 1922 and spread
incoming post-office orders amongst its member companies according to a
quota system. Nevertheless, a further phase of concentration began at the
end of the 1920s. AEG, which had already obtained a majority holding in
Mix & Genest AG[42] in 1921 with the aim of strengthening its position in the
communication-engineering sector, was involved in 1929 in the formation
of Standard Elektrizitäts Gesellschaft AG.[43] Not just AEG, but also Felten
& Guilleaume, Tekade, and Philips all brought shares in C. Lorenz AG into
the holding company, which was run by I.T. & T. In the following year,
Standard Elektrizitäts Gesellschaft obtained a majority of the shares in
Telephonfabrik vorm. J. Berliner and, thus, a share in the Reichspost business. However, this did nothing to diminish Siemens's dominance, particularly as Siemens & Halske had extended the reach of its influence directly
through Telefonapparatefabrik E. Zwietusch & Co. and Bayerische

Telephonewerke (which it took over in 1926), and indirectly through its finance company Elektrische Licht- und Kraftanlagen AG at DeTeWe. In the incandescent-lamp industry, a pattern of standardized bulk sales in conjunction with heavy capital requirements had established itself quickly and favoured large-scale production. As Europe's biggest manufacturer of incandescent lamps, Osram GmbH, founded in 1920 under the joint participation of Auer-Gesellschaft, AEG, and Siemens, not only dominated the German market but also enjoyed a prominent position in foreign markets as a member of the international Phoebus cartel. Next to Osram, only the company Julius Pintsch AG was of real significance as an independent enterprise in the German marketplace. In wireless telegraphy, Siemens and AEG, the two all-rounders, had held the key position since the founding of Telefunken GmbH in 1903, a position made all the more secure through the founding of Deutsche Betriebsgesellschaft für drahtlose Telegraphie mbH, or Debeg, in 1911. In 1922, the companies C. Lorenz AG and Dr. Erich F. Huth AG united under the leadership of Telefunken to form Rundfunk GmbH. Their objective was to split the market for broadcasting transmitter and receiver installations in Germany between them by exploiting the tube patents of Austrian physicist Robert von Lieben, applying quotas to orders, and undertaking a mutual exchange of licences. In the field of meter production, the obligatory transition to more efficient, mass production and the considerable investment needs led in 1925 to the founding of a quota allocation cartel, the Verband deutscher Elektrizitätsfabriken e.V.; 75 per cent of sales went to three companies: SSW and AEG, and Bergmann-Elektricitäts-Werke, in which the first two companies had investments.[44] During the subsequent process of development, additional concentration took place as AEG and SSW took over the other enterprises, and by 1933 production was split almost fully between the two. One of the areas that underwent the greatest degree of concentration was battery manufacture. The two giants, AEG and Siemens, had taken stakes in the leading manufacturer, Accumulatoren-Fabrik AG (AFA), in 1980 having themselves encountered a number of technical problems in the manufacturing process and decided to terminate their own production. In the 1920s, AFA, which in the mean time had gained control of newer smaller enterprises, controlled almost 80 per cent of battery production in Germany.[45] In the interwar period Robert Bosch AG had a generally secure position in the field of electric automobile equipment. The company had a share of more than 90 per cent in the spark plugs market, and its share in the remaining market segments lay in excess of 70 per cent. AEG made attempts to break into this market, but these were warded off successfully. It is also worth mentioning that medical equipment engineering, railway safety engineering, and electrotechnical carbon products were all the fields in which the dominant companies were under Siemens's influence (see Fig. 6.5).

148

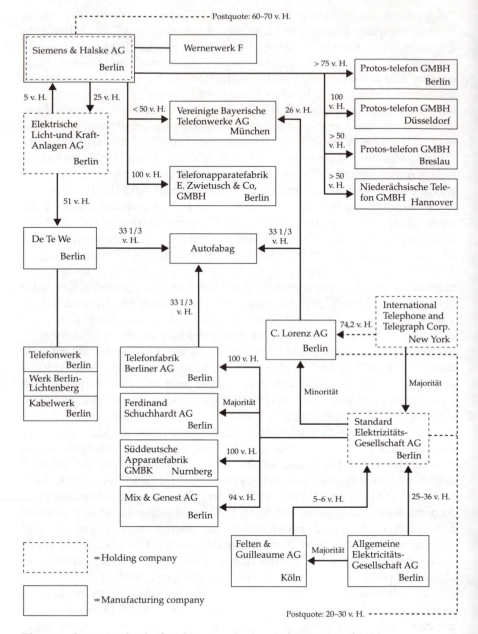

Fig. 6.5. *Concentration in the telecommunications industry around 1930.*

When Siemens and AEG, as well as the other large German industrial complexes, were faced after the First World War with the problem of regaining and expanding their pre-war position (and, in Siemens's case, of protecting its family interests, too), they had two alternatives— the formation of a joint horizontal combination or of a vertical combination with coal, iron, steel, and heavy engineering interests.[46] As both concerns thought obtaining raw material to be decisive, and that regulation of competition or the raising of profitability were secondary to that problem, Siemens and AEG opted for a combination with heavy industry immediately after the First World War.[47] In 1920, Siemens-Rheinelbe-Schuckert-Union (SRSU) was founded to surmount the difficulties of supplying the Siemens-Schuckertwerke with dynamo sheets and other heavy materials. SRSU was intended to free its participating companies from cyclical influences and guarantee them stable profitability. The *Interessengemeinschaft* (community of interests) with the Stinnes companies provided for a mutual exchange of shares and directors between Siemens & Halske AG, Gelsenkirchener Bergwerks AG, Deutsch-Luxemburgische Bergwerks- und Hüttengesellschaft, and Elektrizitäts-AG form. Schuckert & Co., and for the pooling of profits among these four concerns in the ration of 1 : 1 : 1 : 0.45 respectively.[48] To give Siemens & Halske equal ranking with the Stinnes companies, its share capital was increased to 260 million marks. The agreement was to last until the year 2000.[49] At the same time AEG entered into a community of interests with the largest German rolling-stock factory, Hofmann-Linke-Werke in Breslau, to invest jointly with it in Lauchhammergesellschaft, a steelworks in Saxony, which was to guarantee AEG's supply of raw materials. Through a stake in the company Rheinmetall Düsseldorf, the AEG-Linke-Hofmann concern that came into being in this way secured for itself connections to the Rheno-Westphalian iron and steel industry, specifically the companies Krupp AG and Otto Wolff, Cologne, and thus achieved a significant status in the field of locomotive and rolling-stock construction.

While AEG's move into other industries like iron and steel or ship-building seems more in line with the company's general strategies, Siemens's participation in this joint venture signified a complete break with its previous rule of remaining independent, and can only be understood in the context of the general economic, social, and political conditions of the immediate post-war period, when there was a fear of nationalization, and everyone hoped to resist better in large combines. By the time the economy stabilized late in 1923, Carl Friedrich von Siemens, the company founder's youngest son, had realized that the profit distribution established in the SRSU contract was unfavourable to Siemens.[50] Although it was not yet formally dissolved, the SRSU in effect failed as an attempt to form a multi-industry vertical trust with Siemens's participation, upon foundation of the Vereinigte Stahlwerke.

The negative experiences with Siemens-Rheinelbe-Schuckert-Union undoubtedly prompted Carl Friedrich von Siemens in the following years to pay heed once again to the company's fundamental rule of limiting its activities to the field of electricals, yet covering all possible segments within that industry.[51] Only in the field of mechanical instruments and apparatus production did the company extend its activities permanently beyond the scope of purely electrical equipment. The use of electricity in the functioning of many instruments and much small manufacturing apparatus was, however, so extensive that the parallel manufacture of small mechanical and electrical instruments and apparatus was a natural and logical development.

The concern's guiding principle of engaging in all areas of electrical engineering while leaving fields outside the central areas of communication engineering and instrument engineering to specialist subsidiaries and affiliates had led to the founding of SSW in 1903. As a result, a large number of affiliates clustered with time around Siemens & Halske AG, the core of the House of Siemens, which can be grouped into manufacturing enterprises engaged in electrical engineering, companies for the promotion of the sale of Siemens products, such as Industrie-Unternehmen AG, or Inag, Deutsche Betriebsgesellschaft für drahtlose Telegraphie and Deutsche Fernkabel-Gesellschaft, and finance and patent companies. Generally taking the legal form of a GmbH, or limited liability company, these companies were intended to improve the speed of activity by loosening up the organization and to move co-responsibility from company management to the individual plants, departments, and offices (see Fig. 6.6.).

In 1928, in addition to the two central companies, S. & H. and SSW, the concern also included Elektrizitäts AG vorm. Schuckert & Co. and Licht- und Kraftanlagen AG as two further main group companies. Both operated as holding and finance companies and were involved in the development and operation of numerous municipal electricity companies and power stations. Through Österreichische Siemens-Schuckert-Werke, Schuckert & Co. and SSW also brought an influence to bear on the involvement in electricity companies in countries in south-east Europe, such as Hungary, Bulgaria, Yugoslavia, and Romania. When it was founded in 1921, Siemens-Bauunion (SBU) concentrated on the construction of power stations, the electrification of railways, the design of subway systems, and other large-scale projects.[52] Osram GmbH was founded in 1920, immediately after the First World War, and brought together the incandescent-lamp manufacturing operations of S. & H., AEG, and Auer. These companies had been exchanging patents for some time, but the close partnership prompted them to pool their manufacturing facilities and their technical know-how, too.[53] The merger left just two further independent suppliers in the incandescent-lamp market—the companies Julius Pintsch and Bergmann. A number of new companies were founded around this

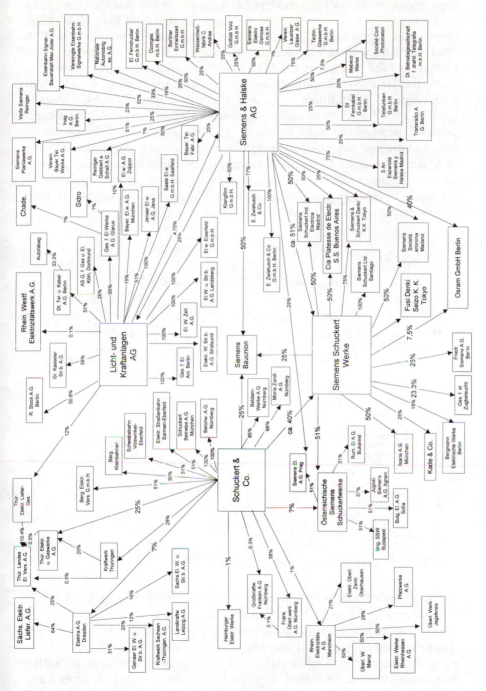

Fig. 6.6. *The structure of the Siemens concern in 1928.*

time, too: Gesellschaft für elektrische Apparate mbH (Gelkap, Electrical Equipment Company)[54] in 1920, Berliner Einheitszeit GmbH in 1924, Siemens-Reiniger-Veifa-Gesellschaft für medizinische Technik mbH[55] in 1925, the Mülheim factory for turbine manufactures[56] taken over from Demag in 1927, Klangfilm GmbH as a combination of interests Siemens, AEG, and Deutsche Grammophon in the production of motion pictures of with sound;[57] in addition, there was Vereinigte Eisenbahn-Signalwerke GmbH (VES)[58] in 1928, as well as the Siemens-Plania AG.[59] All these companies[60] were either joint ventures in the tradition of Telefunken, as Siemens did not hesitate to join forces if advantages, particularly in the technical field, could be gained through co-operating with other concerns, or were intended to serve the regulation of markets in certain segments. At the same time, they allowed Siemens & Halske to concentrate its own efforts on the company's central divisions (see Fig. 6.7.).

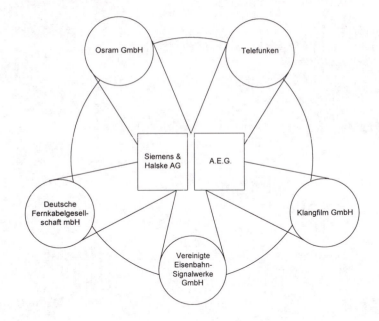

Fig. 6.7. *Major joint ventures of Siemens and AEG, 1929.*

   This renewed concentration in the electrical engineering sector was also the reason why Siemens decided in 1927 to sell its Protos automobile production, originally begun in 1906, to AEG, which incurred heavy losses in that field soon after, and to concentrate the available resources on the company's key activities,[61] while AEG continued its diversification, collecting a sizeable number of subsidiaries and affiliates in various, often non-electricity-related, industries.

Divesting various companies in the 1920s, many as limited liability companies, which under German law had few disclosure requirements, Siemens & Halske increasingly assumed the character of a holding company. This development was further accelerated in the 1930s, when Siemens Apparate- und Maschinen-GmbH (SAM, Siemens Equipment and Machinery Company)[62] was founded to improve the processing of military orders through a unified marketing organization. Even against the background of the war economy, Siemens was keen to limit its production programme for as long as possible to civilian products and to restrict its production of armaments- and war-effort-related items exclusively to the company's traditional field of electrical engineering. The only exception to this was the production of aero-engines, which began at the start of the 1920s and was placed in the hands of a separate company, Brandenburgische Motorenwerke GmbH, in 1936, which was then sold off at the start of 1939 to Bayerische Motorenwerke, but at a high loss on paper.[63]

The structure of the AEG group in 1922 likewise centred on a combination of associated companies, holding companies, and subsidiaries. The company's widely scattered shareholdings were administered by a number of different institutions that served as holding companies, like Bank für electrische Unternehmungen, Zurich, Electrizitäts-Lieferungs-Gesellschaft, Berlin, Gesellschaft für elektrische Unternehmungen, Berlin, Elektrizitäts AG vorm. W. Lahmeyer & Co., Frankfurt am Main, and Bank für elektrische Werte, Berlin. What all these companies had in common was that they held stakes both in industrial enterprises and in electricity plants and railways.[64]

Unlike Siemens, AEG did not confine its activities to the electricals nor did it do much pioneering in research. Financial operations and patent licence agreements accounted largely for its growth. Companies were acquired in the most diverse fields, which greatly increased the problem of managing the complex. Due to over-expansion the company was in financial difficulties several times, which also led to General Electric taking an interest in AEG.

It can certainly be attributed to the differences in the development of the two giants that from 1925 on AEG constantly proposed greater co-operation, with the eventual aim of a complete merger. Even though Carl Friedrich von Siemens could see some benefits in that, it never got that far in spite of numerous meetings and constant discussions between 1925 and 1932. Siemens did not want to give up its name, saw no real way to achieve equal status, and, being aware of AEG's increasing financial troubles, wanted to wait, because its bargaining position had to improve. The two companies' interests met, however, when they both decided to take full control of Bergmann-Elektrizitätswerke and to reduce that firm's line of production. This kind of thing was a frequent occurrence during the course of the Great Depression and at the same time constituted a return to an approach that had been typical around the turn of the century. These two big companies joined forces here and there to buy up, close down, or bring a permanent influence to bear on competitors who had attained a certain level of production. In much the same way as in the case of Bergmann-Elektrizitätswerke, SSW and AEG decided in 1931 to buy up the stock of Maffei-Schwartzkopff, a company engaged in the manufacture of electric locomotives, with the express purpose of liquidating it. In the case of Bergmann, both companies succeeded in increasing their shareholdings considerably with the aim of achieving a controlling influence on the management of the company, which had proved a difficult competitor at the end of the 1920s because of its low-priced heavy machinery.[65]

Compared to Siemens and AEG the other business groups in the German electrical industry were of lesser importance, even though some specialized firms dominated sections of the industry, the most important being Robert Bosch. The firm later included in its production programme all types of electrical equipment for cars and aeroplanes, fuel injection equipment for diesel engines, radios, etc. In 1936 Bosch and Siemens signed an agreement designating their specific 'fields of interest' and stating that they should not compete against each other in their respective fields.[66]

While the power engineering sector of the electrical industry was heavily regulated by four global players who succeeded in shutting out outsiders, the situation in the fast-growing communication engineering sector, at least in the 1920s, was different. As small firms in the German communication engineering industry found themselves in a situation which 'was characterized by Siemens' near monopoly of postal business and unprofitableness of business in other communication engineering sectors',[67] it was fairly easy for foreign capital to gain ground in the German communication engineering industry, which was also a result of the failure of Siemens and AEG to come to an understanding in establishing a second major German group in the field. In 1928 talks between Siemens and AEG had concentrated on plans 'for the joint creation of a major telephone business by amalgamating smaller companies . . . Neither of the two parties is to negotiate with other small German companies without keeping close contact with the other.'[58] Thus, in 1929, AEG's interest in gaining a foothold in the profitable communication engineering business and I.T. & T.'s interest in obtaining access to the German market met and led to the founding of Standard Elektrizitäts-Gesellschaft.[69] In the 1930s I.T. & T. controlled more than twenty firms in the telecommunications and wireless field. As a result of the Depression the companies that were controlled by I.T. & T. ran up high losses which finally had to be consolidated by a drastic capital reduction. Due to the heavy losses of about 20 million reichsmarks during the Depression, the share capital had to be reduced to

5 million reichsmarks and the participating certificates were declared null and void.[70] Nevertheless another reduction to 50,000 reichsmarks was necessary in 1934, before the share capital was raised again to 6 million reichsmarks.[71] In 1934, I.T. & T. made an agreement with Siemens, which was in part intermediated by General Electric, and stipulated that the latter company would manufacture 60 per cent and Mix & Genest 40 per cent of the Reichspost orders.[72] All lawsuits were stopped. The willingness of I.T. & T. to come to an understanding was certainly influenced by the dramatic decline in its sales and profits, a development that is also reflected in general by the production figures of the American electrical industry.

Business Groups and Germany's Electrical Industry after the Second World War

During the course of the Allies' deconcentration and decartelization efforts following the Second World War, it was discussed in principle whether to include the large electrical concerns, because the two companies S. & H. and SSW, each of which employed more than 10,000 people, did, on the face of it, merit the suspicions of concentration expressed by the Allies. With the exception of one instance of proceedings against Robert Bosch GmbH,[73] the electrical industry remained untouched by deconcentration measures owing mainly to the fact that the Allies recognized that the existence of large corporate units next to smaller speciality companies was simply a characteristic of the electrical industry.[74] Decartelization measures in Germany ultimately remained limited to the coal, iron, and steel industries and the chemicals industry, and focused mainly on the big concerns Vereinigte Stahlwerke and IG Farben, and Germany's major banks, all of which appeared to have been involved to a particularly large extent in the war economy and the armaments industry.[75]

During the post-war years, the tendency persisted within the electrical industry to seek opportunities for growth primarily within the same sector, and not without good reason, because perspectives for possible applications in this field continued to be promising. Within the circle of the ten largest electrical companies, roughly 8 per cent of sales in the period 1954–60 were apportionable to other groups of industry, although seven of the companies had extended the scope of their operations to include other sectors. Among all groups of industry, electrical engineering accounted for 7.6 per cent of Germany total industrial revenue in 1960, ranking fourth, and the ten largest electrical companies accounted for 38.4 per cent of the total revenue within their industry, a medium-to-high figure in comparison with other sectors of industry.[76] After rising steadily through to 1975, this figure for the top ten companies levelled out at roughly 48 per cent, a figure which, in the light of a general increase in concentration in the upper category of companies throughout all sectors of industry, is in line with the general trend. However, the high number of companies involved overall in electrical engineering reflects the specific market structure (already mentioned above) and its combination of a small number of large companies and a large number of small companies.[77]

In the post-war period the Siemens concern remained the leading enterprise and continued to dominate the German market. When an amendment to German stock corporation law in the 1960s made provisions for a change in the legal status of dependent affiliates, the three companies Siemens & Halske, Siemens-Schuckertwerke, and Siemens-Reiniger-Werke merged in 1966 to form Siemens AG. One consequence of this merger was the reorganization of the organizational structure into six groups, to which five divisions were assigned.[78] Co-operation between Siemens and AEG also continued when, in 1969, the two companies began two joint ventures: Kraftwerk Union AG (KWU), which combined their interests in the field of nuclear energy, and Transformatoren Union AG (TU). In 1977 Siemens took over AEG's 50 per cent share in Kraftwerk Union and a further 25 per cent share in Transformatoren Union. One year later Osram GmbH was absorbed fully into Siemens AG when General Electric's share was purchased.[79]

Disregarding those companies majority-owned by foreign corporations, Robert Bosch GmbH, Bosch-Siemens-Hausgeräte GmbH (founded in 1967), and Grundig AG[80] successfully stood their ground in 1972 alongside Siemens and AEG-Telefunken[81] in the ranks of Germany's 100 largest industrial enterprises. Robert Bosch GmbH was fully family-owned; in Grundig AG's case, the family had a majority holding; and in Bosch-Siemens-Hausgeräte GmbH's case, each of its founding companies owned 50 per cent. By contrast, both Siemens and AEG-Telefunken had widely spread majority holdings.[82] During the 1980s two new companies, Bergmann-Elektrizitätswerke AG and Telefonbau und Normalzeit Lehner & Co., entered the German top 100. Robert Bosch GmbH owned 31 per cent of Telefonbau und Normalzeit, and AEG-Telefunken owned roughly a further 10 per cent. In 1984 the company was included in Robert Bosch GmbH's consolidated financial statement, which moved the latter up into the top ten German industrial corporations. The majority of Bergmann-Elektrizitätswerke AG's stock was held by three major German enterprises: Siemens owned at least 37.06 per cent, and Deutsche Bank and Bayerische Vereinsbank each held at least 25 per cent of the capital stock.[83]

In 1986, marked changes took place at the top of Germany's rankings for the biggest industrial corporations when Daimler-Benz moved up to the number one position by acquiring a majority in AEG AG.[84] Germany's two leading electrical companies from this time on in terms of sales, Siemens (ranked fourth among Germany's industrial companies in 1990) and Robert Bosch (ranked eighth in 1990), were able to strengthen their standing in terms of sales, both Europe-wide and world-wide: in 1990 Siemens and Bosch ranked ninth and twenty-eighth respectively in Europe, and twenty-fourth and fifty-fourth in the world (see Table 6.1).

In terms of the degree of diversification within the electrical industry, the picture is varied. According to the Monopolies Commission, Siemens was active in three, and Robert Bosch GmbH in four, different industries in 1992/3, which indicated either horizontal or vertical integration. With the exception of ABB, which—like Siemens—was involved in three different industries, all other electrical companies concentrated solely on their specific field.[86] In a comparison of the extent of integration through joint undertakings among Germany's top 100 industrial enterprises, the electrical industry was of relatively low significance at 6.6 per cent, while at the same time Siemens, involved in no less than nineteen joint ventures, showed a high degree of integration during the 1992/3 accounting period. Just three of the 100 enterprises included in the analysis were involved in more than fifteen joint undertakings (see Table 6.2.).[87]

The relationship between banks and industry and the resulting concentration has been the subject of public debate in Germany for more than a century.[88] The disputes, which centred on the provision of loans, participation in non-bank enterprises, proxy voting power, and seats held by banks on supervisory boards, are of far less significance to the large electrical corporations in Germany: banks do not have any holdings worth mentioning, because these corporations are either primarily family-owned or the holdings are widely spread. However, it is important to mention the problem of interlocking personal relationships between individual companies, which indicate a concentration of economic power.

Conclusion

An examination of the development of Germany's electrical industry and its business groups following the so-called second wave of industrialization in the latter part of the nineteenth century shows parallels with contemporary and typically ideal development tendencies, but, at the same time, a number of differences which can only be attributed to the specific requirements of this relatively young sector of industry. If Germany has been viewed traditionally (before this century, even) as the classic land of the cartels, this view only applies to a limited degree to the electrical industry, since the heterogeneity of the goods it manufactured precluded

Table 6.1. *Germany's top thirty industrial companies according to their turnover rankings*

Company	1972	1974	1976	1978	1980	1982	1984	1986	1988	1990	turnover 1990 (million marks)
Daimler-Benz AG	3	5	3	4	2	2	4	1	1	1	85,500
Volkswagen AG	1	4	4	3	3	4	2	2	2	2	68,061
Siemens AG	2	6	6	2	4	3	3	4	3	3	63,185
Veba AG	5	2	2	2	2	2	2	3	4	4	54,591
BASF AG	6	3	5	6	7	7	5	6	5	5	46,623
Hoechst	87	7	7	713	13	13	13	10	11	6	44,862
RWE AG	11	14	11	8	8	8	6	5	6	7	44,235
Bayer AG	10	9	10	10	12	11	11	8	8	8	41,643
Thyssen AG	4	1	2	5	5	5	7	7	7	9	36,185
Robert Bosch GmbH	22	27	24	22	22	22	16	12	9	10	31,824
BMW AG	48	60	37	29	33	24	17	14	10	11	27,178
Mannesmann AG	19	13	14	16	17	17	20	20	15	12	23,943
Adam Opel AG	12	33	16	15	19	18	18	16	12	13	23,708
Ruhrkohle AG	9	8	9	9	11	12	9	9	12	14	22,921
Ford-Werke AG	16	31	17	17	24	20	19	13	13	15	20,754
Metallgesellschaft	23	22	25	24	21	25	25	24	24	16	19,827
Viag	68	49	47	51	43	42	50	52	47	17	19,423
Preussag	58	53	64	62	59	64	54	59	40	18	19,046
MAN	15	18	18	19	15	15	22	21	18	19	18,937
Fried. Krupp	13	15	15	14	14	14	14	17	17	20	15,570
Degussa	56	40	44	39	31	33	29	25	25	21	13,925
IBM Germany GmbH	25	34	27	28	32	27	21	22	21	22	13,324
German Shell	18	12	12	13	10	10	8	11	16	23	12,788
Hoesch	29	21	26	27	30	35	41	35	30	24	12,570
DEA/Texaco	35	26	29	32	28	29	27	36	27	25	12,442
Ruhrgas	72	70	41	34	20	16	15	18	31	26	12,193
Henkel	42	46	48	52	55	58	52	56	58	27	12,017
Siemens Nixdorf								61	66	28	11,500
ESSO	14	10	8	11	9	9	10	15	19	29	11,479
German Unilever	21	20	22	23	29	30	30	34	35	30	9,538

Source: Monopolkommission, Hauptgutachten 1988/89, 240 ff.

Table 6.2. *Interlocking relationships among the big nine in electricals*

Company	No. of joint ventures with other companies									
	(1)	(2)	(3)	(4)	(5)	(6)	(7)	(8)	(9)	Total
1 Siemens		7	5	0	1	9	7	2	3	34
2 AEG	7		4	0	0	4	3	1	4	23
3 Robert Bosch	5	4		1	0	5	2	1	6	24
4 IBM Germany	0	0	1		0	1	0	0	1	3
5 Philips Germany	1	0	0	0		0	1	0	0	2
6 BBC	9	4	5	1	0		5	2	4	30
7 SEL	7	3	2	0	1	5		3	1	22
8 Grundig	2	1	1	0	0	2	3		0	9
9 Bosch-Siemens-Hausgeräte	3	4	6	1	0	4	1	0		19

to a large extent this kind of regulation of production and sales. When the general trend moved towards the extensive formation of groups at the beginning of the twentieth century and again, more intensively, in the 1920s, the electrical industry was involved to a considerable degree. The intensity of research and development efforts, combined with long lead times and immense capital requirements, led from the outset to a tendency towards large corporate units. It is in no small part due to this that the electrical industry was concentrated in a small number of the world's countries and, without exception, was dominated by a small number of large companies. Initially a means of gaining access to the money market in Germany during the *Gründerjahre*, the stock corporation as a legal form served more and more frequently in subsequent years as an instrument of organization and supervision for large groups of companies. In Germany, just as in the USA, it was the capital- and management-intensive industries that demonstrated the greatest degree of functional integration and diversification of products at the start of the twentieth century.

Since early days, the enterprises Siemens and AEG have been representatives of a duopolitical market structure. Above all, Siemens was able to exploit economies of scale and scope, thanks to the degree to which it diversified, while the breadth of the spectrum of applications always allowed a large number of other companies—small, specialist enterprises—to become established and, within their own lines of business, make use of the advantages of economies of scale or mass production. Precisely the breadth of the field of applications for electrical products would have made horizontal diversification appropriate, but expansion both vertically and horizontally of the production programme remained within a narrow band. Integration of the raw materials supply failed when Siemens-Rheinelbe-Schuckert-Union and the Linke-AEG-Lauchhammer group failed to survive the period of high inflation. But this served to confirm the House of Siemens's traditional policy of only working in the field of electrical engineering, and in the period that followed the company reverted to this principle and abandoned its involvement in areas that were too far removed from its core business. By contrast, AEG had placed considerable emphasis on outside growth from the outset and had consciously pursued this strategy. This led to numerous instances of participation, not all of which had any real link to the electrical industry. In need of emphasis in this context is that a conglomerate corporate structure was typical neither for the electrical industry nor for any other sector of industry in Germany. Typical, however, were the numerous interlocking relationships, in the form of either joint ventures, equity stakes, cartels, agreements, or the exchange of patents and licences. The two big players, Siemens and AEG, were frequently involved, either singly, or jointly.

NOTES

1. Cf. Alfred D. Chandler, *The Visible Hand: The Managerial Revolution in American Business* (Cambridge, Mass., 1980), 498. Chandler showed that once companies have reached an advanced stage of development, further expansion not only leads to greater functional integration but also to a diversification of products. He describes as prerequisites and consequences of this process of development the transition from a personal enterprise through the intermediate form of an entrepreneurial enterprise to a managerial enterprise; the criteria for classification are the varying degrees of involvement of owners and employed managers in long- and short-term corporate decisions. According to Chandler, increasingly complex organizational structures develop at the same time, which ultimately can only be countered through a form of corporate organization based on the division of labour and the transition from a single-unit to a multi-unit corporation.

   The price mechanism as a guarantee of the allocation, monitoring, and co-ordination as fundamental economic functions is thus gradually replaced by hierarchically structured corporate administrations and by agreements between the market's participants. Adam Smith's invisible hand gives way to Alfred D. Chandler's visible hand: functions regulated originally via the market mechanism operating between two individual and partially specialized companies are taken care of by managers within a company and, thus, quasi-internalized.

   Viewed economically, the aforementioned processes of development lead to economies of scale and economies of scope. This conforms to the general realization in economics and business administration that technical indivisibility

often demands a minimum size in order to be able to manufacture economically. These are joined by economies of speed, a concept little researched to
date in the field of business science, which arise as a result of improved and
routine transactions between highly interdependent corporate units.

2. Cf. Chandler, *Visible Hand*; Alfred D. Chandler, 'The Structure of American
   Industry in the Twentieth Century: A Historical Overview', *Business History
   Review*, 43 (1969), 255–98.

3. Cf. Alfred D. Chandler, *Scale and Scope* (Cambridge, Mass., 1990), in which the
   author's chapter headings for the United States ('Competitive Managerial
   Capitalism'), Great Britain ('Personal Capitalism'), and Germany
   ('Cooperative Managerial Capitalism') already indicate the relevant directions
   of development. For a discussion of country-specific manifestations, cf.
   Chandler, *Visible Hand*, 498–500, and the related discussion in J. Kocka and
   H. Siegrist, 'Die hundert größten deutschen Industrieunternehmen im späten
   19. und frühen 20. Jahrhundert: Expansion, Diversifikation und Integration im
   internationalen Vergleich', in N. Horn and J. Kocka (eds.), *Recht und
   Entwicklung swe. Großunternehmen im 19. und frühen 20. Jahrhundert* (Göttingen,
   1979), 89–96.

4. Cf. Hidemasa Morikawa, 'The Development of Multi-industrial Concentration
   in Modern Japan', in Hans Pohl (ed.), *The Concentration Process in the Entrepreneurial Economy since the Late 19th Century* (*Zeitschrift für Unternehmensgeschichte*, 55) (Stuttgart, 1988), 49–66; Norbert Voack, 'Die japanischen
   zaibatsu und die Konzentration wirtschaftlicher Macht in ihren Händen'
   (Diss., Erlangen-Nürnberg 1960).

5. Cf. Kocka and Siegrist, 'Industrieunternehmen', 95.

6. Cf. Hirschmeier, 'Development', 152 f.; Voack, 'Zaibatsu', 214 f.; Morikawa,
   'Development', 58; Lawrence G. Franko, *Die japanischen multinationalen
   Konzerne: Herausforderung und westliche Gegenstrategien* (Frankfurt, 1984), 64–6.

7. Cf. Helmut Arndt and Günter Ollenhauer, 'Begriff und Arten der
   Konzentration', in Helmut Arndt (ed.), *Die Konzentration in der Wirtschaft*
   (*Schriften des Vereins für Socialpolitik*, NS 20/1) (Berlin, 1960), 3–39, here 7.

8. Concerns or (German) *Konzerne* were multisubsidiary organizations in which
   a parent company controlled the financial and strategic direction of otherwise
   legally independent firms. The parent company could take various forms.
   Sometimes it was an official holding company or a community of interest
   (*Interessengemeinschaft*, or IG). Often it was a core firm run by a powerful entrepreneurial figure.

9. Cf. Arndt and Ollenhauer, 'Begriff', 29.

10. The theory of electricity as a science developed at the end of the 18th cent. from
    the observation and interpretation of physical phenomena and represented an
    entirely new field of physics, where up to that time mechanics and the initial
    investigations of thermodynamics had constituted the predominant activities.
    Within two centuries the basic laws concerning electricity were discovered
    and investigated and electricity grew into a position where it could be put into
    use in a variety of practical applications as a new form of energy. Just as the
    overall process of economic growth since the middle of the 19th cent. was self-
    funding due to the primary and secondary effects of income and capacity
    effects, so too the development of the electrical industry was stimulated by the

escalating opportunities in the product technology of this very branch. Machines and instruments were invented, developed, and manufactured for the production, storage, transmission, and transformation of electrical energy into other forms of energy. Due to the development of additional branches in this field as a result of research and inventions, new additional capabilities for applications continually opened up to electricity. Consequently today electrical engineering is directly or indirectly intimately connected with all spheres of our daily life. Accordingly, to the present time, the elasticity of growth in the world market for electrical and electronic products and services has shown a positive trend. With a value of some 2,600 billion marks in 1990, the world market in electrical and electronic equipment is one of the largest markets, and with a share of 12% of the manufacturing industry, the electrical industry occupies an impressive second place.

11. Long before the 1871 unification German technical training was one of the most systematic in the world. As early as 1828, a chemical laboratory was established at the University of Geißen, from which a series of discoveries of decisive importance for the German chemical industry originated. By 1872, the University of Munich had more graduate research chemists than there were in all of England.

12. For the early history of the company under Werner von Siemens, cf. Wilfried Feldenkirchen, *Werner von Siemens: Inventor and International Entrepreneur* (Columbus, Oh., 1994).

13. For the history of AEG cf. Allgemeine Electrizitäts-Gesellschaft (ed.), *50 Jahre AEG* (n.p., n.d.), and Hermann Bücher, 'Beitrag zur wirtschaftlichen Geschichte der AEG, 1941'. Speech given on 10 Nov. 1941, in the AEG factory Brunnenstraße.

14. Cf. Jürgen Kocka, 'Siemens und der aufhaltsame Aufstieg der AEG', *Tradition*, 17 (1972), 125–14; for a characterization of the patriarchal owner-manager, cf. J. Kocka, 'Industrielles Management: Konzeption und Modelle, in Deutschland vor 1914', *Vierteljahrschrift für Sozial;-und Wirtschaftsgeschichte*, 56; (1969), 336, 354–6; for information on the influence of bureaucratic traditions in German industry, cf. Jürgen Kocka, 'Family and Bureaucracy in German Industrial Management, 1850–1914: Siemens in Comparative Perspective', *Business History Review*, 45 (1971), 133–56.

15. Cf. Siemens archives (SAA) 4/Lf 529; 33/Lm 126; 33/Lm 126; 51/Lt 270; 68/Ld 851; 68/Li 156; 68/Li 190; Deutsche Bank archives Siemens & Halske files S 1347; 1348.

16. Cf. Rudolf Hilferding, *Das Finanzkapital* (end end. Vienna, 1920) and Otto Jeidels, *Das Verhältnis der deutschen Großbanken zur Industrie unter besonderer Berücksichtigung der Eisenindustrie* (Leipzig, 1905).

17. Cf. Jürgen Kocka, *Unternehmer in der deutschen Industrialisierung* (Göttingen, 1975), 100–5 (general information on the relationship between banks and industry); Volker Wellhöner, *Großbanken und Gorßindustrie im Kaiserreich* (Göttingen, 1989), 212–35.

18. Cf. Kocka, *Unternehmer*, 100; H. Pohl, 'Zur Geschichte von Organisation und Leitung deutscher Großunternehmen seit dem 19. Jahrhundert', *Zeitschrift für Unternehmensgeschichte*, 26 (1981), 165 f.; Chandler, *Scale and Scope*, 473.

19. BOT = Build-Own-Transfer; BOO=Build-Own-Operate.

20. Cf. Wolfgang König, 'Die technische und wirtschaftliche Stellung der deutschen und britischen Elektroindustrie zwischen 1880 und 1900', *Technikgeschichte*, 53 (1987), 221–9, here 225 f.
21. For further information on the founding, see Franz Fasolt, *Sie sieben Elektrizitätsgesellschaften, ihre Entwicklung und Unternehmertätigkeit* (Dresden, 1904), 33–6, 47–9, 70.
22. Cf. König, 'Stellung', 225.
23. Cf. Siemens archives 69/Lr 515; 11/Le 862, '50 years of AEG', 149 f. See also notes by Felix Deutsch in the Leo Baeck-Institute, New York.
24. Cf. P. Czada, *Die Berliner Elektroindustrie in der Weimarer Zeit* (Berlin, 1969), 50.
25. Cf. Siemens archives 69/Lr 515.
26. Cf. Siemens archives 4/Lf 540.
27. Cf. Franz Findeisen, *Unternehmensform als Rentabilitätsfaktor* (Berlin, 1924), 128; Erich Brandstetter, 'Finanzierungsmethoden in der deutschen elektrotechnischen Industrie' (diss. Gießen, 1930), 63.
28. Cf. Kocka, 'Family', 152.
29. Cf. Deutsche Bank archives, Bergmann files S 129; Siemens archives 4/Lf 544; 4/Lf 796.
30. Telefunken was the dominant firm in the German radio industry. It held almost all the important German patents and had numerous licensing arrangements with large firms in other countries throughout the world. The other radio firms in Germany were sublicensed to use the Telefunken patents for which Telefunken had a licence.
31. Cf. National Archives RG 260 ED Box 171.
32. See Siemens archives 50/Lo 768, 50/Lf 570, and 11/Lb 751, Berliner Papers
33. For an account of the effects, see Siemens archives 11/Lg 713, Franke Papers.
34. See Siemens archives 4/Lf 591; 20/Ls 958.
35. For the effects of the Versailles Treaty in this respect, see the *Geschäftsberichte des Zentralverband der deutschen Elektroindustries: Geschäftsberichte* (n.p., n.d.), and Siemens archives 11/Lf 291, Köttgen Papers; 4/Lf 647. Also see Harm Schröter, *Außenpolitik und Wirtschaftsinteresse: Skandinavien im außenwirtschaftlichen Kalkül Deutschlands und Großbritanniens 1918–1939* (Frankfurt am Main, 1983), 323–8.
36. Cf. Siemens archives 4/Lh 296; 4/Lh 945: Speech by Carl Friedrich von Siemens in New York on 21 Oct. 1931.
37. Cf. Siemens archives 16/Lh 262; 29/Le 932; 32/Lm 860; 61/Lf 109; 68/Li 278.
38. Cf. Siemens archives 4/Lf 529; 4/Lf 793; 11/Lg 742, Franke Papers; 23/Lh 689; National Archives Omgus RG 260 17/242-2/4.
39. According to Gert Hautsch, 'Der Elektrokonzern AEG-Telefunken: Untersuchungen zum Verhältnis von Wirtschaft und Politik am Beispiel eines westdeutschen Großunternehmens' (Diss. Bremen, 1982), 34.
40. Cf. National Archives Omgus RG 260 Ec Div Dec Br. 17/2413/25. Here a number of 1,000 cartels is given, which is misleading, as the American investigators also included licensing agreements and did not distinguish between cartels and such licensing agreements. The German cartel register mentioned 67 cartels in the German electrical industry by the end of 1935. Cf. Siemens archives 54/Lp 983.
41. Cf. Wilfried Feldenkirchen, *Siemens 1918–1945* (Munich, 1995).

42. AEG directly owned 25% of the stock; the Bank elektrischer Werte held a further 25.69%, of which 66.79% was owned by AEG. Cf. Siemens archives, uncatalogued records in intermediate archive.

43. Cf. Siemens archives, supervisory board meeting of 28 Jan. 1931; National Archives RG 260 Omgus 17/227-3/2; 17/242-2/4; National Archives RG 407 Box 1049; Felten & Guilleaume Archives B III/55.

44. Cf. Siemens archives 15/Lr 314.

45. Cf. Siemens archives 11/Lf 101, Köttgen Papers.

46. As early as 1908 Siemens & Halske had built a foundry for light moulded metal products; after the war it added plants producing dye, paper, porcelain, plywood, and wood shavings. Cf. Wilfried Feldenkirchen, 'Big Business in Interwar Germany: Organizational Innovation at Vereinigte Stahlwerke, IG Farben, and Siemens', *Business History Review*, 61 (1987), 444.

47. Cf. Siemens archives 54/Li 240; 11/Lf 472, Köttgen Papers.

48. Cf. National Archives RG 260 ED 11/27-3/10, 'German industrial complexes: The Siemens complex'.

49. Cf. Siemens archives 4/Lf 548; 4/Lf 635; 4/Lf 811; 4/Lh 960; 4/Lt 398.

50. Cf. Siemens archives 4/Lf 548; 4/Lf 635 and 54/Li 240.

51. See the comments by Carl Friedrich von Siemens on this basic rule of his company policy. For example, dated 11 Mar. 1927; see National Archives RG 260 Omgus Ec Div Dec Br 17/241-3/7; Carl Friedrich von Siemens to von Witzleben on 22 May 1930; see Siemens archives 11.43/Lm 391, Witzleben Papers; Carl Friedrich von Siemens to von Buol on 22 May 1993; see Siemens archives 4/Lt 398.

52. For information on the founding and development of SBU, see Siemens archives 11/Le 545, Jessen Papers; 12/Lh 583; National Archives RG 260 ED 11/27-3/10; Feldenkirchen, *Siemens 1918–1945*, 366–9.

53. For a history of Osram GmbH, see Siemens archives 54/Li 776; 11/Le 830, Jessen Papers; 54/Li 258; National Archives RG 260 ED 11/27-3/29; RG 466 Box 59 Exhibit 164; Feldenkirchen, *Siemens 1918–1945*, ch. 6.

54. For the development of Gelap, see Siemens archives 17/Lt 371; 29/Lc 776; 68/Li 182; Feldenkirchen, *Siemens 1918–1945*, 380 f. Gelap was founded as an independent company in order to avoid burdening the rest of Siemens with the controls established by the Versailles Treaty for factories producing war material. See Siemens archives 4/Lt 398.

55. See Siemens archives 11/Le 549, Jessen Papers; 68/Li 200; Feldenkirchen, *Siemens 1918–1945*, 369–75.

56. See Siemens archives 21/Lg 573; 34/Ll 674 and 68/Li 250.

57. For the development of Klangfilm, see Siemens archives 68/Li 280 and 4/Lf 706. In 1941, by a participation exchange agreement, AEG gained complete control over Telefunken, while Siemens took over Bergmann Elektrizitäts-Werke AG, Vereinigte Eisenbahn-Signalwerke GmbH, Klangfilm GmbH, and Deutsche Grammophon GmbH. Cf. Feldenkirchen, *Siemens 1918–1945*, 350–3.

58. See Siemens archives 21/Lp 625 and 68/Li 920–1.

59. In 1928 Siemens, together with Rütgerswerke AG, formed Siemens-Planiawerke AG für Kohlenfabrikate, in which Siemens had the controlling share, to manufacture carbon and graphite products. See Siemens archives 11/Lg 713, Franke Papers; 47/Lg 790.

60. For detailed information on the core companies and participations, see Anon., *Siemens 1935* (Berlin, 1935).

61. For a history of Siemens' automobile business and the reasons leading to its sale, see Siemens archives 47/Lg 768; Feldenkirchen, *Siemens 1918–1945*, 299–306.

62. For a history of SAM, see Siemens archives 68/Li 182.

63. For a further history of the Brandenburgische Motorenwerke, see Siemens archives 11/Li 390, von Buol Papers; 68/Li 172.

64. See the overview in Paul Ufermann and Carl Hüglin, *Die AEG: Eine Darstellung des Konzerns der Allgemeinen Elektrizitäts-Gesellschaft* (Berlin, 1992), 101–28.

65. Cf. Siemens 4/Lf 544; 4/Lf 548; 4/LF 796; 11/Lf 314, 381 and 389, Köttgen Papers.

66. Cf. Feldenkirchen, *Siemens 1918–1945*, ch. 4.

67. See Siemens archives 23/Lh 689.

68. For further details about the negotiations see unregistered papers in the Siemens archives; National Archives RG 260 Box 1047.

69. According to statements made by I.T. & T. officials after the war, the company went on the German market 'in order to force an understanding with S & H and AEG with regard to the South American market'. Cf. National Archives RG 260 ED 17/227-3/2; 17/242-2/4.

70. Cf. Felten & Guilleaume Archives B III/55.

71. Cf. National Archives RG 407 Box 1049; Felten & Guilleaume Archives B III/55.

72. Cf. Siemens archives 4/Lt 398; 4/Lf 701.

73. Cf. Horst Freude, 'Wirtschaftliche Machtzusammenballungen und ihre Entflechtungen: Vergleichende Darstellung der Verhältnisse in den USA und Deutschland' (Diss. Mannheim, 1951), 41–3; Wernhard Möschel, *Entflechtungen im Recht der Wettbewerbsbeschränkungen: Eine vergleichende rechtspolitische Studie* (Tübingen, 1979), 4.

74. Cf. Bernhard Plettner, *Abenteuer Elektrotechnik: Siemens und die Entwicklung der Elektrotechnik seit 1945* (Munich, 1994), 51.

75. Cf. Günther Schulz, 'Die Entflechtungsmaßnahmen und ihre wirtschaftliche Bedeutung', in: Hand Pohl (ed.), *Kartelle und Kartellgesetzgebung in Praxis und Rechtsprechung vom 19. Jahrhundert bis zur Gegenwart* (Stuttgart, 1985), 210–22; Harald Winkel, *Die Wirtschaft im geteilten Deutschland 1945–1970* (Wiesebaden, 1974), 49–52.

76. Report on the results of an examination of concentration in industry, dated 29 Feb. 1964, and provided by the Bundesamt für gewerbliche Wirtschaft in Frankfurt am Main (Bundestagsdrucksache IV/2320, 25, 38 f., 48 f. (Anlagenband)); this examination constituted the first comprehensive representation of the circumstances of concentration in Germany industry and has been updated systematically since 1973 in Monopolies Commission reports (*Hauptgutachten der Monopolkommission*).

77. Cf. W. Feldenkirchen, 'Competition Policy in Germany', *Business and Economic History*, 21 (1992), 263.

78. Cf. Plettner, *Abenteuer*, 162.

79. Cf. Sigfrid von Weiher and Herbert Goetzeler, *Weg und Wirken der Siemens-Werke im Fortschritt der Elektrotechnik 1847–1980* (Wiesbaden, 1981), 128.

80. Cf. *Monopolkommission, Hauptgutachten 1973/75*, 112–14.
81. Telefunken-Gesellschaft merged with its parent, AEG, in 1966 to form the corporate unit AEG-Telefunken (taken from Weiher and Goetzeler, *Weg*, 93).
82. *Monopolkommission, Hauptgutachten 1982/83*, 106–13.
83. *Monopolkommission, Hauptgutachten 1984/85*, 257, 289, and 295.
84. *Monopolkommission, Hauptgutachten 1986/87*, 117.
85. *Monopolkommission, Hauptgutachten 1990/91*, 178 and 183.
86. Derived from *Monopolkommission, Hauptgutachten 1992/93*, 118–22.
87. *Monopolkommission, Hauptgutachten 1992/93*, 217 f. and 222.
88. Cf. for the current debate Hans E. Büschgen, 'Zeitgeschichtliche Problemfelder des Bankwesens der Bundesrepublik Deutschland', in Institute für bankhistorische Forschung e.V. (ed.), *Deutsche Bankengeschichte*, III (Frankfurt am Main, 1983), 351–409, here 360–7, and relevant sections in the *Monopolkommission, Hauptgutachten*.

7

A Path to the Corporate Group in Japan:
Mitsubishi Heavy Industries and its Group Formation

TAKAO SHIBA

Introduction

In academic discussion of Japanese business groups, the companies most often used as cases are those in mass-production, assembly-type industries, such as motor vehicles or electronics. This is no doubt due to the fact that companies in these industries tend to have large numbers of subsidiaries, but there are many companies with substantial business groups that are situated in other industries. One such industry is heavy equipment (i.e. shipbuilding and custom machinery), in which participants also tend to be surrounded by groups of subsidiaries. The formation processes of these groups, however, along with their essential character, are rather different from those of the mass-production assemblers' groups. This chapter will illustrate the case of Mitsubishi Heavy Industries Co., Ltd. (MHI hereafter) in order to provide a reference for comparison.

MHI started out in shipbuilding, an industry that was originally characterized by a low level of reliance on outside companies. Shipyards were established in several locations from early on, and MHI was initially a kind of federation of these shipyards. Additionally, the company itself was, until the end of the Second World War, a member firm of the Mitsubishi zaibatsu, which controlled other companies in a variety of industries and which exercised considerable power within the Japanese economy. These three characteristics continued to influence the nature of MHI for a long period, resulting in a special pattern of group formation that we will examine here as it developed through the mid-1960s.

Pre-merger Relations Between Mitsubishi Shipbuilding & Engineering and Outside Companies

In April 1934 Japan's largest shipbuilder, Mitsubishi Shipbuilding & Engineering Co., Ltd. (MSE), changed its name to Mitsubishi Heavy Industries Co., Ltd. (MHI), and, two months later, merged with its subsidiary, the Mitsubishi Aircraft Company (MAC). Accordingly, the newly renamed and reorganized MHI added the manufacture of aircraft and tanks, formerly undertaken by MAC, to its business. At this point, MHI was already involved in the production of electrical power generation equipment, rolling stock, and speciality steel, along with various machinery and metal products (in addition to ships, of course), and the merger meant that it was now active in virtually all industrial areas relating to machinery and metal. This explains why it chose the new name Mitsubishi Heavy Industries. Assets totalled some 140 million yen, making it in actuality the third largest Japanese manufacturing organization.[1] Notwithstanding its size, however, virtually all production was carried out at its six plants or works, and it had not formed supplementary subsidiaries. Neither had it sought to purchase stock in outside companies to place them under its control. This state of affairs was not peculiar to MHI, but was characteristic of Japanese shipbuilding enterprises of the time.

The start of Japan's modern shipbuilding industry can be traced to the pre-Meiji period when the country was still under the control of the Edo Bakufu government, but it was not until the Meiji Restoration that private firms became involved. The government, which had been itself managing a number of shipyards, sold off all of these except the ones required by the Navy to private entrepreneurs. The founders of such well-known Japanese shipbuilders as Ishikawajima-Harima Heavy Industries Co., Ltd., Kawasaki Heavy Industries Co., Ltd., and MHI all purchased their first shipyards from the government during the 1870s and 1880s, thereby establishing themselves in the industry. They were followed in the 1890s by others who established modern shipbuilding operations on their own, but both of these groups faced the same two major difficulties. The first was the insufficient level of fundamental related industries, and the second was the small size of the market.

The British shipbuilding industry, then the foremost in the world, was based on existing machinery and steel industries. This meant that hull construction was essentially an assembly process and could be undertaken with a comparatively small capital investment (Pollard and Robertson 1979). In Japan, however, because the shipbuilding industry was born before the development of the necessary supporting industries, the fundamental structure for the British-type assembly approach was lacking. This was compounded by extremely limited domestic demand for modern ships. While the British yards were able to produce large numbers of tramps, demand for commercial vessels in Japan was almost exclusively for government-subsidized large liners with few orders for tramps. Thus, the Japanese shipyards could not hope to survive in such a small market by producing ships alone (Chida and Davies 1990).

In surviving its passage between a Scylla of a limited industrial base and a Charybdis of a tiny market, the Japanese shipbuilding industry acquired a number of distinctive managerial characteristics. In compensating for the deficiencies of fundamental related industries, the shipbuilders themselves were forced to set about producing almost all required equipment, machinery, and parts. Consequently, they became not only assemblers, but also makers of a wide variety of related items. On the other hand, in order to overcome the limitations of low demand, they also sought to apply their abilities to the production of iron and steel frame products for non-shipping, land-based needs. This led to diversification into machinery and metal products virtually from the beginning, and reliance on non-shipping items was accentuated in waves following the business cycle. It was the shipbuilders' expertise in shipping-related machinery, equipment, and metal products that permitted this flexibility, but production of items for land-based applications occasionally required additional non-shipping-related apparatus and technology, and the shipyards naturally found it necessary to incorporate these as well (Echigo 1956).

Because of the conditions surrounding its birth, the Japanese shipbuilding industry maintained a plethora of production equipment and technology for metalworking and machinery manufacture. This, in turn, meant that, until about the First World War, the shipbuilders were at the forefront of Japan's overall machinery industry, with other types of machinery makers lagging far behind. This being the case, they hardly felt the need to place other machinery makers under their control. The major shipbuilders produced internally everything that they needed, and, if there was something that they could not make, it simply meant that the item in question was unavailable domestically and had to be imported. Purchasing stock in other companies, then, was not seen to have much merit, and this situation continued essentially unchanged until after the First World War.

With the outbreak of the First World War, the Japanese shipbuilding industry grew rapidly and accumulated vast profits. The major companies used these funds for subsequent diversification into fields such as motor vehicles and aircraft, electrical equipment, and the operation of shipping lines. Creation of subsidiary companies was seen in a few cases, but, except for these, the industry did not see any real movement toward group formation for some time (Kaneko 1964).

MHI was not unusual in this sense, but this did not mean there was a complete lack of subsidiaries, related companies, or spin-offs. MAC (Mitsubishi Aircraft Company), which MHI had absorbed in 1934, was

itself spun off from MSE (Mitsubishi Shipbuilding & Engineering, the predecessor of MHI) in 1920, and Mitsubishi Electric Manufacturing Co., Ltd.
(MEM) had been spun off from MSE in 1921. It might be an overstatement,
then, to say that MSE/MHI did not seek to have subsidiaries. Still, the
decision to spin off these two companies was influenced more by outside
factors than by internal policy.

MSE/MHI, it should be remembered, was not a stand-alone entity; it
was one of many companies controlled by the Iwasaki family through the
Mitsubishi zaibatsu. The Mitsubishi zaibatsu had its origins in the shipping business of Yataro Iwasaki in the mid-1870s. The original shipping
business was sold in the mid-1880s after Yataro's death, but his successors
set about continuing in the businesses of mining, finance, shipbuilding,
etc., that Yataro had branched into before his passing. It was the shipbuilding business that was the origin of MSE/MHI. The Iwasaki family
went on to add first real estate and then trading to their impressive list of
business involvements, and, in order to control this empire effectively,
they set up Mitsubishi Goshi in 1893 with the various businesses functioning as departments.

Mitsubishi Goshi then reorganized itself into main operating divisions
in 1908, with large amounts of authority assigned to the division chiefs.
However, important decisions such as those relating to capital expendi-
tures still had to be referred to the central office. The shipbuilding division
had also become an operating division, and its treatment was no different
in this regard. In the late 1910s Mitsubishi Goshi further decentralized its
major operating divisions, establishing them as independent joint-stock
companies. The first of these new companies was the shipbuilding division, established as Mitsubishi Shipbuilding and Engineering Co., Ltd. in
1917, independent of the Mitsubishi Goshi. Subsequently, independent
companies were also formed from the steel, warehousing, trading, and
other divisions, and Mitsubishi Goshi was consequently transformed into
a holding company. The agglomeration of businesses under the aegis of
Mitsubishi Goshi was known as the Mitsubishi zaibatsu (Mishima 1989;
Morikawa 1992).

Thus, while MSE was an individual company, its managers did not have
completely free decision-making power. Significant MSE decisions
required the assent of the zaibatsu headquarters, and actions that did not
take into account the overall zaibatsu structure were not likely to be
approved (Mishima 1981). The formation of the two aforementioned subsidiaries, for example, took place because of overall zaibatsu priorities
rather than because of particular MSE preference. That MSE became
involved in aircraft production at all was due to decisions handed down
from headquarters (Kyu-nainen-kai 1969), and it is thought that the spin-
off of MAC was also related to headquarters manœuvring (Fujita 1985).
The separation of MSE's electrical division into a subsidiary company has

a similar background, and, while the two 'subsidiaries' were technically owned by MSE, Mitsubishi Goshi treated them more or less the same as it did MSE itself. Prior to the 1934 merger, MSE also held controlling interests in two additional companies: Nippon Kogaku (now Nikon), and Nippon Battery (Japan Storage Battery). However, the primary reasons for these stockholding arrangements also had more to do with the needs of the headquarters than with operational factors at MSE (Iwasaki 1957).

Group Formation during the Second World War

As we have seen, until the absorption of MAC, MSE did not seek to control a large number of subsidiaries and did not have a particular internal policy to spin off divisions. This state of affairs derived from the independent nature of the shipbuilding industry, but MSE had even less need than other industry participants to control subsidiaries. That is, MSE was significantly ahead of its competitors in terms of both technology and production equipment, and was even further ahead of general machinery makers. In addition, MSE had three large-scale works capable of mutual complementary supply.

The shipbuilding operations of Mitsubishi Goshi began with the Nagasaki Shipyards, located at the far western tip of Japan. The company subsequently set up another shipyard at the commercial port of Kobe in 1905, and a third in the western Japanese fishing centre of Shimonoseki in 1914. This left it with an effective shipbuilding and repair network in western Japan. Of the three shipyards, the Nagasaki Shipyards had the highest level of shipbuilding technology, while the Kobe Shipyards started as a repair centre and only later began building medium-sized vessels and a variety of machinery. Mitsubishi's involvement in aircraft and electrical equipment can be traced to the Kobe Shipyards. Meanwhile, the Shimonoseki facility served primarily to build and repair fishing vessels. In cases where one of the three could not itself supply a particular item of machinery or metal product that it needed, it could commission production to one of the other two, and such transactions were regularly undertaken (Nishinarita 1978; 1980). When none of the three could supply the requisite item, it often meant that the equipment was not to be had domestically and would have to be imported. Seen in this way, MSE can be described as a federation composed of three relatively independent production centers, and it can also be seen that it had little need to place outside companies under its control. Of course, corporate action is not entirely linked to production, but functions such as real estate transactions and finance were the domains of other zaibatsu member firms, and MSE was not faced with the need to develop such functions on its own. It can be rightly noted that MSE had a large number of transaction partners in which it held stock, but these stockholdings were rather small and were not related to management *per se* (Shiba 1986).

It was the merger in 1934 that brought about a change in MSE/MHI's relationships with outside companies. From that time onward, MHI helped found firms without direct connections to the zaibatsu headquarters, invested in existing companies through stock purchase, and made sufficient such stock purchases so that it came to control some of these companies. As a result, the number of MHI subsidiaries increased, and, at least superficially, it began to form a group. The relationships involved, however, were not strong enough to justify calling it a corporate group at first, because even at this time there was little specific need to create subsidiaries or to control their management.

The number of firms controlled by MHI increased by twenty-five between 1934 and 1941 (Shiba 1986: 182–7), and of these MHI clearly controlled three and sent in managers. These were subsidiaries in the true sense of the word, but in two of these cases the motivation for control came from outside. The two were shipbuilding operations in the colonies, whose management had been consigned to MHI by colonial governments, thereby in effect making them subsidiaries. In the cases of the non-controlled companies, MHI's motivations were even weaker. For instance, minority stakes were held in nine non-manufacturing companies, mostly at the insistence of industry associations and the government, in the hopes that Mitsubishi economic influence would affect them positively (Shiba 1986: 181). Even its holdings in the manufacturing sector were not particularly aggressive. As of 1941, MHI had holdings in fifteen manufacturing companies, but the majority of these were cases in which the issuing companies themselves desired to align themselves with MHI (Shiba 1986: 188–9).

Much more striking from the perspective of capital than its stockholdings in other companies was the dramatic expansion of MSE/MHI's own internal facilities. If we include a factory specializing in torpedoes that had been established in 1917, MSE had a total of four production facilities just prior to its merger in 1934. The merger brought this number to six, with the addition of the former MAC's Nagoya Aircraft Works and its Tokyo Engineering Works. By 1941, the total was eleven, including two more aircraft plants, two more shipbuilding facilities, and a speciality steel plant. During the same period, construction was begun on two additional facilities for rolling stock and motor vehicles. Further, demand for increased production, particularly the strategic weapons of aircraft and tanks, was mounting *vis-à-vis* the existing facilities. Hence, the company embarked upon an ambitious building programme (Shiba 1994), but new factories brought new problems.

The crux of the matter was that aircraft and tank production required a wide variety of parts in massive amounts that MHI could not hope to turn out by itself. It was for this reason that the company came to rely on a large number of subcontractors (Shiba 1987), something that it had never done before, and this provided the impetus for the establishment of production relations with many outside manufacturing firms. The pressure for output was not so strong at first, however, and MHI did not feel the necessity to cement its relationships with parts makers through stock purchases. Rather, the parts makers themselves tended to want MHI to hold blocks of their shares. This was because stable relations with an entity as large and well connected with the military as MHI was thought to be helpful in securing ever scarcer supplies of labour and materials. In response to these requests, MHI purchased holdings in a large number of these manufacturing firms (Shiba 1986: 188–9).

In the mid-1930s MHI's stakes in other companies can be seen to be on the rise, indicating at first glance the formation of a corporate group, but it was not until the Japanese wartime economy entered a new phase that such a group would actually be constructed.

In December 1941 Japan, which had already been at war with China for several years, opened hostilities with the USA and Britain as well. As these events are well known, we need not dwell on them at length here. Suffice it to say that, although the war went well for Japan at first, the Japanese fighting forces became comparatively weaker and weaker from the summer of 1942, until the positions of attacker and defender were reversed. During this process, huge numbers of planes were shot down and vast amounts of military supplies were sent to the bottom of the ocean. As a result, higher and higher production levels for aircraft and military supplies were demanded, and shortages of materials made themselves felt in an island nation that had lost control of the sea. Producers of military items, then, sought a way out of the uncomfortable situation caused by the enormous pressure from the Army and Navy to boost output, on the one hand, and the lack of materials, equipment, and labour on the other, by deepening relations with capable parts makers. It was at this point that military producers utilized stock purchases to strengthen ties with these parts manufacturers. Mitsubishi was no exception; from about 1942 it began to discard its previous passive approach and actively to place emphasis on strategic stock purchases. From 1942 onward, MHI acquired stakes in twenty companies in the machinery and metal industries; ten of these were purchased at the smaller companies' request, but the other ten were sought by MHI. Additionally, MHI increased stakes in four other companies in which it previously held shares, but over which it now felt the need to increase its influence (Shiba 1986: 190).

As illustrated in Table 7.1, MHI, which had had only a very few subsidiaries through the 1930s, by the end of the war had come to control a large number of companies in the machinery and metal industries. This

Table 7.1. *Mitsubishi Heavy Industries group during the Second World War*

	% of holdings
Matsunawa Metals Industries	85.8
Unzen Firebrick	72.8
Taiwan Dockyard	66.0
Mitsubishi Manchuria Engineering	62.5
Wakayama Iron Works	60.0
Hishiya Store	53.3
Hiroshima Casting Industry	48.7
Kyushu Tools Manufacturing	45.5
Ikegai Automobile Manufacturing	31.7
Omi Aircraft Manufacturing	31.0
Nihon Architectural-Steel Manufacturing	30.3
Teikoku Aircraft Manufacturing	30.0
Mitsubishi Wooden Airplane Manufacturing	30.0
Nippon Press Industries	28.7
Korea Heavy Industries	28.7
Diesel Engineering	26.8
Ezaki Iron Works	25.0
Suzuka Transport	24.6
Nagoya Screw Manufacturing	22.7
Metallic Dry Plate Manufacturing	21.5
Seki Machine Manufacturing	20.0
Nippon Electric Bulb	20.0

Source: Report to the General Headquarters for the Allied Powers from Mitsubishi Heavy Industries Co., Ltd.

marked the appearance of a more cohesive group, although it should be noted that ties with the bulk of the member firms had been made necessary by the needs of expanding aircraft and tank production. With shipbuilding and machinery, internal production remained the rule, as it had from the beginning.

Defeat and Group Dissolution

With Japan's surrender to the Allied Powers on 15 August 1945, Japanese firms were confronted with previously unknown difficulties. They had exerted themselves in efforts to meet state-imposed production targets, and had expanded production equipment to unheard-of levels. While these efforts proved unsuccessful, the firms had been guaranteed substantial revenues by the government to compensate them for risk. However, the occupying forces did not recognize the validity of wartime profits, and put pressure on the Japanese government not to pay these obligations. In the end, while payments were made, equivalent amounts were collected in taxes, thereby making the guarantees meaningless. Not only that, many companies had lost substantial amounts of production equipment through bombing raids, losses that put great pressure on their finances. Finally, lucrative military contracts were no longer available; even companies that still had the equipment and could find the materials to convert to consumer demand quickly discovered that the purchasing power of people who had suffered total defeat was not particularly substantial.

Along with the problems associated with production and finance, bigger companies found themselves facing the larger question of survival as the General Headquarters for the Allied Powers (GHQ) sought to modify the existing enterprise system drastically. The policy of economic demilitarization (Miwa 1989) consisted specifically of the dissolution of the zaibatsu, the encouragement of organized labour, and land reform. The first of these was the most immediately significant for Japanese industry. As is pointed out by Professor Suzuki, stock held by the zaibatsu headquarters companies and by the zaibatsu families was forcibly sold, and their controlling power over enterprise (which had already considerably declined during the war) was decisively broken. Ownership of the major companies underwent major change, as companies were forced to sell their holdings and larger companies were threatened with dissolution. This effectively meant the disbanding of the groups that had been constructed around major firms since the 1930s (Shimotani 1991).

MHI was treated fairly harshly by reason of its having been the number one military supplier and being the foremost member of the machinery and metal (i.e. weapons) industries (Mochikabu 1951). It was forced to dispose of all of the holdings that it had acquired prior to the end of the war, and it was split up into three separate entities.

MHI was identified as a holding company in December 1946, and all of its shareholdings were ordered turned over to the Holding Company Liquidation Committee, the executive organization for zaibatsu dissolution. At the time of Japan's defeat, MHI held a total of about 2.714 million shares in 86 companies for a total book value of some 125 million yen (Mitsubishi n.d.).[2] This accounted for approximately 17 per cent of MHI's total paid-in capital of 750 million yen. Accordingly, it lost the shares that it had acquired in various manufacturers during the war, and the group that it had formed was eliminated.

Plans were also being laid for the company's disintegration. The Holding Company Liquidation Committee, which took the view that MHI 'limits competition in Japan's shipbuilding and other industries, and has the power to block opportunities for other individual entities to participate', concluded that this 'power to block opportunities' would have to be eliminated in order to safeguard the public good (Mochikabu 1951). This decision was not announced until later, but MHI, which was well aware of the plans in store for the zaibatsu, drew up its own separation plan in March 1946, originally suggesting the creation of three companies in the areas of shipbuilding, machinery manufacture, and rolling stock. GHQ is said not to have given any clear answer regarding this first proposal, and MHI continued to develop further plans for its own breakup, watching GHQ reaction closely all the while. The second plan called for the creation of five shipbuilding companies, a rolling stock maker, a machinery and equipment maker, and a company composed of the former aircraft-related assets, for a total of eight. GHQ did not respond clearly to this plan either, so MHI next came up with a suggestion that it be divided into thirteen different entities, and, seeing the many companies into which Mitsubishi Trading Co., Ltd. and Mitsui Bussan Co., Ltd. were split up, even formed an extreme version that called for each factory to be made into a separate entity. At this point MHI controlled a total of twenty-three factories, having constructed quite a number during the war to add to its total, but also having closed some as well, and the extreme version of the breakup plan naturally called for twenty-three separate companies. The MHI managers realized that, even if twenty-three such companies were formed, many of them would face major difficulties, and wanted to keep the number of firms resulting from the breakup as small as possible. In April 1948 they approached GHQ yet again with a plan for six companies: three in shipbuilding, and one each in machinery, rolling stock, and motor vehicles. Having got no further with this version, they went back with a plan that denied the need for breakup at all. In response to this, GHQ ordered the creation of three regional companies, in the eastern, central, and western (Kyushu) regions (Mitsubishi 1990: 32–9).

The fact that this process took such a long time reflects the state of mind of the MHI managers. While they were resigned to a breakup, it is clear that they preferred it to occur along product lines. If we set aside the twenty-three-company plan as simply unrealistic, we can see that all of the proposals they submitted were based on the three divisions of shipbuilding, machinery, and land transport. It is especially significant that, even in versions where other divisions were to be kept together, it was shipbuilding that was to be divided into separate companies. This indicates the high level of independence of the individual shipyards. The second plan, for example, called for five shipbuilding companies, and this roughly corresponds to the six shipyards (including Hiroshima, which was constructed during the war) that MHI was operating at the time (Mitsubishi 1956: 371). In effect, the shipyards had maintained the independence that they had inherited from earlier days when MSE had been more or less a federation of the three main shipbuilding locations. Thus, while the other divisions were affected by the requirement to sell off stock in related companies and disband the MHI group, shipbuilding took this relatively calmly. In fact, because GHQ had forbidden tank and aircraft manufacture anyway, there was no particular need to keep the group together anymore. In other words, the MHI group was destined to come unglued even without the forced disposal of stockholdings.

Post-dissolution Group Reorganization

In January 1950 the former MHI was liquidated and its assets divided among three new companies simultaneously established along the geographic lines previously mentioned. The new companies took the rather bland but none the less appropriate names of East Japan Heavy Industries Co., Ltd. (EJHI), Mid-Japan Heavy Industries Co., Ltd. (MJHI), and West Japan Heavy Industries Co., Ltd. (WJHI). WJHI centred on the Nagasaki Shipyards, and was primarily a shipbuilder. MJHI, which initially had its headquarters at the Kobe Shipyards but shortly moved to Tokyo, also included former aircraft plants in Nagoya and Okayama and a rolling stock plant in Okayama as well. These made MJHI the most diversified of the three. EJHI was centred on the Yokohama Shipyards, and included two former tank factories and a smaller shipyard as well (Mitsubishi 1990: 41).

The three companies changed their names in 1952, inserting the Mitsubishi name once more. Japanese companies had been forbidden by GHQ to use the company names and trademarks of their zaibatsu forebears, but use of the former names became possible from 1951 as the Occupation came to a close and Japan again established peaceful relations with most of the Allied Powers. Accordingly, WJHI became Mitsubishi Shipbuilding, Ltd. (MSL); MJHI became Shin Mitsubishi Heavy Industries, Ltd. (SMHI); and EJHI became Mitsubishi Nippon Heavy Industries, Ltd. (MNHI) (Mitsubishi 1990: 45).

None of the three renamed companies had any subsidiaries at all immediately following their founding, as they were completely prohibited by Occupation policy from owning stock of any kind (East Japan 1950). However, this restriction was also relaxed in the summer of 1951, one year after the breakup (Mitsubishi 1967a: 646), and it was from this point that the three companies began to hold shares in other companies. At first their holdings consisted of shares in financial institutions, transaction partners, and the splinter trading companies that resulted from the break-up of the huge zaibatsu trading company Mitsubishi Shoji (East Japan 1951; Mid-Japan 1951; West Japan 1951), but MJHI and MNHI immediately established subsidiaries and held their stock. WJHI, on the other hand, had no subsidiaries until a year after it had changed its name to MSL.

Takao Shiba

The three MHI offshoots once again had subsidiaries but, interestingly, the central Japan company (SMHI) began an active programme of group formation, as opposed to the eastern and western companies (MNHI and MSL), which formed hardly any new subsidiaries. As indicated in Table 7.2, SMHI created a new subsidiary in each of the fiscal years 1952 and 1953, and established six more in fiscal 1954. By fiscal 1962 the company had gone on to have a total of twenty-five subsidiaries. In comparison, while MSL had set up one new subsidiary in 1957, it broke off relations with another the following year, thus having only one in fiscal 1962. It then established a new subsidiary in fiscal 1963, giving it a grand total of two. Meanwhile EJHI, having changed its name to MNHI, merged two of its subsidiaries in fiscal 1953, thus having only one in fiscal 1960. Subsequently it began to form others, but had only five as of fiscal 1963.

As previously noted, SMHI was the most diversified of the three, and this was the reason that it embarked on its ambitious program of subsidiary creation. The Kobe Shipyards had been a centre for MHI diversification from before the war, and itself produced a wide variety of items. The company also included the Nagoya Engineering Works and the

Table 7.2. *Subsidiaries of Mitsubishi Shipbuilding, Shin Mitsubishi Heavy Industries, and Mitsubishi Nippon Heavy Industries*

Fiscal year	MSL			SMHI			MNHI		
	+	−	T	+	−	T	+	−	T
1951	—	—	—	2	—	2	2	—	2
1952	—	—	—	1	—	3	—	—	2
1953	1	—	1	1	—	4	—	1	1
1954	—	—	1	6	—	10	—	—	1
1955	—	—	1	1	—	11	—	—	1
1956	—	—	1	1	—	12	—	—	1
1957	1	—	2	2	2	12	—	—	1
1958	—	1	1	1	—	13	—	—	1
1959	—	—	1	1	—	14	—	—	1
1960	—	—	1	5	2	17	1	—	2
1961	—	—	1	4	—	21	—	—	2
1962	—	—	1	4	—	25	1	—	3
1963	—	—	1	1	16	10	—	—	3

Note: +   = increase
      −   = decrease
      T   = total
      MSL = Mitsubishi Shipbuilding, Ltd.
      SMHI = Shin Mitsubishi Heavy Industries, Ltd.
      MNHI = Mitsubishi Nippon Heavy Industries, Ltd.
Source: *Yuka shoken hokokusho* [*securities reports*] of each company.

Mizushima Engineering Works (Okayama), both former aircraft plants, along with the Kyoto Engineering Works, a former aircraft parts facility, and the Mihara Locomotive Works. The latter was permitted to carry on its former activities of rolling-stock production because of the importance of railway vehicles to the recovery of the post-war economy, but the aircraft plants were flatly forbidden by GHQ to engage in their former lines of business. The Nagoya Works responded at first by turning out pots and pans, followed by bus bodies and scooters, and later by agricultural and marine engines, industrial engines, and refrigeration equipment (Mitsubishi 1967*b*: 543). The Mizushima Works began producing small three-wheeled trucks, and this business was going well by the time MJHI was established (Mitsubishi 1967*b*: 601). The Kyoto Engineering Works, after initially building buses, began from the autumn of 1949 to concentrate on diesel engines for motor vehicles and on engine valves (Mitsubishi Motor 1993: 873–4). That is, the former aircraft plants became devoted to production associated with motor vehicles and machinery for civilian applications, and these businesses expanded along with the general recovery of the Japanese economy. However, because these products had to be sold directly to a large number of users, MJHI was required to set up a national sales network. This resulted in a large number of subsidiaries, as the company established sales companies and appointed regional sales agents (Mitsubishi Motor 1993: 195).

Not all of the subsidiaries were sales companies; other examples included manufacturers, service and installation organizations, and subcontractors for shipbuilding (Mitsubishi 1990: 393; Kobe Shipyard 1981: 231–40), but these were relatively few in number. Rather, the number of sales subsidiaries increased as the company expanded its range and output of products. The need for subsidiaries connected with the automotive and mechanical equipment businesses of SMHI (formerly MJHI) is in contrast to the lack of this need in relation to the shipbuilding and heavy equipment businesses. Just as MHI had felt little pressure to maintain subsidiaries before the 1934 merger, SMHI did not require subsidiaries in connection with these older product lines.

That being said, however, major changes in the business environment with regard to the shipbuilding and heavy equipment industries had occurred in the transition from the pre-war period to the post-war era. In shipbuilding in particular, the pre-war period had seen only domestic sales, whereas post-war expansion into international markets saw dramatic increases in the numbers of vessels being constructed (Chida and Davies 1990). This in turn required the shipbuilders to adopt systems that would allow large-scale production, leading to the utilization of large numbers of subcontractors. Still, the majority of the latter were very small firms that were assigned some part of the construction work within the shipyard of the larger company. The shipyards also used many subcontractors for the supply of processed materials, but precision requirements were not as high as for vehicles or aircraft, making barriers to entry rather low (Kaneko 1964: 504). These companies also tended to remain small, and there was no real need to make major purchases of their stock.

SMHI used large numbers of subcontractors at all of its facilities, with about 200 involved at the Kobe Shipyards in 1962 (Mitsubishi 1967*b*: 532) and 282 at the Nagoya Works (Mitsubishi 1967*b*: 553). The Mizushima Works, responsible mostly for vehicle production, also had many subcontractors, with 74 recorded in 1961 (Mitsubishi Motor, 1993, 713). In order to strengthen these many subcontractors, SMHI served as a guarantor for loans from financial institutions, provided direct financing itself, and also purchased subcontractors' shares. However, the total amount of these subcontractor-bound investments and financing arrangements for the five years from fiscal 1958 to fiscal 1963 came to a mere 10 per cent of SMHI's total loans and investments for fiscal 1958 (Mitsubishi 1967*b*: 271)—clearly not a very large figure. Whatever stockholdings SMHI maintained were not particularly significant.

As in the case of SMHI, which did form a group but which did not have many subsidiaries of note in the shipbuilding and heavy equipment fields, MSL (Mitsubishi Shipbuilding, Ltd., formerly WJHI) had almost no subsidiaries. MSL had concentrated on shipbuilding, and, while it did branch out later, it did not become as diversified as SMHI. Accordingly, it contented itself with a single subsidiary in the area of real estate and building maintenance (Mitsubishi Shipbuilding various years).

Meanwhile, it appears incongruous that SMHI had a large number of sales subsidiaries connected with its motor vehicle business, while MNHI (Mitsubishi Nippon Heavy Industries, formerly EJHI) had very few. The latter had been established with the Tokyo Engineering Works and the Kawasaki Engineering Works, along with a small shipyard and a few other factories that were later closed. The Tokyo Engineering Works, which had produced tanks during the war, redirected itself to the manufacture of bulldozers, tractors, etc. The Kawasaki Engineering Works, which had been engaged in the production of small military boat engines, was originally built just prior to the war for the assembly of buses and trucks (Shiba 1995). As soon as the war ended the facility immediately reverted to its original purpose of making buses and trucks. The Tokyo Engineering Works functioned for a time as a repair depot for US military vehicles, but this relationship proved only temporary. It then merged organizationally with the Kawasaki Works, and began production of dump trucks, tanks for the Japanese self-defence forces, and the like. MNHI also began making passenger automobiles and light trucks, and production expanded progressively. This raised the same issue as SMHI had experienced, namely that of a dealer network, but MNHI took a somewhat different approach. While SMHI built up its own dealer net-work, MNHI chose to split off its sales division altogether. Thus, in March 1950 MNHI bought 90 per cent of the stock of Fuso Motor Sales Ltd. (Fuso), which had been established previously by its bus and truck deal-ers. Subsequently, the dealer network subsidiaries comparable to those of SMHI were placed under the auspices of Fuso (Mitsubishi Motor 1993: 873). This resulted in the formation of a group of 'sub-subsidiaries', but, as before, the group was connected with motor vehicles and not with ship-building or heavy equipment.

Conclusion

In June 1964 the three fragments of the former MHI (MSL, SMHI, and MNHI) were reunited into a new Mitsubishi Heavy Industries Co., Ltd. (new MHI). The reason for the combination was concern over impending capital liberalization and the future competitiveness of Japanese firms in the heavy equipment industry, along with the fact that the three sister companies had advanced into essentially the same areas. It was rational, then, for their managers to seek to eliminate overlapping investment and R. & D. through the unification of the three. There was a strong feeling that the company, which had formerly been one, should be put back together, and the managers of other former Mitsubishi zaibatsu-derived companies also desired a strong heavy industries core company in the corporate com-plex that was then being reassembled (Mitsubishi 1990: 56). These factors worked in favour of the recombination.

As of the end of September 1964, there were only nineteen legal sub-sidiaries (control of 50 per cent or more) held by the new MHI (Mitsubishi 1964). This figure rises to fifty-five, however, when affiliated companies (defined here as those in which holdings are 25 per cent or more) are counted in (Mitsubishi 1990: 387). The scope of the current chapter has not allowed consideration of all the legal subsidiaries, but the majority of these were involved in vehicles, air conditioning and heating equipment, agri-cultural equipment, etc., and close examination of these companies would not affect the overall course of the discussion. From the late 1960s, how-ever, the number of legal subsidiaries began to rise substantially, reaching thirty-nine by the end of March 1975 (Mitsubishi 1976). Some former sub-sidiaries also disappeared during this period, indicating the formation of a large number of new subsidiaries. These new post-1964 subsidiaries can be roughly classified into three types: those formed in response to changes in the business environment or entry into new fields (e.g. the spin-off of Mitsubishi Motors Corp.), those resulting from joint ventures with over-seas companies (e.g. Caterpillar Mitsubishi Co., Ltd., which took over production of bulldozers, etc.), and those formed in order to undertake the managerial rescue of transaction partners.

The first of these major trends in the formation of subsidiaries, that of environmental change and the entry of new businesses, can be seen to be common in a certain sense to the three MHI fragment companies even before their recombination into the new MHI. Their entry into the fields of motor vehicles and industrial engines was responsible for the creation of a number of subsidiaries, and this can also be seen to have been the motivating factor in the formation of the old pre-war and wartime MHI group.

In summary, the former structure of a federation among relatively independent, self-sufficient entities did not require the formation of subsidiaries as an organizational necessity. What created the need for subsidiaries, then, was entry into new fields that could not be properly addressed by existing structures.

NOTES

1. The largest Japanese manufacturing company at this time was Japan Steel, which had been formed in the same year as MHI through the merger of a state-run steel mill and five private steel companies, and which had total assets of approximately 440 million yen. The next largest company was Oji Paper with assets of about 320 million yen, followed by Nippon Chisso, a chemical producer with assets of over 150 million yen. However, Nippon Chisso, as related by Prof. Shimotani, was also a holding company with shares in many affiliates. With this point taken into consideration, MHI was effectively the third largest manufacturer (Showa 1935).
2. References to 'Mitsubishi' are keyed to Mitsubishi Heavy Industries, Co., Ltd. in the References.

BIBLIOGRAPHY

Chida, Tomohei, and Davies, Peter N., (1990), *The Japanese Shipping and Shipbuilding Industries: A History of their Modern Growth*, London.

East Japan Heavy Industries Co., Ltd. (1950), *Yuka shoken hokoku-sho* [*Securities Report*] for the first half of fiscal 1950, Tokyo, Ministry of Finance.

—— (1951), *Yuka shoken hokoku-sho* [*Securities Report*] for the second half of fiscal 1950, Tokyo: Ministry of Finance.

Echigo, Kazunori (1956), *Nihon zosen kogyoron* [*The Shipbuilding Industry in Japan*], Tokyo.

Fujita, Nobuhisa (1985), 'Keiei senryaku no tenkai: Nihon o chushin to shite' ['The Development of Business Strategies in Japan'], in Ryukoku Daigaku

Keieigakubu Shuppan Iinkai [Ryukoku University Department of Business Administration Publishing Committee] (ed.), *Gendai kigyo keieiron* [*Modern Business Management*], Tokyo.

Koyata Iwasaki Den Hensan Iinkai [The Editorial Committee for the Biography of Koyata Iwasaki] (ed.) (1957), *Iwasaki Koyata Den* [*A Biography of Koyata Iwasaki*], Tokyo.

Kaneko, Eiichi (ed.) (1964), *Gendai Nihon sangyo hatten-shi, ix Zosen* [*History of the Development of Modern Japanese Industries, ix: Shipbuilding*], Tokyo.

Kobe Shipyard of Mitsubishi Heavy Industries Co., Ltd. (ed.) (1981), *Mitsubishi Kobe Zosensho 75 nen-shi* [*A 75-Year History of the Mitsubishi Kobe Shipyard*], Kobe.

Kyu-nainen-kai [Association of Members of the Department of Internal Combustion Engines] (ed.) (1969), *Kobe Mitsubishi Nainenki 53 nen-shi* [*53-Year History of the Kobe Shipyards Department of Internal Combustion Engines*], Kobe.

Mid-Japan Heavy Industries Co., Ltd. (1951), *Yuka shoken hokoku-sho* [*Securities Report*] for the second half of fiscal 1950, Tokyo, Ministry of Finance.

Mishima, Yasuo (ed.((1981), *Nihon zaibatsu keieishi: Mitsubishi zaibatsu* [*Business History of Japanese Zaibatsu: Mitsubishi Zaibatsu*], Tokyo.

—— (1989), *The Mitsubishi: Its Challenge and Strategy*, Greenwich.

Mitsubishi Heavy Industries Co., Ltd. (n.d.), *Report to the General Headquarters for the Allied Powers from Mitsubishi Heavy Industries Co., Ltd.* (Supreme Commander for the Allied Powers, Economic and Science Section, Zaibatsu Corporation File), Tokyo.

—— (ed.) (1956), *Mitsubishi Jukogyo Kabushiki Kaisha-shi* [*A History of Mitsubishi Heavy Industries Co., Ltd.*], Tokyo.

—— (1964), *Yuka shoken hokoku-sho* [*Securities Report*] for the first half of fiscal 1964, Tokyo: Ministry of Finance.

—— (ed.) (1967a), *Mitsubishi Zosen Kabushiki Kaisha-shi* [*A History of Mitsubishi Shipbuilding, Ltd.*], Tokyo.

—— (ed.) (1967b), *Shin Mitsubishi Jukogyo Kabushiki Kaisha-shi* [*A History of New Mitsubishi Heavy Industries, Ltd.*), Tokyo.

—— (1976), *Yuka shoken hokoku-sho* [*Securities Report*] for fiscal 1975, Tokyo: Ministry of Finance.

—— (ed.) (1990), *Umi ni sora ni, soshite uchu he: zoku Mitsubishi Jukogyo Kabushiki Kaisha-shi 1964–1989* [*To the Sea, to the Sky, and to Space: A History of Mitsubishi Heavy Industries Co., Ltd., ii: 1964 to 1989*], Tokyo.

Mitsubishi Motor Corporation (ed.) (1993), *Mitsubishi Jidosha Kogyo Kabushiki Kaisha-shi* [*A History of Mitsubishi Motor Corporation*], Tokyo.

Mitsubishi Shipbuilding Co., Ltd. (various years), *Yuka shoken hokoku-sho* [*Securities Reports*], Tokyo, Ministry of Finance.

Miwa, Ryouichi (1989), 'Sengo minshuka to keizai saiken' ['Post-war Democratization of Japan and Economic Reconstruction'], in Takafusa Nakamura (ed.), '*Keikaku ka' to 'minshu ka'* ['*Planning*' and '*Democratization*'], Tokyo.

Mochikabu Kaisha Seiri Iinkai [Holding Company Liquidation Committee], (ed.) (1951), *Nihon zaibatsu to sono kaitai* [*Japanese Zaibatsu and their Liquidation*], Tokyo.

Morikawa, Hidemasa (1992), *Zaibatsu: The Rise and Fall of the Family Enterprise Group in Japan*, Tokyo.

Nakagawa, Keiichiro, Morikawa, Hidemasa, and Yui, Tsunehiko (eds.) (1981), *Kindai Nihon keieishi no kiso chishiki* [*Introduction to the Business History of Modern Japan*], Tokyo: Yuhikaku.

Nishinarita, Yutaka (1978), 'Nichiro senso-go ni okeru zaibatsu zosen kigyo no keiei kozo to roshi-kankei: Mitsubishi Zosen no baai' ['Managerial Structure and Industrial Relations in Zaibatsu Shipbuilding Firms Following the Russo-Japanese War: The Case of Mitsubishi Shipyards'] (No. 1), *Ryukoku daigaku keizai-keiei-ronshu* [*Journal of Economic and Business Studies of Ryukoku University*], 18/3.

—— (1980), 'Dai-ichji senso-ki ni okeru Mitsubishi Zaibatsu no zosen-gyo: Mitsubishi Zosen no baai' ['The Shipbuilding of Mitsubishi Zaibatsu in the First World War'] (No. 1), *Ryukoku daigaku keizai-keiei-ronshu* [*Journal of Economic and Business Studies of Ryukoku University*], 19/4.

Pollard, Sydney, and Robertson, Paul (1979), *The British Shipbuilding Industry: 1870–1914*, Cambridge.

Shiba, Takao (1986), 'Senji taiseiki ni okeru zaibatsukei jukogyo kigyo no kabushiki shoyu no kozo: Mitsubishi Jukogyo Kabushiki Kaisha no baai' ['The Character of Stock Investment by Mitsubishi Heavy Industries, Ltd. during the Second World War'), *Osaka Daigaku Keizaigaku* [*Osaka University Economic Review*], 35/4.

—— (1987), 'Sensha seisan no hensen' ['A History of Tank Production'], in Yasuo Mishima *et al.*, *Dai Niji Taisen to Mitsubishi Zaibatsu* [*Mitsubishi Zaibatsu during the Second World War*], Tokyo.

—— (1994), 'Business Activities of Japanese Manufacturing Industries during World War II', in Jun Sakudo and Takao Shiba (eds.), *World War II and the Transformation of Business Systems*, Tokyo.

—— (1995), 'Mitsubishi's Pre-war Motor Vehicle Manufacturing Business', *KSU Economic and Business Review*, 21.

Shimotani, Masahiro (1991), 'Corporate Groups and Keiretsu in Japan', *Japanese Yearbook on Business History*.

Showa 10 nendo kabushiki nenkan [*1935 Stock Yearbook*] (1935), Tokyo.

West Japan Heavy Industries Co., Ltd. (1951), *Yuka shoken hokoku-sho* [*Securities Report*] for the second half of fiscal 1950, Tokyo: Ministry of Finance.

PART III

ASSEMBLER–SUPPLIER RELATIONS

8

'Japanese-Style' Supplier Relationships in the American Auto Industry, 1895–1920

SUSAN HELPER AND DAVID HOCHFELDER

In recent years, US automakers have moved toward closer relationships with their suppliers. In particular, Ford and Chrysler have moved away from historically adversarial dealings with suppliers toward relationships which are long-term and are characterized by rich flows of information for joint projects such as product development and technical assistance.

This transformation has been seen by the popular press and by the managers making this change as an imitation of the Japanese, and as a move away from traditional American practice. However, evidence indicates that many of the features of these so-called 'Japanese-style' customer–supplier relationships were present in the US auto industry before 1920.

This chapter traces the evolution of supplier relations in three successive stages: fast market growth and segmentation in the auto industry before 1908, mass production and vertical integration between 1909 and 1920, and consolidation from the early 1920s to the late 1930s. We argue that suppliers enjoyed close and co-operative ties with automakers before 1908, while their relationships grew increasingly adversarial between 1909 and 1920. This transitional period proved decisive in changing supplier relations, and subsequently industry consolidation cemented these patterns into place for decades to come.

The US auto industry turned out just over 60,000 vehicles in 1908; by 1920 output topped the 2 million mark.[1] This remarkable growth paralleled the Japanese vehicle industry in the 1950s and 1960s, when production leaped from 68,000 in 1955 to over 7 million in 1973. Both US and Japanese automakers in these periods acted to protect their supplier networks to ensure low prices and continued access to sorely needed parts.[2]

The authors wish to thank John Grabowski of the Western Reserve Historical Society for his invaluable help with manuscript sources and Ken Hirano for his incisive comments on an earlier draft of this chapter.

But they did so in different ways. American automakers after 1909 moved away from co-operative ties, choosing a combination of vertical integration and arm's-length relationships with outside suppliers. On the other hand, Japanese automakers in the 1950s and 1960s 'quasi-internalized' their suppliers, drawing them into their keiretsu groups in which specialized parts firms enjoyed semi-exclusive, long-term commitments from the parent assemblers.[3]

This essay concludes with an explanation for the divergent paths taken by the American and Japanese industries. By doing so we aim to illuminate the differences between business groups in the two countries and to add to the growing literature on comparative business structures.[4]

Rising Demand and Market Differentiation: The US Auto Industry to 1908

Pioneering American builders turned out about 300 automobiles between 1886 and 1898, nearly all of an experimental nature. Just before the turn of the century, demand for automobiles grew and makers increasingly standardized their designs and outsourced more parts. Suppliers with experience in mass-producing vehicle components sought to enter this expanding new market. Bicycle parts makers offered items like bolts and small forgings, and carriage suppliers modified their lamps and bearings to fit the automobile. These companies began marketing to the new industry in 1898 an 1899. In those years, many of the pioneering parts suppliers sprang up in the Northeast, the first centre of the American automobile industry. These firms included Boston's Gray & Davis Co., which made automobile lamps starting in 1897; Utica's Weston-Mott Co., which shifted from bicycle wheels to motor car wheels in 1898; and Newark's Hyatt Roller Bearing Co., which sold its first automobile bearings to the pioneering firm of Haynes-Apperson in 1899.[5] Locomobile of Newton, Massachusetts, an industry leader in steam vehicles, moved to secure its sources of supply as early as 1899. At the end of that year the firm expanded into the plant of a failed competitor and bought out its supplier of drop forgings. It also contracted with a maker of steam boiler regulators to 'furnish engines to the full of the capacity of that concern. All of these plants are being operated at full tilt and . . . the Newton factory would eventually be used for assembling only.'[6]

Locomobile's early efforts to secure its sources of supply showed the growing importance of a supplier base for the new industry as it moved from experimentation to commercial production. As it did, makers found it more economical to turn to outside suppliers for many parts they had formerly made themselves. Over the next several years, the parts industry grew in sophistication and supplied automakers with everything from bolts to complete chassis. Seventeen automakers (5 making gasoline-powered cars, 4 turning out steam-powered machines, and 8 producing electric vehicles) exhibited at the first national auto show held in Chicago in early 1901, but 24 parts makers and 4 parts jobbers displayed everything from headlights and batteries to transmissions and complete running gears.'[7]

Demand for automobiles increased steadily after the turn of the century. About two dozen makers produced just over 4,000 automobiles in 1900. In 1908, about 150 companies sold 65,000 passenger cars, ranging in price from $650 to over $5,000.[8] Over the course of these nine years the automobile market mushroomed in volume and number of manufacturers and segmented according to price.

The development of the low-priced runabout, a rugged and dependable car selling for hundreds, instead of thousands, of dollars, placed the automobile within reach of many more consumers. When Henry Ford announced his plans for his Model N runabout, forerunner to the Model T, in the trade press in early 1906, he was one of the few makers who foresaw the enormous demand for a 'light, low-priced car with an up-to-date engine of sample horsepower . . . one where a chauffeur will not be absolutely necessary either as a driver or because of his mechanical skill'.[9] Ford was hugely successful and the Model T remained the best-selling car in the world until the mid-1920s.

Few car builders agreed with Ford. Most held that 'prices should be maintained' in order to take full advantage of the period's exploding demand, and they regarded the production of a low-priced car for the mass market as 'unjustifiable and suicidal', as Ford characterized their views.[10] As Fig. 8.1 shows, in 1903 about 75 per cent of the cars on the market sold for under $1,375, with about 45 per cent in the $875 to $1,375 range. As demand increased after 1903, many builders abandoned the low-priced segment of the market and targeted their products to those who could afford a distinctive and luxurious car. By 1907, sales of cars costing under $1,375 plummeted to less than 40 per cent of the market; conversely, builders such as Winton who marketed exclusively to the wealthy and charged over $2,775 for their vehicles accounted for about a quarter of sales.[11] By way of comparison, the typical non-farm labourer of 1904 brought home $540 for the year, and the average physician of this time earned between $1,000 and $1,500.[12] For all except the well-to-do, an automobile represented a large expenditure relative to income.

This market structure helped to shape relations between makers and suppliers. Most builders of low- and mid-priced vehicles assembled their products out of equipment bought from suppliers, while builders in the luxury market fabricated most of their components themselves. A typical mid-priced car contained an outsourced motor, transmission, carburetor,

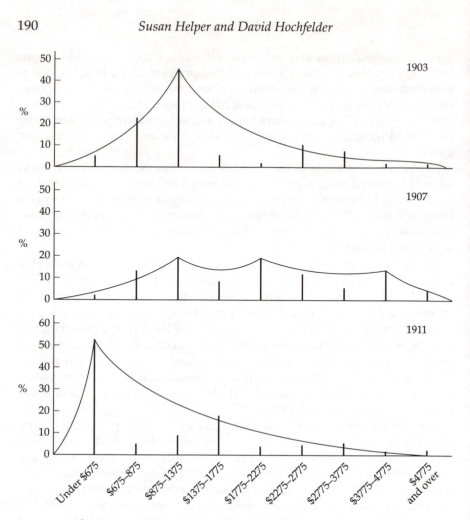

Source: Ralph Epstein, *The Automobile Industry* (Chicago: A. W. Shaw Co., 1928), 100.

Fig. 8.1. *Percentage of unit volume versus price class for cars 1903, 1907, and 1911.*

electrical system, and axles. Many manufacturers, like the short-lived Daisy Automobile Co. of Flint, Michigan, merely placed a body onto an outsourced chassis. In the summer of 1902 that firm announced its plans to build its first 100 cars, 'a standard machine in all respects'. The firm's founders resolved 'not to waste time or money in experimental work . . . While the body design will be somewhat original in many respects, the remainder of the parts will be secured from makers of standard parts, all of which can be assembled without delay.'[13] Even Henry Ford began business that following year in much the same fashion, with only $28,000 in capital. The Dodge brothers, owners of a local machine shop, supplied him with completed chassis to which he merely added bodies, wheels, and tyres.[14] Ford, unlike Daisy, designed much of the chassis which the Dodges fabricated for him.

The Daisy Automobile Co., Henry Ford, and dozens of other low- and mid-priced builders thus relied heavily on an expanding supplier base during their critical early years. Assemblers like Daisy who did not want to expend much engineering effort bought major components from suppliers like the Lindsay Automobile Parts Co. That Indianapolis supplier of transmissions, motors, and running gears[15] took out full-page advertisements in the 1902 and 1903 trade press, boldly asking car builders: 'DID IT EVER OCCUR TO YOU that you can save both time and money by getting our complete running gear . . . ? DON'T WASTE YOUR TIME trying to build gasoline motors, when you can get them from us for less money than you can make them yourself.' The firm also offered to equip their running gears with bodies, requiring the car maker only to label and sell the completed vehicle.[16] Figs. 8.2, 8.3, and 8.4 show advertisements from suppliers of that era.

Other firms repeated Lindsay's sales pitch. Andrew Lee Dyke, owner of the Auto Supply Co., was an automobile pioneer who built St Louis's first car in 1898, and who authored a popular series of repair manuals during the first two decades of the century. He abandoned car building in 1899 and foresaw 'that the automobile supply business would become a distinct branch' of the industry. Although 'there was at the time but a small demand' for auto parts, he was the 'first in America' to dedicate his firm solely to supplying the emerging industry. Dyke, like Lindsay, produced complete running gears, 'and from the way orders are being received it is safe to assume that there will be a hundred or two new automobiles in the country that were never inside a factory other than Dyke's'. The Neustadt-Perry Co. of St Louis conducted a similar business and marketed 'designs of steam and gasoline carriages for which it makes complete sets of parts. . . . The company will furnish the buyer with assembling blueprints.'[17] In the first years of the century, the prospective automobile builder needed only to purchase completed cars from Lindsay or Dyke, or kits from Neustadt-Perry. Few builders went to that extreme, but the option nevertheless existed.

The activities of Lindsay, Dyke, and Neustadt-Perry revealed the porous boundary between supplier and assembler. These firms were a bit of both, since they sold completed cars and kits but did not market the vehicles themselves. Other early entrepreneurs moved freely across this boundary. George Holley, for instance, gained a 'considerable reputation' with his one-cylinder car, the Holley Motorette. But he gave up auto building to focus on carburation, one of the critical design problems in early gasoline engines, and he became a leading manufacturer of carburetors by 1905. In 1902 Henry Leland made technical improvements in the engine which he supplied to the Olds Motor Works, boosting its output to 10.25

DID IT

EVER OCCUR TO YOU

that you can save both time and money by getting our complete running gear for Gasoline or Electric Automobiles with chain drive?

WE MAKE GEARS.

WE DO GEAR CUTTING.

Lindsay's Rear Axle, for Gasoline or Electric Automobiles with Chain Drive.

ANOTHER THING

we would like to call your attention to, is the fact that we make a running gear for Electric Automobiles with SPECIAL REAR AXLE to which the motor may be directly attached.

THINK IT OVER!

DON'T WASTE YOUR TIME

trying to build gasoline motors, when you can get them from us for less money than you can make them yourself.

WE GUARANTEE THEM, TOO!

5 H. P. GASOLINE MOTOR.

Lindsay Automobile Parts Co.

INDIANAPOLIS, ... INDIANA

Source: *Motor Age* (8 Jan. 1903), 29.

Fig. 8.2. *Advertisement for Lindsay running gears, motors, and axles for electric automobiles.*

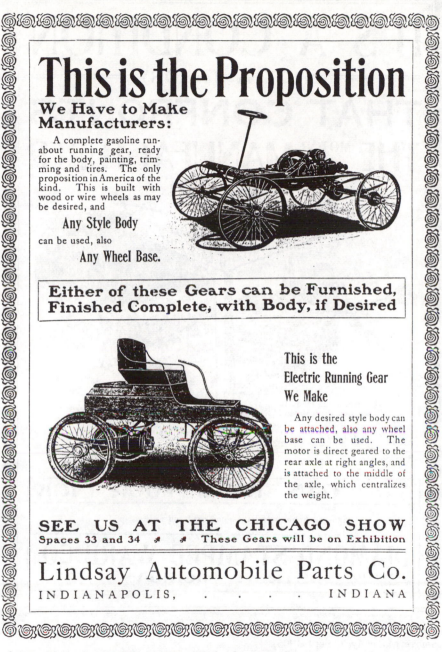

Source: Motor Age (12 Feb. 1903), inside back cover.

Fig. 8.3. *Advertisement for Lindsay running gears and completed cars.*

Source: Motor Age (7 Sept. 1905).

Fig. 8.4. *Advertisement warning automobile assemblers of the dangers of placing late parts orders.*

horsepower. Ransom Olds refused to accept the more powerful engine because it would have required radical changes in his car's design, thus prompting Leland to go into the automobile business for himself. Leland's Cadillac, the first mass-produced car with truly interchangeable parts, won fame for its excellent design and solid construction.[18]

These early suppliers experienced two forms of competition. On the one hand they competed with rival parts firms for orders from many low- and mid-priced builders who outsourced major components. In this case, parts makers sold what Takahiro Fujimoto has termed 'supplier proprietary parts', components for which the supplier carried out almost all of the design, development, and manufacturing.[19] As the experiences of George Holley and Henry Leland made clear, suppliers of this sort were important sources of innovation in the early industry. Parts makers and auto builders probably shared little engineering information, co-operating only as required to fit the components into the completed vehicle. It seems likely that Henry Leland and Ransom Olds maintained this type of relationship and failed to discuss key engineering issues. A closer collaboration between the two men might have led Leland to keep in mind the limitation of the Oldsmobile's construction as he designed his improved engine; alternatively, Olds might have engineered his car with an eye toward future improvements.

Suppliers also competed with builders, usually high-priced luxury automakers, who often manufactured their own components. To secure business from firms like Cleveland's Winton Motor Carriage Co., parts makers needed to convince them to buy their parts instead. In this case, suppliers provided that Fujimoto has called 'black box parts', components for which suppliers and assemblers shared many aspects of their design and development.[20] Typically, the assembler was responsible for basic design parameters such as cost–performance trade-offs and the integration of the part into the overall vehicle design. The supplier in turn designed the component to meet the automaker's general requirements. Such collaboration required a rich flow of technical information and capital between parts maker and auto builder. Winton maintained this kind of relationship with the Cleveland Cap Screw Company, the forerunner of TRW Inc. Alexander Winton, like most other car makers at the turn of the century, experienced difficulty in obtaining a valve which functioned effectively. As Frederick C. Crawford, a later president of TRW, reminisced fifty years later, Winton 'had great trouble making valves. . . . [T]he poppet valve is a lump on top of a stem. He screwed them on, and he riveted them on, and he cut them out of steel, but they didn't work.'[21] In 1903 Charles Thompson, an engineer at Cleveland Cap Screw who later became president, invented an automobile valve in which a nickel-steel head was electrically welded to a carbon-steel stem. This production method resulted in a low-cost, high-performance, and reliable valve. Alexander

Winton became the firm's first valve customer. Cleveland Cap Screw at this time lacked the machinery to produce all of the valves that Winton required, so Winton invested $25,000 to buy the machinery necessary to get his orders produced. Convinced of the success of the valve design and anxious to protect this vital source of supply, Winton secured majority ownership of Cleveland Cap Screw and became its president.

Fujimoto has identified a third type of component, 'detail-controlled parts', parts for which the automaker retained responsibility for the part's entire design. In this case, the assembler treated suppliers 'as nothing more than providers of production capacity', hiring them to produce components to detailed design drawings and manufacturing specifications.[22] Little evidence of this type of component can be found from the first decade of commercial automobile production. Design drawings in this period probably required some interpretation and communication, and suppliers and assemblers often collaborated during the design and fabrication of important components.

Assemblers had relatively little power over their suppliers, especially during boom years and for components which required a measure of manufacturing skill. This arose from the fact that automobile parts orders accounted for a small proportion of business for most forges, foundries, and machine shops. In 1903, for instance, several builders in the growing auto city of Toledo, Ohio faced the threat of production holdups due to delays in obtaining crucial forgings. Low-volume automakers who placed small orders waited as long as sixty days for their shipments. The editor of *Motor Age* lamented, 'The forge plants, busy with great orders for heavy work, turn a deaf ear to the demands of the automobile maker. Only such people as Olds and Winton, ordering from 800 to 3000 pieces from a single die, are worth catering to.' He found that Toledo factories 'ready to ship dozens of vehicles are unable to ship one. With about 300 parts to be incorporated the maker believes himself practically ready when he discovers that part 236 is missing.' Such dependence upon tardy suppliers was not just 'exasperating', but threatened the solvency of many builders as well. 'Customers must wait. Capital must remain tied up. Profits must decrease—perhaps to be totally absorbed.' The editor advised 'the prospective manufacturer . . . to inquire carefully' into these 'troubles experienced every day' by automobile builders.[23]

Automakers of this period depended upon their suppliers for more than just timely deliveries. Parts firms also provided vital financial support to many makers during their critical start-up years. Indeed, the majority of assemblers owed their survival to the supplier infrastructure. Lawrence Seltzer, an early historian of the industry, noted that parts makers assumed much of the fixed and working capital burdens in this period. Most makers entered the automobile business with little investment in fixed plant. Because they relied upon 'the previous development . . . of standardized interchangeable parts manufacture', all many automobile makers needed to do was 'the assembling of the major components and the sale of the completed vehicle'. In short, the prospective automaker 'required neither large plant nor elaborate equipment' as 'specialized automobile factories . . . were not essential' for quantity production.[24] Most companies began business in rented quarters and with little specialized machinery.

Parts makers eased much of the working capital costs of the early automobile firms as well. Parts firms extended thirty- to ninety-day credit on orders, a much longer time than that required to assemble and sell the finished car. At the same time, most car builders required their dealers to advance cash deposits when placing orders and to pay in full upon delivery.[25] Many suppliers also accepted stock for payment in lieu of cash. Thompson Products, the prominent maker of valves in this period, made it 'common practice . . . to accept a customer's stock or other securities in liquidation of a delinquent account'.[26]

Low entry barriers—minimal technical expertise, few fixed plant requirements, and favourable credit agreements—coupled with exploding demand, allowed over one hundred automakers to enter the industry by 1908. However, many of these firms were undercapitalized and unable to ride out economic downturns. Those auto companies which existed on 'the thinnest of equities' failed during the depression of 1907; these failures only increased the 'hostile conservatism' of bankers and shrank the credit they extended to the rest of the industry.[27] Looking back on 1907 and 1908, automobile pioneer Benjamin Briscoe recalled that easy entry into the industry encouraged 'manufacturing gamblers', speculators who 'had adopted methods that were described as "plunging" ', to try their hand at automaking. These 'piratical . . . "skimmers" . . . did not have a worthy car or any manufacturing ability', but succeeded at selling large amounts of watered stock with very little to back it. Briscoe acknowledged the pivotal role that parts suppliers had played in the auto industry's early years, but he also blamed them for bringing a 'great deal of discredit upon the industry' by 'encouraging into the business undercapitalized concerns and inexperienced makers'.[28]

Briscoe's depiction of such 'plungers' and 'skimmers' applied to many firms selling in the lower and middle segments of the price spectrum; that is, those producers able to enter the market with little capital or technical ability. Luxury makers, on the other hand, assured prospective buyers of their financial stability and conservative management practices while proudly proclaiming their vehicle's technical superiority over lower-priced cars. Producing distinctive, individualized autos with craftsman-like care, they asserted that assembling from outsourced components detracted from a vehicle's uniqueness and quality. A 1904 advertising brochure for Winton automobiles, for instance, took the prospective buyer

on a mental tour of the factory floor to underscore the care and workmanship that went into every component. This account impressed upon the
buyer that Winton made everything from its rough castings to its sump-
tuous upholstery, and it concluded by noting the patient care which went
into the 30 to 36 labour hours of final assembly.[29] In a promotional piece
from 1908, Alexander Winton said, 'I believe that every maker ought to be
personally responsible for the cars that leave his factory, and it gives me
pleasure to assume that responsibility for Winton cars, because I know to
the minutest detail of what they are made, and how they are made.'[30]

These pronouncements were a little exaggerated. As his relationship
with Cleveland Cap Screw showed, Winton bought many parts from 'specialists', but only those 'in which he has absolute confidence'.[31] In addition
to buying all of his valves from Cleveland Cap Screw, Winton gave a
Cleveland supplier of drop forgings a sole-source contract for 16,000 con-
necting rod ends and turn buckles in 1903.[32] The company's 1906 Model K
used Holley carburettors, but returned to an in-house design a year later.[33]
Winton selected suppliers with great care, and subjected their components
to severe engineering and road tests before placing orders.[34]

No automaker, then, was entirely self-sufficient: behind each stood a
network of suppliers which provided components, technical innovations,
and financial support. As consumer demand for automobiles grew, many
automakers moved to safeguard their sources of supply. By 1909, two
strategies emerged: (1) vertical integration, the acquisition of independent
parts makers or the expansion of in-house components production; and (2)
reducing dependence on specific suppliers by promoting standardization.

Mass Production and Vertical Integration: 1909–1920

In many ways the automobile industry came of age in 1909. That year's
sales of 128,000 passenger cars were twice those of 1980. Until 1920 annual
sales increased 30 per cent or more, nearly doubling again in 1912 and
1916. In 1917 automobile production reached about 1,750,000 cars despite
America's involvement in the First World War and the shift to war production.[35] The year 1909, and the few months bracketing it, witnessed
major reorganizations which soon led to the consolidation of market
power in the hands of a few automakers, especially Ford and General
Motors. Within the next ten years those two companies accounted respectively for one-half and one-fifth of production volume.

These trends—exploding consumer demand and centralization of final
market power—affected relations between automakers and suppliers in
two important ways. First, automobile producers did not compete with
each other so much for sales—there was enough consumer demand to go

around—as for raw materials and components, chronically in short supply during this period. Second, the high-volume producers began using their strong market positions, first to protect their sources of supply and then to gain the upper hand in their dealings with suppliers. By 1920 the major automakers had created a fiercely competitive parts industry which was largely at their mercy.

Alfred Sloan recalled the common worry among automakers during his years as president of Hyatt Roller Bearing, that 'lack of one tiny part might hold up [an] assembly line. That fear was the nightmare of the business.'[36] Builders who assembled their cars from outsourced components encountered such hold-ups more often than vertically integrated makers. Shortages of raw materials like steel were equally serious problems, especially after 1915, when American industry geared up for war production. The auto industry was unable to secure steel shipments while railways, construction companies, and munitions plants which placed much larger orders got timely deliveries. Because parts makers consumed relatively small amounts of steel, they were forced to pay higher prices and to wait longer for deliveries than most other steel consumers. Many suppliers passed on these higher prices and longer lead times to their customers. As a result, an assembled car of this period cost about 20 per cent more than a manufactured car of comparable quality and design.[37]

Because of these difficulties in obtaining components and steel, the larger assemblers who could afford the fixed and working capital burdens began to produce more of their parts themselves. There existed two paths to vertical integration: expansion of the home factory, and the acquisition of independent parts makers. Henry Ford chose the first and William Durant chose the second alternative.

Late in 1908 Henry Ford unveiled his plans for his famous Model T. He sold over 10,000 of them in 1909, making him the largest automobile producer in the world. The economic and technological imperatives of 'Fordism' necessitated centralized control over all phases of manufacturing, assembling, and selling. This strategy was enormously successful for about two decades, giving Ford undisputed dominance in the low-priced market segment and making him the world's largest automobile producer. The production and marketing inflexibilities of Ford's policy became apparent only in the mid-1920s under pressure from more diversified makers like General Motors.

The reason usually given for Ford's vertical integration was his desire to attain greater economies of scale and scope, and so to reduce manufacturing costs. The logic of mass production of interchangeable parts required specialized machinery and a regimented division of labour. Ford extended such regimentation to his suppliers, 'most of whom came to make a single component of the product'. Many suppliers moved to Detroit to devote themselves exclusively to the growing automaker. Because many parts makers depended upon Ford orders for the bulk of their business, the company regarded them almost as wholly owned subsidiaries. Ford 'purchased materials for its components-makers, reorganized their manufacturing processes, supervised their larger policies, and, in some cases, aided them in financing production'. From its opening in 1909, the River Rouge plant was so dependent upon . . . its specialized suppliers that its own operations were frequently within thirty minutes of suspension because of tardy deliveries of parts or materials'.[38]

The John R. Keim Mills of Buffalo, New York was one such supplier. Since 1908, Keim had been Ford's major supplier of pressed steel parts for the body and chassis of the Model T. By 1910, when Ford bought out the works, the automaker had largely quasi-internalized Keim. Ford not only sent production specialists to Buffalo to assist with mass-production techniques, but also invested heavily in machinery necessary to produce Ford's orders. The companies jointly developed a method for making pressed steel axle housings and crankcases. According to historian John B. Rae, by 1910 the automaker 'was so deeply involved' in the Keim organization 'that it was simpler to buy the organization outright' instead of financing its further expansion to meet Ford's orders.[39] Ford secured the plant for $570,000, 'a bargain with or without the Keim Mills and their machinery', since he acquired the management expertise of William Knudsen, who went on to direct the expansion of Ford's assembly-line methods; W. H. Smith, an expert in deploying machine tools for mass production; and John R. Lee, later the head of the notorious sociological department.[40] After a strike in 1912, Ford moved to assure his supply of these important components. He moved the machinery and key managers to Detroit and integrated them into his plant's daily operations; he left the troublesome work-force back in Buffalo.

When Ford opened its new Highland Park plant in 1914, the company moved to bring almost all components production in-house. Writing in the late 1920s, the economist Lawrence Seltzer found that this vertical integration was a gradual process, 'for the Company needed the resources of its suppliers to sustain the volume of its output'. Ford slowly took over components production 'because parts-manufacture was so lucrative, and because supervision of independent concerns under the purchase system proved difficult'. Ford understood the logic and techniques of mass production, and ploughed his profits into specialized tooling and material handling equipment. The cost savings which resulted from Ford's strategy were impressive, and the components which Ford took in-house ranged from bolts to transmissions formerly provided by the Dodge brothers.[41] Historian John Rae has also claimed that Henry Ford sought self-sufficiency 'partly because he believed it made for greater economy and efficiency but also partly because he just disliked being dependent on anyone else'.[42]

At about the same time that Henry Ford introduced the Model T, William C. Durant was consolidating several automobile builders and parts firms into the General Motors Company. He pursued a different route to vertical integration, that of decentralized divisions run as separate profit centres. Under this arrangement, General Motors produced several lines of cars and owned many captive parts subsidiaries.

While Ford retained tight control over all phases of his far-flung operations, Durant envisioned General Motors as a loosely bound collection of auto companies and supporting parts firms.[43] Whereas Ford sought to mass-produce only one model and to increase sales by reducing price, Durant hedged his bets by acquiring companies with radically different designs. He recalled, 'I was for getting every kind of car in sight, playing safe all along the line.'[44] GM's organization chart reflected Durant's shotgun approach; by 1910, the company owned a controlling interest in twelve automobile manufacturers and about a dozen parts firms.

Durant saw the importance of acquiring parts subsidiaries because GM's automobile divisions assembled their vehicles and depended to a great extent upon their outside suppliers. He was well aware of the industry's chronic difficulties in obtaining components and steel, and he felt it imperative to safeguard important sources of supply in this business climate. The parts firms he acquired made components such as axles, transmissions, engines, bodies, ignition systems, lamps, and rims.[45]

By late 1910 Durant's programme of aggressive expansion had overextended the financial resources of the company. General Motors owed banks about $2,700,000 and other creditors between $4 million, and $5 million. In November a banking syndicate gained control of GM, promising 'a reorganization of the management', and removed Durant from all decision-making; 'a restriction of enthusiasm', ceasing all acquisitions of the sort which had led to this crisis.[46] Shunted aside at GM, Durant obtained control of the newly formed Chevrolet Motor Company in 1913. Chevrolet was instantly successful and sold nearly 16,000 vehicles in its first two years. Durant took his share of the profits and began buying General Motors stock in early 1915. By late autumn, he and his allies owned enough stock to regain control. He once again embarked on a policy of expansion, forming in May 1916 the United Motors Corporation as a wholly owned parts subsidiary of GM. Durant saw United Motors partly as a good investment but mainly as a way to ensure GM's sources of supply. As with the parts companies which Durant had bought when he was president of GM before 1910, the nine subsidiaries which made up United Motors produced components which were not widely available on the arm's-length market: ignition and lighting systems, ball and roller bearings, horns, differential gears, radiators, wire wheels, and demountable rims.

While Ford and General Motors dominated the low- and mid-priced markets between 1909 and 1920, room remained for dozens of smaller firms. Smaller makers experienced the same pressures on their supply bases, but they were forced to pursue different strategies. Each maker's market position—its production volume and its price class—helped shape its dealings with suppliers.

Luxury builders like Winton also were heavily integrated, but for a different reason. While the mass producers needed assured sources of supply to prevent production hold-ups, luxury producers made their own parts because they marketed their cars as unique and distinctive. In 1913 Alexander Winton claimed that he could 'easily quadruple' his output by reducing the price of his six-cylinder model from $3,250 to $2,500. But he chose not to, since 'it would be necessary for us to cut down quality, to skimp on workmanship, or, worse still, to assemble parts from other factories, instead of *building the car ourselves*. . . . Winton Six merit is individual and exclusive.'[47] In another advertisement Winton boldly announced that 'the production of automobiles by the assembling method is basically wrong . . . [T]he assembler is controlled by the parts maker; the principal is ruled by the subordinate. . . . [T]he assembler is a parts manufacturer's selling agent, a mere middleman, an economic intruder.'[48]

Winton's pronouncements led potential customers to believe that he fabricated almost everything entering into his car. While he did produce the majority of his components, he still relied on a supplier network for items like bearings, axles, carburettors, and ignition and lighting systems. Perhaps the key difference between Winton and mid-priced assemblers was the care he took in choosing his components and the firms supplying them. The firm's engineering records between 1910 and 1914 show that Winton engineers put prospective components through a battery of harsh tests in the shop and on the road, tests in which the supplier's chief engineer often participated. In May and June 1914 Winton personnel subjected a Delco lighting and ignition unit to three weeks of factory and road tests, culminating in a three-day road test between the Delco plant in Dayton, Ohio and the Winton factory in Cleveland. Charles Kettering accompanied the Winton people for about 30 miles and returned to Dayton, but a second Delco engineer made the entire trip to Cleveland. Later in that year, three Winton owners returned their cars to the Detroit dealership with problems in their Bosch ignition and lighting systems. As a result of their complaints, two Bosch engineers, including their chief engineer, spent a day assisting the Winton men in identifying the trouble.[49]

Most automakers were neither luxury builders nor high-volume producers. Unlike Winton, these firms outsourced most of their components; unlike Ford and General Motors they could bring little final-market power to bear on parts makers. For them, co-operative relations with suppliers were imperative. Standardization of components by the Society of Automobile Engineers (SAE) was the main strategy by which the smaller makers obtained smooth working relationships with their suppliers.

Howard Coffin, vice-president of Hudson Motor Car, launched the standardization programme during his term as president of the SAE IN 1910. These standards placed automobile making on a more rational footing, cutting back, for example, the number of sizes of lock washers from 800 to 16 and types of steel tubing from 1,600 to 210. Before standardization, a firm wishing to change its supplier of carburettors or spark plugs often needed to redesign its engine to do so.[50] But as John Rae has noted, standardization 'was more than a matter of technical convenience; it was of critical business importance to the small manufacturers who were dependent on outside supplying firms for their parts'. Before standardization, an automaker found it difficult to find another source of supply if a key supplier went out of business; conversely, suppliers were left with thousands of dollars in unusable inventory if one of their customers failed. Because standardization held clear benefits for smaller firms like Hudson, they 'were the most ardent supporters' of standardization while the 'big firms were inclined to stand aloof'.[51]

Reflecting on four years of SAE standardization, W. G. Wall, chief engineer of the National Motor Vehicle Co., found that it was 'easier and cheaper' to buy standardized parts, and that 'time of delivery is very materially shortened, which often prevents costly and wasteful delays'. The chief engineers of Lozier, Woods, and Waverly all agreed with Wall. D. Ferguson of Pierce-Arrow also found that standardization helped his firm to obtain proper grades of steel and aluminium. Before standardization, Pierce-Arrow wrote its own metallurgical specifications. As these often conflicted with those of the steel mills and foundries, 'endless correspondence resulted, [and] frequently a compromise had to be accepted, as few of the large producers cared to cater to individual requirements unless the tonnage involved was very great'. When mills 'consented' to take special orders, 'they charged excessively' and delivered so far behind schedule that Pierce-Arrow could often 'get more prompt shipments from the foreign houses'. Moreover, 'most of the drop forge companies had never heard of heat treatment'. With widespread recognition of the SAE standards for raw materials, Pierce-Arrow's requirements were 'supplied promptly by a dozen different houses'.[52]

Parts makers supplying these smaller firms also benefited from standardization. In early 1906, E. W. Lewis, sales manager for the Timken Roller Bearing Co., hoped that 'the day will soon come when there will be some standardization of axle sizes and type of construction, so that it might be possible to get out more than two axles alike'.[53] Eight years later H. W. Alden, the company's chief engineer, found that 'the adoption of the S.A.E. has been of very considerable benefit to us. . . . While it is a difficult matter to figure out in dollars and cents the actual savings . . . it is very easy to notice the saving in confusion and complication of parts going through the plant.'[54]

While all suppliers who sold to several auto companies benefited in a similar manner, Timken's product line gave it several advantages over most other parts makers. Timken produced axles and tapered roller bearings, specialized components which required skilled labourers, special alloys, and specialized machinery. These requirements placed their manufacture out of the reach of all except the very largest automakers. The integral place of Timken's products in the automobile meant that a car builder could not have switched to another supplier without redesigning the vehicle.

Timken engineers therefore worked closely with their customer's engineers, especially during the design phase of a vehicle's development. Timken's advertisements continually stressed its engineering skill and its close technical ties to its customers; one piece told the prospective automobile owner that 'Timken axles in your car, no matter what its size or price, were selected and installed only after many conferences between Timken engineers and the engineers of the car builder.'[55] In 1917 the company told automakers that they could not include Timken axles 'merely to furnish a selling point; *they must be built in*—not tagged on'. Timken refused 'to deliver motor-car axles except on definite assurance from the car builder that the car on the street will carry out the promise of the car on paper'. To assure that the finished vehicle matched its design drawings, Timken 'insist[ed] upon knowing' the weight of the car, the size and output of the engine, the chassis'; weight distribution, and 'all other details of construction which in the slightest degree' affected how the axles functioned as integral parts of the completed car.[56]

It is inconceivable today for a parts firm to review assembly drawings before agreeing to supply an automaker. That Timken could do so before 1920 brings out some interesting implications. Obviously Timken brought to bear a great deal of technical knowledge in its relations with its clients. Since Timken insisted on checking designs, the firm evidently placed little trust in the engineering abilities of some of its customers. In this case, suppliers like Timken, rather than automakers, stood at the locus of technical innovation. Timken took responsibility for the axle's design, but its incorporation into the finished vehicle required much exchange of technical information between supplier and builder.

Another advantage which Timken enjoyed was its diversified customer base. In 1910 Timken-Detroit Axle sold to 35 automobile manufacturers and 30 truck makers; only one, Cadillac, was a high-volume maker. In that same year, Timken Roller Bearing sold to 86 automakers, 41 truck companies, 8 transmission builders, and several rail car and heavy equipment manufacturers. This large customer list ensured that its fortunes were not tied to the fates of one or two makers and helped the firm to retain its status as an independent supplier.

The history of Hyatt Roller Bearing Company, a New Jersey firm producing a part much like Timken's, had a different outcome. Until 1916 Hyatt had been riding the crest of the auto industry's phenomenal growth and had expanded its works to meet automakers' massive demand for bearings. As Alfred Sloan later recalled in his autobiography, the firm sold to about fifteen auto companies; however, Ford made up the majority of Hyatt's business, with General Motors accounting for most of the remainder. 'Suppose', Sloan worried, 'one or the other or both decided to make their own bearings? The Hyatt Roller Bearing Company might find itself with a plant far bigger than it could use and nowhere to go for new business.' Realizing that this placed the firm in a 'desperate situation', Sloan saw that he could not much longer 'remain in the same status of apparent independence'. He rejected affiliation with Ford, seeing 'no way to place the business under the wing' of the giant company while retaining a scrap of autonomy. So, when Durant proposed buying out Hyatt, Sloan was more than ready to listen.[57] Hyatt Roller Bearing Company became a division of Durant's United Motors Corporation in 1916.

Control of key patents also helped many parts firms to retain their independence. The Steel Products Company, a forerunner to today's TRW, owned a cluster of patents which gave it a virtual monopoly on the manufacture of welded automobile components. These patents ensured that over 90 per cent of all valves—except those in Ford cars, which used a different design—were purchased from Steel Products. As the firm's president Charles Thompson recounted in the early 1930s, '[T]he entire valve business enjoyed by the Steel Products Company' in 1916 'was attributable to the ownership of patents and patent rights, and to that alone'.[58]

But patent rights did not guarantee their owner an exclusive business. In 1914 Schweppe and Wilt, a Detroit manufacturing firm, obtained a patent on the manufacture of drag links, an electrically welded component used in the steering mechanism. As TRW president Frederick Crawford recalled, Schweppe and Wilt 'had no alternative but to grant some licenses under its process'. Already by 1916 'it had become almost standard practice among the automobile companies to insist that a supplier of automobile parts make available to them additional sources of supply' in order to avoid 'a complete tie-up of the automobile companies' production'. Because of its monopoly on drag links, Schweppe and Wilt fell into 'great disrepute with purchasing agents' and its relations with its customers 'were becoming more and more strained'. In early 1917, Schweppe and Wilt licensed Steel Products and another company to make drag links under its patent, but it kept for itself the lion's share of the business, and only 'outwardly met the objections of the automobile companies'.[59]

In 1919 the automakers discovered that Schweppe and Wilt had been fixing its licensees' prices and production volumes, a practice which its customers bitterly protested. Instead of providing more liberal licensing arrangements to other parts firms, the Detroit company attempted to reassert its monopoly. It served notice to automobile manufacturers who bought drag links from other suppliers that they were liable for damages by reason of their failure to buy from Schweppe and Wilt. Buick, 'at that time one of the principal customers' of Steel Products, was one of the auto companies notified. Buick peremptorily told Steel Products to resolve the infringement controversy otherwise 'it would be compelled to transfer its business elsewhere'.[60] Seeking to avoid legal entanglements and the loss of an important customer, Steel Products ended the issue in April 1920 by buying out Schweppe and Wilt 'at an exorbitant price solely in order to acquire that company's drag link patents'. Because Schweppe and Wilt's actions had so infuriated the automobile industry, Steel Products 'inherited ill will to such a degree that it was confronted with a real problem among its customers'.[61]

Industry Consolidation after 1920

By 1920 the automobile industry had gained enough control over its supplier base to demand that key parts makers share proprietary technology, such as basic patents, with customers and competitors alike. Such a demand was unthinkable in 1909. Two trends during these twelve years, the industry's fast growth and its consolidation in the hands of high-volume producers, had shifted market power from suppliers to automakers. What began around 1909 as a series of defensive moves to avoid production hold-ups became by 1920 an aggressive and successful attempt to create a subordinate parts industry. In order to preserve their final-product market rents, the large automakers refashioned the components industry into two sectors: captive subsidiaries who produced specialized parts, and financially independent firms who competed fiercely for commodity parts orders. Automobile manufacturers after 1920 dealt with their outside suppliers at arm's length, awarding them short-term contracts on the basis of price. Automakers increasingly required suppliers to produce components according to the automakers' blueprints, leaving little room for suppliers' innovations.

By 1920 the accelerating trends toward increased centralization and vertical integration had become apparent. Even though about eighty firms produced passenger cars in commercial quantities, Ford and General Motors produced respectively one-half and one-fifth of the industry's volume. Barriers to entry were rising. As one observer noted, 'The day is past when a concern with a few hundred thousand dollars can undertake the manufacture of a $1500 car. . . . The low priced cars are practically all in the hands of a few big manufacturers.' By this time industry consolidation had all but eliminated 'the possibilities of the lower-priced assembled products of 4 and 5 years ago'. Only the medium- and high-price segments remained for the smaller firms.[62]

Smaller producers were already at a significant price disadvantage compared with their high-volume counterparts. This handicap became telling during the recession of 1920 and 1921. Until 1920 demand had increased steadily, often spectacularly, from year to year, but toward the end of that year demand suddenly slumped. Except for the war year of 1918, 1921's production of about 1.5 million cars was the lowest in six years. As John Rae has noted, the recession caught many of these smaller manufacturers 'badly overextended.'[63] Even General Motors teetered on the edge of insolvency. This downturn forced over fifty smaller builders into bankruptcy between 1922 and 1926.

The large automakers stayed afloat by cutting prices and passing the cuts along to their suppliers. When Henry Ford slashed his prices in late 1920, he demanded deep reductions, in some cases 35 per cent to 40 per cent, from his suppliers.[64] Those firms unwilling to grant these concessions suddenly found their contracts cancelled. The editor of *Automotive Industries* blasted builders like Ford in November 1920 for regarding a parts order 'merely as a memorandum of intent' subject to cancellation 'according to the drift of the trade'. While builders were justified in seeking price reductions from their suppliers, they should still have given parts firms 'a hearing as to whether they can reduce their prices without a loss'. Concluded the editor, 'Whatever may be the legality of a sales contract, it implies a moral obligation not to destroy the other party to it, if that can be avoided.'[65]

Although demand picked up after 1922, the number of manufacturers continued to fall. Production reached almost 4 million passenger cars in 1926, but only forty-four automobile producers remained in business. In that year the 'Big Three' (Ford, General Motors, and the recently formed Chrysler) held 75 per cent of the market. The five largest 'Independents' (Hudson, Nash, Packard, Studebaker, and Willys-Overland) held three-quarters of the remaining 25 per cent. That left roughly 6 per cent of the automobile market to the smallest thirty-six firms. Automobile production peaked at about 5.5 million cars in 1929, but the Great Depression hit the industry hard; production declined to 1.3 million in 1932, the lowest volume since 1915. When demand picked up in the late 1930s, only eight firms remained; by 1939 the 'Big Three' accounted for 90 per cent of the market and the five surviving 'Independents' fought over the last 10 per cent.

The firms which survived the 1920s and the 1930s deployed their final market power to strengthen and to extend their control over the parts industry. The interwar years made permanent the trends in supplier relations begun between 1909 and 1920; While the degree of vertical integration rose and fell with demand conditions, automobile companies would revise their adversarial relations with their outside suppliers only when their market shares eroded.

Conclusion: 'Japanese-Style' Supplier Relations?

Several examples of quasi-internal relationships between assemblers and suppliers existed in the early American auto industry. Ford established a supplier network between 1909 and 1914 in which specialized parts firms shipped their orders 'just-in-time'. The giant automaker took equity positions in many of its parts firms, and provided capital and expertise to reorganize their manufacturing operations. The Keim Mills in Buffalo was one such supplier. Similarly, General Motors owned a controlling interest in Fisher Body Corporation for several years, only buying it outright in 1926. During the 1910s and 1920s, the large makers moved away from quasi-internalization and toward a mixture of vertical integration and arm's-length (and often adversarial) relations with outside suppliers. They did so for two reasons. Acquisition of independent parts firms acted to block competitors' access to key sources of components. Automakers also employed competitive, short-term, price-based bidding to increase and to preserve their share of final-product market rents, usually at the expense of their outside suppliers.

The Japanese auto industry between 1955 and 1970 experienced the same dramatic explosion in demand that the US industry did from 1909 to 1920. But Japanese assemblers chose to strengthen rather than abandon their quasi-internal ties to their suppliers. Some of this divergence is due to historical and cultural factors; Japan industrialized later than and under far different circumstances from the United States. American anti-trust legislation and business culture placed limits on interfirm co-operation, while Japanese law and business culture encouraged it.

But economics played a role as well. Most importantly, quasi-internalization assisted Japanese assemblers in overcoming the perennial capital shortage in the auto industry of the 1950s.[65] Although the Japanese industry grew quickly, neither Toyota nor Nissan could match the booming sales that gave Henry Ford the power to buy out the Keim Mills and the Dodge brothers, and to build the massive River Rouge plant. Japanese firms were also unable to raise capital through the stock or bond markets, as did Durant and the DuPonts at General Motors. Using external suppliers gave the industry more access to capital than vertical integration would have, because it brought in more informal sources of funds. By the time automakers were able to generate significant amounts of internal funds, they had already developed skills and attitudes necessary to manage a system of 'governance by trust'; the benefits of vertical integration were correspondingly reduced.

The degree of industry consolidation also shaped the different forms of supplier relations chosen by American and Japanese automakers. While the Big Three (Ford, GM, and Chrysler) have dominated the US market since the 1920s, ten Japanese automakers today produce a combined output only slightly larger than the total US production. The high level of concentration in the USA produced correspondingly high profit margins, giving the Big Three an incentive to avoid sharing their profits with suppliers, even at the cost of overall reductions in social efficiency. Therefore, the Big Three created a competitive market for automotive inputs, because the increased profits the automakers received due to suppliers' low margins outweighed the disadvantages of reduced supplier investment and quality levels.[66]

The Japanese industry has relied on business groups (customer and suppliers tied together by partial equity ownership) and on keiretsu (long-term trading relationships not cemented with equity ties).[67] The early American industry had important similarities to this pattern. Customers and suppliers often entered into long-term relationships involving close consultation and some degree of exclusivity. But important differences existed as well. Whereas Japanese subcontractors are often referred to as 'children' of the 'parent' automakers, in the early American industry this dependency was reversed. Suppliers provided automakers in the first decade of this century with capital, proprietary knowledge, and technical assistance. Accordingly, the current trend toward more co-operative supplier relations in the US auto industry seems like a return to this earlier pattern.

To some commentators, Japanese business groups and keiretsu promote technical and economic development while safeguarding industry stability. Others see them as unfair and restrictive, as barriers which prevent new firms from entering an industry. Early US automaking seems to have combined the best of both a keiretsu and a competitive market. Fledgling car builders drew upon the financial strength of their suppliers through long-term trading relations; conversely, suppliers such as Hyatt had enough assured demand to invest in fixed capital like specialized machinery and research laboratories. Such close collaboration fuelled innovation, as it allowed both sides to solve technical problems and to improve the product's quality. But these ties were fluid enough to preserve many of the benefits of a competitive marketplace. Automakers profited from their suppliers' technical expertise gained in other industries such as carriage-building and bicycle parts, and entry into the industry, either as supplier or assembler, was relatively easy.

After 1920, the industry increasingly combined the worst features of keiretsu and competitive markets.[68] Vertical integration gave the automakers stability but removed incentives for dynamism. Outside suppliers lacked the capital to make the investments necessary for innovation.

Moreover, automakers lowered the barriers to entry into the parts business by taking design and engineering functions in-house and by requiring suppliers to deliver piece parts rather than sub-assemblies. These practices led to severe problems in uniting product and process.[69]

NOTES

1. Lawrence H. Seltzer, *A Financial History of the American Automobile Industry* (Boston: Houghton Mifflin Company, 1928), 75.
2. See Hirofumi Ueda's article in this volume, 'The Subcontracting System and Business Groups: The Case of the Japanese Automotive Industry', for a thorough discussion of the Japanese industry in this period.
3. For a discussion of quasi-internalization of parts suppliers in the Japanese motor vehicle industry, see Masahiro Shimotani's piece in this volume, 'The History and Structure of Business Groups in Japan'.
4. See, for example, Alfred D. Chandler, *Scale and Scope: The Dynamics of Industrial Capitalism* (Cambridge, Mass.: Harvard University Press, 1990); Michael Gerlach, *Alliance Capitalism: The Social Organization of Japanese Business* (Berkeley: University of California Press, 1992); and W. Mark Fruin, *The Japanese Enterprise System: Competitive Strategies and Cooperative Structures* (Oxford: Clarendon Press, 1992).
5. 'Great Oaks from Little Acorns Grow', *Motor Age*, (21 Jan. 1915), 110–11. Alfred Sloan, Jr., *Adventures of a White Collar Man*, ed. Boyden Sparks (New York: Doubleday, Doran & Co., 1941), 26–7 and 91–9.
6. 'Manufacture in New England', *Motor Age*, 1/1 (12 Sept. 1899), 4–5.
7. 'Success at Chicago Show', *Motor Age*, 4/2 (28 Mar. 1901), 3–21.
8. The Olds Motor Works made 1,400 cars priced at $650 each in 1900, accounting for about 35% of all US production. See Seltzer, *Financial History*, 19 and 75.
9. Henry Ford, 'Arranging to Build 20,000 Runabouts', *Automobile*, 14/2 (11 Jan. 1906), 107.
10. Ibid.
11. Ralph Epstein, *The Automobile Industry: Its Economic and Commercial Development* (Chicago: A. W. Shaw Company, 1928), 100.
12. Paul Starr, *The Social Transformation of American Medicine* (New York: Basic Books, 1982), 84–5.
13. 'Another Builder in Michigan', *Motor Age*, 2/9 (28 Aug. 1902), 21.
14. Seltzer, *Financial History*, 19–22.
15. A running gear was essentially an underframe and steering mechanism but did not include an engine or transmission.
16. *Motor Age*, (8 Jan. 1903), 29 and (12 Feb. 1903), inside back cover. Capitals in original advertisement.
17. 'Two of Neustadt's Latest Outfits', *Motor Age*, 1/26 (26 June 1902), 12.
18. Nathan Rosenberg, *Perspectives on Technology* (New York: Cambridge University Press, 1976); and Richard Langlois and Paul Robertson, 'Innovation and Vertical Integration in the American Automobile Industry, 1900–1940',

Working Paper (Department of Economics and Management, University College, University of New South Wales, Canberra), 13.

19. We borrow these parts classifications, and the consequent character of technical information flow, from Takahiro Fujimoto, 'The Origin and Evolution of the "Black Box Parts" Practice in the Japanese Auto Industry', in Shiomi, Haruhito, and Wada, Kazuo (eds.), *Fordism Transformed* (Oxford: Oxford University Press, 1995), pp. 184–7.

20. Ibid.

21. 'Affidavit of Frederick C. Crawford', pp. 1–2, Container 2, Folder 5, TRW Collection.

22. Ibid. 3–4.

23. 'Automobile Production in Toledo', *Motor Age*, 3/12 (19 Mar. 1903), 13.

24. Seltzer, *Financial History*, 19–20.

25. Ibid. 20–1.

26. Frank K. Dossett, 'Physical and Economic History: Highlights, 1895–1955', typed manuscript (1955), 76. TRW Inc. Records, MSS 3942, Western Reserve Historical Society, Container 21, Histories and Indexes. In Feb. 1933, for instance, the Board of Directors advised the management to sell 291 shares of the struggling Marmon Motor Company's stock, valued at about $3,000, 'at whatever price the officers were able to obtain'.

27. Seltzer, *Financial History*, 31.

28. Benjamin Briscoe, 'The Inside Story of General Motors', *Detroit Saturday Night*, 15, 22, 29 Jan. and 5 Feb. 1921, as quoted in Seltzer, *Financial History*, 32–3.

29. George S. Davis, 'Making Winton Motor Carriages' (Cleveland: The Winton Motor Carriage Co., 1904). Sales brochure found in the 1904 Winton Marque File. The Western Reserve Historical Society, Cleveland, holds these marque files.

30. *Auto Era*, 8/1 (Sept. 1908), 9.

31. 'The Automobile Industry in Ohio', *Motor Age*, 5/8 (31 Oct. 1901).

32. 'Hussey Progress', *Motor Age*, 4/7 (13 Aug. 1903), 14.

343. 'Winton Model K: An American Motor Car of Exceptional Merit' (Cleveland: The Winton Motor Carriage Co., 1906), sales brochure found in the 1906 Winton Marque File; and advertisement for Winton Type XIV, *Country Life In America* (Apr. 1907), 696, found in the 1907 Winton Marque File.

34. 'Engineering Data and Laboratory Records, Engineering Dept., The Winton Motor Car. Co.', 1910–14 gives details of these tests. Winton Marque Files, Western Reserve Historical Society.

35. Federal Trade Commission, *Report on Motor Vehicle Industry* (Washington: United States Government Printing Office, 1939), 22.

36. Sloan, *Adventures of a White Collar Man*, 94.

37. 'The Truth about Materials', *Automobile*, 34/6 (10 Feb. 1916), 265–6.

38. Seltzer, *Financial History*, 100.

39. John B. Rae, *American Automobile Manufacturers: The First Forty Years* (Philadelphia: The Chilton Company, 1959), 106.

40. Ibid. 107.

41. Ibid. 100–1.

42. Ibid. 106.

43. For a thorough treatment of the financial history of General Motors during this period, including Durant's ouster in 1910 and his resumption of control in 1916, see Seltzer, *Financial History*, ch. iv.

44. William C. Durant, as quoted ibid. 157.
45. See ibid. 154 for a list of Durant's holdings at the end of 1910.
46. Ibid. 162.
47. 'Big Output or Big Merit?', *Auto Era*, 12/12 (Aug. 1913), 3–4. Italics in original.
48. 'Why Assembling Is Basically Wrong', *Auto Era*, 13/4 (Dec. 1913), 3–4.
49. 'Engineering Data and Laboratory Records' (Cleveland: Engineering Dept., The Winton Motor Car Co., 1910–14), 618–24 and 647–8; Winton Marque Files, Western Reserve Historical Society, Cleveland.
50. Epstein, *The Automobile Industry*, 41 and 184.
51. Rae, *American Automobile Manufacturers*, 79–80. For a full treatment, see also G. Thompson, 'Intercompany Technical Standardization in the Early American Automobile Industry', *Journal of Economic History*, 14 (Winter 1954), 1–20.
52. 'Makers Save by Using S.A.E. Standards', *Automobile*, 31/2 (9 July 1914), 74–5.
53. E. W. Lewis, 'Standardization of Axles', *Automobile*, 14/2 (11 Jan. 1906), 104.
54. 'Makers Save by Using S.A.E. Standards'.
55. Timken advertisement, *Auto Era*, 15/6 (Feb. 1916), advertisement section at back of issue.
56. 'Does the Car Agree with the Blue Prints?', advertisement in *Auto Era*, 16/2 (Aug. 1917), inside back cover.
57. Sloan, *Adventures of a White Collar Man*, 86 and 93–4.
58. 'Deposition of Charles E. Thompson', p. 9, Container 2, Interoffice Memos, 1946–63; Folder 5, 1919–20 Tax Return Depositions, TRW Collection.
59. 'Affidavit of Frederick C. Crawford', pp. 1–2, Container 2, Folder 5, TRW Collection.
60. Tax Return Notes, Container 2, Folder 4, 1919–20 Tax Return Memos, TRW Collection.
61. 'Affidavit of Frederick C. Crawford'.
62. J. Edward Schipper, 'Engineering and Merchandising in 1920 Show', *Automotive Industries*, 42/2 (8 Jan. 1920), 52.
63. Rae, *American Automobile Manufacturers*, 136.
64. 'Ford Gets Concessions from Parts Factories', *Automotive Industries*, 43/25 (25 Nov. 1920), 1094.
65. 'Contracts and Prices', *Automotive Industries*, 43/21 (18 Nov. 1920), 1034.
66. Susan Helper, 'Comparative Supplier Relations in the US and Japanese Auto Industries: An Exit/Voice Approach', *Business and Economic History*, 19 (1990), 160.
67. For an explanation of why firms with market power—like the Big Three—might find it profit-maximizing to have inefficiently short contracts with their suppliers, see Susan Helper and David Levine, 'Long-Term Supplier Relations and Product-Market Structure', *Journal of Law, Economics, and Organization*, 8 (1992), 561–81.
68. This classification is from Masahiro Shimotani, 'Corporate Groups and Keiretsu in Japan', *Japanese Yearbook on Business History*, 8 (1991), 8–19. For a detailed English-language study of supplier relations in the Japanese auto industry, see Toshihiro Nishiguchi, *Strategic Industrial Sourcing: The Japanese Advantage* (New York: Oxford University Press, 1994).
69. For a discussion of the American auto industry after the period under study in this chapter, see Susan Helper, 'Strategy and Irreversibility in Supplier

Relations: The Case of the U.S. Automobile Industry', *Business History Review*, 65 (Winter 1991), 781–824.

70. Even when innovations were available, powerful automakers chose not to use them. For example, Henry Ford refused to make engine blocks for his Model A out of aluminium because he did not wish to deal with Alcoa, a monopoly supplier. See Margaret Graham and Bettye Pruitt, *R&D for Industry: A Century of Technical Innovation at ALCOA* (New York, 1990), 148.

REFERENCES

Manuscript sources

TRW Inc. Records, 1900–69, MSS 3942, Western Reserve Historical Society, Cleveland.

Winton Motor Carriage Company Marque Files, 1904 to 1917. These files, arranged by year and model, include explosion blueprints, bills of materials, sales brochures, and advertisements. The marque files also contain Alexander Winton's patent records, and the laboratory records of the Engineering Department, 1910–14.

Automobile trade periodicals

Motor Era (published monthly by the Winton Motor Carriage Company, Cleveland), 2–16 (Sept. 1902–Aug. 1917).

Automobile (becomes *Automotive Industries* in Jan. 1918) (New York), 14–23 (Jan. 1906–Dec. 1920).

Cycle and Automobile Trade Journal, 12 (July–Dec. 1907, and 1915).

Motor Age (Chicago), 1–10 (Sept. 1899–Dec. 1906).

Published sources

Chandler, Alfred, *Scale and Scope: The Dynamics of Industrial Capitalism* (Cambridge, Mass.: Harvard University Press, 1990).

Epstein, Ralph, *The Automobile Industry: Its Economic and Commercial Development* (Chicago: A. W. Shaw Company, 1928).

Federal Trade Commission, *Report on Motor Vehicle Industry* (Washington: United States Government Printing Office, 1939).

Fruin, W. Mark, *The Japanese Enterprise System: Competitive Strategies and Cooperative Structures* (Oxford: Clarendon Press, 1992).

Fujimoto, Takahiro, 'The Origin and Evolution of the "Black Box Parts" Practice in the Japanese Auto Industry', in Shiomi, Haruhito, and Wada, Kazuo (eds.), *Fordism Transformed* (Oxford: Oxford University Press, 1995), pp. 184–7.

Gerlach, Michael, *Alliance Capitalism: The Social Organization of Japanese Business* (Berkeley and Los Angeles: University of California Press, 1992).

Graham, Margaret, and Pruitt, Bettye, *R&D for Industry: A Century of Technical Innovation at ALCOA* (New York, 1990), 148.

Helper, Susan, 'Comparative Supplier Relations in the US and Japanese Auto Industries: An Exit/Voice Approach', *Business and Economic History*, 19 (1990).

—— 'Strategy and Irreversibility in Supplier Relations: The Case of the U.S. Automobile Industry', *Business History Review*, 65 (Winter 1991).

—— and Levine, David, 'Long-Term Supplier Relations and Product-Market Structure', *Journal of Law, Economics, and Organization*, 8 (1992).

Langlois, Richard, and Robertson, Paul, 'Innovation and Vertical Integration in the American Automobile Industry, 1900–1940', Working Paper (Department of Economics and Management, University College, University of New South Wales, Canberra).

Nishiguchi, Toshihiro, *Strategic Industrial Sourcing: The Japanese Advantage* (New York: Oxford University Press, 1994).

Rae, John B., *American Automobile Manufacturers: The First Forty Years* (Philadelphia: The Chilton Company, 1959).

Rosenberg, Nathan, *Perspectives on Technology* (New York: Cambridge University Press, 1982).

Seltzer, Lawrence, *A Financial History of the American Automobile Industry* (Boston: Houghton Mifflin Company, 1928).

Shimotani, Masahiro, 'Corporate Groups and Keiretsu in Japan', *Japanese Yearbook on Business History*, 8 (1991).

Sloan, Alfred, *Adventures of a White Collar Man*, ed. Boyden Sparks (New York: Doubleday, Doran & Company, 1941).

Starr, Paul, *The Social Transformation of American Medicine* (New York: Basic Books, 1982).

Thompson, G., 'Intercompany Technical Standardization in the Early American Automobile Industry', *Journal of Economic History*, 14 (Winter 1954).

9

The Subcontracting System and Business Groups:
The Case of the Japanese Automotive Industry

HIROFUMI UEDA

Thesis and Methods

This chapter will examine the formation of the subcontracting production system and the development of business groups within the Japanese automotive industry. In the current context, however, the term 'business group' is distinct both from horizontal-type agglomerations of companies with cross-shareholdings and from vertical-type corporate groups consisting of a central parent company accompanied by diversified subsidiaries. Rather, what is meant is an organization resulting from a collection of parts suppliers surrounding an automotive assembler. There is typically a very large number of suppliers providing parts to a given assembler, and so the designation 'group member' is applied only to those companies that have either received capital investment from the assembler or maintain unusually strong business ties. Accordingly, those independent parts suppliers that do not have a particularly close affiliation with the assembler are not considered to be members of that assembler's group.

In considering the historical formation of relations between makers and group members, changes in these relationships, and the emergence of various representative features, there are a number of points that require attention. Primary among these points is the fact that, as illustrated in Table 9.1, not only can parts suppliers be divided into group members and independent makers, but group members can be further subdivided into three types depending on the combination of capital relations, transactional relations, corporate origins, and content of production. Type 1 (Central Group Companies) consists of subsidiaries and of associates

Table 9.1. *Types of group companies in the 1980s*

Type of company	Capital affiliation	Origin	Business relations	Size	Transactions with other assemblers	Type of manufacturer[a]	No. of Cos. in co-op. association	
							Toyota	Mazda
1. Central	Strong	Part of assembler	Strong	Med.–large	Many for large	I	13	6
2. Keiretsu	Strong	Independent	Strong	Med.–large	Many	I	14	7
3. Subcontractors	Weak or none	Independent	Strong	Small–med.	Few	I or II	56	42
Other suppliers[b]	Weak or none	Independent	Weak	Med.–large	Many	I	80	121

[a] Of type of manufacturer, I is the manufacturer which specializes by product as specialized parts or components, and II is the manufacturer which specializes by manufacturing process such as stamping, casting, machining, or others.

[b] Of Mazda's other suppliers, one-third are members of other assemblers' groups.

(typically with the assembler being the primary stockholder) that form the core of the group. Type 2 (Keiretsu Group Companies) includes those affiliated suppliers having a capital affiliation and close relations in terms of personnel. These tend to be formerly independent large or medium-sized companies. Type 3 (Subcontracting Group Companies) is made up of those subcontractors that have no capital ties but nevertheless maintain strong business ties. While group size varies depending on the assembler, group members typically make up one quarter to one half of the companies belonging to an assembler's 'co-operative association'.

This method of group classification allows a contextual understanding of the distinctive features of each type, and is helpful in making a historical observation of business groups in the auto industry. Both the process of group formation and the ranking of the various groups are also closely related to group type.

Secondly, there are several items relating to the comparison of relations between group members and auto assemblers. It is important, for example, to consider the significance of the existence of a group from the standpoint both of the members and of the assembler. Stable transactions, often pointed out as characteristic of the relationship, had different meanings for members and for assemblers, and these meanings changed over time.

Further, it is necessary to view the relationships between automakers and group members within the context of assemblers' market positions. Co-operative associations featuring stable transactions had already been established by Toyota and Nissan by the mid-1950s, and their group compositions naturally differ from those of other assemblers struggling simultaneously to expand their scale of production and to secure reliable parts suppliers.

In addition, regardless of capital affiliations, assemblers undertook control of suppliers using a combination of factors including technology, production, quality, and management. However, the nature of this comprehensive control shifted according to the period, the technological proficiency of the supplier concerned, and general economic conditions. Hence, it will be more productive to consider the total influence of these issues rather than attempting to analyse each one separately.

For convenience, the period under consideration will be divided into four phases, corresponding to the development of the overall Japanese economy. The first phase runs from before the Second World War through to the end of the war; the second phase consists of the war recovery years, 1945 to 1954; the third phase is that of rapid economic growth from 1955 to 1973; and the fourth phase is that of stable growth, 1974–90.

From Pre-war to War's End

The Domestication of the Automotive Industry

Although the Japanese automotive industry has its roots in the early part of the century, it was not until the 1920s that it started up in earnest with the establishment of factories by Ford and GM. At first, the Ford and GM factories imported all parts from the USA, but it soon became necessary to procure parts locally owing to foreign exchange conditions. This process began with nurturing of spare parts producers, and was later widened to include original equipment.

The need for domestication of the industry had already been recognized by the military authorities during the First World War. It was only at the start of the 1930s, however, that this recognition was translated into concrete form, as Japan's invasion of China grew in significance. The Automobile Industry Act was promulgated in 1936, and it provided a definite direction for policy by requiring government permission to engage in motor vehicle assembly and parts making operations. It established the foundation for mass production of completely domestic vehicles, and sought to meet both defence and industrial needs. The domestication of parts manufacture was absolutely essential to the domestication of the overall industry, and this theme was taken up as a policy issue when the Automobile Industry Act was being passed. The Ministry of Commerce and Industry, predecessor to today's Ministry of International Trade and Industry, worked on two methods of organization for proceeding with parts domestication: specialist (independent) makers, and subcontractors (Ueda 1993).

First, Qualified Auto Parts Registration Regulations were instituted in March 1938. As the name suggests, these regulations called for the registration of qualified parts with the Minister of Commerce and Industry, thus encouraging domestic parts-making by independent makers whose products would be used generally by the assemblers. As of June 1941 there were 61 categories of registered parts, and a total of 167 approved manufacturers. A number of comprehensive electrical equipment makers are included in this figure, but it also contains many specialist auto parts makers that have continued their operations through to the present day, indicating that a substantial body of specialist makers had already emerged by this time.

Second, guidance and development of subcontracting firms enjoying close ties with vehicle makers were also given attention, and it became the policy of the Ministry of Commerce and Industry to promote measures aimed at strengthening subcontracting relationships and carried out with the assistance of assemblers. These included necessary financing, loan of equipment, assistance with materials supply, help with capacity expansion, and a system of designation by assemblers that would guarantee subcontractors a certain amount of business. As will be noted later, these kinds of guidance and development policies were expanded to the entire machinery industry as the war economy of the early 1940s took shape, making the automotive industry an important model for wider application.[1]

While the dual-pronged approach of specialist and subcontracting makers was generally followed, it can be seen that the parts procurement policies of the established assemblers (Nissan, Toyota, and Isuzu) differed significantly. The specialist makers were consistently relied upon for general-use parts, but assemblers took different approaches to forged and pressed parts. While Nissan essentially sought to conduct start-to-finish production on its own, Toyota and Isuzu actively utilized smaller subcontracting factories (Nihon Jidosha 1979: 79–86).

However, the outbreak of the Second World War in Europe in 1939 caused Toyota to issue a document entitled 'Future Managerial Direction', indicating changes in purchasing policy. Specifically, it refers to increased internalization of production, in order both to raise the utilization rate of the company's new Koromo plant and to improve the quality of parts. As a result, the number of parts purchased from outside dropped from 700 to 570 in January 1940, and a goal was established to reduce the figure further to 380 and the value of the purchases to one-third of their former level (Toyota 1967: 172–82). During the initial stages of its development, the auto industry was plagued by quality problems with parts, and this did not serve to strengthen relations between assembler and outside parts makers.

The Controlled Wartime Economy

Subcontracting controls and the reorganization of the parts industry

From the end of the 1930s to the year 1940, Japan began to set up a wartime economy as a result of a number of changes in the international environment, including the outbreak of war in Europe, the deepening of its own conflict in China, and worsening relations with the United States. Domestication and increased capacity of the entire machinery industry, with automotive vehicles at the forefront, rapidly became important issues. Let us first examine the impact on the auto industry of subcontractor control policies and organizational measures with regard to parts production (Ueda 1987; 1995; Friedman 1988; Nishiguchi 1994).

Of particular importance in the wartime reorganization and development of the machinery industry were the Guidelines for the Development of Machinery and Steel Industries, released in December 1940 with the goal of increasing production capacity through systematic specialization. There were three major aims to the Guidelines: first, final assembly factories, specialist parts factories, and subcontractor factories were to be categorized by area of speciality in order to take advantage of expertise most effectively. Second, a system of direct intervention was to be set up in order to establish and/or cement relations between assemblers and specific subcontractor factories. Subcontracting activities were to be permitted only upon application by the entities concerned and subsequent approval. Third, when a formal subcontracting relationship had been established and approved, the parties were to become mutually obligated. That is, the assembler became obligated to provide a stable amount of orders to the subcontractor and to provide guidance and assistance, while the subcontractor became obligated to associate itself with the assembler and not to undertake production for other companies. These obligations were intended to breed mutual trust and reliance, and to result in a stable system of production. Later, 'subcontracting' would be referred to as 'co-operation', as in 'co-operating factory' or 'co-operative relationship'.

The Guidelines helped push forward more specific and stronger subcontracting controls, although actual conditions of enforcement were not necessarily according to plan. The most significant obstacle was that neither assemblers nor subcontractors were much in favour of such inflexible and binding ties. As a result, Toyota had only six subcontractor factories in 1941, and Nissan five.

Automotive parts makers were divided at this time into three categories: the group of approved makers already mentioned (73 companies); makers belonging to the prefectural Auto Parts Manufacturers Unions of Tokyo, Kanagawa, Aichi, Osaka, and Hyogo Prefectures (204 companies); and other independent makers. The third category of 'others' consisted of subcontractors to specific assemblers, while those in the first and second categories supplied parts to several assemblers simultaneously and were organized into the overarching Federation of Auto Parts Manufacturers Union. As stipulated in the August 1941 Guidelines for the Development of the Auto Parts Industry, these specialist makers were placed under the auspices of a newly created control organization known as the Japan Auto Parts Union. The goal of this reorganization effort was to realize further increases in production capacities by effecting the principle of 'one factory, one part', and at the same time to guard against an excess of parts makers by requiring that they be appointed by the Ministry of Commerce and Industry.

Suppliers and the breakdown of vehicle production

During the war, just as had been the case in the 1930s, the trend was toward parts production taking place in two distinct types of factories: the smaller factories aligned with assemblers in subcontracting relationships, and the medium-sized factories of the specialist makers that were expected to form the backbone of mass production. In fact, however, automotive production steadily declined from its peak in 1941. This was because auto-related manufacturers were mobilized into other fields, particularly the aircraft industry, which had wartime priority. The auto assemblers themselves were pressed into aircraft production, and the specialist parts makers were redirected towards aircraft parts manufacture. Meanwhile, many subcontractor factories, having enjoyed close relations with their respective assemblers for several years, were mobilized in turn as primary and secondary subcontractors for aircraft parts.

The war saw vehicle assemblers engage in expanded production of non-automotive items, and the number of their suppliers temporarily increased. For example, as noted in Table 9.2, Toyota had 149 subcontractors as of 1944, including specialist makers. For the most part, however, the nature of these supplier relationships was temporary, differing from post-war supplier organization; few of these entities continued their relationships with Toyota beyond the war. Eventually, the inflexible division of labour forced upon the wartime auto industry by subcontractor controls fell apart with the collapse of the industry itself and with ultimate defeat in 1945.

The germination of group alignments

While the rigid, government-monitored systematic specialization of the auto industry did not survive the war, patterns for post-war group

Table 9.2. *Changes in the number of Toyota suppliers*

Location	1944[a]	1958[b]	Number continuing
Aichi Prefecture	55	73	19
Other Tokai	9	7	2
Tokyo Prefecture	43	37 (24)	8
Other Kanto	11	5 (4)	3
Osaka Prefecture	19	11 (8)	1
Other Kinki	6	4 (2)	2
Other	2	1	
Unspecified	4		
Total	149	140 (121)	35

Note: Tokai, Kanto, and Kinki are the names of the regions surrounding Aichi, Tokyo, and Osaka prefectures.

[a] The 1944 figures indicate the number of co-operative companies.

[b] The 1958 figures indicate the number of Kyohokai association members. The figures in parentheses for 1958 eliminate overlap among different parts of the same companies.

Source: Compiled from Toyota (1958).

alignment can be found in the wartime period. One of these patterns, while limited in the number of actual cases, consists of parts makers developing capital ties with assemblers. While such group capital ties were present in other industries as well, such as the aircraft industry, they played a particularly important role in the post-war revival of the auto industry.[2] Another example is the formation of 'co-operative associations' from among the ranks of subcontractors. The oldest of these was formed in 1939, around Toyota, and originally consisted of about twenty companies. Many of the small factories located near Toyota that were originally part of the association continued after the war to maintain strong ties with Toyota as subcontracting group companies. Originally formed as a kind of social club, the association began about 1943 to gather information, perform factory diagnostic functions for members, sponsor technical exchange, etc. It was at this time also that the association was renamed the Kyohokai, a name that in Japanese simultaneously indicates co-operation with Toyota and suggests group prosperity. During the war, these kinds of associations served to iron out difficulties between assemblers and subcontractors, and they were formed at most major assemblers with the encouragement of the government. When the war ended, however, the great majority of them were disbanded. Toyota's Kyohokai is one example of the few such associations that continued their activities into the post-war period (Ueda 1993).

Summary

The pre-war automotive industry finally started on the road to domestication in the late 1930s, and individual automakers began to expand their operations, reaching a peak in 1941. After this, however, output began to decline. While a broad division of labour, or systematic specialization structure, began to be formed in the industry from about 1940, the subsequent decline turned into a collapse, complicating business relationships. Although the government sought through its parts industry development policies to institute an efficient systematic specialization by strengthening subcontractors and subcontracting relationships on the one hand, and by encouraging mass production at specialist parts makers on the other, these plans were frustrated by the war. The germination of groups can be seen in the wartime period, but it was not until after the war that significant improvements in both output and quality, resulting from implementation of the original policy goals of specialization and group formation, were to come about.

Post-war Recovery (1945–1954)

Post-war Confusion and the Auto Parts Industry

The auto parts industry was thrown into a state of confusion following Japan's defeat, as were the other branches of the machinery sector. Many parts makers that had been occupied mainly with aircraft parts production for military demand shifted their capacity to civilian demand for auto parts, meaning that the original pre-war auto parts makers were joined by a host of new entrants. Additionally, many parts manufacturing operations were begun after the war. Thus, there were three types of makers: (1) those that had been occupied before the war with auto parts production, were pressed into aircraft parts production during the war, and subsequently returned to making auto parts; (2) those that had been producing parts for other industries prior to and during the war, and that switched over to auto parts subsequently; and (3) those that were founded after the war for the manufacture of auto parts, or that diversified from some unrelated industry.

However, because the recovery of the auto industry itself was delayed, parts manufacture did not expand very rapidly, and those companies that had chosen the auto parts business found themselves forced to produce household goods and daily necessities in order to survive. Meanwhile, management conditions at auto assemblers were generally bad, and payments to parts makers for actual parts production were often late. These conditions aggravated the industry's state of confusion.

It was the series of special procurement orders for the Korean War that fuelled a quick turnaround in this state of affairs. The effects of the special procurement orders were felt particularly strongly in the automotive assembly and parts industries, and not only led to larger orders and the possibility of solid business conditions for assemblers and parts makers, but also provided a stream of profits that was reinvested in equipment and that allowed the building up of mass-production capabilities.

Keiretsu Diagnosis

Outside ordering in the post-war period

The level of orders placed by assemblers with outside parts makers for production and processing at the time of the post-war recovery is thought to have been high, as high as it was prior to the war, but its extent depended on the individual firm. According to a survey carried out in 1947, while in-house production was the rule at Nissan, Isuzu tended to rely heavily on suppliers for a major portion of required processing and was then utilizing 152 of them (Kokumin Keizai 1947). The previously mentioned policy differences between the two companies can be seen to have continued beyond the war.

While conditions concerning outside ordering varied with individual assemblers, levels of outside ordering increased for all assemblers with the recovery of production, and the number of suppliers utilized also rose. In the case of Toyota, for example, forty-eight new suppliers were added to the total in the decade or so following the war (see Table 9.3). Additionally, some of the relationships that had been broken off during the war were later restored. The question of how to build supplier relationships came to be recognized as an important issue for the assemblers during the movement towards mass production that followed the Korean War. It was during this period that the system of keiretsu diagnosis was implemented as an important part of contemporary government policy *vis-à-vis* small and medium-sized business.

Keiretsu diagnosis at Nissan's Yokohama plant

Keiretsu diagnosis was aimed at analysing conditions and problems at both assembler plants and subcontractor factories, improving relations between the two and pointing the way towards solutions to difficulties with materials or finances at the subcontractors, and boosting the effectiveness of systematically specialized assembler–supplier relations, particularly for assembler plants. Toyota led the way, instituting keiretsu diagnosis from 1952 to 1953 in the three regions around Nagoya, Osaka, and Tokyo (Tokai, Kansai, and Kanto). Accordingly, Toyota carried out factory diagnosis at subcontractors, learned methods for evaluating these firms, and undertook changes in its ordering methods, while its subcontractors acquired competitive awareness and began to take up rationalization more earnestly. These changes had significant effects on the relationships between Toyota and the subcontractors (Wada 1991).

To obtain a view of the contemporary state of subcontractor relations, however, let us consider the case of the Nissan Yokohama plant, which underwent keiretsu diagnosis in 1953, as detailed in the official keiretsu diagnosis report issued in 1955 by the Kanagawa Prefectural Manufacturing and Commerce Guidance Center. (Yokohama is the prefectural capital of Kanagawa Prefecture.) At the time, Nissan was making outside parts purchases from some 400 firms, and the dependence of the Yokohama plant on outside parts, as measured by the ratio of their value to the total cost of the finished product, was determined to be approximately 35 per cent. There were 193 'co-operative factories', 135 of which were in nearby Tokyo Prefecture and 9 of which were in Kanagawa Prefecture itself, accounting for 90 per cent of the total. The keiretsu diagnosis was applied to 60 of these, each having an average work force of 57,

Table 9.3. *Starting dates for transactions with Toyota Kyohokai association members*

	1939	1940–4	1945–9	1950–4	1955–9	1960–4	1965–	Total
Central Group Company	1	1	7	1	1			11
Keiretsu Group Company	3	2	5	2				12
Subcon. Group Company	14	5	7	8	3	4	2	41
Total	18	8	19	11	4	4	2	64
Other suppliers	19	3	10	8	8	2	2	52
Total	37	11	29	19	12	6	2	116

Notes: Type of company based on standards of late 1980s.
Does not include unspecified figures.
The discrepancy between Tables 9.2 and 9.3 in the numbers of pre-war/wartime companies is due to the cutting off of transactional relationships in 1944.
Source: Compiled from Toyota (1967).

meaning that they were rather small compared to most primary parts makers. Of the 60, 43 can be confirmed to have been members of Nissan's co-operative association, the Takarakai, as late as 1964. About half had done business with Nissan before the war. Nine of the firms depended on Nissan for 90 per cent or more of their business, 18 of them for 70 to 90 per cent, 13 of them for 50 to 70 per cent, 14 of them for 20 to 50 per cent, and six of them for 20 per cent or less, indicating that two-thirds of the total had a dependence ratio of 50 per cent or greater. These can be considered subcontractor/group companies according to the model proposed earlier.

The diagnosis report shows that many of the managers of the subcontractor factories came from technical backgrounds, and thus tended to lack interest in production control and overall management. The report identifies needs for clearer management direction, better-established (personnel) organization, managerial planning and scientific management principles, improved time management, and more attention to production management. With regard to the Yokohama plant's utilization of its subcontractors, the report suggests a more planned approach to selecting subcontractors, and an unofficial but concrete indication of intended subcontracting policy. Concerning subcontractor control, a general shift from outside order management to subcontractor management is recommended, as is increased efficiency in dealing with individual relationships. The suggested shift from outside order management to subcontractor management is not merely indicative of purchasing prices and volumes, it also includes the need to grasp the overall managerial situations at subcontractor firms, and the need for increased efficiency in dealing with individual relationships includes the effective use of the co-operative association and the improvement of purchasing operations. Additionally, a wide variety of advice was given to the Yokohama plant concerning other aspects of purchasing and ordering, improvement of subcontractor production, and subcontractor factory management.

As a result of this keiretsu diagnosis, targeted subcontractor factories increased their efforts at rationalization, and Nissan itself carried on its own factory diagnoses and inspections. It also reorganized its co-operative association into the Takarakai in 1957, laying the foundation for future development and expansion. The sum of these changes certainly had an impact on specialization, just as at Toyota, and they can be seen as preparation for formation of the close relationships between assemblers and subcontractors that occurred in the later period of rapid economic growth. Still, in comparison with Toyota, the influence of the keiretsu diagnosis-induced control measures with regard to subcontractor factories was not especially great. In addition to issues bound up with Nissan's traditional view of outside purchasing, the timing of a major labour dispute in 1953 also had an impact.

Other keiretsu diagnoses were later carried out by post-war assembler entrants Daihatsu Motor Co., Ltd. (from 1956 to 1957), and Mitsubishi Motor Corp. (then Shin Mitsubishi Heavy Industries) in 1961 at its Mizushima Works.

Summary

The opportunity presented by the special procurements associated with the Korean War led to expanded production in Japan's auto industry, and the industry entered a new phase of formation of a systematic specialization structure. Parts makers that had connections to the pre-war period were joined by newly established makers. On the other hand, many of the temporary wartime suppliers were unable to continue their relationships beyond the war's end, and a new system of specialization came about under new conditions (see Table 9.2).[3] In the midst of these changes, Toyota, Nissan, and some of their small and medium-sized suppliers, particularly those with high levels of dependence, sought to improve their mutual relations through keiretsu diagnoses. This process illuminated issues concerning ordering on the part of the assemblers and concerning general and production management on the part of subcontractors, and highlighted the need for a more general approach to subcontractor relations and management by assemblers. It also heightened awareness of the need for improved competitive and rationalization efforts by the subcontractors, and resulted in stronger mutual relations.

Rapid Economic Growth (1955–1973)

Rapid Economic Growth and the Auto Industry

The period of rapid economic growth was a time of amazing progress for the Japanese auto industry. Annual production soared from 68,000 vehicles in 1955 to over 7 million in 1973, with passenger automobile output jumping from just over 20,000 to 4.47 million over the same period. Naturally, this sudden and continued growth had important ramifications for the auto parts industry; the value of parts production rocketed from about 3.4 billion yen in 1955 to over 116.1 billion yen in 1970.

This huge increase in volume was also accompanied by dramatic improvements in the quality of output, and by significant shifts toward modernization and specialization as well. The various parts makers actively sought to improve technology, production rationalization, and quality control, and their forward-looking management policies were given support by government policy in the form of the Machinery

Industry Promotion Temporary Measures Law (Odaka *et al.* 1988: 85–8). At the same time, these trends were given further impetus in the early 1960s by impending trade and capital liberalization. The rate of introduction of machine equipment by auto parts makers also moved forward rapidly: machinery that was less than five years old accounted for only 30 per cent of the total in 1955, but it rose to 56 per cent in 1965.

There are also changes to be seen during this period in the specialization structure that existed between assemblers and parts makers. While the parts makers improved their technological and production capabilities through modernization and specialization, this did not lead directly to more managerial independence. Rather, there was a strong tendency during the period of rapid economic growth for assemblers to take (or increase) equity positions in parts makers, thereby drawing them into their respective keiretsu groups and reorganizing the specialization structure. Capital liberalization had a particularly strong effect on this trend, which continued through the late 1960s. Also, the utilization by primary parts makers of secondary makers led to further reinforcement and expansion of systematic specialization in the overall industry.

Changes in Systematic Specialization in Response to Mass Production

The most important element in the changes that took place in the structure of specialization in response to mass production was the need for a stable supply of parts. In the case of Toyota, however, as can be seen in Table 9.3, supplier network development had been virtually completed by about 1960, and it subsequently embarked on efforts to raise international competitiveness by lowering costs, improving quality, and bringing about synchronous production (Nihon Jinbun 1963; Toyota 1987; Nissan 1967).

With regard to cost, pressure placed by Toyota on co-operative factories to lower parts costs was extremely high even from the very beginning of rapid economic growth. Unit prices paid by Toyota to some suppliers declined by as much as 16 per cent between 1956 and 1959. Nissan also obtained favourable results from a programme implemented from 1961 to 1962 aimed at improving management, factory layout, and value analysis at Takarakai member companies.

Concerning quality, Toyota began a series of measures aimed at strengthening quality control activities at co-operative firms, prompted by its 1961 decision to adopt company-wide total quality control, including the formation of a supplier quality control research body in 1960, and the establishment of the Tokai (Nagoya region) Kyohokai Quality Control Committee in 1961.

Nissan began its 'synchronization experiment' in 1963, setting up a system that encouraged co-operative suppliers to link their materials purchasing, production, and deliveries directly to Nissan's output. Toyota also began working on synchronous parts production from about 1960, realizing simultaneous (just-in-time) deliveries of body parts in 1963, and expanding the system to cover all parts purchases in 1966 (Cusumano 1985: 248–61).

An important point concerning the pressure put on co-operative companies for reduced costs as volumes expanded is that it was not simply a matter of demanding lower unit prices. Rather, assemblers were active in recommending ways that suppliers could cut their own costs. Unit costs for parts makers were calculated on the basis of number of operations, and on an hourly rate that varied according to the individual parts maker, meaning that reductions in the number of operations were directly linked to reductions in manufacturing costs (Ueda 1987; Smitka 1991: 140–2). As noted earlier, Toyota and Nissan recognized through keiretsu diagnosis in the early 1950s the need for evaluation based on a complete understanding of their co-operative subcontractors' managerial and production conditions, and this recognition is evident in the promotion of reduced costs through evaluation and reduction of actual unit costs.

For the most part, parts makers responded to this reorganization of the specialization structure with technological change. The rate of introduction of new equipment during the period of rapid economic growth is striking, and, even allowing for differences relating to the scale of individual firms, this process can be observed throughout the industry. Further, accompanying the introduction of new equipment, there was a reorganization of work towards the flow model. In order to respond to the needs stemming from mass production for stable supply, lower unit prices, higher quality, and production synchronization, parts makers pushed forward with technological change through the introduction of new equipment and flow production methods that corresponded to individual corporate characteristics.

The 'technological revolution', consisting primarily of the introduction, adaptation, and integration of foreign technology, brought specialist parts makers a step closer to international levels. The revolution also affected what were formerly small-scale specialized process subcontractors making pressed, forged, and cast parts, causing them to become specialist parts makers of special function parts.

Improvements in production management and in quality and cost control had their foundation in the technological revolution, thereby further increasing the efficiency of the intra-industry division of labour. Additionally, stable relations with assemblers and the rapid growth of the automotive industry were important factors allowing parts makers to push forward along the road of technological change. With stable relations and rapid growth held as basic assumptions, parts makers were able to invest aggressively in new equipment, improve technological capabilities, expand the scale of production, and otherwise continue with overall modernization efforts.

The Reorganization of Systematic Specialization, and the Keiretsu

Capital liberalization and the reorganization of systematic specialization

Systematic specialization in the auto industry, influenced by capital liberalization from the mid-1960s, entered a new phase of adjustment. In expectation of direct competition from foreign companies as a result of liberalization, Toyota saw reinforcement of its suppliers as an important priority, and provided assistance for the improvement of financial conditions, productivity-based profitability, and personnel and capital ties with itself. Nissan also saw the need for its parts suppliers to be 'transformed into a cooperate complex maintaining international competitiveness in management, technology, and all other facets, achieving an internal structure capable of demonstrating overall group efficiency'. Accordingly, it established a Corporate Consulting Office in 1967, which, in addition to offering concrete assistance and guidance, sought to 'improve overall group efficiency through the education of managers and the resulting qualitative improvements in parts makers'. The assemblers were reinforcing their ties with parts makers, and forming a solid specialization structure able to withstand capital liberalization (Toyota 1987; Nissan 1975).

Specifically, reorganization during this period consisted of mergers among suppliers, repositioning and ranking of suppliers, and keiretsu formation through capital participation. While there were a few mergers of large parts makers, such as the combination of Aichi Kogyo and Shinkawa Kogyo (both Toyota suppliers) into Aisin Seiki in 1965, or the merger of independent Ichikawa Seisakusho and Hakkosha to form Ichikoh Industries in 1968, the far greater number was of smaller-scale firms. Repositioning and ranking took place mostly in the Nissan organization, particularly with the 1966 merger of Prince with Nissan. Most Prince suppliers were repositioned as secondary or tertiary suppliers to existing Nissan parts makers. As a consequence, only 16 of the approximately 300 members of Prince's former co-operative association joined Nissan's co-operative Takarakai.

Capital keiretsu formation

From 1968 Nissan had been actively taking equity positions in its medium-sized Takarakai member suppliers in order to promote improved corporate vigour and the building up of outside factories that would perform with the responsiveness of internal units. Then, in response to the 1971 crisis atmosphere in which other domestic and foreign parts makers began to take stakes in affiliated and non-keiretsu parts makers, Nissan boosted its capital investments in those makers with which it already had capital ties, invested in and arranged mutual shareholding with suppliers whose supply capabilities it determined were threatened by the capital participation of other entities, and stepped up its activities with regard to mutual shareholding and capital participation in companies that were involved in particularly sensitive technological areas (Nissan 1975: 79; Cusumano 1985: 252–61; Odaka *et al.* 1988: 256–7).

A similar tendency can be seen at Toyota as well, so that investments in major parts makers by Nissan, Toyota, and foreign parts makers accelerated from the late 1960s. This period also saw expansion of scale and capital increases at medium-sized parts makers. Some had their stock listed on exchanges, and these capital increases and listings provided additional opportunities for capital participation. As a result of the capital keiretsu formation process from the late 1960s to the early 1970s, Toyota and Nissan each incorporated a number of formerly independent parts makers and subcontractors into their groups.

There are at least three points concerning this process, however, that must be noted. First, cases in which assemblers became the top-ranking shareholders and sent in high-level managers to undertake straightforward keiretsu formation must be distinguished from cases in which the level of capital participation was not necessarily high, and participation in management was low-key. Second, capital investment was not always made solely by assemblers, but also in concert with major group affiliates, or by group affiliates on their own. In the last-named case, the parts makers receiving the investment often became *de facto* members of these group affiliates' own keiretsu organizations, being then positioned as secondary parts makers with respect to the assemblers. Third, Nissan pushed forward with keiretsu formation more aggressively than Toyota did. This was because of the relative weakness of the generality of its group affiliates, as well as the relative weakness of its own supplier management abilities.

Structural reorganization of the co-operative associations and the formation of groups

Following the reorganization of the specialization structure described above, the assemblers set out in the late 1960s to reshape the structures of their co-operative associations, as noted in Table 9.4. Aside from Toyota's Kyohokai, which had visible pre-war ties, most of the co-operative associations had started after the war as social organizations, and had tended to develop along such lines. All of the assemblers, from about 1960 onward, had sought to reinforce their respective co-operative associations, providing them with the means to strengthen assembler ties with co-operative companies, and to develop further their individual capabilities. Also,

Table 9.4. *Co-operative associations of the assemblers*

Maker	Established[a]	Number of association members			
		Mid-1960s	1975	1985	1975–85
Toyota[b]	1939	114	129	135	−4, +11
Nissan[b]	1954	102	110	102	−12, +4
Mitsubishi	1966	355	340	333	−56, +49
Isuzu	1962	228	276	279	−41, +44
Fuji (Subaru)[c]	1958	—	174	202	−69, +97

[a] In some cases, predecessor associations existed before the dates of establishment listed here.
[b] Figures for Toyota and Nissan are for the Tokai Kyohokai and Takarakai (associations of subcontractors) respectively.
[c] There were two associations for Fuji; the figure for 1975 is the total of both (eliminating overlaps), and the figure for 1985 is from their combination and reorganization in 1986.
Source: Compiled from Auto Trade Journal (1972), and official company histories.

along with the expansion of primary makers there was an expansion in, the utilization of secondary makers, and the formation of co-operative associations of these secondary makers took place during the period of rapid economic growth (Odaka *et al.* 1988: 257–8, 260).

Thus, from among their co-operative association members, assemblers formed core groups consisting primarily of suppliers with pronounced capital and/or business ties. Aside from Nissan, where separate organizations were set up for specialist (independent) makers and subcontracting makers, the two types are generally mixed together, and most specialist makers belong to several different co-operative associations.[4] Specialist parts makers expanded their production capacities through equipment investment, and required similar expansion on the part of their transaction partners (assemblers) in order to make full use of their capabilities. The same can be said of the major keiretsu-affiliated parts makers. An important issue having to do with co-operative association structure, then, is that, apart from the specialist makers, the subcontractors and group companies of the other assemblers were rather small in comparison with those of Toyota and Nissan. As will be subsequently explained, while Toyota and Nissan had basically completed building their associations and groups, the other assemblers found themselves required to continue their readjustment in the 1970s and beyond (Smitka 1991).

Formation of the 1960s-Style Specialized Production System

Parallel to the process of systematic specialization and development in response to mass production, the actual items being produced by the parts makers were also undergoing change. While equipment investment was being undertaken to keep up with expanded scale and output, improvements were also being made in technology, production methods, quality, and management. Quality control, value analysis, and industrial engineering techniques were being transmitted to the suppliers via guidance from assemblers and the co-operative associations, and a specialized production system came to be formed between the assemblers and suppliers.

The 1960s form of this specialized production system was fundamentally different, however, from that of the post-oil crisis 1970s and 1980s, as represented by Toyota. For example, although Toyota was already using its well-known kanban system for parts deliveries by the mid-1960s, many parts makers simply kept their own stocks and supplied Toyota's needs out of these, meaning that parts inventories were often merely shifted from Toyota to the suppliers. Traditional mass production techniques, involving large equipment investments and accompanying stocks of output, were effective in the 1960s, but were modified in the 1970s, following the oil crisis. This modification was the result of the need for a new type of specialized production system, one that would respond to demands for further rationalization and product diversification.

Summary

During the period of rapid economic growth, in which the expansion of output in the auto industry was particularly marked, the relationships between assemblers and suppliers also changed significantly. The development of systematic specialization, dependent on technological revolution on the part of suppliers, its post-1965 reorganization in the face of capital liberalization, and the formation of the 1960s-type specialist production system in response to mass production all took place during this period. The assemblers reinforced their respective co-operative associations of suppliers, and formed groups of companies having especially significant capital and business ties. Although keiretsu formation led to changes in the type and number of group members, the membership of Nissan's and Toyota's co-operative associations did not expand very much during the process of rapid economic growth. Needs for expanded production were not met by increasing the number of suppliers, but rather by expanding the scale of production at existing suppliers. Assemblers maintained stable relations with suppliers, and, assuming their continuation, suppliers were able to push ahead with technological change and modernization of production. This is what permitted suppliers to respond to rapid growth in the auto industry with shifts to mass production and specialization. Japanese parts makers, well behind their Western counterparts technologically, used stable transactional relationships to catch up and become internationally competitive. Further, as primary suppliers responded to the need for expanded output, new levels of secondary and tertiary suppliers were formed. As this chain of production was strengthened, the group surrounding each assembler was also made stronger, on the basis of the assumption of systematically specialized production.

Certain points concerning the period of rapid economic growth, however, must be kept in mind. First, the formation of systematic specialization structures by each assembler was not indicative of completely exclusive relationships between assemblers and suppliers. Rather, large suppliers, including core group members, set about expanding their customer bases. This was necessary in order to take full advantage of production equipment investments; it allowed the large independents to expand, and was accepted by the assemblers in light of the need to control costs. It was the existence of these large-scale suppliers that made mass production possible for the post-war entrant assemblers, who in turn provided expansion opportunities for the suppliers. Accordingly, while stable relations were assumed between assemblers and their suppliers, these did not generally preclude business relations between suppliers and other assemblers.[5]

Second, the formation of systematized specialist production systems around each maker was targeted as a problem for contemporary government policy. An influential agency of the Ministry of International Trade and Industry (MITI) compiled a 'Passenger Car Sub-committee Interim Report' in 1962, stating the need for an industry structure capable of mass production based on specialization, and suggesting that assemblers avoid purchasing from their own group companies. For the healthy development of the industry, the report recommended, less constricted transactions were necessary. The actual growth of the industry, however, far exceeded then-current expectations, and suppliers were able to undertake mass production even within specific assembler-dedicated specialized production structures. Also, as noted earlier, even assembler-dedicated group members increasingly supplied other assemblers. Consequently, the reinforcement of capital, personnel, and production ties between assemblers and their group companies proceeded simultaneously with the expansion of group companies' own customer bases and output.

The Period of Stable Growth (1974–1990)

Issues for the Specialized Production System under Stable Growth

Following the oil crisis, the Japanese auto industry grappled with a number of issues related to renewed international competitiveness, including cost and quality control, wide-variety small-lot production methods, and a production system that would allow shorter development times. Accordingly, the specialized production system formed with suppliers was once again reshaped to meet these needs. Toyota was best able to undertake these changes in its version of the specialized production system, and provides a useful perspective on the overall changes that rippled through the industry during this period.

The Reshaping of the Specialized Production System at Toyota

The introduction of the Toyota production system at suppliers

The Toyota production system, which formed the basis for the lean production system that characterized the Japanese auto industry in the 1970s and beyond, was already put into practice at Toyota by the 1960s. In the 1970s, Toyota both implemented the system more completely and encouraged its implementation at its primary suppliers. However, it was not simultaneously implemented at all suppliers. Instead, there was a clear timing differential according to supplier type. As presented in Table 9.5, the introduction of the kanban technique, an important indicator of Toyota production system implementation, was completed earliest at core group companies, spreading thereafter to keiretsu group companies, subcontractor group companies, and finally to independent producers. In order for group companies to answer the challenges put forth by the post-oil shock managerial crisis and the new issues for parts production, the older 1960s-type production methods were revised and the Toyota production methods were quickly implemented. Possible reasons for the early group company implementation are the deep contact on a daily basis between these companies and Toyota, and Toyota's aggressive approach to production management. In addition, Toyota's in-house version of the Deming Prize, the Toyota Quality Control Prize, was initiated in 1969, and Toyota accordingly provided strong guidance in terms of quality, production, and cost management. The prize had undoubted influence on those companies eligible to win it, the ranks of medium-sized and smaller suppliers.

Following the oil shock, the Toyota production system was introduced at suppliers, particularly group companies, and homogenization of the system advanced to the primary supplier level. What had taken place during the period of rapid economic growth was no more than the improvement of the efficiency of deliveries from primary suppliers, with comparatively little effect on the internal operations of the suppliers themselves. In comparison, the mid-1970s and later years resulted in the formation of the 1980s-type specialist production system, meaning the establishment of a unified system of production, intrinsically different from what emerged in the period of rapid economic growth.

Table 9.5. *Introduction of the kanban system at Toyota group companies*

Stage	Period when kanban system was introduced				Total
	>1970	1971–5	1976–80	1981–4	
Core group company					
Delivery	5				
Production	4	1			5
Purchase	1	3	1		
Keiretsu affiliate					
Delivery	4	3			
Production	3	4	1		8
Purchase	2	2	3		
Subcontractor					
Delivery	18	6	6	1	
Production	10	8	12	1	32
Purchase	6	5	10	5	
Other supplier					
Delivery	10	11	4	2	
Production		2	18	10	40
Purchase			9	4	

Notes: 1. The stages of kanban implementation are as follows: delivery indicates that a kanban label is used when parts are delivered to Toyota, production indicates that kanban labels are used during production in the company's own plant, and purchase indicates that kanban labels are required to be used on shipments from downline suppliers.
2. 'Total' figures include firms that had not fully completed kanban implementation at the time of evaluation.

Source: (Shiomi 1985).

Group companies and labour relations

Fig. 9.1 describes the structure of the group-wide labour federations composed of individual unions at parts makers and dealers under each assembler, which themselves come together under the Confederation of Japan Automobile Workers' Unions (CJAW). In the case of Toyota, there is the Federation of All Toyota Workers' Unions (FATWU), to which belong the unions at seventy-nine group manufacturing companies, as well as the unions at their own affiliates, and this organization covers 60 per cent of the Toyota group companies. FATWU was the result of a reorganization that accompanied the formation of the CJAW in 1972, and stems originally from ties between unions at assemblers and group companies that began in the 1950s, but which progressively took on new significance as a co-operative organization.

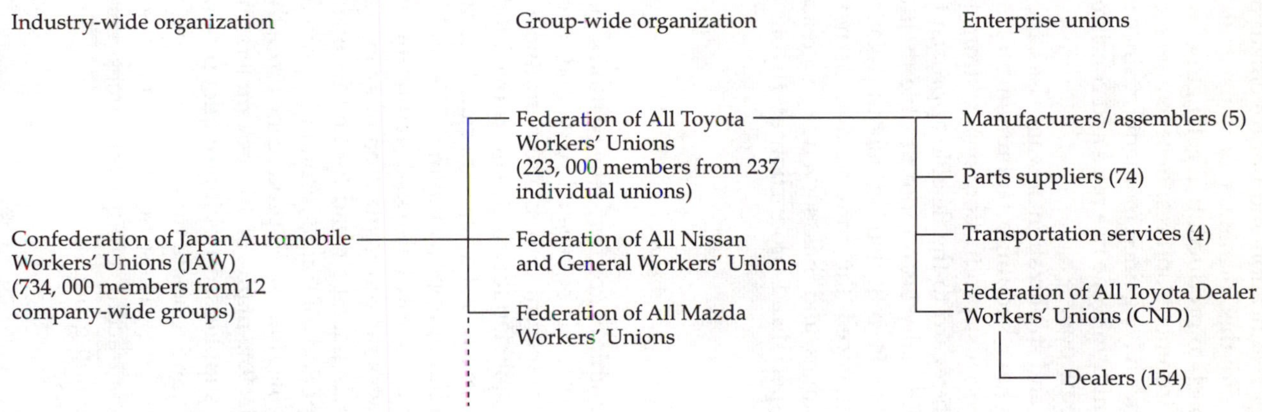

Industry-wide organization

Group-wide organization

Enterprise unions

Confederation of Japan Automobile Workers' Unions (JAW) (734, 000 members from 12 company-wide groups)

Federation of All Toyota Workers' Unions (223, 000 members from 237 individual unions)

Federation of All Nissan and General Workers' Unions

Federation of All Mazda Workers' Unions

Manufacturers / assemblers (5)

Parts suppliers (74)

Transportation services (4)

Federation of All Toyota Dealer Workers' Unions (CND)

Dealers (154)

Note: CND is a symbol name of the Federation of All Toyota Workers' Unions, and stands for 'Challenge for New Development'.

Source: Federation of All Toyota Workers' Unions, Union Activities (Dec. 1988).

Fig. 9.1. *Confederation of Japan Automobile Workers' Unions and Federation of All Toyota Workers' Unions.*

First, FATWU places emphasis on 'providing broad goals for activities by individual members'. These include unified wage demands, the establishment of minimums for rectification and improvement of differentials in working conditions, and the formation of consistent policies with regard to a flexible approach to production (e.g. length of working hours, job rotation, working environment, and response to new technology). Co-operative FATWU activities have gained momentum since the mid-1970s, with visible progress in uniform wage rise rates and consistent policies for a flexible approach to production.

Second, the unification and stabilization of wage rises, the development of consistent policies, etc. have had important ramifications for the stable anchoring of the new specialist production system from the mid-1970s onward. Particularly with regard to the flexible approach to production, Toyota unions have traditionally been more flexible than their counterparts at Nissan, and this is reflected in labour relations at group companies. This has influenced the introduction of new production systems at group companies and has served to increase the overall efficiency of systematic specialized production at Toyota (Totsuka and Hyodo 1991).

Summary

By taking Toyota as an example of groups in the post-oil shock auto industry, we can observe that relations between Toyota and its group companies, from the standpoint of the unification of the production system and labour relations, took a major step forward. This proved to be an important foundation for the reforming of Toyota's specialist production system so as to meet the new conditions apparent in the 1970s and later years.

That Toyota took this way forward also had significant effects on other assemblers. One of these was the reorganization of group companies. As mentioned previously, each assembler had formed its own co-operative association during the period of rapid economic growth, and these included many small and medium-sized producers. From the 1970s to the 1980s, as shown in Table 9.4, many of the assemblers, mostly lower-ranked, reorganized their suppliers, dropping smaller producers from the ranks of primary suppliers and repositioning stronger parts makers as co-operative association members. These lower-ranked assemblers compressed the layer of subcontracting group companies, correspondingly increasing purchases from non-group suppliers.

Conclusion

By way of a conclusion to the foregoing consideration of groups in the Japanese automotive industry from the pre-war period to the 1980s, the following four points deserve mention.

The first concerns the timing of group formation by assemblers. Ever since the pre-war period, when domestication was being promoted through government policy, close relations between assemblers and subcontractors have continued to be an important issue. However, it was not until the 1950s and beyond that even front-runners Toyota and Nissan were able to position some of their suppliers solidly as subcontractors, undertaking managerial integration and developing along with them in a unified manner. Other assemblers did not achieve this until even later. Further, even after groups, including subcontractors, had been formed, they continued to be reshaped in response to prevalent conditions. This is demonstrated by the subsequent incorporation into keiretsu and group organizations of subcontractors, group companies, and independent makers, often through capital participation, and by the reorganizations undertaken by the middle-ranking and lower-ranking assemblers of their own groups from the 1970s onward. These reorganizations both reduced the number of small-scale subcontractors and recognized other assemblers' group companies as co-operative association members, thus reflecting significant differences in group strength between the front-runners and the rest of the pack.

The second is that the type of managerial integration extended to group companies differed by period. During the period of rapid economic growth, the realization of stable supply required higher production, better quality, and lower costs, and these were the issues that were focused upon. Precise management of methods of production was not yet called for. After the oil crisis, however, as seen in the case of Toyota, the unification of production methods moved forward, and the level of managerial integration shifted upward.

The third concerns the reasons why, although there are significant differences among firms in the Japanese auto industry, each assembler formed a body of subcontractors and group companies around itself and pushed forward with managerial integration. The Japanese assemblers, which had taken up the issue of their subcontractors' development and management since before the war, continued afterwards to build up systematic specialization through close relations with subcontractors, as demonstrated by post-war keiretsu diagnosis. Accordingly, the assemblers did not endeavour to expand the ranks of their subcontractors during the period of rapid economic growth, but instead concentrated on realizing a mass-production structure capable of stable supply through the growth of existing suppliers. This was reasonable under contemporary conditions from the standpoints of the assemblers' costs of managing their subcontractors, and of the subcontractors' capabilities to undertake major technological change in support of mass production. Assemblers expanded orders placed with particular subcontractors, and subcontractors responded by making the requisite investments in equipment and expanding the scale of production. Then, as the industry grew more rapidly, assemblers and subcontractors continued to strengthen their mutual ties, allowing continued development and growth.

Finally, the development of major independent specialist parts makers that could supply multiple assemblers simultaneously, along with the establishment of cross-group business relations by large group companies, proceeded as part of a set along with the original trend toward group formation. Competition among group and non-group suppliers, as well as the ability of group companies to supply other assemblers with marginal production, helped to assist group companies' own rationalization efforts and boosted productivity. Additionally, the availability of parts supply from independent suppliers or from large group suppliers had great significance with regard to increased production expansion on the part of middle and lower-ranked assemblers. This means that groups in the Japanese automotive industry developed in tandem with the existence of extra-group transactions and non-group companies.

NOTES

1. The Yazaki group, Topy Industries, Tokyo Radiator Mfg., and NGK Spark Plug (see Odaka *et al.* 1988) were all registered parts manufacturers at this time. Additionally, Kojima Press Industry provides a good contemporary example of subcontractor relations with assemblers.
2. For example, with Toyota-linked companies, Toyoda Seiko (which can be identified as the predecessor to Toyota Auto Body, Toyoda Machine Works, and Aichi Seiko) and Tokai Aircraft and Toshin Aircraft (which preceded Aisin Seiki) were established. Also, in the case of Isuzu (then known as Jizel Jidosha Kogyo) the years from 1943 to 1945 saw the consolidation of control over parts makers in order to secure stable deliveries (Isuzu 1988: 87).
3. In the cases of Toyota and Nissan, as of the mid-1950s about half of the suppliers had been doing business with the assemblers since prior to the Second World War, but this ratio is rather lower for assemblers that started up auto production later. For example, of the 56 suppliers to Daihatsu that underwent keiretsu diagnosis in 1956, only 8 had pre-war business connections.
4. Nissan undertook a reorganization of its co-operative associations in Oct. 1990, integrating them into the single Nisshokai.
5. It should be noted, however, that the boundary separating the Toyota and

Nissan group companies was rather clearly marked, and the major suppliers of one did not do business with the other.

REFERENCES

Auto Trade Journal (ed.) (1972), *Nihon no jidosha buhin kogyo 1972 nendo-ban* [*The Auto Parts Manufacturing Industry in Japan, Fiscal Year 1972*], Tokyo: Auto Trade Journal, Inc.

Cusumano, Michael A. (1985), *The Japanese Automobile Industry: Technology & Management at Nissan and Toyota*, Cambridge, Mass.: Harvard University Press.

Friedman, David (1988), *The Misunderstood Miracle: Industrial Development and Political Change in Japan*, Ithaca, NY: Cornell University Press.

Isuzu Motors Co., Ltd. (1988), *Isuzu jidosha 50 nen-shi* [*A 50-Year History of Isuzu Motors*], Tokyo.

Kokumin Keizai Kenkyu Kyokai, Kinzoku Kogyo Chosakai [People's Economic Research Association, Committee for Metal Industries] (ed.) (1947), *Kigyo jittai chosa hokokusho 9 ogata jidosha hen* [*Report No. 9 on Company Conditions: Large Vehicle Edition*], Tokyo.

Nihon Jidosha Kogyo-kai [Japan Automobile Industry Association] (1979), *Nihon jidosha kogyo-shi gyosei kiroku-shu* [*Administrative Records of the Japan Automobile Industry Association*], Tokyo.

Nihon Jinbun Kagakkai [The Japanese Association for Human Science] (ed.) (1963), *Gijutsu kakushin no shakaiteki eikyo* [*The Social Ramifications of Technological Progress*], Tokyo: Tokyo Daigaku Shuppankai.

Nishiguchi, Toshihiro (1994), *Strategic Industrial Sourcing: The Japanese Advantage*, New York: Oxford University Press.

Nissan Motor Corp. (1967), *Nissan jidosha 30-nen-shi* [*A 30-Year History of Nissan Motor*], Tokyo.

—— (1975), *Nissan jidosha sha-shi 1964–1973* [*A Corporate History of Nissan Motor: 1964–1973*], Tokyo.

Odaka, Konosuke, *et al.* (1988), *The Automobile Industry in Japan: A Study of Ancillary Firm Development*, Tokyo: Kinokuniya.

Shiromi, Haruhito, 'Kigyo group no kanri-teki togo: Nihon jidosha sangyo ni okeru buhintorihiki no jissho kenkyu' ['Managerial Integration of Kigyo Groups: A Case Study on Parts Transactions in the Japanese Automotive Industry'], *Oikonomika* (Nagoya City University), 22/1 (June), 25–6.

Smitka, Michael J. (1991), *Competitive Ties: Subcontracting in the Japanese Automotive Industry*, New York: Columbia University Press.

Totsuka, H., and Hyodo, K. (eds.) (1991), *Roshi kankei no tenkan to sentaku: Nihon no jidosha sangyo* [*The Development of Labour Relations: The Japanese Auto Industry*], Tokyo: Nihon Hyronsha.

Toyota Motor Corp. (1958), *Toyota jidosha 20 nen-shi* [*A 20-Year History of Toyota Motor*].

—— (1967), *Toyota jidosha 30 nen-shi* [*A 30-Year History of Toyota Motor*].

Toyota Motor Corp. (1987), *Sozo kagiri naku; Toyota jidosha 50 nen-shi* [*Creation without Limit: A 50-Year History of Toyota Motor*].

Ueda, Hirofumi (1987), 'Senji tosei keizai to shita-uke-sei no tenkai ['Development of the Subcontracting System under the Wartime Controlled Economy'], in *Senji keizai* [*The Wartime Economy*], Tokyo: Yamakawa Shoten.

—— (1993), '1930 nendai kohan no shita-uke seisaku no tenkai' ['The Development of Subcontracting Policy in the Late 1930s'], *Kikan keizai kenkyu* [*Quarterly Economic Research*], 6/3, Dec.

—— (1995), 'Senji keizai-ka no shita-uke-kyoryoku kogyo seisaku no keisei' ['Policy for Rationalization of the Subcontracting System under the Wartime Economy'], in Akira Hara (ed.), *Nihon no senji keizai* [*Japan's Wartime Economy: Planning and Markets*], Tokyo: Tokyo Daigaku Shuppankai.

—— *et al.* (1987), 'Industrial Structures in Japan (Part 2): The Pricing of Procured Parts and Services in the Automobile and Electrical/Electronics Industries', *Annals of the Institute of Social Science*, 29.

Wada, K. (1991), 'The Development of Tiered Inter-firm Relationships in the Automobile Industry: A Case Study of the Toyota Motor Company', *Japanese Yearbook on Business History*, 8.

PART IV

JAPANESE BUSINESS GROUPS

10

The Organizational Logic of Business Groups:
Evidence from the Zaibatsu

MICHAEL L. GERLACH

Every economy faces an ongoing set of decisions concerning the optimal organization of its business activities. Firms acquire other firms, they sell corporate assets, they form strategic alliances, and they spin off their factories and divisions as independent enterprises—all in response to changing technological and market opportunities. In so doing, they help to establish boundaries around business units and define the interrelationships among those units.

Special attention has been devoted in recent years to distinctive features of Japanese economic organization, and in particular to the ways in which firms in Japan have crafted alternatives to traditional arm's-length markets or vertically integrated hierarchies.[1] But the reality is that these alternative forms are by no means unique to Japan. Whether termed alliances, networks, hybrids, or intermediate forms, both the business press and students of organization have recognized the increased importance of the loosening of organizational boundaries in many sectors in advanced industrial economies, and especially in the complex networks of alliance that constitute Silicon Valley and other areas of intensive high technology activity.

The starting point for this chapter is the observation that the common interest among Japan specialists and organizational theorists is no coincidence. That is, both the emerging industrial structure of Japan that resulted in the present-day keiretsu and the emerging structure of contemporary high technology that has resulted in strategic alliances share similar origins: they have arisen to resolve the co-ordination and governance problems created by undeveloped markets of the sort common in dynamic and innovative sectors of the economy. Phrased differently, business groups and strategic alliances are both the natural outcome of conditions of rapid and unpredictable industrial development and technological change.

This chapter is intended to expand on and develop this linkage. First, I introduce a simple framework for understanding the logic of economic organization under conditions of industrial and technological change. These conditions, I argue, lead to the loosening of firm boundaries and the rise of business networks as viable and efficient organizational forms. Next, I consider this framework in the context of Japan's pre-war business groupings, the zaibatsu. Zaibatsu evolution is shown to result from the interplay of two competing forces—operational fragmentation into multiple satellite companies at the technological frontier, along with strategic centralization among important financial, commercial, and administrative activities that support development along that frontier. This results in very different growth patterns at the firm level, with financial institutions growing primarily through business consolidations and technology-oriented firms through an expanding network of satellite operations. Overall growth in the zaibatsu, for this reason, tends to be asymmetric, with new member firms coming mostly from industrial firms' expansion into frontier fields. More detailed analyses suggest at least two major advantages to growth through satellite formation over vertical integration—creation of a less bureaucratic and more entrepreneurial environment, and facilitation of strategic partnering with other firms.

What Factors Loosen Firm Boundaries?

Firms have three broad options in how they organize the various activities necessary for them to carry out their business: they may contract through market transactions with external suppliers; they may carry out the activities in-house, including by purchasing outside suppliers and integrating them into their own internal structure; and they may craft a variety of intermediate arrangements that combine features of both. There is nothing inevitable about the choice of form that is made for any given activity, although there are factors that push in one direction or another. What are these factors?

The limits of arm's-length market contracting were first addressed in Coase's (1937) classic article on the nature of the firm, and later developed in the important theoretical work of Williamson (1975; 1985) and the business histories of Chandler (1962; 1977; 1992). As these writers have argued, there are costs to relying on decentralized and impersonal markets where significant co-ordination and governance economies exist. This has given rise to vertical integration and internal hierarchies as mechanisms for reducing transactions costs and developing co-ordinational efficiencies. With the rise of the large-scale corporation, both in the USA and elsewhere, the visible hand has become as important as the invisible hand in the organization of competitive economies.

Far less well developed, both conceptually and empirically, are the factors that determine whether business activities will be carried out within internal hierarchies or through inter-organizational alliances. Although it is beyond the scope of this chapter to develop a general theory of alliance, we do briefly consider here two considerations that such a theory is likely to have. First, the theory will have to tackle the nature and extent of bureaucratic costs and the limits to internal hierarchy—factors that push firms to rely on other firms rather than carrying out all activities in-house. Second, the theory must help to determine the importance of these factors across different types of activities in order to establish the comparative costs of alternative modes of organization in various industries.

As corporations grow, so too do a variety of organizational inefficiencies. The pathologies of large-scale organization are a staple of both the theoretical and popular literature on companies and corporate management. Many firms, such as IBM and General Motors, have found that they are slower than their smaller and more nimble competitors to make important strategic decisions, to introduce innovative new technologies, and to respond to changing consumer demands. The arguments will be familiar to readers and there is no need to belabour the point.

Firms can at least partially mitigate these problems by choosing to limit their size and scope through the substitution of inter-organizational co-operation for internal hierarchy. Interfirm co-operation that involves long-term, dense networks of information sharing and co-ordination introduces at least some of the advantages enjoyed by firms. But it does so while keeping down firm size and allowing firms to focus on those activities they do best. It is true that alliance forms do not provide the same degree of control that is enjoyed by internal hierarchy, and for this reason many activities do take place within firms.[2] But they do help to keep their partner firms within reasonable size and scope limits.

This argument takes us part-way to our goal of understanding the distinctive advantages to alliance or network forms of organization. But further development is needed in understanding just *where* the limits to organization are likely to be most severe. Industries vary considerably in the extent of inter-organizational co-operation, just as they vary in ways that affect the size and scope of the enterprise. What determines, then, how organizations set their boundaries?

First, and perhaps most important, is the rate of change in underlying technological and market conditions. Dynamic situations create opportunities, as well as dangers, that have important economic implications. As Levinthal puts it:

Instances of technological discontinuity and, more generally, of market disequilibria, are occasions for the establishment of potentially long-enduring competitive positions. While business strategy is of importance even in situations of stable market conditions, the opportunity to fundamentally change ones [sic] competitive position is far greater at times of change when former sources of competitive advantage decay and new opportunities for establishing competitive position emerge. (Levinthal 1992: 427)

Not all firms are equally well suited to manage these conditions, however. Smaller and newer firms, for example, are often better positioned to exploit the entrepreneurial opportunities these conditions create because of their flexible structures and greater incentives for employees. As we see below, one way that larger, established firms in Japan have tried to manage this problem is to spin off new businesses, in response to changing technological and market opportunities, while limiting the size and scope of the enterprise. They have built in adaptability by relying on networks of co-operation rather than carrying out activities in-house.

What this means is that firm boundaries will tend to be looser where industries are undergoing rapid change. This perspective is consistent with much of the contemporary literature on strategic alliances. A number of writers in recent years have described joint ventures, cross-licensing agreements, and other co-operative forms as flexible organizations that allow firms with complementary strengths to experiment with new technological, organizational, and marketing strategies. As Mody (1992) argues in a recent review, these forms are being pushed by two different forms of disequilibrium conditions: (1) technology push (as new technologies emerge, the opportunities for experimenting with various combinations increase); and (2) demand pull (pressures of competition force firms to differentiate their products and bring them to market more quickly).

A second factor determining sectoral differences in the organization of activities is what we might term an industry's 'complexity.' Complexity refers to the range of skills and capabilities necessary to complete all activities in the value chain, from initial research through various intermediate manufacturing stages to final product sales. Complex chains have many transactional interfaces and require broad sets of skills—designing a computer and its software, for example, is not the same as manufacturing its components or marketing final systems. Complex activities test the organizational limits of individual firms and make it impossible for them to carry out all activities in-house. Instead we will find various forms of inter-firm co-ordination at different points along the way.

Industries vary considerably in how dynamic and complex their activity sets are. Motor vehicles and electronics, for example, both involve complex assembly operations requiring dozens or even hundreds of product transformations among many workers—within factories, between factories, and across companies. But they differ in the rate with which the requisite skill sets are changing, with technologies and market positions considerably more stable in automobiles than in electronics. In contrast, financial institutions represent relatively low scores for both complexity and dynamism, at least in relation to large and diverse industrial firms. These institutions require broad, macroeconomic data and good knowledge of specific firms and industries. But the organizational routines they use to follow these are well established and systematic. That is, localized information conditions do not generally have a fundamental impact on the know-how base of the firm as a whole.

As we see in the following section, these differences are reflected in the patterns of growth that occurred within the zaibatsu. While financial institutions grew primarily through business consolidation (mergers and acquisitions), ensuring a centralized structure and close ties to the home office, industrial firms tended to grow through the formation of more loosely connected satellite enterprises. As a result of these patterns, overall zaibatsu growth was asymmetric, with most new member firms coming from leading-edge industries.

Organizational Logic of the Zaibatsu

One of the implications of the preceding discussion is that economic organization under conditions of technological and market change will vary substantially from that under stable conditions. Dynamic conditions are prevalent, of course, within industries at the global technological frontier. But they are also prevalent within any rapidly developing economy, including those (e.g. in pre-war and early post-war Japan) that are catching up to more advanced economies. Firms in developing economies are continually innovating—crafting combinations that differ substantially from pre-existing arrangements—even if those firms do benefit from the ability to borrow technologies, production processes, and organizational models from other countries.

Japan's rapid development throughout much of the modern era helps to explain why organizational boundaries have remained so flexible and why growth through satellite operations has often been the preferred form. Equally important has been the interdependent development among these partially fragmented enterprises—the ways in which financial, commercial, and industrial ties fostered and reinforced their collective growth. Together these represent two competing forces that shaped the evolution of the zaibatsu, and continue to shape the post-war keiretsu—strategic centralization and operational decentralization. The result has been a network structure that had emerged in Japan in its important details by the 1930s, long before Japan's keiretsu had gained their current notoriety.

Strategic centralization determined the zaibatsu's ability to reallocate resources among enterprises based on some notion of collective interest. It was the leading zaibatsu that had the financial wherewithal, the political connections, and the overseas contacts to promote development of Japan's frontier industries—buying foreign technology and product licences, funding learning missions to and from Japan, investing in supply and distribution infrastructure, and investing in plant and equipment. Three institutions were vital in this: the group bank helped to raise capital that was used in expansion projects; the group trading firm provided international and overseas intelligence and resource support; and the head office co-ordinated overall resource allocation through a small team of decision-makers.

Equally importantly, however, while the centralized head office managed overall strategic decisions over resource allocation, it often allowed considerable autonomy to managers at the level of the enterprise or line of business over just how those resources would be allocated, especially during Japan's rapid diversification in the 1920s and 1930s. This *operational decentralization* was intended to permit rapid expansion of promising technological and market areas through the localized focusing of entrepreneurial activities and strategic partnerships. This is best represented by the process of creating new enterprises organizationally segregated from the head office—a process termed here 'satellite formation'.[3]

Strategic centralization and operational decentralization operate as centripetal and centrifugal forces that work continually to define and redefine organizational boundaries as groups and their member firms grow and evolve over time. Just how these processes operate is addressed in this section through analysis of the growth and evolution of the zaibatsu, with a special focus on two groups: Sumitomo and Furukawa. First, we compare the overall patterns of growth in these groups, finding similar patterns of satellite-based development of frontier industries but also seeing that Furukawa's more limited diversification resulted from its failure to develop an effective strategic core. Next we explore sectoral variations in growth and diversification based on firm-level patterns. These demonstrate that financial and industrial firms grew through very different processes, with financial enterprises consolidating through acquisitions into a concentrated strategic centre and industrial firms fragmenting into looser satellite networks. Third, we explore these differences in more detail by analysing the organizational advantages to industrial firms of satellite-based growth over vertical integration.

Overview of growth and diversification in the Sumitomo and Furukawa groups

Growth and diversification, especially at Japan's technological frontier, were a driving force behind the organizational changes that the zaibatsu underwent in the decades leading up the Second World War. As is well known, zaibatsu-affiliated firms were instrumental in developing Japan's frontier industries—from the introduction of new metal and chemical manufacturing processes to the development of an electrical machinery industry to the expansion into overseas markets (Lockwood 1968; Ohkawa and Rosovsky 1973). By the 1930s, companies linked either to the old, family-based zaibatsu (e.g. Mitsui, Mitsubishi, and Sumitomo) or the new, industrial zaibatsu (e.g., the Nissan group) were involved in all major industries in Japan, and held leading positions in most.

The growth and diversification reflected here, I argue, was the product of a balancing of strategic advantages enjoyed by the zaibatsu as a centralized resource allocator with an ongoing process of decentralizing operational decisions through the formation of new, partially autonomous enterprises. Among the most important of the head office's centralized resources were capital reserves made possible by successful mines, profitable landholdings, exclusive licences for the development of new regions, etc. These operations served as 'cash cows', the excess from which could be funnelled into promising new ventures. Another important strategic resource was management talent and experience, which could be allocated to promising ventures through information sharing and the dispatch of trained personnel. A third was political connections, as zaibatsu leadership used their relations to politicians and bureaucrats to gain exclusive business licences, subsidies, and government contracts.

Balancing these centralizing forces were an equally powerful set of decentralizing forces. Managerial aggressiveness and entrepreneurial initiative reflected the extraordinary investment opportunities made possible by the new technologies, industries, and markets offered by Japan's opening to the West. The zaibatsu and their affiliates were by far the heaviest investors in developing overseas branch offices to handle imports and exports, in the licensing of the latest technologies from Europe and the USA, and in other risky investments. But in order to harness these investments within their increasingly far-flung empires, they also found they had to grant freedoms to enterprise managers not necessary during their earlier years.

In the case of the Sumitomo and Furukawa groups, we see each set of forces at work, but we also see important differences that were the product of their distinctive organizational evolution. Both companies diversified out of a core base in copper mining operations—the Besshi mine in the case of Sumitomo and the Ashio mine in the case of Furukawa. These highly productive operations (the two largest in Japan) were to serve as an important source of investment capital during the rapid-growth years beginning in the late 1800s. In addition, they served as an important source of accumulated know-how that could be used in new fields—both related (where the know-how was technology- or industry-specific) and unrelated (where the know-how was generic).

Both groups used these capital reserves and know-how base to expand aggressively into the related industries in serial fashion, at each point creating a new satellite organization to handle the responsibilities. Among these 'techno-organizational chains' were those that ran between mining, refined metal, wire production, electrical machinery, chemicals, and iron and steel, as depicted in Fig. 10.1. In both groups, the most important chain ran from the copper mining operations through copper refining and wire production to electrical machinery production. In the case of Sumitomo, this was tied to the formation of Sumitomo Electric, Sumitomo Machinery, and the later adoption of Nippon Electric (NEC) as major affiliate. In the case of Furukawa, this satellite series ran from Furukawa Electric to the Fuji Electric joint venture with Siemens to a later spin-off from Fuji Electric, Fujitsu.

MINING → REFINED METALS → WIRE PRODUCTION → ELECT. MACHINERY

    → CHEMICALS (Sumitomo only)

    → IRON AND STEEL (Sumitomo only)

Fig. 10.1. *The dominant techno-organizational chains in the Sumitomo and Furukawa zaibatsu during the pre-war period.*

Of the two groups, Sumitomo was by far the more aggressive and successful diversifier overall, both into related and unrelated areas. Sumitomo's full-scale diversification out of mining began with the establishment of Sumitomo Bank in 1895, which within ten years of founding had become the third largest bank in Japan (after Mitsui and Dai-Ichi). Sumitomo also diversified at the turn of the century into the iron and steel industry, with the establishment of Japan's first cast steel mill and open hearth furnace, an operation that later was incorporated as part of Sumitomo Metal Industries, one of Japan's steel giants. Although both groups attempted to diversify into chemicals from the Taisho period on, only Sumitomo's diversification was fully successful, resulting in the creation of Sumitomo Chemical, then and now one of Japan's largest chemical companies.

Diversification in Furukawa was much slower and more limited. Although, as Japan's largest copper producer, it had amassed a substantial storehouse of capital, it continued to focus its activities on copper-related operations until well into the Taisho period (1912–26). In the late 1800s and early 1900s, at a time when Mitsui, Mitsubishi, and Sumitomo were moving rapidly into unrelated businesses, Furukawa continued to focus on vertical and horizontal integration—purchasing and expanding mines, producing copper and electric wire, mining coal used to run its refineries, and expanding refinery operations themselves. As a result, it never grew into the kind of group that could rival the other three.[4]

How do we explain these differences? An important reason lies in Sumitomo's early effort to diversify into banking, which provided it with a strategic core of support operations for its broad diversification during the rapid expansion in the interwar period. After its founding, the Sumitomo Bank grew quickly, resulting in a bank that ranked among Japan's top five by the early 1900s and has served as an important source of capital for affiliated enterprises throughout the remainder of this century. In contrast, Furukawa did not finally move into banking until 1917, with the founding of Tokyo Furukawa. But its late start kept it small relative to its counterpart in Sumitomo. At the time of founding, it comprised only 5 million yen in share capital (compared to 30 million); 13.5 million in deposits (compared to 187.6 million); and 15.3 million in loans (compared to 120.1 million) (Morikawa 1992: 137–8).

A second reason can be located in the effects of Furukawa's failure to develop strategic support operations in overseas commerce. Mitsui dominated this area for much of the pre-war period, controlling roughly one-third of all Japan's international trade and using these operations to promote its affiliated businesses. Furukawa attempted to expand its international operations by spinning off its marketing arm as Furukawa Trading in 1917. This operated as a successful operation for a number of years, but speculative grain transactions in its Dalian branch led to about 58 million yen in losses and to its later bankruptcy. This event reinforced Furukawa's conservatism about expansion out of its mining and machinery core, and prevented it from developing the kind of international and overseas support network that might have compensated for its small financial core.

The net result of these differences is evident in subsequent group evolution. By the 1930s, Sumitomo had an elaborate network of affiliates involved in a wide range of industries, while Furukawa's activities remained limited to a few operations centered on mining, metals, and machinery. The Sumitomo zaibatsu, as seen in Fig. 10.2, was organized within a multi-satellite structure of directly and indirectly related enterprises, often referred to (borrowing from the German) as a 'konzern'. In this structure, the head office typically controlled a substantial share of each venture's total equity and retained a number of seats on its board; it maintained strong claims on the revenue stream the venture company created; and in some cases it also managed the affiliate's top-level personnel decisions. But balanced against this central strategic function, as we see below, was a recognition of an important degree of enterprise autonomy.

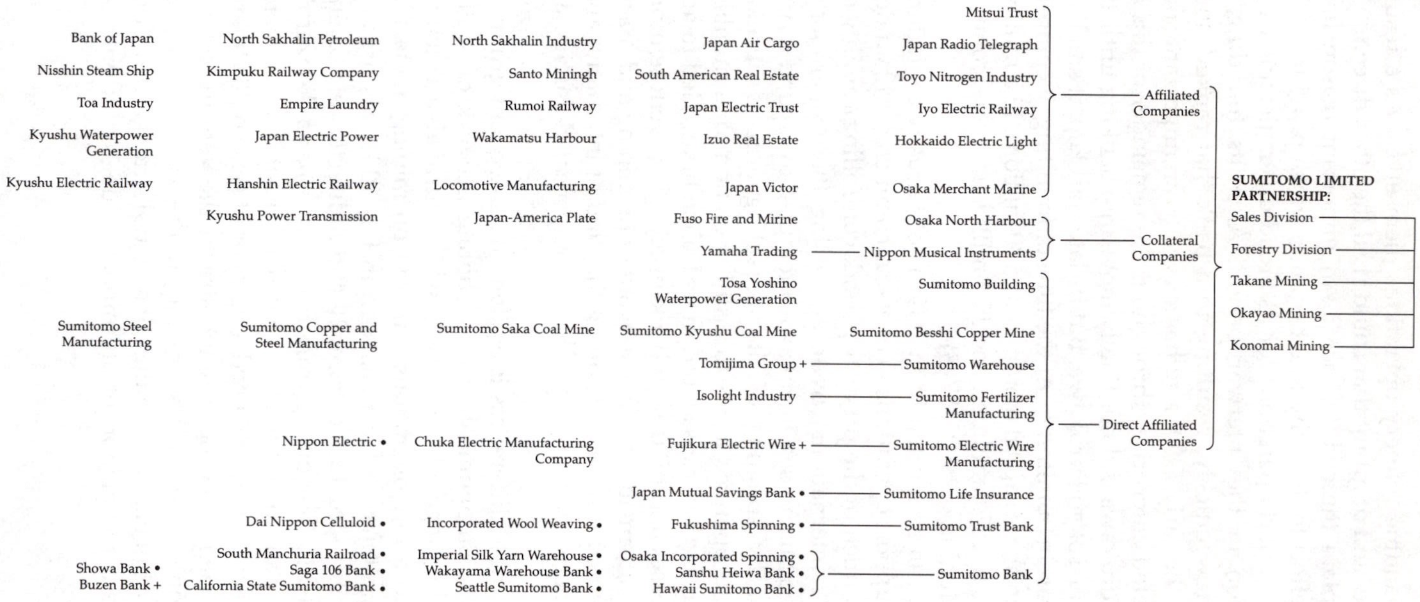

SUMITOMO LIMITED PARTNERSHIP:

Sales Division
Forestry Division
Takane Mining
Okayao Mining
Konomai Mining

Affiliated Companies

Mitsui Trust
Japan Radio Telegraph
Toyo Nitrogen Industry
Iyo Electric Railway
Hokkaido Electric Light
Osaka Merchant Marine

Collateral Companies

Osaka North Harbour
Nippon Musical Instruments
Sumitomo Building

Direct Affiliated Companies

Sumitomo Besshi Copper Mine
Sumitomo Warehouse
Sumitomo Fertilizer Manufacturing
Sumitomo Electric Wire Manufacturing
Sumitomo Life Insurance
Sumitomo Trust Bank
Sumitomo Bank

Bank of Japan
Nisshin Steam Ship
Toa Industry
Kyushu Waterpower Generation
Kyushu Electric Railway
Hanshin Electric Railway
Kyushu Power Transmission

North Sakhalin Petroleum
Kimpuku Railway Company
Empire Laundry
Japan Electric Power

Japan Air Cargo
South American Real Estate
Japan Electric Trust
Izuo Real Estate
Japan Victor
Fuso Fire and Mirine
Yamaha Trading
Tosa Yoshino Waterpower Generation

Japan-America Plate
Locomotive Manufacturing

North Sakhalin Industry
Santo Miningh
Rumoi Railway
Wakamatsu Harbour

Sumitomo Steel Manufacturing
Sumitomo Copper and Steel Manufacturing
Sumitomo Saka Coal Mine
Sumitomo Kyushu Coal Mine
Tomijima Group +
Isolight Industry

Nippon Electric •
Chuka Electric Manufacturing Company
Fujikura Electric Wire +

Dai Nippon Celluloid •
Incorporated Wool Weaving •
Japan Mutual Savings Bank •
Fukushima Spinning •

Showa Bank •
Buzen Bank +
South Manchuria Railroad •
Saga 106 Bank •
California State Sumitomo Bank •
Imperial Silk Yarn Warehouse •
Wakayama Warehouse Bank •
Seattle Sumitomo Bank •
Osaka Incorporated Spinning •
Sanshu Heiwa Bank •
Hawaii Sumitomo Bank •

Note: • indicates that Sumitomo's control over a company is definite.
Unmarked indicates that Sumitomo's control is less than definite.
+ indicates that Sumitomo's control is not classified as any of the above.

Source: Miyamoto (1976: 61).

Fig. 10.2. *The organization of the Sumitomo konzern (c. 1930).*

Sectoral variations in organizational growth

Additional evidence for the importance of the dual processes of strategic centralization and operational decentralization comes from a detailed analysis of the patterns of organizational growth and diversification at the level of individual enterprises within the zaibatsu. Consider the following four modes of growth: internal expansion of the core organization's own operations; external acquisition of another organization's operations; the spinning off of new ventures from the core organization; and strategic partnering with other organizations. Among these four modes, depicted in Table 10.1, the first two, internal expansion and external acquisition, maintain tight boundaries around the core organization's operations and a continuation of a centralized organizational structure under a unitary command centre. (They differ primarily in whether the operations were generated internally or not—factors that were determined by the availability of resources and the strategic vision of the organization.) The other two, spin-offs and strategic partnerships, result in the loosening of organizational boundaries, the decentralization of important managerial activities, and a weakening of control by the core company over operations.

All four of these growth modes were important within the zaibatsu at various points in time, but they were not equally distributed across activities or industries. As Figs. 10.3 and 10.4 clearly demonstrate, the predominant growth pattern within Japan's largest financial institutions (represented here by Sumitomo Bank and Dai-Ichi Kangyo Bank) is one of strategic consolidation—from multiple banks to a single bank through a chain of mergers and acquisitions. Although some city banks (including Sumitomo) began through the splitting off of financial operations from the original zaibatsu family enterprises, they grew largely through acquisitions in the late Taisho and early Showa periods (1920s and 1930s). That is, once the basic division from the head office was established, the financial institution continued to expand without significant further division.

In sharp contrast, as evidenced in the organizational trees for NEC and Fujitsu, industrial firms at Japan's technological frontier have tended to grow through an atomizing process of satellite formation.[5] This process,

Table 10.1. *Modes of organizational growth and diversification*

	Internally generated	Externally generated
Strategic centralization (tight boundaries)	Internal expansion	Merger/acquisition
Operational decentralization (loose boundaries)	Spin-offs	Strategic partnering

256

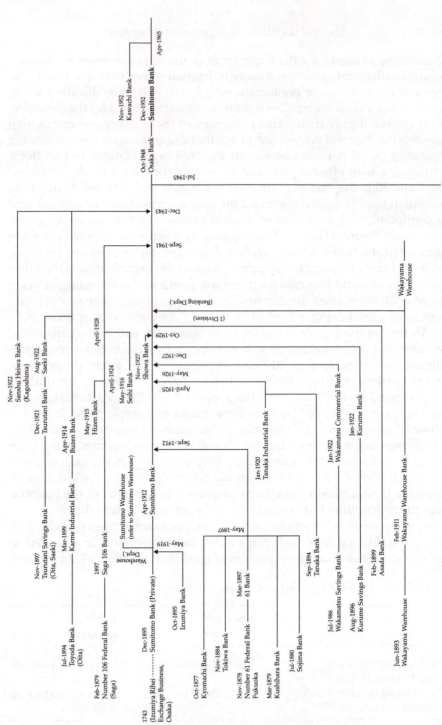

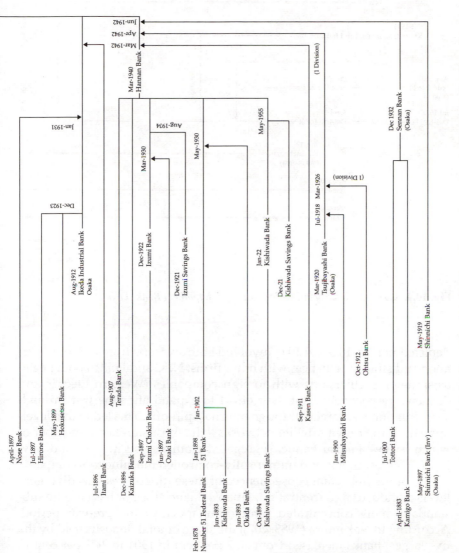

Sources: Sumitomo Bank (1926: 240; 1955a: 182; 1955b: 405, 116, 56; 1955c: 34; 1965: 198; 1979: 14, 687, 107).

Fig. 10.3. *Company history of Sumitomo Bank.*

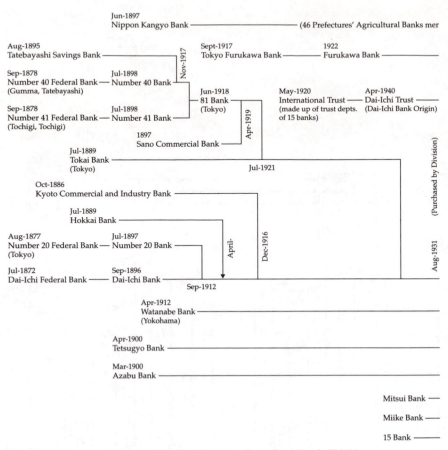

Fig. 10.4. *Company history of Dai-Ichi Kangyo (hypothec) Bank (DKB).*

depicted in Figs. 10.5 and 10.6, involved both spin-offs from the core operation and strategic alliances with other firms. NEC and Fujitsu both began
as strategic partnerships with foreign companies (Western Electric and
Siemens, respectively). But their effort to expand after the war through
segmentation was largely through internal spin-offs. This led to the development of their own satellite networks—the most significant member of
which is now Fujitsu Fanuc, segregated from Fujitsu in 1972 and now
Japan's largest robots and numerically-controlled machine tool company.

One of the important consequences of these differences was divergent
levels of industrial concentration. Japan's financial sector has become substantially more concentrated throughout much of the pre-war period.
According to Nakamura (1983: 207), the share of total deposits held by the
five largest banks increased from 20.7 per cent in 1901 to 24.1 per cent in

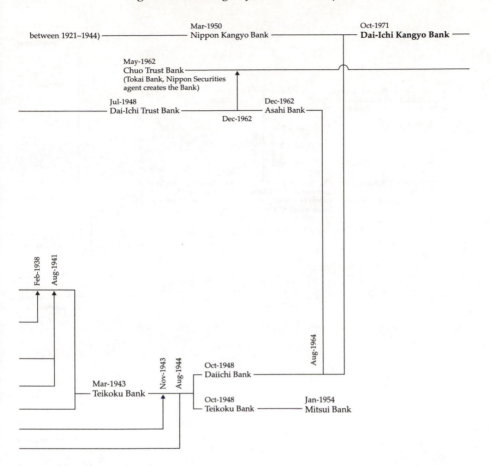

1925 to 41.8 per cent in 1940, while their share of loans went up even faster, from 12.0 per cent to 18.4 per cent to 57.1 per cent. In contrast, he finds, industrial concentration in nearly all sectors actually declined during the rapid diversification of the 1920s and 1930s.

A second consequence of these differing growth patterns is that the development of the zaibatsu as a whole was asymmetric. The strategic core was marked by internal growth among a few key players closely tied to the head office—several major financial institutions and a major trading company were the extent of this core in even the largest groups. In contrast, the operational frontier was marked by continual expansion into new fields through ongoing satellite formation. For this reason, by far the most important source of growth in business activities and in the formation of affiliated companies was the decentralized expansion and diversification of 'venture businesses' intended to exploit new technologies and markets.

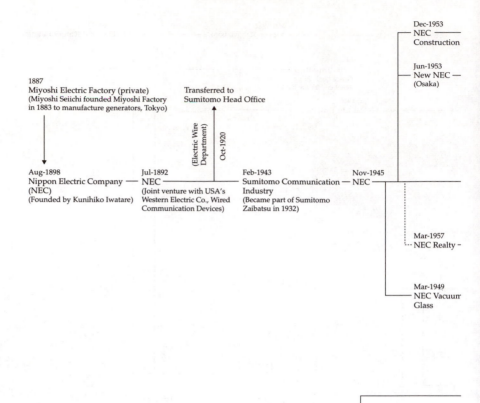

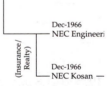

Source: Nippon Electric Company (1958*a*: 63; 1958*b*: 598; 1969: 79).

Fig 10.5. *Company history of Nippon Electric Company (NEC).*

Consider the process of organizational growth in Sumitomo. At present, there are twenty core companies in the group, as defined by membership in the group presidents' council, the Hakusuikai. More detailed analysis of the foundings of these companies reveals two important facts. First, new firms were formed primarily through spin-offs from the core operation, with all but seven of the twenty resulting from intentional spin-offs, either from the head office or from other satellite firms. Among the seven that were not spin-offs, three (Sumitomo Bakelite, NEC, and Nippon Sheet Glass) started independently but built ties to Sumitomo during the pre-

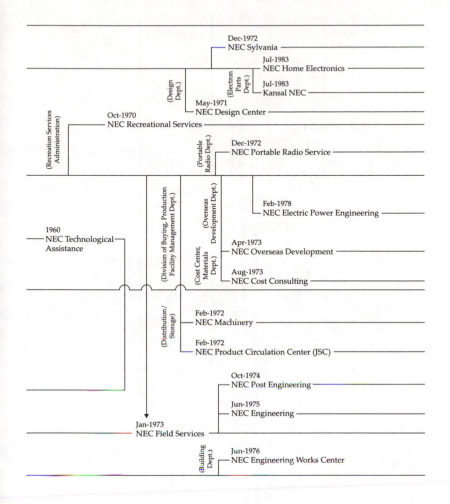

war period, and an additional two (Sumitomo Forestry and Sumitomo Realty) were created out of the remains of the head office after the post-war zaibatsu dissolution. Second, all of the industrial spin-offs (Sumitomo Coal Mining, Sumitomo Metal Mining, Sumitomo Construction, Sumitomo Chemical, Sumitomo Electric, Sumitomo Metal Industries, Sumitomo Heavy Industries, and Sumitomo Light Metals) were the direct or indirect result of Sumitomo's operations in a small number of interrelated industries—mining operations during the Meiji period, and chemical, metal, and machinery businesses later. It was these sectors that were the leading edge of Sumitomo's operations, the primary source of new member firms during its pre-war diversification.

262

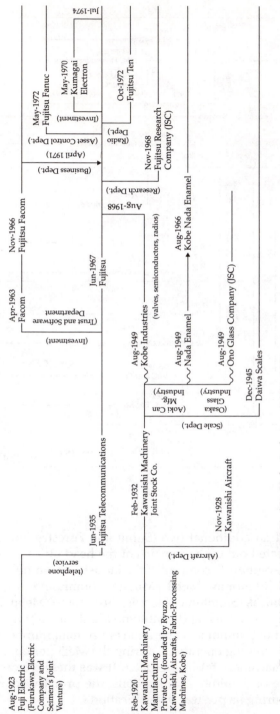

Source: Fujitsu (1964: 206; 1976: 203, 33); Kobe Industry (1976: 119).

Fig. 10.6. Company history of Fujitsu.

The Advantages to Satellite Organization

The significance of these divergent processes of growth raises a fundamental question in the logic of the zaibatsu: why grow through fragmentation of the organization? The reasons begin in the complex and dynamic technical and market conditions structured into frontier industries. These conditions imposed considerable demands on the resource and administrative core of the zaibatsu. Owing to high rates of growth in many key sectors, as well as the importance of establishing early entry to gain competitive advantage, capital investment requirements were enormous. At the same time, head office employees often had little experience in the technical and market requirements of emerging industries, and were often more adept at managing financial and strategic affairs (monitoring subsidiary accounts, cultivating political relationships, etc.) than they were at handling local operations.

By segregating activities, the head office was able to accomplish two important objectives. First, it provided greater autonomy for localized decisions and incentives to operate and created a more entrepreneurial environment in the satellite operation. Second, it facilitated strategic partnering by creating an independent location in which to focus partner-related activities. Gradually emerging from this was a natural organizational division of labour, with a decentralized network of industrial firms taking care of the complex logistics involved in managing diverse technological and industrial activities and the head office taking on the functions of overall strategic planning and resource allocation.

Building in independence and flexibility

As a rule, large-scale organizational systems are structured around standardized products and processes, and employees are encouraged to focus on the observance of rules and procedures rather than on acting independently or entrepreneurially. While this can be an advantage in stable settings, where reliability and cost containment are primary goals, it works against the organization's ability to deal with rapid technological and industrial change. A partial solution to this problem is to decentralize those operations in frontier areas by segregating them from the core operation, granting them a degree of autonomy to develop new and more appropriate procedures to follow, and providing strong managerial incentives toward venture growth. A degree of control is no doubt given up by the head office. But the underlying logic is that the agency costs produced by a weakened administrative control structure are often less important than the organizational flexibility and entrepreneurial initiative that result.

This process of satellite formation took place as a dynamic process in the zaibatsu. As new ventures gained experience, developed outside business relations, and trained their own workers, they gained a corresponding degree of independence from the core firm. In practice, this process typically evolved through several stages. The venture establishes its earliest identity as an internal division of the head office or one of its satellites. As new markets and technologies open business opportunities outside the core firm's basic lines of business, the strategy shifts toward segregating the operation as an independent entity, leading to full-scale incorporation. Significantly, this segregation typically took place through the spinning off of whole units, either divisions or factories. This suggests that it is not only differentiation from the core firm that is important; the internal coherence of the venture itself is also a factor. Over time, if the venture is successful, its ties to the core firm (both control and resource) gradually weaken and it begins to build its own satellite network.

Managers in the head office increasingly removed themselves from the day-to-day running of most subsidiary operations—especially those unrelated to its strategic and cash-cow operations. By the 1930s, less than half of the top management in most satellites came from the head office, and an internally promoted managing director (*senmu* or *jyoomu*) was in charge of day-to-day administration. In the case of Sumitomo, for example, Sumitomo Tomozumi, the president of the partnership, withdrew from the position of the president in Sumitomo Steel Mill and Sumitomo Electric Wire, and served only as the president of the group's bank, the warehouse, and the trust bank. As a Sumitomo executive explained in 1928: 'Each branch operation has its own authority to pursue actively business activities. Under our decentralized organization, these operations can be flexible. The head office must support the affiliates, but cannot ultimately regulate or control them' (translated from Miyamoto and Sakudo 1979: 356).

To be sure, the partial loss of control resulting from the segregating of operations was an ever-present danger. In Morikawa's (1980) detailed discussion of Mitsui's trading operations during the Taisho period, for example, we find a continuing tension between the head office and local branch managers over personnel matters, the kind of products to be promoted, and other important business decisions. But this account also makes clear that Mitsui's loss of central control was countered by a corresponding set of advantages in the form of increased entrepreneurial initiative and organizational flexibility. Mitsui, like other successful groups, managed this tension by acknowledging the advantages of maintaining loosened control over an expanding empire.

Two other examples involving the Furukawa group reinforce this logic. The rapidly expanding operations of Furukawa Electric in the early 1920s continued to be held back by the lack of financial and strategic support from a conservative head office that was still trying to recover from its losses in the trading business and from the recession that followed the

First World War. Although Siemens of Germany had agreed to enter a broad-ranging technical tie-up with Furukawa, the head office backed out at the last minute. Rather than abandon the project, the top management of Furukawa Electric agreed *independently* to sign the contract, leading to the establishment of a new enterprise, Fuji Electric, in 1925. Of the original capitalization of 10 million yen, 3 million yen came from Siemens and an additional 4 million yen from Furukawa-related companies, but none from the head office. It was not until the end of 1928, several years later, that the head office bought any shares in the company. The new venture also sought additional capital through loans from outside financial institutions (Dai-Ichi Bank, Mitsui Bank, Mitsubishi Bank, and Mitsui Trust Bank) rather than relying on the limited resources of the Furukawa Bank. And in terms of management, the new venture's first president was brought in not from the head office, but from a textile company outside the group (Morikawa 1980: 130).

Another example of Furukawa Electric's independent initiative came in its diversification into the aluminium business. Beginning in 1919, Furukawa had been working in a technical partnership with British Aluminium for the production of aluminium cables. As this business expanded, the top management of Furukawa Electric proposed to the head office of Furukawa that it build an aluminium refinery with which to supply the venture. Once again, the Furukawa head office opposed the move, expressing concern about the financial liabilities it might entail. On the surface, Furukawa Electric obeyed this order by appearing to discontinue the research it was already doing in collaboration with a syndicate of several other Japanese firms. But independently it was moving to expand this research, which it did by bringing in funding from the Mitsui, Mitsubishi and Taiwan Electric Power company. In 1935, Japan Aluminium Corporation (Nihon Arumi Kabushiki Gaisha) was established, and soon became one of Japan's major producers (Morikawa 1980: 132).

Facilitating strategic partnering

A second major advantage of satellite-based growth is its usefulness in the building of relations outside of the group. By segregating operations, the zaibatsu were able to create a coherent organizational focus for localized strategic alliances with other companies. The partner firm's investments, personnel, and other resource contributions could be directed toward a limited set of activities. This had the advantages of concentrating the partner's efforts while at the same time protecting the core firm from undue external influence by the partner over its own operations. In addition, the resulting operation was freer than the core firm to pursue new markets and customers (especially those involving firms that might, due to strategic conflicts, be reluctant to deal directly with the parent firm).

The history of Japan's technological development is a history of strategic partnering, both domestic and international. Among Japan's leading C. & C. (computers and communications) firms, for example, most can trace their history to partnerships involving foreign firms. One producer, NEC, was founded in 1899 as a joint venture between Western Electric and a small Tokyo-based broadcasting equipment manufacturer by the name of Nippon Denki. A second, Fujitsu, maintained close connections to Siemens through its parent company Fuji Electric, which was itself a joint venture between Siemens and Furukawa Electric (as noted above). Two other companies, Toshiba and Mitsubishi Electric, received substantial technical assistance and capital investment from foreign partners (General Electric and Westinghouse, respectively).

Also important were strategic partnerships with domestic firms, as evidenced in the growth of Sumitomo Chemical. During the pre-war period, Japan Dyestuffs (Nihon Senryo) had been in close relation with Sumitomo Chemical as the buyer of tar products from Sumitomo's coke oven. Sumitomo Chemical increased its shares in the company and by 1937 controlled half of the total. In addition, it also dispatched the general director (*riji*) from its head office to take over as the director of the board of governors and as an administrator in its partner.

During the post-war period, Sumitomo Chemical continued to expand its outside relations. As Fig. 10.7 indicates, by the 1950s, Sumitomo had established an elaborate network of relations with other companies across a broad range of fields. Among these ventures were linkages to textile companies, oil producers, iron and other metal producers, cosmetics firms, as well as various chemical companies. The capital structures of the ventures were similarly diverse, with some ventures based on a 50 : 50 split between Sumitomo Chemical and its partner and other ventures dominated by one partner or the other. But in any case, by decentralizing these investments to a satellite venture, each partner firm was able to focus its efforts on specific business activities while otherwise remaining independent.

It becomes clear from this evidence that business relations among zaibatsu-affiliated enterprises was far from exclusive. Wray's (1984) study of the evolution of the Mitsubishi group's flagship company, Nippon Yusen Kaisha (NYK), for example, demonstrates that from its beginning, NYK consciously balanced the interests of the larger zaibatsu with its own strategic concerns. Among its shareholders and creditors over time were Mitsui, Yasuda, and Dai-Ichi banks, and in the pre-war period it felt sufficiently independent to terminate contracts it had held with Mitsubishi Shipbuilding. Indeed, Wray attributes much of the success of the NYK during its early years to strategic relationships outside its own zaibatsu. He refers to these as 'business alliances' involving importing firms, trading companies, shipping firms, industrial producers, and banks: 'The company's major innovation prior to World War I, the opening of the lightly subsidized Calcutta line, demonstrated the key to further expansion to be the business alliances in which the NYK joined with other Japanese firms in quest of their corporate goals' (p. 516).

A more fine-grained analysis of the independent business relations created through strategic partnering is available for the Fuji Electric joint venture between Siemens and Furukawa Electric. In the first volume of its company history, Fuji Electric provides a detailed listing of unit sales of major products (power generators, turbine engines, etc.) during both the pre-war and early post-war periods. (This represents the most detailed historical records on company trading relations that the author has been able to locate.) As seen in the figures reported in Table 10.2, it is clear that Fuji Electric sold the vast majority of its output outside the Furukawa group in both the pre-war and post-war periods, with the leading purchasers being power utility companies.

In summary, satellite formation served as an important means of accomplishing several objectives in the zaibatsu. It imparted a greater sense of managerial autonomy and organizational flexibility than would otherwise have existed by limiting the size and scope of the firm as it entered new fields. It also provided an organizational focus for strategic partnering

Table 10.2. *Business relationships with affiliated and unaffiliated companies: unit sales of large-scale industrial products by Fuji Electric, 1924–1956*

Customer	1924–45		1946–56	
	No.	%	No.	%
Affiliated companies				
Furukawa Co.	14	5.6	4	1.4
Furukawa Electric	0	0.0	1	0.4
Other firms in the present-day DKB group	8	3.2	34	12.1
Subtotal	22	8.7	39	13.8
Unaffiliated companies				
Firms in one of the other 5 bank groups[a]	30	11.9	51	18.1
All others (e.g. public utilities)	200	79.4	192	68.1
Subtotal	230	91.3	243	86.2
TOTAL	252		282	

Note: Numbers represent total units sold of large-scale industrial products (power generators, turbine engines, etc.).

[a] These groups are Mitsui, Mitsubishi, Sumitomo, Fuyo, and Sanwa.

Source: Calculated from data provided in *Fuji Denki shashi, 1923–1956*.

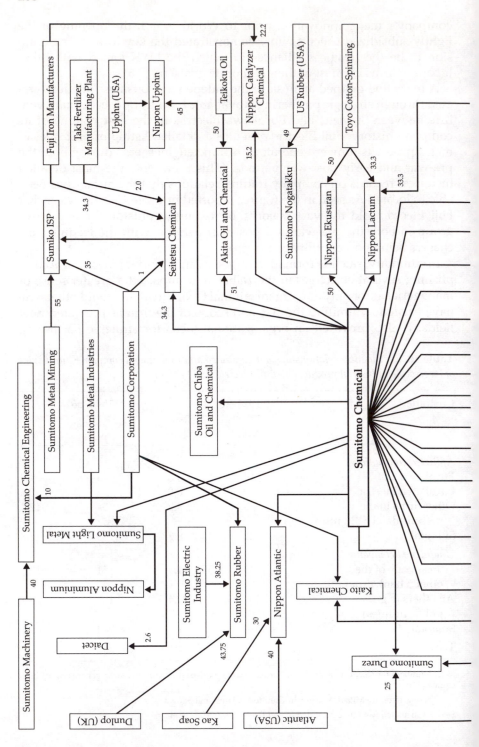

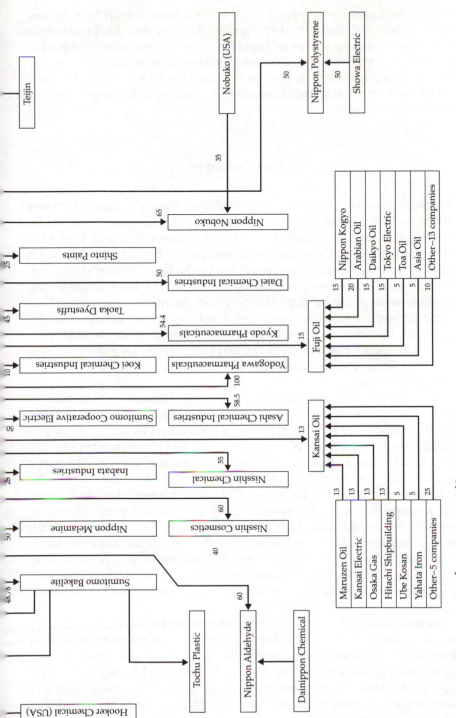

Note: Numbers represent the percentage of investments.

Source: Noguchi, Tasaku (1968), *Sumitomo Konzern*, p. 215. Tokyo: Shinhyoron.

Fig. 10.7. *Sumitomo Chemical and associated business enterprises.*

activities, and used the independence thereby created to help develop new markets involving unaffiliated enterprises. The fact that this process was most common among industrial firms at Japan's technological and market frontier is no surprise. These were the fields in which conditions were continually changing (requiring flexible responses) and where know-how and markets were most dispersed (requiring strategic linkages across an array of firms and industries).

Conclusion

This chapter has considered the organizational logic of Japanese business groups, with a special focus on the growth and diversification of the zaibatsu. This logic, I suggested, flowed out of two competing dynamics. The importance of strategic centralization came in the integrated decision making and resource allocation provided by the head office and key supporting institutions (banks and trading companies). In this way, important decisions were made by a strategically and financially wise, as well as politically well-connected, cadre of head office executives. Equally important, however, was the force toward operational decentralization, with the attendant advantages of creating entrepreneurial initiative, organizational flexibility, and close ties to strategic partners associated with satellite formation.

What this means is that the evolution of the zaibatsu as an organizational form and of Japanese industrial structure more generally involved several distinctive regularities. Financial institutions tended to grow primarily through acquisition of other operations and to retain very close ties to the head office. In part, scale growth was practical because this was a sector in which technologies were simple and industrial conditions relatively stable. In addition, business consolidation meant that banks were well positioned to act as the powerful and concentrated strategic core for group firms. In contrast, industrial firms faced conditions that often resulted in a very different pattern of growth. Those firms that were developing new technologies and entering fast-growing markets were more likely to grow through the formation of more loosely organized satellite groupings—either through spin-offs from the core firm or through strategic partnerships with other firms.

The balancing of these twin forces continues into Japan's contemporary business groups. On the one hand, Japan's best-performing and most innovative sectors (such as motor vehicles, computers, and consumer electronics) are dominated by firms that rely heavily on close ties to key strategic institutions, notably banks. Among the leading computers and communications companies, for example, all have retained close ties to major intermarket groups, or corporate complexes, use their banks as an important source of capital and other services, and act as core members in their group's information councils (Gerlach 1992). On the other hand, the rapidly changing technological and market conditions that underlie these industries have forced these firms to grow and diversify through an expanding network of satellite operations (Aoki 1987). This dynamic process ensures that business groups are by no means an outmoded remnant of Japan's feudal past or its late-developer status. While the ongoing restructuring of the Japanese economy away from heavy industry toward complex assembly industries will no doubt have important implications for the predominant modes of organizing, the logic of group-based organization remains a compelling one.

NOTES

1. The best-known of these intermediate forms, of course, are the keiretsu. In the past several years alone, at least five book-length studies of enterprise groupings have been published in English: Fruin (1992), Gerlach (1992), Nishiguchi (1994), Sako (1992), and Smitka (1991).
2. One of the common concerns among managers (and one which in my experience is especially common among Americans) is that their firms risk giving up control over strategic assets when they develop those assets through collaborative ventures.
3. Other writers have referred to these segregated operations as subsidiaries. I have chosen the term satellite to imply the frontier character of many of these ventures and the possibility that with growth, they would become substantial, semi-autonomous entities in their own right. These growth processes differentiate satellite enterprises from subsidiaries in their more usual connotation (e.g., foreign branches within a company's distribution channel).
4. Although Furukawa did not develop on its own into a broader zaibatsu, it did consolidate important ties that it had maintained since the 1800s with the Dai-Ichi Bank and its affiliates during the postwar period to create the core of what is now the DKB group.
5. This is not to say that mergers and acquisitions are never used by these firms, for they are. But it is to say that their distinctive significance comes in the ways in which their growth through satellite formation has dominated new venture creation in Japan.

REFERENCES

Aoki, Masahiko (1987), 'The Japanese Firm in Transition', in Kozo Yamamura and Yasukichi Yasuba (eds.) *The Political Economy of Japan*, vol. i. Stanford, Calif.: Stanford University Press.

Chandler, Alfred D. (1962), *Strategy and Structure*, Cambridge, Mass.: MIT Press.

—— (1977), *The Visible Hand: The Managerial Revolution in American Business*, Cambridge, Mass.: Harvard University Press.

—— (1992), 'Organizational Capabilities and the Economic History of the Industrial Enterprise', *Journal of Economic Perspectives*, 6/3.

Coase, Ronald H. (1937), 'The Nature of the Firm', *Economica*, 4.

Fruin, Mark (1992), *The Japanese Enterprise System: Competitive Strategies and Cooperative Structures*, Oxford: Oxford University Press.

Fujitsu (1964), *Company History*.

—— (1976), *Company History*, ii: *1961–1975*.

Gerlach, Michael L. (1992), *Alliance Capitalism: The Social Organization of Japanese Business*, Berkeley and Los Angeles: University of California Press.

Hatakeyama, Hideki (1988), *Sumitomo zaibatsu seiritsu-shi no kenkyu* [*Research on the History of the Founding of Sumitomo Zaibatsu*], Tokyo: Dobunkan.

Kobe Industry (1976), *Kobe Industry History*.

Levinthal, Daniel A. (1992), *Administrative Science Quarterly*.

Lockwood, William W. (1968), *The Economic Development of Japan: Growth and Structural Change*, Princeton: Princeton University Press.

Miyamoto, Mataji, and Sakudo, Yotaro (eds.) (1979), *Sumitomo no keieishi-teki kenkyuu* [*Research on the Economic History of Sumitomo*], Tokyo: Jikkyo Shuppan.

Mody, Ashoka (1993), 'Learning through Alliances', *Journal of Economic Behavior and Organization*, 20.

Morikawa, Hidemasa (1980), *Zaibatsu no keieishi-teki kenkyu* [*Research on the Business History of Zaibatsu*], Tokyo: Toyo Keizai.

—— (1992), *Zaibatsu: The Rise and Fall of Family Enterprise Groups in Japan*, Tokyo: University of Tokyo Press.

Nippon Electric Company (1958a), *NEC 60 Year History*.

—— (1958b), *NEC 40th Edition*.

—— (1969), *70 Year History (1899–1969)*.

Nishiguchi, Toshihiro (1994), *Strategic Industrial Sourcing: The Japanese Advantage*, New York: Oxford University Press.

Ohkawa, Kazushi, and Rosovsky, Henry (1973), *Japanese Economic Growth: Trend Acceleration in the Twentieth Century*, Stanford, Calif.: Stanford University Press.

Sako, Mari (1992), *Prices, Quality and Trust: Inter-firm Relations in Britain and Japan*, Cambridge: Cambridge University Press.

Smitka, Michael J. (1991), *Competitive Ties: Subcontracting in the Japanese Automotive Industry*, New York: Columbia University Press.

Sumitomo Bank (1926), *Sumitomo Bank 30 Year History*.

—— (1955a), *Sumitomo Bank Short History*.

—— (1955b), *Sumitomo Bank History*.

—— (1955c), *History of 60 Years 1895–1955*.

—— (1965), *Sumitomo Bank History Continued*.

—— (1979), *History of 80 Years*.

Williamson, Oliver E. (1975), *Markets and Hierarchies: Analysis and Antitrust Implications*, New York: Free Press.

—— (1985), *The Economic Institutions of Capitalism*, New York: The Free Press.

Wray, William D. (1984), *Mitsubishi and the N.Y.K., 1870–1914: Business Strategy in the Japanese Shipping Industry*, Cambridge, Mass.: Council on East Asian Studies, Harvard University.

Yasuoka, Shigeaki (1976), *Nihon no zaibatsu [Japan's Zaibatsu]*, Tokyo: Nihon Keizai Shimbun.

11
Learning to Work Together:
Adaptation and the Japanese Firm

W. MARK FRUIN

After we enter the world, we adapt to it. Indeed, after creation, adaptation is the most basic fact of life for organizations no less than individuals. As soon as organizations are founded and for as long as they exist, they adapt and continue to adapt. Given this imperative, it is also evident that organizational learning is the primary means whereby both large and small adaptation, planned and unplanned change, take place in firms. Yet, in spite of the significance of adaptation and learning, it is surprising how little attention has been paid to these concepts in most theories of the firm.

This oversight may be particularly unfortunate with respect to studies of the Japanese firm. The large Japanese firm, with its personnel policies favouring long-term employment and seniority-weighted remuneration, its patterns of stable shareholding and relational contracting, and its operational interdependency with groups of related firms, subsidiaries, and affiliates, as discussed throughout this volume as corporate clusters and groups, may be among the best examples of the need to 'adapt or fail'. All of these organizational features tend to shield Japanese firms from market forces, especially in factor markets but also in product markets, and to reinforce emphases on adaptation and learning, so much so that many scholars have argued for a distinctive pattern of corporate organization in late-industrializing Japan based on these features (Levine and Kawada 1980; Dore 1987; Nakagawa and Yui 1983; Cole 1989; Fruin 1992).

Obviously, when thinking about firms in Japan, both allocative and adaptive efficiencies are important. Yet, because allocative efficiency models of the firm assume a high level of efficiency in capital and factor markets or in terms of how resources are redistributed within firms, there is good reason to question their primacy in Japan. One of the most distinctive outcomes of the personnel, shareholding, and contracting policies

This chapter benefited from the helpful comments of Dr Masao Nakamura, University of British Columbia.

of large Japanese firms is the degree to which these policies limit the ability of firms to exchange or convert their assets in the marketplace.

By restraining this option, given policies of long-lasting human resources, relational contracting, non-contested corporate control, and long-term interfirm transacting within a finite group of cognate firms, Japanese firms have to pay even more attention to modifying and renewing the resources that they already have. Spinning out non-core divisions and forming joint ventures with non-core activities are two ways of retaining this focus within parent firms. Above all, the strategy of large Japanese firms is based on adaptation, incremental learning, and innovation based on existing resources.

Allocative Efficiency Models

Given these strategic and operational emphases, the extent to which models of allocative efficiency are normative in Japan (as elsewhere) with respect to theories of the firm is surprising. Such models come in three basic varieties. First, there are models where firms are assessed relative to the cost of capital and net present value calculations (Grossman and Hart 1980; Eccles and White 1986). The overriding presumption of these models is that managers of firms seek either to minimize the cost of capital or to maximize the net present value of their assets. In either calculation, the market determines cost and value.

In a second model, the agency model of the firm, firms are depicted as a nexus of contracts involving principal–agent bargaining; the purpose of bargaining is to create a structure of incentives and a set of conditions that maximize performance. Performance is usually measured by financial criteria (Jensen and Meckling 1976; Fama 1980). A third and related model is concerned with how large industrial firms are organized and how the costs of organizing affect performance. In this model, firms are described as mini-capital markets where funds are disbursed according to the best possible returns on the internal cost of capital (Chandler 1962; 1977; 1990; Williamson 1970; 1975; 1985).

In other words, models of allocative efficiency, whether financial models of net present value, managerial models of principal–agent bargaining, or models of how costs of organizing affect corporate strategy and operations, are predicated on market-based tests of performance. Net present value calculations, for example, assume that firms are an amalgamation of the values of individual parts of a company. Principal–agent theories attempt to find ways of modelling the incentives and contractual safeguards needed to get others to behave in desired ways. Multidivisional firms (M-Form) and other organizationally complex corporations, operating as mini-capital markets, are said to allocate funds in accordance with the best, that is, the most profitable, internal use of funds.

While such theories may reflect how the performance of firms in leading Western economies are evaluated and rewarded, *and there are major debates about this* (Porter 1992), they are not appropriate when describing or evaluating the behaviour of most major Japanese firms. In other words, allocative efficiency models of the firm should not be considered normative in Japan. Instead, adaptation, both internal and external, reigns supreme because of the relative unimportance of shareholder rights, a general absence of full-blown M-Form firms, and the prevalence of network forms of industrial organization where technical and functional interdependencies create strong forces favouring mutual adjustment and information exchange between firms, often unsecured by interfirm shareholding (Fruin 1992; Fruin and Nishiguchi 1992; Gerlach 1987; 1992). Adaptation, not allocation, is the driving force for corporate change in Japan, and in no way does adaptation seek optimality.

Financial Markets and Organizational Development

The rise of the New York stock exchange, a *sine qua non* for allocative models of organizational efficiency, occurred only once, more than a century ago, and affected directly only a handful of the world's leading industrial firms. Remember that the degree to which American firms have raised funds openly through markets like the New York stock exchange is unparalleled in the history of capitalist enterprise. Sources of capitalist financing were much more constrained in Europe; witness the importance of Lloyd's of London and other private sources of capital for British industrialization and the main bank functions of German and Belgian banks in bankrolling industrial firms in those countries and their colonies (Chandler 1990).

Japan is closer to the European than to the American model of corporate financing. In other words, the financial context of industrialism was coloured by a scarcity of investment capital and, therefore, its high cost. Non-equity-based forms of capitalization, such as debentures, credit, and unsecured notes, were common, as was a reliance on co-operation as a means of competition within business groupings. In time, the prevalence of such arrangements within business groups has given rise to a number of stylized facts about the nature of corporate rights in Japan. Paul Sheard writes on the subject in the following way:

It is felt that Japanese firms pay more attention to the interests of employees and other stakeholders, rather than having their objective function dictated by shareholders, and tend to structure their input and output relations under long-term arrangements rather than rely on open markets. (Sheard 1994*b*: 215)

Japanese individuals hold ownership claims on firms mainly in indirect form, through various forms of intermediary, e.g. banks and insurance companies. (Sheard 1994*b*: 227)

Adaptation as a Source of Efficiency

Allocative efficiency and cost of capital models miss the point of organizational adaptation and learning models of the firm, especially in countries like Japan where the degree to which corporate funds could be raised publicly has been severely constrained. Accordingly, the exchange of executive or technical personnel and the establishment of supplier associations and presidents' councils within business groups in Japan, for example, are neither 'hostage-taking' surrogates nor analogous to the monitoring function of financial models of corporate governance (Hoshi *et al.* 1990*a*; 1990*b*). Instead, their purpose is to provide information, make suggestions, and monitor policy formation processes as a means of promoting more effective inter-organizational adaptation and learning.

In order to accomplish these ends—that is, more effective adaptation and learning—a variety of interfirm governance mechanisms, such as supplier associations, supplier grading schemes, exchanges of engineering and managerial personnel, shareholding, technology diffusion practices, and dedicated training programmes like Total Quality Management (TQM) and Total Productivity Management (TPM) seminars for the mutual adoption of technology and know-how, have appeared. All of these—associations, schemes, seminars, forums, training programmes, exchange activities, personnel policies, campaigns, and other forms of information exchange and knowledge sharing—are designed to help firms and enterprises organize, manage, co-ordinate, enhance, and reinforce mutually beneficial trading relations in the absence of clear-cut market-based means for doing so.

For such reasons and others, Japanese industrial firms are rather different in structure and strategy from their Western counterparts. In general, it can be demonstrated that Japanese firms are smaller, less vertically integrated, and less broadly diversified than their Western, particularly American, counterparts. Since firms are relatively smaller and more specialized in Japan, interactive learning effects in a value-adding chain are larger and, thus, the transactional costs associated with this decentralized model of industrial and corporate organization may be lowered (Fruin 1992, 1995).

The reasons for such differences are historical. Whether one takes a view that structure follows strategy or that strategy follows structure, the consequences of these historical differences in market characteristics, the institutional environment, and late development make Japanese firms markedly different from their Western counterparts in organizational size, structure, conduct, and performance.

The Japanese Enterprise System argues that, because of these developmental differences, there are three strong forms of industrial organization in Japan: factory, firm, and interfirm network. For industrial firms, factories are the engine of technology transfer and transformation; firms manage, plan, and co-ordinate the core resources of the firm; and interfirm networks provide inputs and handle outputs that flow to and from firms and factories. In this view, firms are organizationally interdependent with factories and other enterprise units; a value chain analysis would find production and distribution functions that are aggregated *within and between firms*. Obviously, where and how boundaries between factories, firms, and networks are located affects the flow of information, the exchange of assets, and the input–output functions of the macro-organizational units involved.

These forms of strong organization—factory, firm, and interfirm network—are part of the deep structure of Japan's system of industrial organization. And because Japanese firms are smaller, less vertically integrated (due to interfirm networks or keiretsu), less broadly diversified (at the two-digit level of SIC classification and also due to the existence of interfirm networks or keiretsu), they are relatively more focused in structure and strategy than comparable American and European firms. Being more focused, however, mandates a strategy of co-operation with other firms in order to realize the size, scale, and transaction cost economies needed to be competitive across the value chain.

Interfirm networks provide breadth of activity and resources. In the past, such networks were often financial in character, but now the bank share of intergroup financing is declining while financing through interfirm shareholding and retained earnings are rising. Intrafirm networks, in addition, provide and stimulate depth of activity. Given the technology-focused thrust of Japanese industrials, the importance of lead or focal factories—the foundations of intrafirm networking—gives Japanese firms a low and dynamic centre of gravity.

In concert, smallish, specialized Japanese firms develop great strength and flexibility by reaching downward to create factories of innovation and adaptability, and reaching outward to augment the resources of single firms with those of other enterprises in network alliances. The core strategy of Japanese firms is *the mobilization of resources at every level of organization*. Such a strategy is logical and consistent within an institutional environment where the assets of corporate groups and complexes at every level of organization are not easily bought and sold.

Accordingly, companies like Toshiba may pursue a strategy designed to maximize economies of scope by mobilizing the resources of numerous factories and affiliated firms while other firms may be more like Toyota Motor, that is, pursuing a strategy that is more scale-oriented, designed to produce a large volume of high-quality, low-cost motor vehicles. In either case, Japanese industrials are working through the same triad of organizational forms—factory, firm, and interfirm network—and, hence, organizational adaptation and learning are more powerful forces for change than are strategies of allocative efficiency.

Some Evidence of Adaptation's Centrality

Using Toshiba, Toyota, and Kikkoman as examples—three firms that I have studied extensively—this section of the chapter is designed to provide some empirical evidence supporting adaptation as a primary and central force for change among major industrial firms in Japan.

Kikkoman and Family Enterprise

The flexibility of the Japanese stem family or *ie* has helped guarantee continuity and ability in family-owned and -managed firms. Because of the overriding importance of stem family preservation and success, the focus of family members in *ie*-based enterprises was more institutional than personal. Institutional performance was far more important than individual power, privilege, and success; riches-to-rags in three generations did not so frequently afflict stem family firms in Japan. Rather, individuals were taught to be restrained in their personal lives and to seek achievement and satisfaction within the context of the family enterprise (Fruin 1983: 10).

In pre-war Japan, stem family-based enterprises were forced most often to turn to banks for loans rather than to equity markets, given the undeveloped and uncertain quality of stock and security markets before the Second World War. As a result, firms, especially family firms, came to depend on loans as the primary means of raising capital with an accompanying result that the control of family firms was not often lessened by the sale of company shares. Accordingly, family control has not been as diluted in Japan as it has been in the United States by a steady reduction in the proportion of company shares that are closely held. Shares have commonly remained closely held in Japan, even if one or several banks have become influential at the level of the board of directors in family firms (Fruin 1983: 10–11).

When the Noreda Shoyu Company, Limited (the precursor of Kikkoman) was founded in 1917, that most traditional yet most malleable and motivating of all institutions—the family—was the rallying point for establishing a new post-cartel business organization. Unlike the cartel, with its emphasis on locale and occupation, the new corporate enterprise focused primarily on family. But these were families that were interrelated genealogically and experienced in the growing sophistication of the soy foods industry.

Seven Mogi families, out of the twenty-two families that had been involved with the cartel on one occasion or another, joined with Horikiri Monjiro and Takanashi Hyozaemon (a direct descendant of the Takanashi Hyozaemon whore first brewed shoyu in Noda in 1661) to form the Noda Shoyu Company in December 1917. Once the new corporation was in place, it required less than seven years for its executives to transform the enterprise from a local soy foods maker into a rural zaibatsu, a family-based, holding company conglomerate, with interests in banking, railways, shipping and storage companies, and in domestic as well as foreign manufacture of a variety of food and food-related products (Fruin 1983: 283–4). Clearly, in the case of Noreda Shoyu, adaptation within the context of the Japanese stem family was the major vehicle of enterprise growth and development during the twentieth century, primarily before the Pacific War but even thereafter.

Toyota Motor Company and Corporate Complexes

In explaining network-based forms of organization in Japan, like Toyota's network of auto parts and sub-assembly suppliers, none of the obvious and often cited reasons—legal, organizational, and financial—for favouring co-operation among numerous independent actors is either convincing or satisfying on its own. Typically, enterprises engaged in collective action strategies in Japan are neither compelled nor paid to co-operate.

For such reasons, network organizations are defined in terms of the nature and quality of the relations that bind actors together. These may be informal and personal, like relations among office friends, and they may be formal and impersonal, such as relations among political action groups which lobby together for government funds and entitlements. Whether informal and personal or formal and impersonal, the nature and quality of relations among groups of otherwise independent and co-operating actors define the boundaries of network organization.

Sheard writes:

Relations in a given *keiretsu* are multi-faceted, involving such aspects as ownership, financing, transfer of intermediate products, movement of personnel, sharing of information, and joint research and product development, even between a given pair of firms. Not only is 'membership' better conceived in terms of a continuum rather than a zero–one condition, it is also better viewed as connoting a vector of attributes rather than a single one. (Sheard 1994*a*: 13)

This is true of highly formalized networks, like Toyota Motor supplier firms, or of loosely organized, informal networks, like Harvard University graduates living and working in Tokyo. The nexus of relations that characterize network organizations may appear enduring, almost transcendental on one end of the temporal scale, and rather temporary, almost transitory, on the other end. So, not only are there many different kinds of network organizations but they coexist and interpenetrate one another spatially and temporally. That diversity and complexity represent the challenge of analysing, interpreting, and comparing corporate groups and complexes as opposed to markets as fundamental ways of organizing human activity.

Again, Sheard argues, 'When an individual firm allocates its input demand (including for distribution inputs), it is not "closing the market", it is organizing its production and distribution system, and presumably doing so in a cost-minimizing way' (Sheard 1994*a*: 37). Also:

If long-term transactions are as prevalent as is suggested, the coordination problem would be largely solved, or at least relative to the problem as it would exist in a period-by-period arms-length trading environment. It is hard to see why government coordination mechanism would be needed on top of that. Government coordination and long-term ties both make sense, but it is hard to see both being needed at the same time, *at least to solve the same coordination problem.* (Sheard 1994*b*: 245; my italics)

The financial ties between Toyota Motor and its first-tier companies, of which there are about 179, are fairly transparent even though intragroup shareholding within the Toyota group of companies may be calculated in various ways. Toyota's financial position in the largest 15 first-tier suppliers averages 24 per cent; in other words, Toyota owns a quarter of the shares of less than 10 per cent of its first-tier suppliers. According to 1986 data, among 27 of Toyota's largest suppliers, the average level of Toyota shareholding was 20.7 per cent. For the entire group of first-tier suppliers, however, the average level of intragroup shareholding is well under 10 per cent (Fruin 1992: 289–90, 299).

In short, financial models of why firms co-operate cannot do justice to the many reasons why firms within the Toyota group of companies might participate in strategies of collective action (Ostrum 1990; Ostrum *et al.* 1992). Except for relatively recent cases of interfirm financing, when proximate and more remote reasons for the buying and selling of shares may be traced, interfirm shareholdings within corporate groupings in Japan are not especially indicative of anything other than prevailing patterns of interfirm financing. And once enterprises are engaged in strategies of interfirm financing within a limited set of actors, firms are likely or be judged and or judge their own performance on the basis of learning and adaptation within the group rather than on cost of capital calculations.

Factories as Engines of Organizational Adaptation at Toshiba

Factories are sources, really, one could say, engines, of adaptive efficiency at Toshiba. Examples of this abound and three such examples are detailed below.

First, the Komukai Works was established on 3 December 1937 in Kawasaki City as a branch parts factory of the Yanagicho Works, then the principal factory of Tokyo Electric Wireless. Tokyo Electric Wireless was itself founded just two years earlier as a speciality producer of wireless radios for Tokyo Electric, one of two progenitors of today's Toshiba Corporation, which joined Shibaura Seisakusho in 1939 to form Tokyo Shibaura Company (Toshiba Corporation 1987).

The Komukai Works grew rapidly, employing as many as 10,000 workers by the end of the Second World War. In 1944 the factory was being depicted on organization charts as the Komukai Works, a principal factory of Tokyo Shibaura Electric. After the war, in August 1949 when Tokyo Shibaura was reorganized, the Komukai Works was listed as the principal factory of the communication products division. By 1952 the Komukai Works boasted 1,230 regular employees and production of 15,000 radios per month. In 1954, however, the principal responsibility for radio production was moved back to the Yanagicho Works to make room for television production at Komukai.

Televisions were one of the big three consumer durables that everyone coveted in the 1950s and 1960s, the other two being washing machines and refrigerators. In 1955 Komukai was running at 1,000 black and white televisions per month but by 1957 production had jumped tenfold. Benefiting from a tremendous increase in corporate capital investment, by 1959 Komukai's production had jumped again to 50,000 units per month.

The jump in television production based on new transistor technology brought thousands of female employees into the workplace. From 1960 to 1970, the Komukai work-force doubled in size, from some 1,200 during the latter half of the 1950s to at least 4,000 during the 1960s. From 1965 to 1970, when female employment was at its peak, roughly half of Komukai's 4,600 workers were women. When production technology allowed for more automation and when transistor and integrated circuit production became more centralized in the 1970s, however, female employment dropped drastically. In the first half of the 1970s, women were no more than one-sixth of Komukai's 2,900 workers, and by the latter half of the decade they were down to 4–5 per cent of the total.

The obligations of long-term employment and steady promotion for regular, mostly male, employees plus the potential loss of production and process technology know-how that had accumulated at Komukai would not allow Toshiba to close the plant or dismiss or transfer its workers.

Instead, responsibility for the design, development, and production of such closely related products as air traffic control radar, multi-purpose radar, rail communications and control equipment, and television broadcast equipment were centralized at Komukai and new product lines as well as parts production associated with various assembly operations located elsewhere were sited at Komukai. Komukai adapted to new market and technical circumstances.

Second, Toshiba's Nagoya Works was founded in 1943. Actually, it had been established earlier in Tokyo as the Oi Works but the core of the factory, about 20 machine tools and 100 workers, was moved to Nagoya in 1943 to escape aerial bombardment, occupying a factory in the Suwa district of Aichi Prefecture that had been owned previously by the Central Spinning Company. When the Nagoya Works started up production of electric drills in earnest in 1944, it had swelled to 361 employees (Toshiba Corporation 1983).

After the war, the Nagoya Works, like most other Toshiba factories, got back on its feet by producing parts for or assembling high-demand consumer products like electric irons, toasters, refrigerators, fans, and washing machines. Through the 1960s and 1970s, Nagoya Works concentrated especially on the last two of these, fans and washing machines, and the range of their production was truly impressive. From 1945 to 1983, for example, the Nagoya Works produced and assembled 240 different kinds of products, including 83 different kinds of fan and 36 different models of washing machine. In other words, although the Nagoya Works prospered as a general maker of consumer electrical goods, it did so by developing a full line of products in relatively narrow lines of business. This strategy, based on what are called economies of scope, is based on the flexible organization and human resource practices of Japanese factories.

Take fans, for instance. The Nagoya Works built desk fans, exhaust fans, floor fans, stand fans, heater fans, car fans, wall fans, revolving fans, salon fans, range top fans, window fans, industrial fans, duct fans, pipe fans, greenhouse fans, heater fans, circulation fans, wireless remote control fans, microfans, dual-purpose fans (a fan during the summer, an air circulator during winter), and so on. That is twenty different kinds of fan, not counting the different models possible for each kind of fan. Admittedly, in many cases the degree of variation between these different sorts of fans may not be great. However, even when the variation is no more than one of dimension, adjustments have to be made in production organization and operations, department management, product distribution, sales, marketing, service, and accounting.

The Nagoya Works illustrates well one of the principal maxims of Japanese manufacturing: instead of making a few things in large volume, make many things in limited numbers. Flexible and adaptable production capabilities are the key to survival at the factory-level of organization.

Otherwise, what a factory makes in volume cannot be long sustained in the marketplace in the face of manœuvring by rival manufacturers and, given a host of other internal factories making products for the firm, the production value of what is manufactured needs to show consistency if not improvement. For both reasons, factories need to be flexible and responsive.

Third, the Fukaya Works, Toshiba's television and picture tube factory, is located in the city of Fukaya, Saitama Prefecture, about two hours from the centre of Tokyo. Toshiba opened the plant in 1969 and, as soon as the production lines began to roll, the factory was engaged in a factory-wide zero defects campaign. From the start, the strategic thrust of the plant was production of picture tubes and televisions, the combination of which in a single plant was and is rather unusual. Obviously, great savings in design and development costs as well as production efficiency may be realized when parts and complete systems are made together. The complexity of combining sub-tasks and systems products prevent the co-location and integration of parts and systems products in most instances. Toshiba, however, chose to defy the odds against an integration of functional and systems requirements at Fukaya and elsewhere (Toshiba Corporation 1989; 1990).

By March 1970, a scant twenty-one months after the plant was opened, the 1,528 employees at Fukaya had rolled the 1 millionth colour picture tube down the production transfer line. Company president Toshio Doko, former president of Ishikawajima-Harima and of the Keidanren, visited the factory to commemorate the hugely successful production of picture tubes at Fukaya. The pace of production progress was so rapid that Fukaya initiated a programme of exchanging information on techniques with other factories in an effort to keep abreast of what was happening generally throughout Toshiba. An open systems approach to organizational learning is based on building iterative, evolutionary pathways of knowledge acquisition and know-how application. Adaptive rather than allocative efficiency is the primary driver of Toshiba's strategy of factory-based organizational adaptation and learning (Fruin, forthcoming b).

Discussion: Co-operation and Adaptive Models of Efficiency

These examples and others suggest the following eight points:

1. Co-operation among profit-seeking firms is possible and, often, desirable. Co-operation can be of several sorts but, most often, co-operation seeks to realize a so-called win/win situation, a situation where all co-operating parties benefit. It is not necessary that all co-operating parties

benefit equally although over the long-term there may be a sequential equity rule that seeks to balance out the benefits of co-operation (Ostrum 1990; Ostrum *et al.* 1992; Sandler 1992).

2. Co-operation is especially common in Japan, given all sorts of inter-firm alliance building there; the frequency of interfirm alliance building was most likely due to the scarce resources and unpredictable course of industrialization at the turn of the twentieth century. Firms learned co-operation as a matter of necessity. Studies of non-human populations, such as animal study groups reported by *Scientific American*, suggest that such ecological determinants may be especially important for co-operation to develop (Holloway 1995).

3. Co-operating companies conduct 'searches' that seek to utilize, not necessarily maximize, resources at their disposal. If they have established patterns of co-operation with other firms, successive 'searches' may include scenarios that depend in critical ways on the resources of other firms (Nelson and Winter 1982; Fruin 1992). Adaptation arising out of the 'search' process does not necessarily seek optimality.

4. Notions of static equilibrium with respect to levels of resource availability and utilization make little sense in models of adaptive efficiency. Not only are a firm's internal resource capabilities evolving but so are those of the set of firms with which it routinely co-operates. Depending on the numbers of firms in a 'co-operation set' and dynamic learning routines within a set, resource availability and utilization are anything but static.

5. Imperfect rather than perfect information is an important trait of adaptation models of the firm. However, because of adaptation, firms, acting singly and together, can accumulate and act on more and more (perfect) information. As the reservoir of accumulated information and routines grows, however, firms are less and less likely to search for alternative routines, policies, and procedures to solve the problems that they face. In other words, searches for solutions are likely to occur within a set of established pathways of co-operation. 'Bounded rationality' limits decision-makers' search to a small subset (within a potentially much larger set) of solutions (Simon 1957; Nelson and Winter 1982).

6. Selection based on search routines does not assume that all selection processes are optimal. Instead, human behaviour is most often habitual, not optimal, rule-reinforcing rather than rule-breaking. Adaptation is the norm rather than the exception in habitual behaviour.

7. Within groups of co-operating firms in Japan, keiretsu, *kigyo shudan*, and *kigyo gurupu*, initial motivations for collective action strategies were rarely financial in character. In other words, incentives to work together, especially before and after the turn of the twentieth century when the original zaibatsu groups were forming or during the interwar and post-war years when the *shinko zaibatsu* and the more recent keiretsu were forming, were not based on cost of capital models of allocative efficiency. (Fruin

1992; Odagiri 1992). Obviously, cost of capital considerations were important but they were not an overwhelming criterion deciding group size or
membership.

8. Once inter-organizational memories with embedded routines and
policies are established, something akin to institutional lock-in happens.
Thereafter, strategies of long duration and inter-organizational resource
mobilization are likely to appear. In other words, adaptation is the principal force for organizational change, anytime and almost anywhere but
especially in Japan where there is no market for corporate control and
where norms of inter-organizational action are well established and
highly esteemed (North 1990; Fruin 1992; Gerlach 1992).

Adaption and the Japanese Firm: Concluding Thoughts

Allocative efficiencies are obviously important in Japan, as elsewhere.
Clearly, managers attempt to get the most for their money and one way of
doing so is by allocating capital to the most attractive uses that are available. What uses are routinely available, however, are limited by past practices, the structures within which managers manage, and the institutional
environment that defines business activity. Given these limitations, allocative efficiencies are more likely to be second-order effects in Japan, playing second fiddle to the greater importance of organizational adaptation
and learning.

Second-order effects can be important, depending on the situation. In
Japan, the systems of interlocking shareholdings and main bank relationships create an institutional framework where the stakeholders in large
Japanese firms constitute a latent or background force, able to block hostile takeover bids from external parties and able to veto collective action
strategies of lower-level corporate coalitions. So, in some situations they
are able to exercise some secondary rights of corporate control, but in
almost all circumstances their actions are reactions. That is, they may be
able to block internal and external initiatives but they are not able to initiate themselves.

With respect to exceptional cases, when some sort of intervention is
called for, Paul Sheard writes:

The typical features of the system can be summarized as follows. When the banking authorities detect a worsening financial position in a financial institution, they
conduct an intensive audit. If it is judged that the institution can remain solvent
and viable in the longer run but requires some managerial assistance and restructuring of operations, typically one or more senior officers from the MOF or BOJ, of
'retiring rank', will take up a senior management position in the institution, even
president or vice-president. (Sheard 1994b: 251)

Allocative models of efficiency do not assume dynamic organizational learning because the sources of efficiency—market competition and principal–agency bargaining—are forces external to the firm. Even the standard profit maximization condition is treated as something external to firms since all firms operate under this condition. Adaptive models of efficiency, by contrast, assume that internal co-ordination, management, and organizational campaigning are among many factors that affect organizational change. Organizations adapt to these factors, not once in a while but more or less often (Liebenstein 1966; 1975; Fruin, forthcoming *b*).

If 80 per cent of the capital investment requirements of most firms are met through retained earnings, and this is seemingly true of large industrial firms world-wide, no matter how the remaining 20 per cent of needs are met, large firms will not act as uninterested agents of minority interests. They will fight to ensure that reinvested earnings reflect the interests of management. Moreover, since the headquarter's function within Japanese firms does not emphasize capital allocation efficiencies and shareholders' rights, as is generally true of Western firms, even the 20 per cent minority reinvestment requirements are likely to emphasize internal standards of performance that are based on adaptive efficiency assumptions.

Surely the ability of the Japanese corporate complexes to move firms from one corporate group to another and to move business activities in, out, and about corporate groups and complexes is related to the lack of a market for corporate control as well as the lack of top executive labour mobility. And, of course, both of these are closely related to the valuation problem. Buying and selling require markets. Viable markets require a reasonable number of buyers and sellers. Many aspects of Japanese corporate groups and complexes are characterized by internal business relations that are not market-like.

While the number of internal transactions between members of corporate complexes and groups may be extremely large, there are not that many buyers and sellers of the intermediate goods and services that make up the bulk of internal transactions. In other words, the organizational flexibility of interfirm groupings and the inter-organizational flexibility of factories, firms, and interfirm networks are related, directly and fundamentally, to the weakness of market forces in the organizational life of many Japanese firms. The co-evolution of firms and interfirm networks has created a functional and strategic interdependency that emphasizes organizational adaptation and learning as the primary means of industrial competition. In Japan as elsewhere, but especially in Japan, adaptation is the fundamental fact of organizational life.

REFERENCES

Alchian, A. A., and H. Demsetz (1972), 'Production, Information Costs, and Economic Organization', *American Economic Review*, 62.

Arthur, W. Brian (1990), 'Positive Feedback in the Economy , *Scientific American*, Feb.

Asanuma, Banri (1992), 'Japanese Manufacturer–Supplier Relationships in International Perspective: The Automobile Case', in Paul Sheard (ed.), *International Adjustment and the Japanese Firm*, Sydney: Allen & Unwin.

Chandler, Alfred D., Jr. (1962), *Strategy and Structure*, Cambridge, Mass.: MIT Press.

—— (1977), *The Visible Hand: The Management Revolution in American Business*, Boston: Harvard University Press.

—— (1990), *Scale and Scope*, Boston: Harvard University Press.

Cole, Robert E. (1989), *Strategies for Learning*, Berkeley and Los Angeles: University of California Press.

Dore, Ronald (1986), *Flexible Rigidities: Industrial Policy and Structural Adjustment in the Japanese Economy 1971–80*, Stanford, Calif.: Stanford University Press.

—— *Taking Japan Seriously*, Stanford, Calif.: Stanford University Press.

Douglas, Mary (1986), *How Institutions Think*, Syracuse, NY: Syracuse University Press.

Eccles, R. G., and H. C. White (1986), 'Firms and Market Interfaces of Profit Center Control', in J. S. Lindenberg, J. S. Coleman, and S. Nowak (eds.), *Approaches to Social Theory*, New York: Russell Sage.

Fama, Eugene F. (1980), 'Agency Problems and the Theory of the Firm', *Journal of Political Economy*.

Fruin, W. Mark (1983), *Kikkoman: Company, Clan, and Community*, Cambridge, Mass.: Harvard University Press.

—— (1992), *The Japanese Enterprise System: Competitive Strategies and Cooperative Structures*, Oxford: Clarendon Press.

—— (1995), 'Competing in the Old Fashioned Way: Localizing and Integrating Knowledge Resource in Fast-to-Market Competition', in J. Liker, J. Ettlie, and J. Campbell (eds.), *Technology Management: America and Japan*, New York: Oxford University Press.

—— (forthcoming a), 'Good Fences Make Good Neighbors: Organizational Property Rights and Permeability in Product Development Strategies in Japan', in Yves Doz (ed.), *Managing Technology and Innovation for Corporate Renewal*, Oxford: Oxford University Press.

—— (forthcoming b), *Knowledge Works: Managing Intellectual Capital at Toshiba*, New York: Oxford University Press.

—— and Nishiguchi, Toshihiro (1993), 'Supplying the Toyota Production System: Intercorporate Organizational Evolution and Supplier Subsystems', in Bruce Kogut (ed.), *Work and Country Competitiveness*, New York: Oxford University Press.

Gerlach, Michael, (1987), 'Business Alliances and the Strategy of the Japanese Firm', *California Management Review*, 30, Fall.

—— (1992), *Alliance Capitalism: The Social Organization of Japanese Business*, Berkeley: University of California Press.

Goto, Akira (1982), 'Business Groups in a Market Economy', *European Economic Review*, 19.

Grossman, S., and Hart, O. (1980), 'Takeover Bids, the Free Rider Problem, and the Theory of the Corporation', *Bell Journal of Economics*, 11.

Hirshleifer, J. (1977), 'Shakespeare vs. Becker on Altruism: The Importance of Having the Last Word', *Journal of Economic Literature*, 15.

Holloway, Marguerite (1995), 'Socializing with Non-naked Mole Rats', *Scientific American*, Jan.

Hoshi, Takeo, Kashyap, Anil, and Scharfstein, David (1990a), 'Bank Monitoring and Investment: Evidence from the Changing Structure of Japanese Corporate Banking Relationships', in R. Glenn Hubbard (ed.), *Asymmetric Information, Corporate Finance and Investment*, Chicago: University of Chicago Press.

—— —— —— (1990b), 'The Role of Banks in Reducing the Costs of Financial Distress in Japan', *Journal of Financial Economics*, 27/1.

Jensen, M. C., and Meckling, W. H. (1976), 'Theory of the Firm: Managerial Behavior, Agency Costs and Ownership Structure, *Journal of Financial Economics*, 3.

Kauffman, Stuart A. (1992), *Origins of Order: Self Organization and Selection in Evolution*, Oxford: Oxford University Press.

Leibenstein, Harvey (1966), 'Allocative Efficiency vs. X-Efficiency', *American Economic Review*, 56.

—— (1975), 'Aspects of the X-Efficiency Theory of the Firm', *Bell Journal of Economics*, 6/2, Autumn.

Levine, Solomon B., and Kawada, Hisashi (1980), *Human Resources in Japanese Industrial Development*, Princeton: Princeton University Press.

March, James G. (1962), 'The Business Firm as a Political Coalition', *Journal of Politics*, 24.

Nakagawa, Keiichiro, and Yui, Tsunehiko (1983) (eds.), *Organization and Management*, Tokyo: Japanese Business History Institute.

Nelson, Richard, and Winter, Sidney G. (1982), *An Evolutionary Theory of Economic Change*, Cambridge, Mass.: Harvard University Press.

North, Douglass C. (1990), *Institutions, Institutional Change and Economic Performance*, Cambridge: Cambridge University Press.

Odagiri, Hiroyuki (1992), *Growth through Competition, Competition through Growth: Strategic Management and the Economy in Japan*, Oxford: Oxford University Press.

Ostrum, Elinor (1990), *Governing the Commons: The Evolution of Institutions for Collective Action*, New York: Cambridge University Press.

—— *et al.* (1992), 'Covenants with and without a Sword: Self-Governance is Possible', *American Political Science Review*, 86/2, June.

Penrose, Edith T. (1959), *The Theory of the Growth of the Firm*, New York: Wiley.

Porter, Michael E. (1992), 'Capital Disadvantage: America's Failing Capital Investment System', *Harvard Business Review*, 70/5.

Sandler, Todd (1992), *Collective Action: Theory and Applications*, Ann Arbor: University of Michigan Press.

Sheard, Paul (1989), 'The Main Bank System and Corporate. Monitoring and Control in Japan', *Journal of Economic Behavior and Organization*, 11.

Sheard, Paul (1994a), 'Long-Termism and the Japanese Firm', in Mitsuaki Okabe (ed.), *The. Structure of the Japanese Economy*, New York: Macmillan Press.

—— (1994b), 'The Role of Government in Different Market Systems: Observations from the Japanese Case', paper given at the Eleventh Economic Research Institute, Economic Planning Agency, Government of Japan, 23–4 Mar. Simon, Herbert (1957), *Administrative Behavior*, New York: Macmillan.

Toshiba Corporation (1983), *Me de miru Nagoya yonjunen no ayumi* [*Forty Years at the Nagoya Works*], Nagoya.

—— (1987), *Toshiba Komukai kojo gojunenshi* [*A Fifty Year History of the Toshiba Komukai Works*], Tokyo.

—— (1989), *Toshiba Fukaya Buraunkan Kojo nijunenshi* [*A Twenty Year History of the Fukaya CRT Works*], n.p.

—— (1990), *Fukaya Kojo Nijugonen no Ayumi* [*Twenty-Five Years at the Fukaya Works*], n.p.

Westney, Eleanor (1987), *Imitation and Innovation*, Harvard Cambridge, Mass.: University Press.

Williamson, Oliver E. (1970), *Corporate Control and Business Behavior*, Englewood Cliffs, NJ: Prentice Hall.

—— (1975), *Markets and Hierarchies: Analysis and Anti-trust Implications*, New York: Free Press.

—— (1985), *The Economic Institutions of Capitalism*, New York: Free Press.

Afterword

MASAHIRO SHIMOTANI AND TAKAO SHIBA

Centralization and Decentralization of Business Organizations

The present volume has examined the formation process of business groups in a number of countries from a variety of standpoints. Naturally, business groups have evolved into distinct and multifaceted forms, given various historical conditions, legal and systemic constraints, and economic motivations. Today, however, in no matter what country, firms can no longer be viewed solely as independent entities. Although differences in degree and structure must certainly be allowed for, it is imperative to look beyond the firm to the increasingly important role being played by business groups.

Generally, as firms grow and correspondingly expand their spheres of influence, they tend to form a plurality of operational units within their organizations, Accordingly, because it becomes increasingly difficult to exercise complete control over the entire organization, these firms must subsequently go on to permit an increased level of decentralization among these units. Such sub-control units are typically formed internally within the organization, and in many cases a number of them are spun off outside the organization. Alternatively, operational units brought in through mergers and acquisitions are decentrally controlled. The more firms expand, the more they tend to become composed of large numbers of semi-autonomous operational units. This is the reason that decentrally structured business groups can be found in all countries, with naturally occurring differences in extent and form.

However, as noted in the historical observation of enterprise organizations provided by the present volume, it must be remembered that firms are centralized organizations first and foremost, regardless of the extent to which they are structured as decentralized business groups. That is, a centralized organizational foundation is assumed prior to determining the degree and form of decentralization; centralization and decentralization cannot be seen as opposite polar conditions. Solidly maintaining central-ized organizational frameworks, firms have long experimented with vari-ous forms of decentralized control mechanisms. If decentralization were to proceed without reference to centralized organization, the organization itself would no doubt quickly disintegrate. It should be emphasized that the birth of business groups is the logical and rational result of efforts to control decentralized operational units centrally.

There are numerous reasons as to why firms are forced to experiment with decentralized techniques. The difficulty accompanying growth of thorough control is an important one, as firms attempt to avoid the ineffi-ciencies of becoming bloated and over-stratified. Another is change in technology, markets, and the legal system. Such changes in the business environment often lead to renewed emphasis on issues such as the speed-ing up of decision-making and the clarification of managerial responsibil-ity via reductions in the scale of operational units. Thus, firms have responded to environmental change by constructing decentralized meth-ods on their centralized foundations. While the present volume clearly shows that the process of formation of business groups is different in dif-ferent countries, this is the result of responses to different business envi-ronments, leading in turn to differing methods of decentralization, and finally to the appearance of differing forms of business groups.

One of the better-known forms of decentralization is the multidivisional organization,[1] which can be seen as the creation of internally decentralized divisions within the firm. Another is the spinning off of subsidiaries, whereby internal operational units are established as entities nominally separate from the parent firm. Spin-offs have been particularly popular in Japan, where virtually all large firms have large numbers of 'child compa-nies' which exist with their 'parents' in the form of corporate groups. In effect, the parent companies are operating holding companies positioned at the apex of the group. In addition, a number of Japanese firms have recently begun to adopt a system of 'internal companies', reflecting a new variation on the decentralization theme.

While large Japanese firms have essentially metamorphosed into oper-ating holding companies, the post-war Anti-Monopoly Law forbids the establishment of pyramid structures headed by pure holding companies. The pre-war period saw the formation of the well-known zaibatsu pyr-amid organizations, overseen by wealthy families: pure holding compa-nies that dominated huge swaths of the Japanese economy. The 'internal company' system is a new organizational attempt to overcome the legal constraints posed by the Anti-Monopoly Law. Firms retain their main operational units internally, but undertake such contrivances as capitaliz-ing them separately, setting up independent boards of directors, and cre-ating independent balance sheets, all aimed at handling operational units as individual companies while retaining the accounting benefits of a large single firm. This allows the parent to essentially transform itself into a pure holding company. The resulting internally defined 'companies' are hybrids, existing in an intermediate form between 'divisions' and 'spin-offs' and consequently are sometimes referred to as 'internal spin-offs'.

The Boundaries of the Firm

The boundaries of the firm bear consideration in relation to any discussion of the distinction between 'internal' and 'external', and this is reflected in the title of the present volume, *Beyond the Firm*. How to define the boundaries of the firm has been the subject of debate since Ronald Coase's path-breaking treatise 'The Nature of the Firm',[2] which opened up a whole new branch of economics known as corporate theory, addressing such important questions posed by Coase as whether markets naturally give rise to firms, and how the limits on size are determined. Today, however, problems related to the boundaries of the firm have less to do with the boundaries of individual firms than with the interfirm relations beyond the firm (e.g. corporate complexes, corporate groups, and keiretsu organizations). This is an area that deserves to be explored more fully, in an economic sense rather than a legal one.

For example, a significant feature of the Japanese economic landscape is the close interrelationship between the nature of peculiarly 'Japanese' interfirm ties and the problem of the borders of the firm. Of course, individual Japanese firms have legally distinct borders as joint-stock companies. Still, many large firms are members of the loose collections referred to as the six major corporate complexes. These ties are established primarily by means of cross-shareholdings, intracomplex transactions, and the presidents' councils, resulting in loose and indefinite 'boundaries'. Meanwhile, they simultaneously embrace multitudes of subsidiaries and affiliates. As seen in the present volume, many of these were formerly internal units that were created through spin-offs. Large Japanese firms (i.e. corporate groups) are not typically agglomerations of acquired companies, but instead tend to be composed of groups of new enterprises formed by spinning off internal operations and hiving off managers.[3] In other words, corporate groups have been formed by means of self-inspired quasi-disintegration through active spinning off, or, alternatively stated, via quasi-externalization of formerly internal units. Large firms are thus organically connected with their subsidiaries, resulting in a new set of boundaries known as the corporate group which exist beyond the firm.

Moreover, large Japanese firms or corporate groups typically maintain a host of nominally external subcontractors and/or dedicated sales channels. The great majority of these subcontractors and sales companies were

originally positioned completely externally; the large firms virtually
absorbed them into their internal structures through long-term recurrent
transactions, convenient terms, and incentives that worked to the advantage of both parties. Through quasi-internalization of formerly external
units, then, new economic boundaries were again created.

Large Japanese firms have pursued both strategies at once, simultaneously spinning off and quasi-externalizing formerly internal units, while
'spinning in' and quasi-internalizing formerly external units, thereby
forming a new set of economic boundaries of the firm that actually exist
beyond the firm. As in Fig. A.1, Japanese firms actually maintain three sets
of boundaries; the firm, the corporate group, and the firm keiretsu. In
addition, many large firms have come together in the form of the loosely
organized six major corporate complexes, thereby forming another set of
boundaries at an even higher level. Thus, Japan's flexible corporate system
rests on a foundation of hierarchical and somewhat ambiguous 'permeable boundaries'.[4]

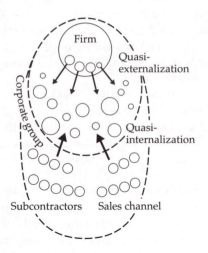

Fig. A.1. *Boundaries of a firm.*

Again, business groups in each country have undergone a variety of
formation processes which have taken place under widely varying conditions. The present volume has approached the classification of the types
and levels of these groups from a standpoint that derives essentially from
Japanese business groups and interfirm relations, examining the formation and existence of business groups in the realm beyond the firm. This is
because business groups can be found in Japan in a variety of types and at
a number of different levels, leading in recent years to considerable international attention to the role of these groups in Japan's economic devel-

opment. In other countries, of course, there are differing historical conditions and legal constraints. Accordingly, the attempt to use the Japanese
framework to view situations existing in other countries is necessarily
experimental, but, we believe, useful in the further promotion of related
work.

NOTES

1. A. Chandler, Jr., *Strategy and Structure: Chapters in the History of the American Industrial Enterprise* (Cambridge, Mass.: MIT Press, 1962).
2. R. Coase, 'The Nature of the Firm', *Economica*, N.S. (1937).
3. M. Aoki, (ed.), *Economic Analysis of the Japanese Firm* (Amsterdam: North-Holland, 1984).
4. M. Fruin, *The Japanese Enterprise System: Competitive Strategies and Cooperative Structures* (Oxford: Clarendon Press, 1992). Note that Fruin uses the term 'permeable boundaries' to describe the borders delineating the focal factory, the firm, and the interfirm network.

INDEX

ABB 157
Accumulatoren-Fabrik AG 147
acquisitions and mergers *see* mergers and acquisitions
adaptation 274–87
AEG 3, 136–42
agency model of the firm 275
AGIP (Azienda Generale Italiana Petroli) 120, 121
Agnelli, A. 112, 128
Aichi Kogyo 230
Aikawa/Nissan 73, 85
Aisin Seiki 230
Alden, H. W. 203
Alfa Romeo 111–12, 127
alliances/partnerships 245, 247, 248
  Belgian business groups 98–100, 104
  zaibatsu 255, 258, 265–7, 270
  see also joint ventures
allocative efficiency models of the firm 275–6, 287
Amato, G. 122, 133 n.
Amatori, F. 3, 109–31, 132 n.
Amoroso, B. 133 n.
ANIC (Oil Hydrogenation National Company) 121
Ansaldo group 110, 113
Anti-Monopoly Law 1947 (Japan) 9, 73, 77, 292
Aoki, M. 271, 295 n.
Arndt, H. 161 n.
Asahi Trust & Banking 80
Asajima, S. 66, 68, 85
Asano zaibatsu 73
assembler-supplier relations 1, 3, 187–240
  Japanese auto industry 22, 187–8, 208, 209, 215–40
  US auto industry 187–210
  see also subcontractor systems
asset tax, Japan 74–6
Auer-Gesellschaft 147
Automatische Fernsprechanlagen-Bau-Gesellschaft 146
automobile industry
  assembler-supplier relationships
    in Japan 3, 22, 187–8, 208, 209, 215–40
    in US 3, 187–210
  Italy 111–12
Automobile Industry Act 1936 (Japan) 218

Azienda Generale Italiana Petroli (AGIP) 120, 121

Balconi, M. 126, 133 n.
Banca Commerciale Italiana 118
Banca Italiana di Sconto 113, 117
Banca Nazionale 114
Bank für elektrische Unternehmungen 139
banks 276
  Belgium 88–90, 91–2, 93
  Germany 139–40, 155, 157
  and Japanese corporate complexes 11, 84–5, 86, 270–1
  and the zaibatsu 60–2, 66–72, 252, 253, 255, 258–9
  see also individual banks
Banque de Bruxelles 89, 90, 91, 96, 97, 100
Banque de l'Indochine 90
Banque de Paris et des Pays-Bas 89, 100
Banque d'Outremer 89, 91
Banque Industrielle Belge 91
BASF AG 158
Bayer AG 158
Bayerische Telephonewerke 147
Bayerische Vereinsbank 156
Belgian Coke and Coking Coal Union 99
Belgian Industrial Coal Agency 99
Belgium, business groups 3, 88–105
Beneduce, A. 117, 118
Bergmann-Elektricitäswerke AG 141, 147, 150, 153, 154, 156
Berliner Einheitszeit GmbH 152
Berliner Handelsgesellschaft 139
Bezza, B. 132 n.
Bigazzi, D. 132 n.
BMW AG 158
Bocciardo, A. 114–15, 118
Boël family 93
Bolle, P. 90
Bondi, M. 112–13, 114
Bonelli, F. 122, 133 n.
Bosch AG 147, 154, 155, 156, 157, 158, 159
Bosch-Siemens-Hausgeräte GmbH 156, 159
Brandenburgische Motorenwerke GmbH 153
Brandstetter, E. 163 n.
Breda, V. S. 114
Brioschi, F. 132 n.
Briscoe, B. 197, 211 n.

Brufina 97, 100
Bücher, H. 162 n.
Build-Own-Transfer (BOT)/Build-own-
    Operate (BOO) businesses 139
Büschgen, H. E. 166 n.
business groups
    Belgium 88–105
    Italy 109–31
    Japan 5–26, 167–82, 245–71
    see also corporate complexes; corporate
        groups; subcontractor systems

Capiau, H. 99
car industry *see* automobile industry
Caracciolo, A. 132 n.
Carnevali, F. 133 n.
Carparelli, A. 132 n.
cartels/cartellization
    Germany 136, 143, 144
    of industrial coal producers, Belgium
        98–9
    see also decartelization
Castronovo, V. 132 n.
centralization 291–2
    in zaibatsu 249–50, 251, 255, 270
chaebol, Korean 3, 31–54
Chandler, A. D. 132 n., 135, 160–1 n., 210 n.,
    246, 275, 295 n.
Chang, C. S. 46, 48, 55 n.
chemical industry
    Italy 115–16, 126
    Samsung diversification into 41–3
    Sumitomo diversification into 252
Chevrolet Motor Company 201
Chida, T. 169, 179
China 35
Chiyoda Bank 78, 79
Choi, J. P. 46, 48, 55 n.
Chrysler motor company 187, 207, 209
Chuo Life Insurance Co. 80
Cianca, E. 132 n.
Cleveland Cap Screw Company 195–6,
    198
coal mining, Belgium 95–100
Coase, R. H. 246, 293, 295 n.
Cockerill steel company 97, 99
Coffin, H. 203
Cole, R. E. 274
Colitti, M. 133 n.
colonies, Belgian banks in 89, 90
Compagnie Mutuelle des Tramways 89
complexity of industries 248
Confederation of Japan Automobile
    Workers' Unions (CJAW) 236
Confinindus holding company 97
contracting, market 246
co-operation among firms 248, 284–6
    see also alliances; joint ventures

co-operative associations, among Japanese
    auto industry suppliers 22–4, 222, 226,
    231–2, 233, 238, 239
Coppé, A. 98
Coppée, E. 99
Coppée family 90, 94–5, 96, 97, 98, 100
Cornigliano corporation 119
corporate complexes 1, 2–3, 31–105
    passim
    Belgium 90
    Japan 5, 7, 11–14, 13, 20, 24, 25–6, 79–86,
        270–1, 280–1, 294
    Korea 31–54
corporate groups 1, 3, 109–82
    Germany 135–60
    Italy 109–31
    Japan 4, 7, 8–10, 13, 14–16, 20, 24–5,
        167–82, 293
Corporate Securities Holdings Limitation
    Law (1946) 73
Cosh, A. 37
Costruzioni Meccaniche di Saronno 111
Cottenier, J. 93
Crawford, F. 105, 205
Cusumano, M. 231
Czada, P. 163 n.

Daems, H. 92, 93
Daewoo chaebol 32, 47
Dai-Ichi Bank 61, 66, 78, 86, 265, 266
    see also Teikoku Bank
Dai-Ichi Kangin complex 11, 12, 85, 86
Dai-Ichi Kangyo Bank 86, 255, 258
Daihatsu 227
Daijyugo National Bank 66
Daimler-Benz 156, 158
Daisy Automobile Co. 190–1
Dan, T. 64
Davies, P. N. 169, 179
Davis, G. S. 211 n.
DEA/Texaco 158
de Benedetti, C. 128
decartelization/deconcentration, of post-
    war German industry 155
decentralization 7, 291–2
    in zaibatsu 250, 251, 255, 270
    see also spin-offs
Degussa (company) 158
Delaet, J. L. 92
Deutsch-Luxemburgische Bergwerks- und
    Hüttengesellschaft 149
Deutsche Bank 139, 156
Deutsche Betriebsgesellschaft für drahtlose
    Telegraphie mbH 147
Deutsche Edison Gesellschaft 139
Deutsche Grammaphon 152
Deutsche Telephonwerke und
    Kabelindustrie AG 146

diversification processes
  Samsung chaebol 34–46
  Sumitomo and Furukawa groups 250–65
Donegani, G. 115, 116
Dore, R. 274
Doria, M. 132 n.
Dossett, F. K. 211 n.
Dubois, G. F. Lepore 133 n.
Dubois, L. 90
Dupont (company) 32
Durant, W. 199, 201, 205, 208
Dyke, A. L. 191

East Japan Heavy Industries (EJHI) 177,
  178, 180
Eccles, R. G. 275
Echigo, K. 169
Edo, H. 78, 83
efficiency
  adaptation as source of 277–9, 284–7
  allocative 275–6, 287
EFIM 127
EGAM 126–7
Eihokai 22
Electrabel 103
electric power industry, Belgium 100–3
electrical industry
  Germany 3, 135–60
  Japan 22–4, 282–4
  see also Furukawa Electric
Electrobel 100–1, 103, 104
Electrorail 100, 101
Elektrische Licht- und Kraftanlagen AG
  147
Elektrische Licht- und Kraftlagen-
  Aktiengesellschaft 140
Elektrizitäts-AG form. S. Schuckert & Co.
  140, 149, 150
Elektrizitätsgesellschaft AG 140
Empain group 90, 91, 94, 101
energy sector
  Belgium 95–103
  see also oil sector
ENI (National Hydrocarbon Corporation)
  3, 111, 119–21, 122, 126, 127, 128, 129,
  130, 131
Epstein, R. 210 n., 212 n.
ESSO 158
European Coal and Steel Community
  (ECSC) 98, 99

family ownership and control 279–80, 292
  Belgium 90, 93–5, 104
  see also zaibatsu
Federation of All Toyota Workers' Unions
  (FATWU) 236, 238
Federation of Auto Parts Manufacturers
  Union (Japan) 220

Feldenkirchen, W. 3, 135–60
Felten & Guilleaume 141
Ferguson, D. 203
Ferruzzi family 128
Fiat 110, 112, 127
financial institutions 248–9
  treasury stock purchases, Japan 78, 81–2
  of zaibatsu 60–1, 66–72, 78
  see also banks
financial markets, and organizational
  development 276–7

Findeisen, F. 163 n.
Finsider group 119, 124, 125–6, 129, 130,
  131
the firm
  boundaries of 293–5
  theories of 275–6
Fisher Body Corporation 208
Ford motor company 187, 189, 190, 191,
  198, 199–200, 201, 205, 206, 207, 208,
  209, 218
Ford-Werke AG 158
Frère, A. 104
Freude, H. 165 n.
Friedman, D. 219
Fruin, M. 3, 210 n., 271 n., 274–87, 295 n.
Fuji, co-operative association 232
Fuji Bank 86
Fuji Electric 252, 265, 266, 267
Fuji Trust & Banking 80
Fujimoto, T. 195, 196, 211 n.
Fujita, N. 170
Fujitsu 252, 255, 258, 262, 266
Fujitsu Fanuc 258
Fujiwara, G. 64
Fukaya Works 284
Furukawa Bank 265
Furukawa Electric 252, 264–5, 266, 267
Furukawa, J. 74, 75
Furukawa Trading 253
Furukawa zaibatsu 73, 85, 251, 252–3, 255,
  258, 262, 264–5, 266, 267
Furuta, S. 61
Fuso Motor Sales Ltd 181
Fuyo complex 11, 12, 85

Gelsenkirchener Bergwerks AG 149
General Electric 153, 155, 156, 266
General Motors (GM) 198, 201, 205, 206,
  207, 208, 209, 218
Gerlach, M. 3, 245–71, 276, 286
Germany
  business groups in electrical industry 3,
  135–60
  economy 1918–45 142–3
Gesellschaft für elektrische Apparate mbH
  152

glass industry, Belgium 92
Goetzeler, H. 165 n.
Gray & Davis Co. 188
Grossman, S. 275
Groupe Bruxelles Lambert (GBL) 104
Grundig AG 156, 159

Han, J.-W. 33, 46, 52, 55 n.
Hart, O. 275
Hashimoto, J. 18, 20
Hattori, T. 46, 49, 55 n.
Haynes-Apperson (company) 188
heavy industry
    Mitsubishi Heavy Industries 167–82
    Samsung diversification into 41–3
    Siemens and AEG combination with 149
Helper, S. 3, 187–210
Henkel (company) 158
Hewlett Packard 33
Hilferding, R. 162 n.
Hochfelder, D. 3, 187–210
Hoechst (company) 158
Hoesch (company) 158
Hofmann-Linke-Werke 149
Hokkaido Colliery & Steamship 63, 64
holding companies
    created by Belgian banks 92, 93
    Japan 8–9
Holding Company Liquidation
    Commission (Japan) 73, 76, 175
Holley, G. 191
Holloway, M. 285
Horn, N. 161 n.
Hoshi, T. 277
Hosono, G. 80
Hudson motor company 207
Hutchinson, W. R. 80
Hyatt Roller Bearing Co. 188, 204–5
Hyozaemon, T. 280
Hyundai chaebol 32, 47

I. T. & T. 146, 154–5
IBM 32
IBM Germany GmbH 158, 159
Ichikawa Seisakusho 230
Ichikoh Industries 230
IFI 128
IG Farben 155
Ilva corporation 110, 112–13, 118, 119
Imai, K. 25
imperfect information 285
interest rates, and value-added margin ratio
    35
International General Electric Co. 65
IRI (Instituto di Ricostruzione Industriale)
    3, 110, 111, 117–19, 122, 124–5, 128, 129,
    130, 131
Isomura, T. 64

Isuzu 219, 223, 232
Italsider 119, 124
Italy, corporate groups 3, 109–31
Itochu (company) 33
Iwasaki family 74, 75–6, 170

Japan 1–2, 3–4
    assembler-supplier (subcontractor)
        relationships 4, 21–4, 25, 26, 180
    auto industry 22, 187–8, 208, 209, 215–40
    corporate complexes 5, 7, 11–14, 20, 24,
        25–6, 79–86, 280–1, 294
    corporate groups 5, 7, 8–10, 13, 14–16, 20,
        24–5, 167–82, 293–4
    electrical industry *see* electrical industry
    keiretsu *see* keiretsu
    shipbuilding industry 168–72, 176,
        179–80
    subsidiary formation 7, 8, 9–10, 169–71,
        172, 173–4, 177–8, 179, 181–2, 292, 293
    zaibatsu *see* zaibatsu
Japan Aluminium Corporation 265
Japan Auto Parts Union 220
Japan Steel Works 68, 182 n.
Japan Storage Battery 171
Jeanjot, P. 90
Jeidels, O. 162 n.
Jensen, M. C. 275
joint ventures 266
    Siemens and AEG 141, 149, 152, 156, 157
    Siemens and Furukawa Electric 267
Joye, P. 94
Jun, J.-W. 33, 46, 52, 55 n.

kanban system, at Toyota group companies
    235, 236
Kanebo group 16
Kanegafuchi Spinning 63, 64
Kaneko, E. 169, 180
Kang, C. K. 3, 46, 48, 50, 55 n.
Kawada, H. 274
Kawasaki Engineering Works 180
Kein Mills 200, 208
keiretsu
    Japanese 1, 2, 6, 25, 47, 209, 216, 217,
        230–1, 233, 280, 285, 294
        capital keiretsu formation 230–1
    Korean 32, 45–6, 47, 50
keiretsu diagnosis, in Japanese auto
    industry 223–7, 229, 239
Kettering, C. 202
Kia Motors 33
Kikkawa, T. 17, 102
Kikkoman 279–80
Kim, Y.-O. 37, 41, 42, 49, 51, 53, 55 n.
Klangfilm GmbH 152
Knudsen, W. 200
Kocka, J. 161 n., 162 n.

Kokumin Life Insurance Co. 80
Komukai Works 282–3
Kong, B. H. 46, 49, 55 n.
König, W. 163 n.
Konzerns 14–16, 19, 24
Korea, chaebol 3, 31–54
Korea Fertilizer Company 41
Kraftwerk Union AG 156
Krupp AG 149, 158
Kurgan-van Hentenryk, G. 3, 88–103
Kyohokai 22, 222, 231
Kyoto Engineering Works 179
Kyu-nainen-kai 170

labour relations, Japanese auto industry
    236–8
Lanerossi company 126
Lanthier, P. 94
Launoit, P.de 97
Lee, J. R. 200
Leland, H. 191, 195
Leopold II, King of Belgium 89
Levine, D. 212 n.
Levine, S. B. 274
Levinthal, D. A. 247–8
Lewis, E. W. 203, 212 n.
LG chaebol 32, 47
Licht und Kraft AG 144, 150
Lieben, R. von 147
Liebenstein, H. 287
Lindsay Automobile Parts Co. 191
Linke-AEG-Lauchhammer 160
Lockwood, W. W. 251
Locomobile 188–9
Lorenz AG 146
Luachhammergesellschaft 149

Machinery Industry Promotion Temporary
    Measures Law (Japan) 227–8
Maffei-Schwartzkopff 154
MAN 158
managerial structures
    Belgian industrial groups 93–5
    Korean chaebol 51–3, 54
    see also family ownership and control
Mannesmann AG 158
Mannheim and Sachsenwerk 144
Marchesi, M. 124
market conditions 247–8
market contracting 246
Maschinenfabrik Esslingen 111
mass production
    in Japanese auto industry 228–30, 233,
        234, 239–40
    in US auto industry 198–9
Matsunaga, Y. 102
Matsushita group 9, 16, 22–4, 33
Mattei, E. 120, 121, 122

Meckling, W. H. 275
Meiji Life Insurance 61
mergers and acquisitions 291
    within zaibatsu 255
Metallgesellschaft 158
Mid-Japan Heavy Industries (MJHI) 177,
    179
Mihara Locomotive Works 179
Mishima, Y. 170
Mitsubishi Aircraft Company (MAC) 168,
    169–70
Mitsubishi Bank 66, 68, 70, 78, 79, 84, 265
Mitsubishi complex 11, 12, 16, 17, 19, 33, 78,
    79, 80, 82, 83, 86
Mitsubishi Electric 84, 266
Mitsubishi Electric Manufacturing (MEM)
    170
Mitsubishi Goshi 170, 171
Mitsubishi Heavy Industries 73, 167–82
Mitsubishi Motor Corporation 227
Mitsubishi Nippon Heavy Industries
    (MNHI) 177, 178, 180–1
Mitsubishi Shipbuilding & Engineering
    (MSE) 168, 170–2
Mitsubishi Shipbuilding Ltd (MSL) 177,
    178, 180, 181, 266
Mitsubishi Trading Co., Ltd. 176
Mitsubishi Trust 70, 80
Mitsubishi zaibatsu 59, 60, 61–2, 78, 167,
    170
    financial institutions 61, 66, 68, 70, 72
    control of subsidiaries 61–2
Mitsui Bank 61, 65–6, 66, 67, 68, 84, 85, 265,
    266
    see also Teikoko Bank
Mitsui Bussan 63, 64, 65, 73, 176
Mitsui complex 11, 12, 16, 17, 18, 19, 78, 79,
    80, 82, 83, 86
Mitsui family 74, 75, 76
Mitsui Life Insurance 69, 80
Mitsui Mining 62–3, 73
Mitsui Real Estate 77–8, 85
Mitsui Trust 69, 80, 265
Mitsui zaibatsu 59, 60, 62–6, 253, 264
    control of subsidiaries 62–6
    financial institutions 68, 69
    see also Mitsui Bank
Miwa, R. 175
Mix & Genest AG 146, 155
Miyamoto, M. 264
Mizushima Engineering Works 179, 180
Mody, A. 248
Molony, B. 15
Monjiro, M. 280
Montecatini corporation 111, 115–16
Montedison corporation 126, 128
Mori group 14
Morikawa, E. 31, 55 n.

Morikawa, H. 16, 20, 161 n., 253, 264, 265
Muto, S. 64
Mutuelle Solvay 101

Nagashima, O. 23
Nagoya Engineering Works (Mitsubishi)
 178, 179, 180
Nagoya Works (Toshiba) 283–4
Nakagawa, K. 274
Nakajima zaibatsu 73
Nash motor company 207
National Coal Office (Belgium) 99
National Hydrocarbon Corporation (ENI)
 111, 119–21, 122, 126, 127, 128, 129, 130,
 131
National Natural Gas Pipeline Company
 (SNAM) 121
Nelson, R. 285
net present value models 275
networks 247, 248
Neustadt-Perry Co. 191
New Konzerns 14–16, 19, 24
Newly Industrializing Economies (NIEs) 35
Nikon 171
Nippon Battery 171
Nippon Chisso 182 n.
Nippon Denki 266
Nippon Electric (NEC) 252, 255, 258, 260, 266
Nippon Kangyo Bank 86
Nippon Kogaku 171
Nippon Steel 73, 84
Nippon Yusen Kaisha (NYK) 266
Nishiguchi, T. 219, 271 n., 276
Nishinarita, Y. 171
Nissan 14, 208, 217, 219, 220, 223, 224–33
 passim
Nitscitsu group 14–15
Noda Shoyu Company 280
Nomura zaibatsu 73, 85
Noreda Shoreyu Company 279–80
North, D. C. 286

Odagiri, H. 11, 286
Odaka, K. 231, 232
Ohkawa, K. 251
Ohtsuki, B. 62, 83
Oil Hydrogenation National Company
 (ANIC) 121
oil sector, Italy 120–1
Oji Paper 63, 64, 182 n.
Okumura, H. 11, 83, 85
Okura, K. 74, 75
Okura zaibatsu 73
Olds Motor Works 191, 195
Olivetti 128
Ollenhauer, G. 161 n.
Olsen, A. J. 133 n.
Opel AG 158

organizational learning 274, 277
Osaka Bank 78, 80
Osaka Sumitomo Marine & Fire Insurance
 61, 71, 80
Oshio, T. 15
Osram GmbH 147, 150, 156
Osti, G. 124, 133 n.
Ostrum, E. 281, 285
ownership structures
 Belgian business groups 90, 92–3, 95–6
 Korean chaebol 46–50, 54
 see also family ownership and control

Packard motor company 207
partnerships *see* alliances
patent rights, US auto industry 205
Pavan, R. 133 n.
Peirce-Arrow 203
Penrose, E. T. 41
Perrone family 113
Petrilli, G. 124
Petrofina 104
Philips Germany 159
Pintsch AG 147, 150
Plettner, B. 165 n.
Pollard, S. 168
Porter, M. E. 133 n., 276
Powerfin 103
Preussag (company) 158
Prince (company) 230
principal-agent theories 275
Protos automobile production 152
Puissant, J. 95, 99, 100

quality control, in Japanese auto industry
 228, 229, 235

Rae, J. B. 200, 203, 207, 211 n., 212 n.
Ranieri, R. 133 n.
Rathenau, E. 137, 139
rent-seeking activity 45
rental costs, and value-added margin ratio
 35
research and development (R&D), Samsung
 33
Rheinmetall Düsseldorf 149
Riken group 14
Robertson, P. 168
Rocca, A. 119
Rosenberg, N. 210 n.
Rosovsky, H. 251
Ruhrgas 158
Ruhrkohle AG 158
Rundfunk GmbH 147
RWE AG 158

Sakamoto, K. 7
Sako, M. 271 n.

Sakudo, Y. 264
Samsung chaebol 3, 31–54
Sandler, T. 285
Sanwa complex 11, 12, 85–6
Saraceno, P. 133 n.
Sato, K. 84
Schipper, J. E. 212 n.
Schneider group 90
Schukert & Co. 140
Schulz, G. 165 n.
Schweizerische Gesellschaft für elektrische
    Industrie 140
Schweizerische Kreditanstalt 139–40
Schweppe and Wilt 205–6
Seika Mining 73
SEL 159
Seltzer, L. 196–7, 200
share ownership *see* stocks and shares
    ownership
Sheard, P. 276–7, 280, 281, 286
Shell (Germany) 158
Shiba, T. 1–4, 3, 167–82, 291–5
Shimada, K. 25, 64
Shimotani, M. 1–26, 45, 175, 291–5
Shin, B. H. 50
Shin Mitsubishi Heavy Industries (SMHI)
    177, 178, 179, 180, 181
Shinkawa Kogyo 230
shipbuilding industry, Japan 168–72, 176,
    179–80
Showa Bank 66
Siegrist, H. 161 n.
Siemens 3, 136–42, 258, 265, 267
Siemens & Halske AG 137, 139, 141, 144,
    146, 149, 150, 152, 153, 156
Siemens Apparate- und Maschinen-GmbH
    153
Siemens Elektrische Betriebe AG 140
Siemens Nixdorf 158
Siemens-Bauunion (SBU) 150
Siemens-Plania AG 152
Siemens-Reiniger-Veifa-gesellschaft für
    medizinische Technik mbH 152
Siemens-Rheinelbe-Schuckert-Union
    (SRSU) 149, 150, 160
Siemens-Schuckertwerke GmbH 140, 141, 156
Sinigaglia, O. 118–19
Sloan, A. 199, 205, 211 n., 212 n.
Smith, W. H. 200
Smitka, M. 229, 232, 271 n.
SNAM (National Natural Gas Pipeline
    Company) 121
Société Belge de Banque 91
Société Générale 88, 89, 91, 92, 93, 94, 96,
    97, 98, 99, 100–1, 103, 104
Société Nationale d'Investissement 103
Society of Automobile Engineers (SAE)
    202–3

Sofina 100
Sofindit 118
'sogo shosha' general trading companies
    11
Solvay, Ernest 90
Solvay family 93
Son, Il-Sun 23
Sony 9
Sonzogno, C. 133 n.
South-East Asia 35
specialization structure in Japanese auto
    industry 220, 221, 228–31, 232–3,
    234–5, 239, 240
spin-offs 255, 258, 260–1, 293
    formation of subsidiaries through 7,
    9–10, 43, 169–70, 292, 293, 294
Sraffa, P. 110, 132 n.
Städtische Elektrizitätswerke 139
Standard Elektrizitäts Gesellschaft AG 146,
    154
standardization, in US auto industry 202–3
Starr, P. 210 n.
state intervention, Italy 110–11, 113–14,
    117–28
Steel Products Company 205, 206
steel sector, Italy 114–15, 118–19, 124–6
stockholding arrangements, of Japanese
    corporate complexes 11
stocks and shares ownership
    cross-shareholding 77, 78–9
    mutual share ownership 77, 84
    treasury stock 77–9
    of zaibatsu 58, 64–5, 68–72
    of former zaibatsu 76–9
strategic alliances *see* alliances
Structural Impediments Initiatives (SII) 1, 5
Studebaker motor company 207
Subaru 232
Subcontracting Factory Assignment System
    23
subcontractor systems 1, 3
    Japan 5, 21–4, 25, 26, 180
    see also assembler-supplier relations
subsidiaries, zaibatsu control of 60–6
subsidiary formation
    Japan 7, 8, 9–10, 169–71, 172, 173–4,
    177–8, 179, 181–2, 292, 293, 294
    Samsung chaebol 43
Suez group 103, 104
Sumitomo Bank 66, 68, 70, 78, 81, 84, 252,
    253, 255, 256–7
Sumitomo Chemical 266, 268–9
Sumitomo complex 12, 13–14, 16, 17, 78, 79,
    80, 82, 83, 86
Sumitomo family 74, 75, 76
Sumitomo Life Insurance 71, 81
Sumitomo Machinery 85
Sumitomo Trust 70, 81

Sumitomo zaibatzu 3, 59, 60, 61, 78, 251–70
    passim
  financial institutions of 61, 66, 68, 71, 72
  control of subsidiaries 61, 62
Sunkyung chaebol 32, 47
Suzuki, K. 3, 59–86, 78, 175

Taisho Marine & Fire Insurance 61
Taiwan Electric Power company 265
Takayanagi, K. 80
Takeda, H. 20
Tanaka, K. 85
Tatsu'uma, Y. 74
taxation of assets, Japan 74–6
technological conditions 247–8
Teikoku Bank 61, 66, 68, 69, 78, 84
Telefonapparatefabrik E. Zweietusch & Co.
    146–7
Telefonbau und Normalzeit Lehner & Co.
    156
Telefunken 141, 142, 147, 163 n.
Telephonfabrik vorm J. Berliner AG 146
Terni corporation 114–15, 118, 125–6
Thompson, C. 195, 205
Thompson Products 197
Thyssen AG 158
Timken Roller Bearing Co. 203–4
Tokio Marine & Fire Insurance 61, 68, 70
Tokyo Electric 282
Tokyo Electric Wireless 282
Tokyo Engineering Works 180
Tokyo Furukawa 253
Tokyo Shibaura Company 282
Tokyo Shibaura Electric 63, 64–5, 73, 84, 282
Tokyo Trust & Banking 80
Tongbang Life Insurance Company 41
Toshiba 266, 278, 282–4
Toyobo group 16
Toyota 9, 22, 208, 217–33 *passim*, 235–6, 237,
    238, 279, 280–1
  unions 236, 237, 238
Tractebel 94, 103
Tractionel 100, 101, 102, 103, 104
Transformatoren Union AG 156
treasury stock 79, 81–2
  illegal purchases of, by zaibatsu
    companies 77–8
Tsuda, H. 85

Ueda, H. 3, 215–40
Unilever (Germany) 158
Union Minière 94
Union-Electrizitätsgesellschaft 140
United Motors Corporation 201, 205
United States, auto industry 187–210

value-added margin ratio (VMR) competi-
    tion 34–5, 37
Vantemsche, G. 91
Veba AG 158
Verband deutscher Elektrizitätsfabriken
    147
Vereinigte Eisenbahn-Signalwerke GmbH
    152
Vereinigte Stahlwerke 155
vertical integration 246
  in US auto industry 199–206, 208, 209
Viag 158
Vickers corporation 113
Vincent, A. 92, 93, 103
Volkswagen AG 158

Wada, K. 224
wages
  Japanese auto industry 238
  and value-added margin ratio 35
Wall, W. G. 203
Warocqué family 96
Weiher, S. von 165 n.
West Japan Heavy Industries (WJHI) 177,
    180
Western Electric 258, 266
Westinghouse 266
Weston-Mott Co. 188
White, H. C. 275
Williamson, O. E. 246, 275
Willys-Overland motor company 207
Winter, S. 285
Winton, A. 202
Winton Motor Carriage Co. 195–6, 197–8,
    202
Wray, W. D. 266

Yamaguchi, K. 64, 65
Yasuda Bank 266
Yasuda zaibatsu 73
Yui, T. 274

zaibatsu 3, 11, 16–21, 59–86, 167, 170,
    249–71, 292
  and the banks (financial institutions)
    60–2, 66–72, 252, 253, 255, 258–9
  control of subsidiaries 60–6
  dissolution of 72–9, 175
  operational decentralization in 250, 251,
    255, 270
  strategic centralization in 249–50, 251,
    255, 270
zaibatsu conversion 18
Zamagni, V. 132 n.